Numerical Methods for Solving Nonlinear Equations

Numerical Methods for Solving Nonlinear Equations

Editors

Maria Isabel Berenguer
Manuel Ruiz Galán

Basel • Beijing • Wuhan • Barcelona • Belgrade • Novi Sad • Cluj • Manchester

Editors
Maria Isabel Berenguer
Department of Applied Mathematics, University of Granada
Granada, Spain

Manuel Ruiz Galán
Department of Applied Mathematics, University of Granada
Granada, Spain

Editorial Office
MDPI
St. Alban-Anlage 66
4052 Basel, Switzerland

This is a reprint of articles from the Special Issue published online in the open access journal *Mathematics* (ISSN 2227-7390) (available at: https://www.mdpi.com/si/mathematics/Numerical_Methods_for_Solving_Nonlinear_Equations).

For citation purposes, cite each article independently as indicated on the article page online and as indicated below:

Lastname, A.A.; Lastname, B.B. Article Title. *Journal Name* **Year**, *Volume Number*, Page Range.

ISBN 978-3-0365-9214-5 (Hbk)
ISBN 978-3-0365-9215-2 (PDF)
doi.org/10.3390/books978-3-0365-9215-2

© 2023 by the authors. Articles in this book are Open Access and distributed under the Creative Commons Attribution (CC BY) license. The book as a whole is distributed by MDPI under the terms and conditions of the Creative Commons Attribution-NonCommercial-NoDerivs (CC BY-NC-ND) license.

Contents

About the Editors . . . . **vii**

Preface . . . . **ix**

Petko D. Proinov and Milena D. Petkova
On the Convergence of a New Family of Multi-Point Ehrlich-Type Iterative Methods for Polynomial Zeros
Reprinted from: *Mathematics* **2021**, *9*, 1640, doi:10.3390/math9141640 . . . . **1**

Li Zhang, Jin Huang, Hu Li and Yifei Wang
Extrapolation Method for Non-Linear Weakly Singular Volterra Integral Equation with Time Delay
Reprinted from: *Mathematics* **2021**, *9*, 1856, doi:10.3390/math9161856 . . . . **17**

María Isabel Berenguer and Manuel Ruiz Galán
An Iterative Algorithm for Approximating the Fixed Point of a Contractive Affine Operator
Reprinted from: *Mathematics* **2022**, *10*, 1012, doi:10.3390/math10071012 . . . . **37**

Juan Zhang and Xiao Luo
Gradient-Based Optimization Algorithm for Solving Sylvester Matrix Equation
Reprinted from: *Mathematics* **2022**, *10*, 1040, doi:10.3390/math10071040 . . . . **47**

Michael I. Argyros, Ioannis K. Argyros, Samundra Regmi and Santhosh George
Generalized Three-Step Numerical Methods for Solving Equations in Banach Spaces
Reprinted from: *Mathematics* **2022**, *10*, 2621, doi:10.3390/math10152621 . . . . **61**

Ioannis K. Argyros, Samundra Regmi, Stepan Shakhno and Halyna Yarmola
A Methodology for Obtaining the Different Convergence Orders of Numerical Method under Weaker Conditions
Reprinted from: *Mathematics* **2022**, *10*, 2931, doi:10.3390/math10162931 . . . . **89**

R. H. Al-Obaidi and M. T. Darvishi
Constructing a Class of Frozen Jacobian Multi-Step Iterative Solvers for Systems of Nonlinear Equations
Reprinted from: *Mathematics* **2022**, *10*, 2952, doi:10.3390/math10162952 . . . . **105**

Khaled Ben Amara, Maria Isabel Berenguer and Aref Jeribi
Approximation of the Fixed Point of the Product of Two Operators in Banach Algebras with Applications to Some Functional Equations
Reprinted from: *Mathematics* **2022**, *10*, 4179, doi:10.3390/math10224179 . . . . **119**

Gholamreza Farahmand, Taher Lotfi, Malik Zaka Ullah and Stanford Shateyi
Finding an Efficient Computational Solution for the Bates Partial Integro-Differential Equation Utilizing the RBF-FD Scheme
Reprinted from: *Mathematics* **2023**, *11*, 1123, doi:10.3390/math11051123 . . . . **137**

Obadah Said Solaiman, Rami Sihwail, Hisham Shehadeh, Ishak Hashim and Kamal Alieyan
Hybrid Newton–Sperm Swarm Optimization Algorithm for Nonlinear Systems
Reprinted from: *Mathematics* **2023**, *11*, 1473, doi:10.3390/math11061473 . . . . **151**

About the Editors

Maria Isabel Berenguer

Maria Isabel Berenguer is an Associate Professor in the Department of Applied Mathematics at the University of Granada, Spain; since 2015, she has also been a member of the university's Institute of Mathematics. She is a notable reviewer, and has published a several articles in well-known journals with high JCR ranking. She has also actively participated in different projects with national or regional funding. Additionally, she has trained young researchers and tutored international doctoral students during their term abroad at the University of Granada. Currently, she is a member of the Editorial Board of MDPI's journal *Mathematics*. Her research interests include applied mathematics, numerical analysis, fixed point theory and inverse problems.

Manuel Ruiz Galán

Manuel Ruiz Galán received his Ph.D. in 1999 from the University of Granada, Spain. Currently, he serves as a Full Professor in the Mathematics Department at the University of Granada, Spain. He has authored more than 60 research papers and book chapters, particularly on topics related to convex and numerical analysis and their applications. He has been a member and principal investigator in several nationally funded projects (Spanish Government). He has served as a Guest Editor for several Special Issues of journals such as *Optimization and Engineering*, *Frontiers in Psychology*, *Mathematical Problems in Engineering*, and the *Journal of Function Spaces and Applications*. Additionally, he is a member of the Editorial Board of MDPI's journal *Mathematics* and the journal *Minimax Inequalities and its Applications*.

Preface

Many problems that emerge in areas such as medicine, biology, economics, finance, or engineering can be described in terms of nonlinear equations or systems of such equations, which can take different forms, from algebraic, differential, integral or integro-differential models to variational inequalities or equilibrium problems. For this reason, nonlinear problems are one of the most interesting fields of study in pure and applied mathematics.

However, there is a lack of direct methods that can facilitate the effective resolution of nonlinear problems, and hence, research interest in their numerical treatment has further consolidated. This Special Issue have collated manuscripts that address the recent advancements in the aforementioned area. It contains 10 articles accepted for publication among the 24 submitted.

Maria Isabel Berenguer and Manuel Ruiz Galán
Editors

Article
On the Convergence of a New Family of Multi-Point Ehrlich-Type Iterative Methods for Polynomial Zeros

Petko D. Proinov * and Milena D. Petkova

Faculty of Mathematics and Informatics, University of Plovdiv Paisii Hilendarski, 24 Tzar Asen, 4000 Plovdiv, Bulgaria; milenapetkova@uni-plovdiv.bg
* Correspondence: proinov@uni-plovdiv.bg

Abstract: In this paper, we construct and study a new family of multi-point Ehrlich-type iterative methods for approximating all the zeros of a uni-variate polynomial simultaneously. The first member of this family is the two-point Ehrlich-type iterative method introduced and studied by Trićković and Petković in 1999. The main purpose of the paper is to provide local and semilocal convergence analysis of the multi-point Ehrlich-type methods. Our local convergence theorem is obtained by an approach that was introduced by the authors in 2020. Two numerical examples are presented to show the applicability of our semilocal convergence theorem.

Keywords: multi-point iterative methods; iteration functions; polynomial zeros; local convergence; error estimates; semilocal convergence

MSC: 65H04

1. Introduction

This work deals with multi-point iterative methods for approximating all the zeros of a polynomial simultaneously. Let us recall that an iterative method for solving a nonlinear equation is called a multi-point method if it can be defined by an iteration of the form

$$x^{(k+1)} = \varphi(x^{(k)}, x^{(k-1)}, \ldots, x^{(k-N)}), \quad k = 0, 1, 2, \ldots,$$

where N is a fixed natural number, and $x^{(0)}, x^{(-1)}, \ldots, x^{(-N)}$ are $N+1$ initial approximations. In the literature, there are multi-point iterative methods for finding a single zero of a nonlinear equation (see, e.g., [1–7]). This study is devoted to the multi-point iterative methods for approximating all the zeros of a polynomial simultaneously (see, e.g., [8–11]).

Let us recall the two most popular iterative methods for simultaneous computation of all the zeros of a polynomial f of degree $n \geq 2$. These are Weierstrass' method [12] and Ehrlich's method [13].

Weierstrass' method is defined by the following iteration:

$$x^{(k+1)} = x^{(k)} - W_f(x^{(k)}), \quad k = 0, 1, 2, \ldots, \qquad (1)$$

where the function $W_f: \mathcal{D} \subset \mathbb{K}^n \to \mathbb{K}^n$ is defined by $W_f(x) = (W_1(x), \ldots, W_n(x))$ with

$$W_i(x) = \frac{f(x_i)}{a_0 \prod_{j \neq i}(x_i - x_j)} \quad (i = 1, \ldots, n), \qquad (2)$$

where $a_0 \in \mathbb{K}$ is the leading coefficient of f and $\mathcal{D}$ denotes the set of all vectors in $\mathbb{K}^n$ with pairwise distinct components. Weierstrass' method (1) has second order of convergence (provided that f has only simple zeros).

Ehrlich's method is defined by the following fixed point iteration:

$$x^{(k+1)} = T(x^{(k)}), \quad k = 0, 1, 2, \ldots, \tag{3}$$

where the iteration function $T \colon \mathbb{K}^n \to \mathbb{K}^n$ is defined by $T(x) = (T_1(x), \ldots, T_n(x))$ with

$$T_i(x) = x_i - \frac{f(x_i)}{f'(x_i) - f(x_i) \sum_{j \neq i} \dfrac{1}{x_i - x_j}} \quad (i = 1, \ldots, n). \tag{4}$$

Ehrlich's method has third order convergence. In 1973, this method was rediscovered by Aberth [14]. In 1970, Börsch-Supan [15] constructed another third-order method for simultaneous computing all the zeros of a polynomial. However in 1982, Werner [16] proved that both Ehrlich's and Börsch-Supan's methods are identical.

In 1999, Trićković and Petković [9] constructed and studied a two-point version of Ehrlich's method. They proved that the two-point Ehrlich-type method has the order of convergence $r = 1 + \sqrt{2}$.

In the present paper, we introduce an infinite sequence of multi-point Ehrlich-type iterative methods. We note that the first member of this family of iterative methods is the two-point Ehrlich-type method constructed in [9]. The main purpose of this paper is to provide a local and semilocal convergence analysis of the multi-point Ehrlich-type methods.

Our local convergence result (Theorem 2) contains the following information: convergence domain; a priori and a posteriori error estimates; convergence order of every method of the family. For instance, we prove that for a given natural number N, the order of convergence of the Nth multi-point Ehrlich-type method is $r = r(N)$, where r is the unique positive solution of the equation

$$1 + 2(t + \ldots + t^N) = t^{N+1}. \tag{5}$$

It follows from this result that the first iterative method ($N = 1$) has the order of convergence $r(1) = 1 + \sqrt{2}$ which coincides with the above mentioned result of Trićković and Petković. We note that each method of the new family has super-quadratic convergence of order $r \in [1 + \sqrt{2}, 3)$. The semilocal convergence result (Theorem 4) states a computer-verifiable initial condition that guarantees fast convergence of the corresponding method of the family.

The paper is structured as follows: In Section 2, we introduce the new family of multi-point iterative methods. Section 3 contains some auxiliary results that underlie the proofs of the main results. In Section 3, we present a local convergence result (Theorem 2) for the iterative methods of the new family. This result contains initial conditions as well as a priori and a posteriori error estimates. In Section 5, we provide a semilocal convergence result (Theorem 4) with computer verifiable initial conditions. Section 6 provides two numerical examples to show the applicability of our semilocal convergence theorem and the convergence behavior of the proposed multi-point iterative methods. The paper ends with a conclusion section.

2. A New Family of Multi-Point Ehrlich-Type Iterative Methods

Throughout the paper $(\mathbb{K}, |\cdot|)$ stands for a valued field with a nontrivial absolute value $|\cdot|$ and $\mathbb{K}[z]$ denotes the ring of uni-variate polynomials over $\mathbb{K}$. The vector space $\mathbb{K}^n$ is equipped with the product topology.

For a given vector $u \in \mathbb{K}^n$, u_i always denotes the ith component of u. For example, if F is a map with values in $\mathbb{K}^n$, then $F_i(x)$ denotes the ith component of the vector $F(x) \in \mathbb{K}^n$. Let us define a binary relation $\#$ on $\mathbb{K}^n$ as follows [17]

$$u \# v \quad \Leftrightarrow \quad u_i \neq v_j \text{ for all } i,j \in I_n \text{ with } i \neq j.$$

Here and throughout the paper, I_n is defined by

$$I_n = \{1, 2, \ldots, n\}.$$

Suppose $f \in \mathbb{K}[z]$ is a polynomial of degree $n \geq 2$. A vector $\xi \in \mathbb{K}^n$ is called a *root vector* of the polynomial f if

$$f(z) = a_0 \prod_{i=1}^{n}(z - \xi_i) \quad \text{for all} \quad z \in \mathbb{K},$$

where $a_0 \in \mathbb{K}$. It is obvious that f possesses a root vector in $\mathbb{K}^n$ if and only if it splits over $\mathbb{K}$.

In the following definition, we introduce a real-value function of two vector variables that plays an essential role in the present study.

Definition 1. *Suppose $f \in \mathbb{K}[z]$ is a polynomial of degree $n \geq 2$. We define an iteration function $\Phi: D_\Phi \subset \mathbb{K}^n \times \mathbb{K}^n \to \mathbb{K}^n$ of two vector variables as follows:*

$$\Phi_i(x, y) = x_i - \frac{f(x_i)}{f'(x_i) - f(x_i) \sum_{j \neq i} \frac{1}{x_i - y_j}} \quad (i = 1, \ldots, n), \tag{6}$$

where D_Φ is defined by

$$D_\Phi = \left\{ (x, y) \in \mathbb{K}^n \times \mathbb{K}^n : x \# y, \ f'(x_i) - f(x_i) \sum_{j \neq i} \frac{1}{x_i - y_j} \neq 0 \ \text{for} \ i \in I_n \right\}. \tag{7}$$

Now the two-point Ehrlich-type root-finding method introduced by Tričković and Petković [9] can be defined by the following iteration

$$x^{(k+1)} = \Phi(x^{(k)}, x^{(k-1)}), \quad k = 0, 1, \ldots \tag{8}$$

with initial approximations $x^{(0)}, x^{(-1)} \in \mathbb{K}^n$.

Theorem 1 (Petković and Tričkovic [9]). *The convergence order of the two-point Ehrlich-type method (8) is $r = 1 + \sqrt{2} \approx 2.414$.*

Based on the function Φ, we define a sequence $(\Phi^{(N)})_{N=1}^{\infty}$ of vector-valued functions such that the Nth function $\Phi^{(N)}$ is a function of $N + 1$ vector variables.

Definition 2. *We define a sequence $(\Phi^{(N)})_{N=0}^{\infty}$ of iteration functions*

$$\Phi^{(N)}: D_N \subset \underbrace{\mathbb{K}^n \times \ldots \times \mathbb{K}^n}_{N+1} \to \mathbb{K}^n$$

recursively by setting $\Phi^{(0)}(x) = x$ and

$$\Phi^{(N)}(x, y, \ldots, z) = \Phi(x, \Phi^{(N-1)}(y, \ldots, z)). \tag{9}$$

The sequence $(D_N)_{N=0}^{\infty}$ of domains is defined also recursively by setting $D_0 = \mathbb{K}^n$ and

$$D_N = \left\{ (x,y,\ldots,z) \in \underbrace{\mathbb{K}^n \times \ldots \times \mathbb{K}^n}_{N+1} : (y,\ldots,z) \in D_{N-1}, \; x \mathbin{\#} \Phi^{(N-1)}(y,\ldots,z) \right. \\ \left. \text{and } f'(x_i) - f(x_i) \sum_{j \neq i} \frac{1}{x_i - \Phi_j^{(N-1)}(y,\ldots,z)} \neq 0 \; \text{ for } \; i \in I_n \right\}. \quad (10)$$

Clearly, the iteration function $\Phi^{(1)}$ coincides with the function Φ.

Definition 3. *Let N be a given natural number, and $x^{(0)}, x^{(-1)}, \ldots, x^{(-N)} \in \mathbb{K}^n$ be $N+1$ initial approximations. We define the Nth iterative method of an infinite sequence of multi-point Ehrlich-type methods by the following iteration*

$$x^{(k+1)} = \Phi^{(N)}(x^{(k)}, x^{(k-1)}, \ldots, x^{(k-N)}), \quad k = 0, 1, \ldots. \quad (11)$$

Note that in the case $N = 1$, the iterative method (11) coincides with the two-point Ehrlich-type method (8).

In Section 4, we present a local convergence theorem (Theorem 2) for the methods (11) with initial conditions that guarantee the convergence to a root vector of f. In the case $N = 1$, this result extends Theorem 1 in several directions.

In Section 5, we present a semilocal convergence theorem (Theorem 4) for the family (11), which is of practical importance.

3. Preliminaries

In this section, we present two basic properties of the iteration function Φ defined in Definition 1, which play an important role in obtaining the main result in Section 4.

In what follows, we assume that $\mathbb{K}^n$ is endowed with the norm $\|\cdot\|_{\infty}$ defined by

$$\|u\|_{\infty} = \max\{|u_1|, \ldots, |u_n|\}$$

and with the cone norm $\|\cdot\|: \mathbb{K}^n \to \mathbb{R}^n$ defined by

$$\|u\| = (|u_1|, \ldots, |u_n|),$$

assuming that $\mathbb{R}^n$ is endowed with the component-wise ordering $\preceq$ defined by

$$u \preceq v \quad \Leftrightarrow \quad u_i \leq v_i \text{ for all } i \in I_n.$$

Furthermore, for two vectors $u \in \mathbb{K}^n$ and $v \in \mathbb{R}^n$, we denote by u/v the vector

$$\frac{u}{v} = \left(\frac{|u_1|}{v_1}, \ldots, \frac{|u_n|}{v_n} \right).$$

We define a function $d: \mathbb{K}^n \to \mathbb{R}^n$ by $d(u) = (d_1(u), \ldots, d_n(u))$ with

$$d_i(u) = \min_{j \neq i} |u_i - u_j| \quad (i = 1, \ldots, n).$$

Lemma 1 ([11]). *Suppose $x, y, \xi \in \mathbb{K}^n$ and ξ is a vector with pairwise distinct components.*

$$|x_i - y_j| \geq (1 - E(x) - E(y)) |\xi_i - \xi_j| \quad \text{for all } i,j \in I_n, \quad (12)$$

where the function $E\colon \mathbb{K}^n \to \mathbb{R}_+$ is defined by

$$E(x) = \left\| \frac{x - \xi}{d(\xi)} \right\|_\infty. \tag{13}$$

Lemma 2. *Suppose $f \in \mathbb{K}[z]$ is a polynomial of degree $n \geq 2$, which splits over $\mathbb{K}$, and $\xi \in \mathbb{K}^n$ is a root vector of f. Let $x, y \in \mathbb{K}^n$ be two vectors such that $x \mathbin{\#} y$. If $f(x_i) \neq 0$ for some $i \in I_n$, then*

$$\frac{f'(x_i)}{f(x_i)} - \sum_{j \neq i} \frac{1}{x_i - y_j} = \frac{1 - \tau_i}{x_i - \xi_i}, \tag{14}$$

where $\tau_i \in \mathbb{K}$ is defined by

$$\tau_i = (x_i - \xi_i) \sum_{j \neq i} \frac{y_j - \xi_j}{(x_i - \xi_j)(x_i - y_j)}. \tag{15}$$

Proof. Since ξ is a root vector of f, we obtain

$$\frac{f'(x_i)}{f(x_i)} - \sum_{j \neq i} \frac{1}{x_i - y_j} = \sum_{j=1}^n \frac{1}{x_i - \xi_j} - \sum_{j \neq i} \frac{1}{x_i - y_j} = \frac{1}{x_i - \xi_i} + \sum_{j \neq i} \left(\frac{1}{x_i - \xi_j} + \frac{1}{x_i - y_j} \right)$$

$$= \frac{1}{x_i - \xi_i} - \sum_{j \neq i} \frac{y_j - \xi_j}{(x_i - \xi_j)(x_i - y_j)} = \frac{1 - \tau_i}{x_i - \xi_i},$$

which proves (14). □

Define the function $\sigma\colon \mathscr{D} \subset \mathbb{K}^n \times \mathbb{K}^n \to \mathbb{R}_+$ by

$$\sigma(x, y) = \frac{(n-1) E(x) E(y)}{(1 - E(x))(1 - E(x) - E(y)) - (n-1) E(x) E(y)} \tag{16}$$

with domain

$$\mathscr{D} = \{(x, y) \in \mathbb{K}^n \times \mathbb{K}^n : (1 - E(x))(1 - E(x) - E(y)) > (n-1) E(x) E(y) \text{ and } E(x) + E(y) < 1\}, \tag{17}$$

where $E\colon \mathbb{K}^n \to \mathbb{R}_+$ is defined by (13).

Lemma 3. *Let $f \in \mathbb{K}[z]$ be a polynomial of degree $n \geq 2$ with n simple zeros in $\mathbb{K}$, and let $\xi \in \mathbb{K}^n$ be a root vector of f. Suppose $x, y \in \mathbb{K}^n$ are two vectors such that $(x, y) \in \mathscr{D}$. Then:*

(i) $(x, y) \in D_\Phi$;
(ii) $\|\Phi(x, y) - \xi\| \preceq \sigma(x, y) \|x - \xi\|$;
(iii) $E(\Phi(x, y)) \leq \sigma(x, y) E(x)$,

where the functions Φ, E and σ are defined by (6), (13) and (16), respectively.

Proof. (i) According to (17), we have $E(x) + E(y) < 1$. Then it follows from Lemma 1 that

$$|x_i - y_j| \geq (1 - E(x)) d_j(\xi) > 0 \tag{18}$$

for every $j \neq i$. This yields $x \mathbin{\#} y$. In view of (7), it remains to prove that

$$f'(x_i) - f(x_i) \sum_{j \neq i} \frac{1}{x_i - y_j} \neq 0 \tag{19}$$

for $i \in I_n$. Let $i \in I_n$ be fixed. We shall consider only the non-trivial case $f(x_i) \neq 0$. In this case, (19) is equivalent to

$$\frac{f'(x_i)}{f(x_i)} - \sum_{j \neq i} \frac{1}{x_i - y_j} \neq 0. \tag{20}$$

On the other hand, it follows from Lemma 2 that (20) is equivalent to $\tau_i \neq 1$, where τ_i is defined by (15). By Lemma 1 with $y = \xi$, we obtain

$$|x_i - \xi_j| \geq (1 - E(x)) d_i(\xi) > 0 \tag{21}$$

for every $j \neq i$. From (15), (18) and (21), we obtain

$$\begin{aligned}
|\tau_i| &\leq |x_i - \xi_i| \sum_{j \neq i} \frac{|y_j - \xi_j|}{|x_i - \xi_j||x_i - y_j|} \tag{22} \\
&\leq \frac{1}{(1 - E(x))(1 - E(x) - E(y))} \frac{|x_i - \xi_i|}{d_i(\xi)} \sum_{j \neq i} \frac{|y_j - \xi_j|}{d_j(\xi)} \\
&\leq \frac{(n-1)E(x)E(y)}{(1 - E(x))(1 - E(x) - E(y))} < 1.
\end{aligned}$$

This implies that $\tau_i \neq 1$ which proves the first claim.

(ii) The second claim is equivalent to

$$|\Phi_i(x, y) - \xi_i| \leq \sigma(x, y) |x_i - \xi_i| \tag{23}$$

for all $i \in I_n$. If $x_i = \xi_i$, then (23) holds trivially. Let $x_i \neq \xi_i$. Then, it follows from (21) that $f(x_i) \neq 0$. It follows from (6), (20) and (14) that

$$\begin{aligned}
\Phi_i(x, y) - \xi_i &= x_i - \xi_i - \left(\frac{f'(x_i)}{f(x_i)} - \sum_{j \neq i} \frac{1}{x_i - y_j} \right)^{-1} \tag{24} \\
&= x_i - \xi_i - \frac{x_i - \xi_i}{1 - \tau_i} = -\frac{\tau_i}{1 - \tau_i}(x_i - \xi_i).
\end{aligned}$$

By (24) and the estimate (22), we obtain

$$\begin{aligned}
|\Phi_i(x, y) - \xi_i| &= \frac{|\tau_i|}{|1 - \tau_i|} |x_i - \xi_i| \leq \frac{|\tau_i|}{1 - |\tau_i|} |x_i - \xi_i| \\
&\leq \frac{(n-1)E(x)E(y)}{(1 - E(x))(1 - E(x) - E(y)) - (n-1)E(x)E(y)} |x_i - \xi_i| \\
&= \sigma(x, y) |x_i - \xi_i|.
\end{aligned}$$

Therefore, (23) holds, which proves the second claim.

(iii) By dividing both sides of the last inequality by $d_i(\xi)$ and taking the max-norm, we obtain the third claim. □

Lemma 4. *Let $f \in \mathbb{K}[z]$ be a polynomial of degree $n \geq 2$ with n simple zeros in $\mathbb{K}$, and let $\xi \in \mathbb{K}^n$ be a root vector of f. Suppose $x, y \in \mathbb{K}^n$ are two vectors satisfying*

$$\max\{E(x), E(y)\} \leq R = \frac{2}{3 + \sqrt{8n - 7}}, \tag{25}$$

where the function $E \colon \mathbb{K}^n \to \mathbb{R}_+$ is defined by (13). Then:

(i) $(x, y) \in \mathscr{D}$;

(ii) $\sigma(x,y) \leq \dfrac{E(x)E(y)}{R^2}$;

(iii) $E(\Phi(x,y)) \leq \dfrac{E(x)^2 E(y)}{R^2}$.

Proof. It follows from (25) that $E(x) + E(y) \leq 2R < 1$ and

$$(1 - E(x))(1 - E(x) - E(y)) - (n-1)E(x)E(y) \geq (1-R)(1-2R) - (n-1)R^2 > 0. \quad (26)$$

Hence, it follows from (17) that $(x,y) \in \mathscr{D}$ which proves the claim (i). It is easy to show that R is the unique positive zero of the function ϕ, defined by

$$\phi(t) = \dfrac{(n-1)t^2}{(1-t)(1-2t) - (n-1)t^2}. \qquad (27)$$

Then, from (16) and (26), we obtain

$$\begin{aligned}
\sigma(x,y) &\leq \dfrac{(n-1)E(x)\,E(y)}{(1-R)(1-2R) - (n-1)R^2} \\
&= \dfrac{(n-1)R^2}{(1-R)(1-2R) - (n-1)R^2} \dfrac{E(x)E(y)}{R^2} \\
&= \phi(R)\dfrac{E(x)E(y)}{R^2} = \dfrac{E(x)E(y)}{R^2},
\end{aligned} \qquad (28)$$

which proves (ii). The claim (iii) follows from Lemma 3 (iii) and claim (ii). □

4. Local Convergence Analysis

In this section, we present a local convergence theorem for the multi-point iterative methods (11). More precisely, we study the local convergence of the multi-point Ehrlich-type methods (11) with respect to the function of the initial conditions $E \colon \mathbb{K}^n \to \mathbb{R}_+$ defined by (13), where $\xi \in \mathbb{K}^n$ is a root vector of a polynomial $f \in \mathbb{K}[z]$.

Definition 4. We define a sequence $(\sigma_N)_{N=1}^{\infty}$ of functions $\sigma_N \colon \mathscr{D}_N \subset \underbrace{\mathbb{K}^n \times \ldots \times \mathbb{K}^n}_{N+1} \to \mathbb{R}$ by

$$\sigma_N(x, y, \ldots, z) = \sigma(x, \Phi^{(N-1)}(y, \ldots, z)), \qquad (29)$$

where σ is defined by (16). The domain $\mathscr{D}_N$ is defined by

$$\begin{aligned}
\mathscr{D}_N = \{(x, y, \ldots, z) &: x \in \mathbb{K}^n,\ (y, \ldots, z) \in D_{N-1},\\
&(1 - E(x))(1 - E(x) - E(\Phi^{(N-1)}(y, \ldots, z))) > (n-1)E(x)E(\Phi^{(N-1)}(y, \ldots, z)),\\
&E(x) + E(\Phi^{(N-1)}(y, \ldots, z)) < 1\},
\end{aligned}$$

and D_N is defined by (10).

Lemma 5. Let $f \in \mathbb{K}[z]$ be a polynomial of degree $n \geq 2$ with n simple zeros in $\mathbb{K}$ and $\xi \in \mathbb{K}^n$ be a root vector of f. Assume $N \geq 1$ and $(x, y, \ldots, z) \in \mathscr{D}_N$. Then:

(i) $(x, y, \ldots, z) \in D_N$;

(ii) $\|\Phi^{(N)}(x, y, \ldots, z) - \xi\| \leq \sigma_N(x, y, \ldots, z)\,\|x - \xi\|$;

(iii) $E(\Phi^{(N)}(x, y, \ldots, z)) \leq \sigma_N(x, y, \ldots, z)\,E(x)$,

where $\Phi^{(N)}$ and σ_N are defined by (9) and (29), respectively.

Proof. Applying Lemma 1 with $y = \Phi^{(N-1)}(y,\ldots,z)$, we obtain (i). It follows from Definition 2, Lemma 3 (ii) and Definition 4 that

$$\|\Phi^{(N)}(x,y,\ldots,z) - \xi\| = \|\Phi(x, \Phi^{(N-1)}(y,\ldots,z)) - \xi\|$$
$$\preceq \sigma(x, \Phi^{(N-1)}(y,\ldots,z))\,\|x - \xi\| = \sigma_N(x,y,\ldots,z)\,\|x - \xi\|,$$

which proves (ii). From Definition 2, Lemma 3 (iii) and Definition 4, we obtain

$$E(\Phi^{(N)}(x,y,\ldots,z)) = E(\Phi(x, \Phi^{(N-1)}(y,\ldots,z)))$$
$$\leq \sigma(x, \Phi^{(N-1)}(y,\ldots,z))\,E(x) = \sigma_N(x,y,\ldots,z)\,E(x),$$

which proves (iii). □

Lemma 6. *Let $f \in \mathbb{K}[z]$ be a polynomial of degree $n \geq 2$ with n simple zeros in $\mathbb{K}$, and let $\xi \in \mathbb{K}^n$ be a root vector of f. Assume $N \geq 1$ and $x,y,\ldots,t,z$ are $N+1$ vectors in $\mathbb{K}^n$ such that*

$$\max\{E(x), E(y),\ldots, E(z)\} \leq R = \frac{2}{3 + \sqrt{8n-7}}, \tag{30}$$

where the function $E \colon \mathbb{K}^n \to \mathbb{R}_+$ is defined by (13). Then:

(i) $(x,y,\ldots,t,z) \in \mathscr{D}_N$;

(ii) $\sigma_N(x,y,\ldots,t,z) \leq \dfrac{E(x)E(y)^2 \ldots E(t)^2 E(z)}{R^{2N}}$;

(iii) $E(\Phi^{(N)}(x,y,\ldots,t,z)) \leq \dfrac{E(x)^2 E(y)^2 \ldots E(t)^2 E(z)}{R^{2N}}$.

Proof. The proof goes by induction on N. In the case $N = 1$, Lemma 6 coincides with Lemma 4. Suppose that for some $N \geq 1$ the three claims of the lemma hold for every $N+1$ vectors $x,y,\ldots,t,z \in \mathbb{K}^n$ satisfying (30). Let $x,y,\ldots,t,z \in \mathbb{K}^n$ be $N+2$ vectors satisfying

$$\max\{E(x), E(y),\ldots, E(t), E(z)\} \leq R.$$

We must prove the following three claims:

$$(x,y,\ldots,t,z) \in \mathscr{D}_{N+1}, \tag{31}$$

$$\sigma_{N+1}(x,y,\ldots,t,z) \leq \frac{E(x)E(y)^2 \ldots E(t)^2 E(z)}{R^{2(N+1)}}, \tag{32}$$

$$E(\Phi^{(N+1)}(x,y,\ldots,z)) \leq \frac{E(x)^2 E(y)^2 \ldots E(t)^2 E(z)}{R^{2(N+1)}}. \tag{33}$$

By induction assumption, we obtain $(y,\ldots,t,z) \in \mathscr{D}_N$. By induction assumption (ii) and (30), we obtain

$$E(x) + E(\Phi^{(N)}(y,\ldots,t,z)) \leq E(x) + E(y)^2 \ldots E(t)^2 E(z)/R^{2N} \leq 2R < 1. \tag{34}$$

By induction assumption, we also have

$$(1 - E(x))(1 - E(x) - E(\Phi^{(N)}(y,\ldots,z))) - (n-1)E(x)E(\Phi^{(N)}(y,\ldots,z))$$
$$> (1-R)(1-2R) - (n-1)R^2 > 0 \tag{35}$$

The inequalities (34) and (35) yield $(x, y, \ldots, z) \in \mathcal{D}_{N+1}$, which proves (31). From Definition 4, Lemma 4 (ii) and induction assumption (ii), we obtain

$$\sigma_{N+1}(x, y, \ldots, z) = \sigma(x, \Phi^{(N)}(y, \ldots, z)) \leq E(x) E(\Phi^{(N)}(y, \ldots, z)/R^2$$
$$\leq E(x)E(y)^2 \ldots E(t)^2 E(z)/R^{2(N+1)},$$

which proves (32). Claim (33) follows from Lemma 5 (ii) and claim (32). □

Now we are ready to state the first main result in this paper.

Theorem 2. *Suppose $f \in \mathbb{K}[z]$ is a polynomial of degree $n \geq 2$ which has n simple zeros in $\mathbb{K}$, $\xi \in \mathbb{K}^n$ is a root vector of f, and $N \in \mathbb{N}$. Let $x^{(0)}, x^{(-1)}, \ldots, x^{(-N)} \in \mathbb{K}^n$ be initial approximations such that*

$$\max_{-N \leq k \leq 0} E(x^{(k)}) < R = \frac{2}{3 + \sqrt{8n - 7}}, \quad (36)$$

where the function $E \colon \mathbb{K}^n \to \mathbb{R}_+$ is defined by (13). Then the multi-point Ehrlich-type iteration (11) is well defined and converges to ξ with order r and error estimates

$$\|x^{(k+1)} - \xi\| \preceq \lambda^{r^{k+N+1} - r^{k+N}} \|x^{(k)} - \xi\| \quad \text{for all } k \geq 0, \quad (37)$$

$$\|x^{(k)} - \xi\| \preceq \lambda^{r^{k+N} - r^N} \|x^{(0)} - \xi\| \quad \text{for all } k \geq 0, \quad (38)$$

where $r = r(N)$ is the unique positive root of the Equation (5), and λ is defined by

$$\lambda = \max_{-N \leq k \leq 0} \left(\frac{E(x^{(k)})}{R} \right)^{1/r^{k+N}}. \quad (39)$$

Proof. First, we will show that the iterative sequence $(x^{(k)})_{k=-N}^{\infty}$ generated by (11) is well defined and the inequality

$$E(x^{(\nu)}) \leq R \lambda^{r^{\nu+N}} \quad (40)$$

holds for every integer $\nu \geq -N$. The proof is by induction. It follows from (39) that (40) holds for $-N \leq \nu \leq 0$. Suppose that for some $k \geq 0$ the iterates $x^{(k)}, x^{(k-1)}, \ldots, x^{(k-N)}$ are well defined and

$$E(x^{(\nu)}) \leq R \lambda^{r^{\nu+N}} \quad \text{for all} \quad k - N \leq \nu \leq k. \quad (41)$$

We shall prove that the iterate $x^{(k+1)}$ is well defined and that it satisfies the inequality (40) with $\nu = k + 1$. It follows from (39) that $0 \leq \lambda < 1$. Hence, from (41) we obtain

$$\max_{k-N \leq \nu \leq k} E(x^{(\nu)}) \leq R.$$

Then by (11), Lemma 6 (iii), (41) and the definition of r, we obtain

$$E(x^{(k+1)}) = E(\Phi^{(N)}(x^{(k)}, x^{(k-1)} \ldots, x^{(k-N)}))$$
$$\leq \left(E(x^{(k)}) E(x^{(k-1)}) \ldots E(x^{(k-N+1)}) \right)^2 E(x^{(k-N)})/R^{2N}$$
$$\leq R \left(\lambda^{r^{k+N}} \lambda^{r^{k+N-1}} \ldots \lambda^{r^{k+1}} \right)^2 \lambda^{r^k} = R \lambda^{r^k(1+2r+\ldots+2r^{N-1}+2r^N)} = R \lambda^{r^{k+N+1}},$$

which completes the induction. By Lemma 6 (ii), (40) and the definition of r, we obtain the following estimate

$$\sigma_N(x^{(k)}, x^{(k-1)}, \ldots, x^{(k-N)}) \leq E(x^{(k)}) \left(E(x^{(k-1)}) \ldots E(x^{(k-N+1)}) \right)^2 E(x^{(k-N)})/R^{2N}$$
$$\leq \lambda^{r^{k+N}} \left(\lambda^{r^{k+N-1}} \ldots \lambda^{r^{k+1}} \right)^2 \lambda^{r^k} = \lambda^{r^k(1+2r+\ldots+2r^{N-1}+r^N)} = \lambda^{r^{k+N+1} - r^{k+N}}.$$

From (11), Lemma 5 (ii) and the last estimate, we obtain

$$\|x^{(k+1)} - \xi\| = \|\Phi^{(N)}(x^{(k)}, x^{(k-1)}, \ldots, x^{(k-N)}) - \xi\|$$
$$\preceq \sigma_N(x^{(k)}, x^{(k-1)}, \ldots, x^{(k-N)}) \|x^{(k)} - \xi\|$$
$$\preceq \lambda^{r^{k+N+1} - r^{k+N}} \|x^{(k)} - \xi\|,$$

which proved the a posteriori estimate (37). The a priori estimate (38) can be easily proved by induction using the estimate (37). Finally, the convergence of the sequence $x^{(k)}$ to a root vector ξ follows from the estimate (38). □

Remark 1. *It can be proved that the sequence $r(N)$, $N = 1, 2, \ldots$, of orders of the multi-point Ehrlich-type methods (11) is an increasing sequence which converges to 3 as $N \to \infty$. In Table 1, one can see the order of convergence $r = r(N)$ for $N = 1, 2, \ldots, 10$.*

Table 1. Values of the convergence order $r = r(N)$ for $N = 1, 2, \ldots, 10$.

N	1	2	3	4	5	6	7	8	9	10
$r(N)$	2.41421	2.83117	2.94771	2.98314	2.99446	2.99816	2.99939	2.99979	2.99993	2.99998

5. Semilocal Convergence Analysis

In this section, we present a semilocal convergence result for the multi-point Ehrlich type methods (11) with respect to the function of initial conditions $E_f \colon \mathcal{D} \subset \mathbb{K}^n \to \mathbb{R}_+$ defined by

$$E_f(x) = \left\| \frac{W_f(x)}{d(x)} \right\|_\infty, \tag{42}$$

where the function $W_f \colon \mathcal{D} \subset \mathbb{K}^n \to \mathbb{K}^n$ is defined by (2). We note that in the last decade, this is the most frequently used function to set the initial approximations of semilocal results for simultaneous methods for polynomial zeros. (see, e.g., [10,11,17–22]).

The new result is obtained as a consequence from the local convergence Theorem 2 by using the following transformation theorem:

Theorem 3 (Proinov [19]). *Let $\mathbb{K}$ be an algebraically closed field, $f \in \mathbb{K}[z]$ be a polynomial of degree $n \geq 2$, and let $x \in \mathbb{K}^n$ be a vector with pairwise distinct components such that*

$$\left\| \frac{W_f(x)}{d(x)} \right\|_\infty < \frac{R(1+R)}{(1+2R)(1+nR)}, \tag{43}$$

where $0 < R \leq 1/(\sqrt{n-1} - 1)$. Then f has only simple zeros in $\mathbb{K}$ and there exists a root vector $\xi \in \mathbb{K}^n$ of f such that

$$\left\| \frac{x - \xi}{d(\xi)} \right\|_\infty < R. \tag{44}$$

Each iterative method for finding simultaneously all roots of a polynomial $f \in \mathbb{K}[z]$ of degree $n \geq 2$ is an iterative method in $\mathbb{K}^n$. It searches the roots $\xi_1, \ldots, \xi_n$ of the polynomial f as a vector $\xi = (\xi_1, \ldots, \xi_n) \in \mathbb{K}^n$. We have noticed in Section 2 that such a vector ξ is called a root vector of f. Clearly, a polynomial can have more than one vector of the roots. On the other hand, we can assume that the vector root is unique up to permutation.

A natural question arises regarding how to measure the distance of an approximation $x \in \mathbb{K}^n$ to the zeros of a polynomial. The first step is to identify all vectors whose components are the same up to permutation. Namely, we define a relation of equivalence

$\equiv$ on $\mathbb{K}^n$ by $x \equiv y$ if the components of x and y are the same up to permutation. Then following [11,20], we define a distance between two vectors $x, y \in \mathbb{K}^n$ as follows

$$\rho(x, y) = \min_{v \equiv y} \|x - v\|_\infty. \tag{45}$$

Note that ρ is a metric on the set of classes of equivalence. For simplicity, we shall identify equivalence classes with their representatives.

In what follows, we consider the convergence in $\mathbb{K}^n$ with respect to the metric ρ. Clearly, if a sequence $x^{(k)}$ in $\mathbb{K}^n$ is convergent to a vector $x \in \mathbb{K}^n$ with respect to the norm $\|\cdot\|$, then it converges to x with respect to the metric ρ. The opposite statement is not true (see [11]).

Before formulating the main result, we recall a technical lemma.

Lemma 7 ([11]). *Let $x, \xi, \bar{\xi} \in \mathbb{K}^n$ be such that $\bar{\xi} \equiv \xi$. Then there exists a vector $\bar{x} \in \mathbb{K}^n$ such that $\bar{x} \equiv x$ and*

$$\left\| \frac{x - \bar{\xi}}{d(\bar{\xi})} \right\|_\infty = \left\| \frac{\bar{x} - \xi}{d(\xi)} \right\|_\infty. \tag{46}$$

Now we can formulate and prove the second main result of this paper.

Theorem 4. *Suppose $\mathbb{K}$ is an algebraically closed field, $f \in \mathbb{K}[z]$ is a polynomial of degree $n \geq 2$ and $N \in \mathbb{N}$. Let $x^{(0)}, x^{(-1)}, \ldots, x^{(-N)} \in \mathbb{K}^n$ be initial approximations satisfying the following condition:*

$$\max_{-N \leq k \leq 0} E_f(x^{(k)}) < R_n = \frac{2(5 + \sqrt{8n - 7})}{(2n + 3 + \sqrt{8n - 7})(7 + \sqrt{8n - 7})}, \tag{47}$$

where the function E_f is defined by (42). Then the polynomial f has only simple zeros and the multi-point Ehrlich-type iteration (11) is well defined and converges (with respect to the metric ρ) to a root vector ξ of f with order of convergence $r = r(N)$, where r is the unique positive solution of the Equation (5).

Proof. The condition (47) can be represented in the form

$$\max_{-N \leq k \leq 0} \left\| \frac{W_f(x)}{d(x)} \right\|_\infty < \frac{R(1 + R)}{(1 + 2R)(1 + nR)}, \tag{48}$$

where R is defined in (36). From Theorem 3 and the inequality (48), we conclude that f has n simple zeros in $\mathbb{K}$ and that there exist root vectors $\xi^{(0)}, \xi^{(-1)}, \ldots \xi^{(-N)} \in \mathbb{K}^n$ such that

$$\max_{-N \leq k \leq 0} \left\| \frac{x^{(k)} - \xi^{(k)}}{d(\xi^{(k)})} \right\|_\infty < R. \tag{49}$$

Let us put $\xi^{(0)} = \xi$. Since $\xi^{(0)}, \xi^{(-1)}, \ldots \xi^{(-N)}$ are root vectors of f, then $\xi^{(k)} \equiv \xi$ for all $k = 0, -1, \ldots, -N$. It follows from Lemma 7 that there exist vectors $\bar{x}^{(0)}, \bar{x}^{(-1)}, \ldots, \bar{x}^{(-N)}$ such that $\bar{x}^{(k)} \equiv x^{(k)}$ and (49) can be represented in the form

$$\max_{-N \leq k \leq 0} \left\| \frac{\bar{x}^{(k)} - \xi}{d(\xi)} \right\|_\infty < R. \tag{50}$$

It follows from Theorem 2 and inequality (50) that the multi-point iterative method (11) with initial approximations $\bar{x}^{(0)}, \bar{x}^{(-1)}, \ldots, \bar{x}^{(-N)}$ is well defined and converges to ξ. Hence, the iteration (11) with initial approximations $x^{(0)}, x^{(-1)}, \ldots, x^{(-N)}$ converges with respect to the metric ρ to the root vector of f. □

The following criterion guarantees the convergence of the methods (11). It is an immediate consequence of Theorem 4.

Corollary 1 (Convergence criterion). *If there exists an integer $m \geq 0$ such that*

$$E_m = \max\{E_f(x^{(m)}), E_f(x^{(m-1)}), \ldots, E_f(x^{(m-N)})\} < R_n, \tag{51}$$

then f has only simple zeros and the multi-point Ehrlich-type iteration (11) converges to a root vector ξ of f.

The next result is an immediate consequence of Theorem 5.1 of [19]. It can be used as a stopping criterion of a large class of iterative methods for approximating all zeros of a polynomial simultaneously.

Theorem 5 (Proinov [19]). *Suppose $\mathbb{K}$ is an algebraically closed field, $f \in \mathbb{K}[z]$ is a polynomial of degree $n \geq 2$ with simple zeros, and $(x^{(k)})_{k=0}^{\infty}$ is a sequence in $\mathbb{K}^n$ consisting of vectors with pairwise distinct components. If $k \geq 0$ is such that*

$$E_f(x^{(k)}) < \mu_n = 1/(n + 2\sqrt{n-1}), \tag{52}$$

then the following a posteriori error estimate holds:

$$\rho(x^{(k)}, \xi) \leq \varepsilon_k = \alpha(E_f(x^{(k)})) \|W_f(x^{(k)})\|_\infty, \tag{53}$$

where the metric ρ is defined by (45), the function E_f is defined by (42), and the function α is defined by

$$\alpha(t) = 2/(1 - (n-2)t + \sqrt{(1-(n-2)t)^2 - 4t}). \tag{54}$$

6. Numerical Examples

In this section, we present two numerical examples in order to show the applicability of Theorem 4. Using the convergence criterion (51), we show that at the beginning of the iterative process it can be proven numerically that the method is convergent under the given initial approximations.

We apply the first four methods of the family (11) for calculating simultaneously all the zeros of the selected polynomials. In each example, we calculate the smallest $m > 0$ that satisfies the convergence criterion (51). In accordance with Theorem 5, we use the following stop criterion

$$E_f(x^{(k)}) < \mu_n \quad \text{and} \quad \varepsilon_k < 10^{-12}, \tag{55}$$

where μ_n and ε_k are defined by (52) and (53), respectively. To see the convergence behavior of the methods, we show in the tables ε_{k+1} in addition to ε_k.

In both examples, we take the same polynomials and initial approximations as in [11], where the initial approximations are chosen quite randomly. This choice gives the opportunity to compare numerically the convergence behavior of the multi-point Ehrlich-type methods with those of the multi-point Weierstrass-type methods which are studied in [11].

To present the calculated approximations of high accuracy, we implemented the corresponding algorithms using the programming package Wolfram Mathematica 10.0 with multiple precision arithmetic.

Example 1. *The first polynomial is*

$$f(z) = z^3 - (2 + 5i)z^2 - (3 - 10i)z + 15i \tag{56}$$

with zeros $-1, 3$ and $5i$ (marked in blue in Figure 1). For $N \in \{1, 2, 3, 4\}$, the initial approximations $x^{(0)}, x^{(-1)}, \ldots, x^{(-N)}$ in $\mathbb{C}^3$ are given in Table 2, where

$$a = (5+i, 7-i, -4.5i), \quad b = (1, -2.7, 4.5i), \quad c = (-5i, 2, 8),$$

$$u = (-10, -5i, 8), \quad v = (i, 3+i, 8).$$

In the case $N = 3$, the initial approximations are marked in red in Figure 1.

Table 2. Initial approximations for Example 1.

N	$x^{(-4)}$	$x^{(-3)}$	$x^{(-2)}$	$x^{(-1)}$	$x^{(0)}$
1	—	—	—	a	b
2	—	—	a	b	c
3	—	a	b	c	u
4	a	b	c	u	v

The numerical results for Example 1 are presented in Table 3. For instance, for the multi-point Ehrlich-type method (11) with $N = 3$, one can see that the convergence condition (51) is satisfied for $m = 6$ which guarantees that the considered method is convergent with order of convergence $r = 2.94771$. The stopping criterion (55) is satisfied for $k = 6$ and at the sixth iteration the guaranteed accuracy is 10^{-16}. At the next seventh iteration, the zeros of the polynomial f are calculated with accuracy 10^{-47}.

Table 3. Convergence behavior for Example 1 ($R_n = 0.125$, $\tau_n = 0.171573$).

N	m	$E_f(x^{(m)})$	k	$E_f(x^{(k)})$	ε_k	ε_{k+1}	r
1	4	0.036247	5	0.000039	9.06336×10^{-14}	1.52321×10^{-32}	2.41421
2	5	0.001957	5	0.001957	5.97453×10^{-17}	5.45631×10^{-48}	2.83117
3	6	0.076062	6	0.076062	2.46336×10^{-16}	1.05897×10^{-47}	2.94771
4	7	0.083021	7	0.083021	6.50717×10^{-17}	3.80803×10^{-51}	2.98314

In Figure 1, we present the trajectories of the approximations generated by the first six iterations of the method (11) for $N = 3$. We observe how each initial approximation, moving along a bizarre trajectory, finds a zero of the polynomial.

Example 2. *The second polynomial is*

$$f(z) = z^7 - 28 z^6 + 322 z^5 - 1960 z^4 + 6769 z^3 - 13132 z^2 + 13068 z - 5040 \quad (57)$$

with zeros $1, 2, 3, 4, 5, 6, 7$ (marked in blue in Figure 2). For given $N \in \{1, 2, 3, 4\}$, the initial approximations $x^{(k)} \in \mathbb{C}^n$ ($k = -N, \ldots, -1, 0$) are chosen with Aberth initial approximations as follows:

$$x_\nu^{(k)} = -\frac{a_1}{n} + R_k \exp(i\theta_\nu), \quad \theta_\nu = \frac{\pi}{n}\left(2\nu - \frac{3}{2}\right), \quad \nu = 1, \ldots, n, \quad (58)$$

where $a_1 = -28$, $n = 7$, $R_k = R + 2 - k$ and $R = 13.7082$. In the case $N = 3$, the initial approximations are marked in red in Figure 2.

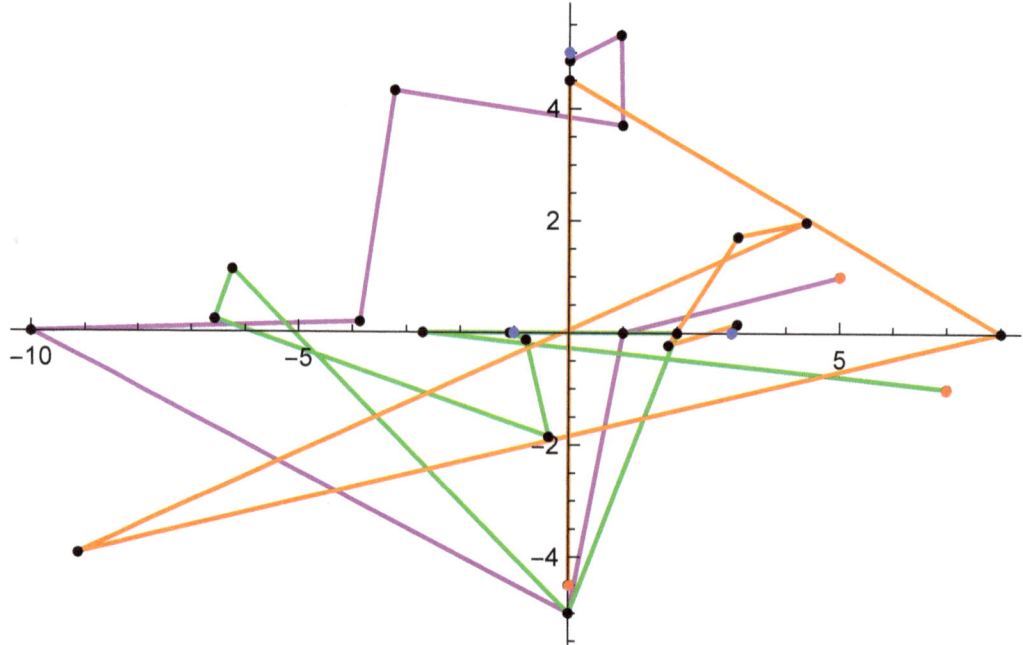

Figure 1. Trajectories of the approximations for Example 1 ($N = 3$).

The numerical results for Example 2 are presented in Table 4. For example, for the multi-point Ehrlich-type method (11) with $N = 3$, the convergence condition (51) is satisfied for $m = 7$ and the stopping criterion (55) is satisfied for $k = 8$ which guarantees an accuracy 10^{-22}. At the next ninth iteration, the zeros of the polynomial f are calculated with accuracy 10^{-65}. In Figure 1, we present the trajectories of the approximations generated by the first seven iterations of the method (11) for $N = 3$. One can see that the trajectories are quite regular in the case of Aberth's initial approximations.

Table 4. Convergence behavior for Example 2 ($R_n = 0.125$, $\tau_n = 0.171573$).

N	m	$E_f(x^{(m)})$	k	$E_f(x^{(k)})$	ε_k	ε_{k+1}
1	18	0.00526	21	3.48544×10^{-10}	4.73454×10^{-16}	1.25695×10^{-38}
2	6	0.01689	8	7.85062×10^{-6}	4.23967×10^{-17}	1.06658×10^{-48}
3	7	0.01348	8	0.00038	1.12167×10^{-22}	6.66169×10^{-65}
4	14	0.03215	14	0.03215	6.61642×10^{-24}	4.98369×10^{-71}

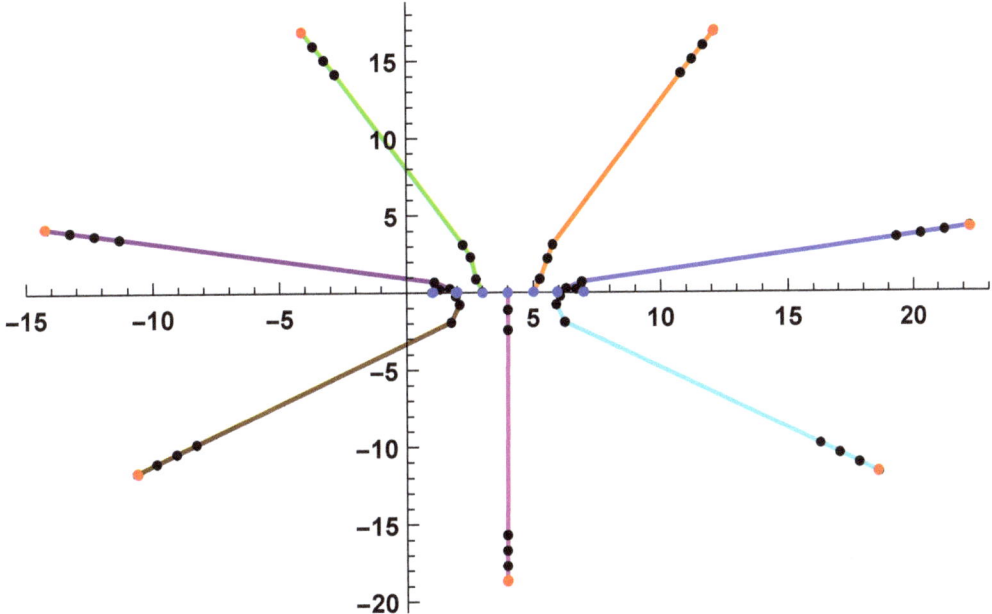

Figure 2. Trajectories of the approximations for Example 2 ($N = 3$).

7. Conclusions

In this paper, we introduced a new family of multi-points iterative methods for approximating all the zeros of a polynomial simultaneously. Let us note that the first member of this family is the two-point Ehrlich-type method introduced in 1999 by Trićković and Petković [9]. Its convergence order is $r = 1 + \sqrt{2}$.

We provide a local and semilocal convergence analysis of the new iterative methods. Our local convergence result (Theorem 2) contains the following information for each method: convergence order; initial conditions that guarantee the convergence; a priori and a posteriori error estimates. In particular, each method of the family has super-quadratic convergence of order $r \in [1 + \sqrt{2}, 3)$. Our semilocal convergence result (Theorem 4) can be used to numerically prove the convergence of each method for a given polynomial and initial approximation.

Finally, we would like to note that the local convergence theorem was obtained by a new approach developed in our previous article [11]. We believe that this approach can be applied to obtain convergence results for other multi-point iterative methods.

Author Contributions: The authors contributed equally to the writing and approved the final manuscript of this paper. Both authors have read and agreed to the published version of the manuscript.

Funding: This research was supported by the National Science Fund of the Bulgarian Ministry of Education and Science under Grant DN 12/12.

Institutional Review Board Statement: Not applicable.

Informed Consent Statement: Not applicable.

Data Availability Statement: Not applicable.

Conflicts of Interest: The authors declares no conflict of interest.

References

1. Stewart, G.W. On the convergence of multipoint iterations. *Numer. Math.* **1994**, *68*, 143–147. [CrossRef]
2. Abu-Alshaikh, I.; Sahin, A. Two-point iterative methods for solving nonlinear equations. *Appl. Math. Comput.* **2006**, *182*, 871–878. [CrossRef]
3. Ignatova, B.; Kyurkchiev, N.; Iliev, A. Multipoint algorithms arising from optimal in the sense of Kung-Traub iterative procedures for numerical solution of nonlinear equations. *Gen. Math. Notes* **2011**, *11*, 45–79.
4. Argyros, I.K.; González, D. Unified majorizing sequences for Traub-type multipoint iterative procedures. *Numer. Algorithms* **2013**, *64*, 549–565. [CrossRef]
5. Tiruneh, A.T.; Ndlela, W.N.; Nkambule, S.J. A two-point Newton method suitable for nonconvergent cases and with super-quadratic convergence. *Adv. Numer. Anal.* **2013**, 687382. [CrossRef]
6. Petković, M.S.; Neta, B.; Petković, L.D.; Džunić, J. Multipoint methods for solving nonlinear equations: A survey. *Appl. Math. Comput.* **2014**, *226*, 635–660. [CrossRef]
7. Amat, S.; Argyros, I.; Busquier, S.; Hernández-Verón, M.A.; Rubio, M.J. A unified convergence analysis for some two-point type methods for nonsmooth operators. *Mathematics* **2019**, *7*, 701. [CrossRef]
8. Kanno, S.; Kjurkchiev, N.V.; Yamamoto, T. On some methods for the simultaneous determination of polynomial zeros. *Jpn. J. Indust. Appl. Math.* **1996**, *13*, 267–288. [CrossRef]
9. Tričković, S.B.; Petković, M.S. Multipoint methods for the determination of multiple zeros of a polynomial. *Novi Sad J. Math.* **1999**, *29*, 221–233.
10. Proinov, P.D.; Petkova, M.D. Convergence of the two-point Weierstrass root-finding method. *Jpn. J. Indust. Appl. Math.* **2014**, *31*, 279–292. [CrossRef]
11. Proinov, P.D.; Petkova, M.D. Local and semilocal convergence of a family of multi-point Weierstrass-type root-finding methods. *Mediterr. J. Math.* **2020**, *17*, 107. [CrossRef]
12. Weierstrass, K. Neuer Beweis des Satzes, dass jede ganze rationale Function einer Veränderlichen dargestellt werden kann als ein Product aus linearen Functionen derselben Veränderlichen. *Sitzungsber. Königl. Akad. Wiss. Berlin* **1891**, *II*, 1085–1101. [CrossRef]
13. Ehrlich, L. A modified Newton method for polynomials. *Commun. ACM* **1967**, *10*, 107–108. [CrossRef]
14. Aberth, O. Iteration methods for finding all zeros of a polynomial simultaneously. *Math. Comput.* **1973**, *27*, 339–344. [CrossRef]
15. Börsch-Supan, W. Residuenabschätzung für Polynom-Nullstellen mittels Lagrange-Interpolation. *Numer. Math.* **1969/70**, *14*, 287–296. [CrossRef]
16. Werner, W. On the simultaneous determination of polynomial roots. In *Iterative Solution of Nonlinear Systems of Equations (Oberwolfach, 1982)*; Springer: Berlin, Germany; New York, NY, USA, 1982; Volume 953, pp. 188–202.
17. Proinov, P.D.; Vasileva, M.T. On the convergence of high-order Ehrlich-type iterative methods for approximating all zeros of a polynomial simultaneously. *J. Inequal. Appl.* **2015**, *2015*, 336. [CrossRef]
18. Proinov, P.D. General convergence theorems for iterative processes and applications to the Weierstrass root-finding method. *J. Complex.* **2016**, *33*, 118–144. [CrossRef]
19. Proinov, P.D. Relationships between different types of initial conditions for simultaneous root finding methods. *Appl. Math. Lett.* **2016**, *52*, 102–111. [CrossRef]
20. Proinov, P.D.; Ivanov, S.I. Convergence analysis of Sakurai-Torii-Sugiura iterative method for simultaneous approximation of polynomial zeros. *J. Comput. Appl. Math.* **2019**, *357*, 56–70. [CrossRef]
21. Cholakov, S.I.; Vasileva, M.T. A convergence analysis of a fourth-order method for computing all zeros of a polynomial simultaneously. *J. Comput. Appl. Math.* **2017**, *321*, 270–283. [CrossRef]
22. Ivanov, S.I. A unified semilocal convergence analysis of a family of iterative algorithms for computing all zeros of a polynomial simultaneously. *Numer. Algorithms* **2017**, *75*, 1193–1204. [CrossRef]

Article

Extrapolation Method for Non-Linear Weakly Singular Volterra Integral Equation with Time Delay [†]

Li Zhang [1], Jin Huang [1,*], Hu Li [2] and Yifei Wang [1]

[1] School of Mathematical Sciences, University of Electronic Science and Technology of China, Chengdu 611731, China; lizhang17@std.uestc.edu.cn (L.Z.); yfwang@std.uestc.edu.cn (Y.W.)
[2] School of Mathematics, Chengdu Normal University, Chengdu 611130, China; 063029@cdnu.edu.cn
* Correspondence: huangj@uestc.edu.cn
[†] This work was supported by the Program of Chengdu Normal University (CS18ZDZ02).

Abstract: This paper proposes an extrapolation method to solve a class of non-linear weakly singular kernel Volterra integral equations with vanishing delay. After the existence and uniqueness of the solution to the original equation are proved, we combine an improved trapezoidal quadrature formula with an interpolation technique to obtain an approximate equation, and then we enhance the error accuracy of the approximate solution using the Richardson extrapolation, on the basis of the asymptotic error expansion. Simultaneously, a posteriori error estimate for the method is derived. Some illustrative examples demonstrating the efficiency of the method are given.

Keywords: weakly singular kernel Volterra integral equation; proportional delay; improved trapezoidal quadrature formula; Richardson extrapolation; posteriori error estimate

1. Introduction

Delay functional equations are often encountered in biological processes, such as the growth of the population and the spread of an epidemic with immigration into the population [1,2], and a time delay can cause the population to fluctuate. In general, some complicated dynamics systems are also modeled by delay integral equations since the delay argument could cause a stable equilibrium to become unstable. The motivation of our work is twofold: one of the reasons is based on the first-kind delay Volterra integral equation (VIE) of the form [3]

$$\int_{qt}^{t} k(t,s)y(s)\mathrm{d}s = f(t), \qquad t \in I := [0,T],$$

which was discussed and transformed into the second-kind equivalent form

$$k(t,t)y(t) - qk(t,qt)y(qt) + \int_{qt}^{t} \frac{\partial k(t,s)}{\partial t}y(s)\mathrm{d}s = f'(t),$$

if $k(t,t) \neq 0$ for $t \in I$, the normal form was given by

$$y(t) = f(t) + y(qt) + \int_{0}^{t} K_1(t,s)y(s)\mathrm{d}s + \int_{0}^{qt} K(t,s)y(s)\mathrm{d}s, \qquad t \in I.$$

There has been some research [4–6] to the following form

$$y(t) = f(t) + \int_{0}^{t} K_1(t,s)y(s)\mathrm{d}s + \int_{0}^{qt} K(t,s)y(s)\mathrm{d}s, \qquad t \in I.$$

Another source of motivation comes from the weakly singular delay VIE [7–9]

$$y(t) = f(t) + \int_0^{qt} \frac{K(t,s)}{(qt-s)^\lambda} G(s,y(s))ds, \quad t \in [0,1],$$

where $\lambda \in (0,1)$, $K(t,s)$ is smooth and $G(s,y(s))$ is a smooth non-linear function. However, there has not yet been investigated for the case where two integral terms are presented, the first integral term is the weakly singular Volterra integral and the second integral terms not only has weak singularity in the left endpoint but also its upper limit is a delay function, which is challenging to calculate. It is the aim of this paper to fill this gap.

With theoretical and computational advances, some numerical methods for delay differential equations [10–13], delay integral equations [14], delay integral–differential equations [15–18], and fractional differential equations with time delay [19–22] have been investigated widely. Here, we consider the following non-linear weakly singular kernel VIE with vanishing delay

$$y(t) = f(t) + \int_0^t s^\lambda k_1(t,s;y(s))ds + \int_0^{\theta(t)} s^\mu k_2(t,s;y(s))ds, \quad t \in I, \quad (1)$$

where $\theta(t) := qt$, $q \in (0,1)$, $\lambda, \mu \in (-1,0)$, $f(t)$, $k_1(t,s;y(s))$, $k_2(t,s;y(s))$ are r ($r \geq 1$, $r \in \mathbf{N}$) times continuously differentiable on I, $D \times \mathbf{R}$, $D_\theta \times \mathbf{R}$, respectively, $D := \{(t,s) : 0 \leq s \leq t \leq T\}$ and $D_\theta := \{(t,s) : 0 \leq s \leq \theta(t) \leq \theta(T), t \in I\}$. Additionally, $k_i(t,s;y(s))$ ($i=1,2$) satisfy the Lipschitz conditions with respect to $y(s)$ on the domains, respectively. That is, for fixed s and t, there are two positive constants L_j ($j=1,2$) which are independent of s and t, such that

$$|k_j(t,s;y(s)) - k_j(t,s;v(s))| \leq L_j|y(s) - v(s)|. \quad (2)$$

Then, Equation (1) possesses a unique solution (see Theorem 1). In this paper, we consider the case where the solution is smooth.

Some numerical investigations of delay VIE have been conducted, such as discontinuous Galerkin methods [23], collocation methods [24–26], the iterative numerical method [27], and the least squares approximation method [28]. In [29], an h_p version of the pseudo-spectral method was analyzed, based on the variational form of a non-linear VIE with vanishing variable delays. The algorithm increased the accuracy by refining the mesh and/or increasing the degree of the polynomial. Mokhtary et al. [7] used a well-conditioned Jacobi spectral Galerkin method for a VIE with weakly singular kernels and proportional delay by solving sparse upper triangular non-linear algebraic systems. In [8], the Chebyshev spectral-collocation method was investigated for the numerical solution of a class of weakly singular VIEs with proportional delay. An error analysis showed that the approximation method could obtain spectral accuracy. Zhang et al. [9] used some variable transformations to change the weakly singular VIE with pantograph delays into new equations defined on $[-1,1]$, and then combined it with the Jacobi orthogonal polynomial.

The extrapolation method has been used extensively [30,31]. We apply the extrapolation method for the solution of the non-linear weakly singular kernel VIE with proportional delay. We prove the existence of the solution to the original equation using an iterative method, while uniqueness is demonstrated by the Gronwall integral inequality. We obtain the approximate equation by using the quadrature method based on the improved trapezoidal quadrature formula, combining the floor technique and the interpolation technique. Then, we solve the approximate equation through an iterative method. The existence of the approximate solution is validated by analyzing the convergence of the iterative sequence, while uniqueness is shown using a discrete Gronwall inequality. In addition, we provide an analysis of the convergence of the approximate solution and obtain the asymptotic expansion of the error. Based on the error asymptotic expansion, the Richardson extrapolation method is applied to enhance the numerical accuracy of the approximate solution. Furthermore, we obtain the posterior error estimate of the method. Numerical experiments effectively support the theoretical analysis, and all the calculations can be easily implemented.

This paper is organized as follows: In Section 2, the existence and uniqueness of the solution for (1) are proven. The numerical algorithm is introduced in Section 3. In Section 4, we prove the existence and uniqueness of the approximate solution. In Section 5, we provide the convergence analysis of the approximate solution. In Section 6, we obtain the asymptotic expansion of error, the corresponding extrapolation technique is used for achieving high precision, and a posteriori error estimate is derived. Numerical examples are described in Section 7. Finally, we outline the conclusions of the paper in Section 8.

2. Existence and Uniqueness of Solution of the Original Equation

In this section, we discuss the existence and uniqueness of the solution of the original equation. There are two cases, $0 \leq t \leq T \leq 1$ and $1 < t \leq T$, that we will discuss in the following.

Lemma 1 ([32]). *Let $y(t)$ and $g(t)$ be non-negative integrable functions, $t \in [0, T]$, $A \geq 0$, satisfying*

$$y(t) \leq A + \int_0^t g(s)y(s)\mathrm{d}s,$$

then, for all $0 \leq t \leq T$,

$$y(t) \leq A e^{\int_0^t g(s)\mathrm{d}s}.$$

Theorem 1. *$f(t)$, $k_1(t,s;y(s))$, $k_2(t,s;y(s))$ are r ($r \geq 1$, $r \in \mathbf{N}$) times continuously differentiable on I, $D \times \mathbf{R}$, $D_\theta \times \mathbf{R}$, respectively. Additionally, assume that $k_i(t,s;y(s))$ $(i = 1,2)$ satisfies the Lipschitz conditions (2), respectively. Then, Equation (1) has a unique solution.*

Proof. We first construct the sequence $\{y_n(t), n \in \mathbf{N}\}$ as follows:

$$y_0(t) = f(t),$$
$$y_n(t) = f(t) + \int_0^t s^\lambda k_1(t,s;y_{n-1}(s))\mathrm{d}s + \int_0^{qt} s^\mu k_2(t,s;y_{n-1}(s))\mathrm{d}s.$$

Let $b = \max\limits_{0 \leq t \leq T} |y_1(t) - y_0(t)|$, $L = \max\{L_1, L_2\}$, $\gamma = \min\{\lambda, \mu\}$.

- **Case I.** For $0 \leq s \leq t \leq T \leq 1$, by means of mathematical induction, when $n = 1$,

$$\begin{aligned}|y_2(t) - y_1(t)| &= \left| \int_0^t s^\lambda \Big(k_1(t,s;y_1(s)) - k_1(t,s;y_0(s))\Big)\mathrm{d}s + \int_0^{qt} s^\mu \Big(k_2(t,s;y_1(s)) - k_2(t,s;y_0(s))\Big)\mathrm{d}s \right| \\ &\leq \int_0^t s^\lambda \left|k_1(t,s;y_1(s)) - k_1(t,s;y_0(s))\right|\mathrm{d}s + \int_0^{qt} s^\mu \left|k_2(t,s;y_1(s)) - k_2(t,s;y_0(s))\right|\mathrm{d}s \\ &\leq \int_0^t L_1 s^\lambda |y_1(s) - y_0(s)| + \int_0^t L_2 s^\mu |y_1(s) - y_0(s)|\mathrm{d}s \\ &\leq \int_0^t (s^\lambda Lb + s^\mu Lb)\mathrm{d}s \\ &\leq 2Lb \int_0^t s^\gamma \mathrm{d}s \\ &= 2Lb \frac{t^{\gamma+1}}{\gamma+1}.\end{aligned} \quad (3)$$

Suppose that the following expression is established when $n = k$,

$$|y_k(t) - y_{k-1}(t)| \leq b \frac{(2L)^{k-1}}{(k-1)!(\gamma+1)^{k-1}} t^{(k-1)(\gamma+1)}. \quad (4)$$

Let $n = k+1$; then,

$$|y_{k+1}(t) - y_k(t)| \leq \int_0^t s^\lambda |k_1(t,s;y_k(s)) - k_1(t,s;y_{k-1}(s))| ds + \int_0^{qt} s^\mu |k_2(t,s;y_k(s)) - k_2(t,s;y_{k-1}(s))| ds$$

$$\leq \int_0^t L_1 s^\lambda |y_k(s) - y_{k-1}(s)| + \int_0^t L_2 s^\mu |y_k(s) - y_{k-1}(s)| ds$$

$$\leq 2L \int_0^t s^\gamma |y_k(s) - y_{k-1}(s)| ds$$

$$\leq b \frac{(2L)^k}{k!(\gamma+1)^k} t^{k(\gamma+1)},$$

that is, the recurrence relation is established when $n = k+1$, then the inequality (4) is also established. Next, we prove that the sequence $y_n(t)$ is a Cauchy sequence,

$$|y_n(t) - y_{n+m}(t)| \leq |y_{n+1}(t) - y_n(t)| + |y_{n+2}(t) - y_{n+1}(t)| + \cdots + |y_{n+m}(t) - y_{n+m-1}(t)|$$

$$\leq b \frac{(2L)^n}{n!(\gamma+1)^n} t^{n(\gamma+1)} + \cdots + b \frac{(2L)^{n+m-1}}{(n+m-1)!(\gamma+1)^{n+m-1}} t^{(n+m-1)(\gamma+1)}$$

$$\leq b \sum_{i=n}^{n+m+1} \left(\frac{2L}{\gamma+1}\right)^i T^{i(\gamma+1)} \frac{1}{i!}.$$

The term $\sum_{i=0}^{\infty} \left(\frac{2L}{\gamma+1}\right)^i T^{i(\gamma+1)} \frac{1}{i!}$ is convergent, so the Cauchy sequence $\{y_n\}_{n \in \mathbb{N}}$ is convergent uniformly to $y(t)$. Thus, $y(t)$ is the solution to Equation (1), the existence is proved.

- **Case II.** For $1 < s \leq t \leq T$, the process is similar. Let $\tilde{\gamma} = \max\{\lambda, \mu\}$, when $n=1$,

$$|y_2(t) - y_1(t)| \leq 2Lb \frac{t^{\tilde{\gamma}+1}}{\tilde{\gamma}+1}. \tag{5}$$

Suppose that the following expression is established when $n = k$,

$$|y_k(t) - y_{k-1}(t)| \leq b \frac{(2L)^{k-1}}{(k-1)!(\tilde{\gamma}+1)^{k-1}} t^{(k-1)(\tilde{\gamma}+1)}. \tag{6}$$

Let $n = k+1$. Then, we have

$$|y_{k+1}(t) - y_k(t)| \leq b \frac{(2L)^k}{k!(\tilde{\gamma}+1)^k} t^{k(\tilde{\gamma}+1)},$$

i.e., the recurrence relation is established when $n = k+1$, such that the inequality (6) is also established. For the sequence $y_n(t)$,

$$|y_n(t) - y_{n+m}(t)| \leq b \sum_{i=n}^{n+m+1} \left(\frac{2L}{\tilde{\gamma}+1}\right)^i T^{i(\tilde{\gamma}+1)} \frac{1}{i!}.$$

Since the term $\sum_{i=0}^{\infty} \left(\frac{2L}{\tilde{\gamma}+1}\right)^i T^{i(\tilde{\gamma}+1)} \frac{1}{i!}$ is convergent, so the Cauchy sequence $\{y_n\}_{n \in \mathbb{N}}$ is convergent uniformly to $y(t)$. Thus, $y(t)$ is the solution to Equation (1), the existence is proved.

Now, we prove that the solution to Equation (1) is unique. Let $y(t)$ and $v(t)$ be two distinct solutions to Equation (1), and denote the difference between them by $w(t) = |y(t) - v(t)|$. We obtain

$$w(t) = \left| \int_0^t s^\lambda \left(k_1(t,s;y(s)) - k_1(t,s;v(s)) \right) ds + \int_0^{qt} s^\mu \left(k_2(t,s;y(s)) - k_2(t,s;v(s)) \right) ds \right|$$

$$\leq \int_0^t s^\lambda \left| k_1(t,s;y(s)) - k_1(t,s;v(s)) \right| ds + \int_0^{qt} s^\mu \left| k_2(t,s;y(s)) - k_2(t,s;v(s)) \right| ds$$

$$\leq \int_0^t L_1 s^\lambda w(s) ds + \int_0^{qt} L_2 s^\mu w(s) ds$$

$$\leq \int_0^t (Ls^\lambda + Ls^\mu) w(s) ds.$$

Let $g(s) = Ls^\lambda + Ls^\mu$, then $g(s)$ is a non-negative integrable function, according to Lemma 1. We obtain $w(t) = 0$, i.e., $y(t) = v(t)$, the solution to Equation (1) is unique. □

3. The Numerical Algorithm

In this section, we first provide some essential lemmas which are useful for the derivation of the approximate equation. Next, the discrete form of Equation (1) is obtained by combining an improved trapezoidal quadrature formula and linear interpolation. Finally, we solve the approximate equation using an iterative method. The process does not have to compute the integrals; hence, the method can be implemented easily.

3.1. Some Lemmas

Lemma 2 ([32]). Let $u \in C^3(0,1)$ and $z = \beta x + (1-\beta)y$ with $\beta \in [0,1]$, $x,y \in [0,T]$. Then,

$$u(z) = \beta u(x) + (1-\beta)u(y) - \frac{\beta(1-\beta)}{2}(x-y)^2 u''(z) + O((x-y)^3). \quad (7)$$

Proof. The Taylor expansion of function $u(x)$ at the point z is

$$\begin{aligned} u(x) &= u(\beta x + (1-\beta)x) \\ &= u(\beta x + (1-\beta)y + (1-\beta)(x-y)) \\ &= u(z + (1-\beta)(x-y)) \\ &= u(z) + (1-\beta)(x-y)u'(z) + \frac{(1-\beta)^2}{2}(x-y)^2 u''(z) + O((x-y)^3). \end{aligned} \quad (8)$$

Similarly, the Taylor expansion of function $u(y)$ at point z is

$$u(y) = u(z - \beta(x-y)) = u(z) - \beta(x-y)u'(z) + \frac{\beta^2}{2}(x-y)^2 u''(z) + O((x-y)^3), \quad (9)$$

combining (8) with (9), the proof is completed. □

Lemma 3 ([33,34]). Let $g(t) \in C^{2\tilde{r}}[a,b]$ ($\tilde{r} \geq 1$, $\tilde{r} \in \mathbb{N}$), $G(t) = (b-t)^\lambda g(t)$, $h = \frac{(b-a)}{N}$, and $t_k = a + kh$ for $k = 0, \cdots, N$, as for the integral $\int_a^b G(t) dt$. Then, the error of the modified trapezoidal integration rule

$$T_N(G) = \frac{h}{2} G(t_0) + h \sum_{j=1}^{N-1} G(t_k) - \zeta(-\lambda) g(b) h^{1+\lambda}, \quad (10)$$

has an asymptotic expansion

$$E_N(G) = \sum_{j=1}^{\bar{r}-1} \frac{B_{2j}}{(2j)!} G^{(2j-1)}(a) h^{2j} + \sum_{j=1}^{2\bar{r}-1} (-1)^j \zeta(-\lambda - j) \frac{g^{(j)}(b) h^{j+\lambda+1}}{(j!)} + O(h^{2\bar{r}}), \quad (11)$$

where $-1 < \lambda < 0$, ζ is the Riemann–Zeta function and B_{2j} represents the Bernoulli numbers.

3.2. The Approximation Process

In this subsection, we describe the numerical method used to find the approximate solution to Equation (1). Let $y(t)$ have continuous partial derivatives up to 3 on I, $f(t)$, $k_1(t,s;y(s))$, $k_2(t,s;y(s))$ are four times continuously differentiable on I, $D \times \mathbf{R}$, $D_\theta \times \mathbf{R}$, respectively. Let $y(t_i)$, y_i denote the exact solution and approximate solution when $t = t_i$, respectively. We divide $I = [0, T]$ into N subintervals with a uniform step size $h = \frac{T}{N}$, $t_i = ih$, $i = 0, 1, \cdots, N$. Let $t = t_i$ in Equation (1). Then,

$$\begin{aligned} y(t_i) &= f(t_i) + \int_0^{t_i} s^\lambda k_1(t_i, s; y(s)) ds + \int_0^{qt_i} s^\mu k_2(t_i, s; y(s)) ds \\ &= f(t_i) + \int_0^{t_i} s^\lambda k_1(t_i, s; y(s)) ds + \int_0^{t_{[qi]}} s^\mu k_2(t_i, s; y(s)) ds + \int_{t_{[qi]}}^{qt_i} s^\mu k_2(t_i, s; y(s)) ds \\ &= f(t_i) + I_1 + I_2 + I_3, \end{aligned} \quad (12)$$

where $[qi]$ denotes the maximum integer less than qi. According to Lemma 3, we have

$$I_1 = \int_0^{t_i} s^\lambda k_1(t_i, s; y(s)) ds \approx -\zeta(-\lambda) k_1(t_i, t_0; y(t_0)) h^{1+\lambda} + h \sum_{k=1}^{i-1} t_k^\lambda k_1(t_i, t_k; y(t_k)) + \frac{h}{2} t_i^\lambda k_1(t_i, t_i; y(t_i)). \quad (13)$$

For I_2 and I_3, there are two cases.

- **Case I.** If $[qi] = 0$, then

$$I_2 = 0;$$

$$I_3 = \int_0^{qt_i} s^\mu k_2(t_i, s; y(s)) ds \approx -\zeta(-\mu)(qt_i)^{1+\mu} k_2(t_i, t_0; y(t_0)) + \frac{qt_i}{2}(qt_i)^\mu k_2(t_i, qt_i; y(qt_i)). \quad (14)$$

- **Case II.** If $[qi] \geq 1$, we obtain

$$I_2 \approx \begin{cases} -\zeta(-\mu) h^{1+\mu} k_2(t_i, t_0; y(t_0)) + \frac{h}{2} t_1^\mu k_2(t_i, t_1; y(t_1)), & [qi] = 1, \\ -\zeta(-\mu) h^{1+\mu} k_2(t_i, t_0; y(t_0)) + h \sum_{k=1}^{[qi]-1} t_k^\mu k_2(t_i, t_k; y(t_k)) + \frac{h}{2} t_{[qi]}^\mu k_2(t_i, t_{[qi]}; y(t_{[qi]})), & [qi] > 1. \end{cases}$$

$$I_3 \approx \frac{qt_i - t_{[qi]}}{2} \left(t_{[qi]}^\mu k_2(t_i, t_{[qi]}; y(t_{[qi]})) + (qt_i)^\mu k_2(t_i, qt_i; y(qt_i)) \right). \quad (15)$$

$y(qt_i)$ can be represented by linear interpolation of the adjacent points $y(t_{[qi]})$ and $y(t_{[qi]+1})$. For the node $t_i = ih$, $i = 0, 1, \cdots, N$, since $[qi] \leq qi \leq [qi] + 1$, we obtain $t_{[qi]} \leq qt_i \leq t_{[qi]+1}$; according to Lemma 2, there exists $\beta_i \in [0, 1]$ such that $qt_i = \beta_i t_{[qi]} + (1 - \beta_i) t_{[qi]+1}$. The value of $\beta_i = 1 + [qi] - qi$ can be calculated easily. Then, the approximate expression of $y(qt_i)$ is

$$y(qt_i) \approx \beta_i y(t_{[qi]}) + (1 - \beta_i) y(t_{[qi]+1}). \quad (16)$$

Then, (15) can be written as

$$I_3 \approx \frac{qt_i - t_{[qi]}}{2} \left(t_{[qi]}^\mu k_2(t_i, t_{[qi]}; y(t_{[qi]})) + (qt_i)^\mu k_2(t_i, qt_i; \beta_i y(t_{[qi]}) + (1 - \beta_i) y(t_{[qi]+1})) \right). \quad (17)$$

The approximation equations are as follows

- **Case I.** When $[qi] = 0$,

$$y_0 = f(t_0);$$

$$y_i \approx f(t_i) - \zeta(-\lambda)k_1(t_i, t_0; y_0)h^{1+\lambda} + h\sum_{k=1}^{i-1} t_k^\lambda k_1(t_i, t_k; y_k) + \frac{h}{2}t_i^\lambda k_1(t_i, t_i; y_i) \quad (18)$$

$$- \zeta(-\mu)(qt_i)^{1+\mu}k_2(t_i, t_0; y_0) + \frac{qt_i}{2}(qt_i)^\mu k_2(t_i, qt_i; \beta_i y_{[qi]} + (1-\beta_i)y_{[qi]+1}).$$

- **Case II.** When $[qi] \geq 1$,

$$y_0 = f(t_0);$$

$$y_i \approx f(t_i) - \zeta(-\lambda)k_1(t_i, t_0; y_0)h^{1+\lambda} + h\sum_{k=1}^{i-1} t_k^\lambda k_1(t_i, t_k; y_k) + \frac{h}{2}t_i^\lambda k_1(t_i, t_i; y_i)$$

$$- \zeta(-\mu)h^{1+\mu}k_2(t_i, t_0; y_0) + \delta_i + \frac{h}{2}t_{[qi]}^\mu k_2(t_i, t_{[qi]}; y_{[qi]}) \quad (19)$$

$$+ \frac{qt_i - t_{[qi]}}{2}\left(t_{[qi]}^\mu k_2(t_i, t_{[qi]}; y_{[qi]}) + (qt_i)^\mu k_2(t_i, qt_i; \beta_i y_{[qi]} + (1-\beta_i)y_{[qi]+1})\right),$$

where

$$\delta_i \approx \begin{cases} 0, & [qi] = 1, \\ h\sum_{k=1}^{[qi]-1} t_k^\mu k_2(t_i, t_k; y_k), & [qi] \geq 2. \end{cases}$$

3.3. Iterative Scheme

Now, the solution of the approximate equation can be solved by an iterative algorithm.

Iterative algorithm

Step 1. Take sufficiently small $\epsilon > 0$ and set $\tilde{y}_0 = f(t_0)$, $i := 1$.
Step 2. Let $\tilde{y}_i^0 = \tilde{y}_{i-1}$, $m := 0$, then we compute y_i^{m+1} ($i \leq N$) as follows:

- **Case I.** When $[qi] = 0$,

$$y_0 = f(t_0);$$

$$y_i^{m+1} \approx f(t_i) - \zeta(-\lambda)k_1(t_i, t_0; \tilde{y}_0)h^{1+\lambda} + h\sum_{k=1}^{i-1} t_k^\lambda k_1(t_i, t_k; \tilde{y}_k) + \frac{h}{2}t_i^\lambda k_1(t_i, t_i; y_i^m) \quad (20)$$

$$- \zeta(-\mu)(qt_i)^{1+\mu}k_2(t_i, t_0; \tilde{y}_0) + \frac{qt_i}{2}(qt_i)^\mu k_2(t_i, qt_i; \beta_i \tilde{y}_{[qi]} + (1-\beta_i)y_{[qi]+1}^{m+1}).$$

- **Case II.** When $[qi] \geq 1$,

$$y_0 = f(t_0);$$

$$y_i^{m+1} \approx f(t_i) - \zeta(-\lambda)k_1(t_i, t_0; \tilde{y}_0)h^{1+\lambda} + h\sum_{k=1}^{i-1} t_k^\lambda k_1(t_i, t_k; \tilde{y}_k) + \frac{h}{2}t_i^\lambda k_1(t_i, t_i; y_i^m)$$

$$- \zeta(-\mu)h^{1+\mu}k_2(t_i, t_0; \tilde{y}_0) + \tilde{\delta}_i + \frac{h}{2}t_{[qi]}^\mu k_2(t_i, t_{[qi]}; \tilde{y}_{[qi]}) \quad (21)$$

$$+ \frac{qt_i - t_{[qi]}}{2}\left(t_{[qi]}^\mu k_2(t_i, t_{[qi]}; \tilde{y}_{[qi]}) + (qt_i)^\mu k_2(t_i, qt_i; \beta_i \tilde{y}_{[qi]} + (1-\beta_i)y_{[qi]+1}^{m+1})\right),$$

where

$$\tilde{\delta}_i \approx \begin{cases} 0, & [qi] = 1, \\ h\sum_{k=1}^{[qi]-1} t_k^\mu k_2(t_i, t_k; \tilde{y}_k), & [qi] \geq 2. \end{cases}$$

Step 3. If $|y_i^{m+1} - y_i^m| \leq \epsilon$, then let $\tilde{y}_i := y_i^{m+1}$ and $i := i+1$, and return to step 2. If otherwise, let $m := m+1$, and return to step 2.

Remark 1. *In Section 3.2, we considered the regularity of $k_i(t,s;y(s))(i=1,2)$ only up to $\tilde{r} = 2$ in Lemma 3, since the desired accuracy has been obtained, and it is sufficient for the subsequent convergence analysis and extrapolation algorithm.*

4. Existence and Uniqueness of the Solution to the Approximate Equation

In this section, we investigate the existence and uniqueness of the solution to the approximate equation. We first introduce the following discrete Gronwall inequality.

Lemma 4 ([35,36]). *Suppose that the non-negative sequence $\{w_n\}$, $n = 0, \cdots, N$, satisfy*

$$w_n \leq h \sum_{k=1}^{n-1} B_k w_k + A, \quad 0 \leq n \leq N, \tag{22}$$

where A and B_k, $k = 1, \cdots, N$ are non-negative constants, $h = 1/N$, when $h \max_{0 \leq k \leq N} w_k \leq \frac{1}{2}$ then we have

$$\max_{0 \leq n \leq N} w_n \leq A \exp(2h \sum_{k=1}^{N} B_k).$$

Theorem 2. *Let $f(t)$, $k_1(t,s;y(s))$, $k_2(t,s;y(s))$ are four times continuously differentiable on I, $D \times \mathbf{R}$, $D_\theta \times \mathbf{R}$, respectively. Additionally, $y(t)$ has continuous partial derivatives up to 3 on I and $k_i(t,s;y(s))$ $(i = 1, 2)$ satisfy Lipschitz conditions (2). Assume that h is sufficiently small, then the solution to Equation (21) exists and is unique.*

Proof. We discuss the existence of the approximate solution under two cases.

- **Case I.** When $[qi] = 0$,

$$|y_i^{m+1} - y_i^m| = \left|\frac{h}{2} t_i^\lambda \left(k_1(t_i, t_i; y_i^m) - k_1(t_i, t_i; y_i^{m-1})\right)\right|$$

$$\leq L_1 \frac{h}{2} t_i^\lambda |y_i^m - y_i^{m-1}|.$$

When h is sufficiently small, such that $L_1 \frac{h}{2} t_i^\lambda \leq \frac{1}{2}$, then $|y_i^{m+1} - y_i^m| \leq \frac{1}{2}|y_i^m - y_i^{m-1}|$ holds. Therefore, the iterative algorithm is convergent and the limit is the solution to the approximation equation. The existence of approximation is proved when $[qi] = 0$. Now, we prove the uniqueness of approximation. Suppose y_i and x_i are both solutions to Equation (20). Denote the absolute differences as $w_i = |y_i - x_i|$. We have

$w_0 = 0,$

$w_i \leq -\zeta(-\lambda)|k_1(t_i, t_0; y_0) - k_1(t_i, t_0; x_0)|h^{1+\lambda} + h \sum_{k=1}^{i-1} t_k^\lambda |k_1(t_i, t_k; y_k) - k_1(t_i, t_k; x_k)|$

$+ \frac{h}{2} t_i^\lambda |k_1(t_i, t_i; y_i) - k_1(t_i, t_i; x_i)| - \zeta(-\mu)(qt_1)^{1+\mu}|k_2(t_i, t_0; y_0) - k_2(t_i, t_0; x_0)|$

$+ \frac{qt_i}{2}(qt_i)^\mu |k_2(t_i, qt_i; \beta_i y_{[qi]} + (1-\beta_i)y_{[qi]+1}) - k_2(t_i, qt_i; \beta_i x_{[qi]} + (1-\beta_i)x_{[qi]+1})|$

$\leq L_1 h \sum_{k=1}^{i-1} t_k^\lambda w_k + L_1 \frac{h}{2} t_i^\lambda w_i + L_2 \frac{qt_i}{2}(qt_i)^\mu (\beta_i w_{[qi]} + (1-\beta_i)w_{[qi]+1})$

$\leq Lh \sum_{k=1}^{i-1} t_k^\lambda w_k + L \frac{h}{2} t_i^\lambda w_i + L \frac{qt_i}{2}(qt_i)^\mu (1-\beta_i)w_1.$ \hfill (23)

where $L = \max\{L_1, L_2\}$. When h is sufficiently small, such that $L_1 \frac{h}{2} t_i^\lambda \leq \frac{1}{2}$, we have

$$w_i \leq 2Lh \sum_{k=1}^{i-1} t_k^\lambda w_k + Lht_i^\lambda w_i + Lqt_i(qt_i)^\mu (1-\beta_i) w_1$$

$$\leq \left[2Lht_k^\lambda + Lh(qt_i)^\mu (1-\beta_i)\right] w_1 + 2Lh \sum_{k=2}^{i-1} t_k^\lambda w_k$$

$$= h \sum_{k=1}^{i-1} B_k w_k,$$

where

$$B_k = \begin{cases} 2Lt_k^\lambda + L(qt_i)^\mu (1-\beta_i), & j = 1, \\ 2Lht_k^\lambda, & j = 2, \cdots, i-1. \end{cases}$$

According to Lemma 4 with $A = 0$, we have $w_i = 0$, i.e., $y_i = x_i$, the solution of Equation (20) is unique.

- **Case II.** For $[qi] > 1$, we consider the following cases.

(1) The first situation is $[qi] + 1 = i$, namely, when $i \leq \frac{1}{1-q}$, we have

$$|y_i^{m+1} - y_i^m| = \left|\frac{h}{2} t_i^\lambda \left(k_1(t_i, t_i; y_i^m) - k_1(t_i, t_i; y_i^{m-1})\right)\right|$$
$$+ \frac{qt_i - t_{[qi]}}{2} (qt_i)^\mu \left|k_2\left(t_i, qt_i; \beta_i \tilde{y}_{[qi]} + (1-\beta_i) y_{[qi]+1}^m\right) - k_2\left(t_i, qt_i; \beta_i \tilde{y}_{[qi]} + (1-\beta_i) y_{[qi]+1}^{m-1}\right)\right|$$
$$\leq L_1 \frac{h}{2} t_i^\lambda |y_i^m - y_i^{m-1}| + L_2 \frac{qt_i - t_{[qi]}}{2} (qt_i)^\mu |(1-\beta_i) y_{[qi]+1}^m - (1-\beta_i) y_{[qi]+1}^{m-1}|$$
$$\leq L \frac{h}{2} \left(t_i^\lambda + (qt_i)^\mu (1-\beta_i)\right) |y_i^m - y_i^{m-1}|.$$

Let the step size h be small enough, such that $L \frac{h}{2} \left(t_i^\lambda + (qt_i)^\mu (1-\beta_i)\right) \leq \frac{1}{2}$. Then, we can determine that $|y_i^{m+1} - y_i^m| \leq \frac{1}{2} |y_i^m - y_i^{m-1}|$ holds.

(2) The second situation is $[qi] + 1 < i$, namely, when $i > \frac{1}{1-q}$, we obtain

$$|y_i^{m+1} - y_i^m| = \left|\frac{h}{2} t_i^\lambda \left(k_1(t_i, t_i; y_i^m) - k_1(t_i, t_i; y_i^{m-1})\right)\right|$$
$$\leq L_1 \frac{h}{2} t_i^\lambda |y_i^m - y_i^{m-1}|$$
$$\leq L \frac{h}{2} t_i^\lambda |y_i^m - y_i^{m-1}|.$$

Let $L \frac{h}{2} t_i^\lambda \leq \frac{1}{2}$ for a sufficiently small h, then $|y_i^{m+1} - y_i^m| \leq \frac{1}{2} |y_i^m - y_i^{m-1}|$ holds.

The above two situations show that the iterative algorithm is convergent and that the limit is the solution to Equation (21).

Next, we prove that the solution to Equation (21) is unique. Suppose y_i and $\tilde{x}_i$ are both solutions to Equation (21). Denote the differences as $\tilde{w}_i = |y_i - \tilde{x}_i|$, $i = 1, \cdots, N$. Then, we have

$\widetilde{w}_0 = 0;$

$$\widetilde{w}_i \leq -\zeta(-\lambda)|k_1(t_i,t_0;y_0) - k_1(t_i,t_0;\widetilde{x}_0)|h^{1+\lambda} + h\sum_{k=1}^{i-1} t_k^\lambda |k_1(t_i,t_k;y_k) - k_1(t_i,t_k;\widetilde{x}_k)|$$

$$+ \frac{h}{2} t_i^\lambda |k_1(t_i,t_i;y_i) - k_1(t_i,t_i;\widetilde{x}_i)| - \zeta(-\mu)h^{1+\mu}|k_2(t_i,t_0;y_0) - k_2(t_i,t_0;\widetilde{x}_0)|$$

$$+ h\sum_{k=1}^{[qi]-1} t_k^\mu |k_2(t_i,t_k;y_k) - k_2(t_i,t_k;\widetilde{x}_k)| + \frac{h}{2} t_{[qi]}^\mu |k_2(t_i,t_{[qi]};y_{[qi]}) - k_2(t_i,t_{[qi]};\widetilde{x}_{[qi]})|$$

$$+ \frac{qt_i - t_{[qi]}}{2}(t_{[qi]}^\mu |k_2(t_i,t_{[qi]};y_{[qi]}) - k_2(t_i,t_{[qi]};\widetilde{x}_{[qi]})|$$

$$+ (qt_i)^\mu |k_2(t_i,qt_i;\beta_i y_{[qi]} + (1-\beta_i)y_{[qi]+1}) - k_2(t_i,qt_i;\beta_i \widetilde{x}_{[qi]} + (1-\beta_i)\widetilde{x}_{[qi]+1}))| \quad (24)$$

$$\leq h\sum_{k=1}^{i-1} t_k^\lambda L_1 \widetilde{w}_k + \frac{h}{2} t_i^\lambda L_1 \widetilde{w}_i + h\sum_{k=1}^{[qi]-1} t_k^\mu L_2 \widetilde{w}_k + \frac{h}{2} t_{[qi]}^\mu L_2 \widetilde{w}_{[qi]}$$

$$+ \frac{qt_i - t_{[qi]}}{2}(t_{[qi]}^\mu L_2 \widetilde{w}_{[qi]} + (qt_i)^\mu L_2(\beta_i \widetilde{w}_{[qi]} + (1-\beta_i)\widetilde{w}_{[qi]+1}))$$

$$\leq Lh\sum_{k=1}^{i-1} t_k^\gamma \widetilde{w}_k + L\frac{h}{2} t_i^\gamma \widetilde{w}_i + Lh\sum_{k=1}^{[qi]-1} t_k^\gamma \widetilde{w}_k + L\frac{h}{2} t_{[qi]}^\gamma \widetilde{w}_{[qi]}$$

$$+ L\frac{h}{2}\left(t_{[qi]}^\gamma \widetilde{w}_{[qi]} + t_{[qi]}^\gamma (\beta_i \widetilde{w}_{[qi]} + (1-\beta_i)\widetilde{w}_{[qi]+1})\right).$$

(1) The first situation is $[qi] + 1 = i$ (i.e., when $i \leq \frac{1}{1-q}$). Then, (24) entails

$$\widetilde{w}_i \leq Lh\sum_{k=1}^{[qi]-1} t_k^\gamma \widetilde{w}_k + Lht_{[qi]}^\gamma \widetilde{w}_{[qi]} + L\frac{h}{2} t_i^\gamma \widetilde{w}_i + Lh\sum_{k=1}^{[qi]-1} t_k^\gamma \widetilde{w}_k + L\frac{h}{2} t_{[qi]}^\gamma \widetilde{w}_{[qi]}$$

$$+ L\frac{h}{2}\left(t_{[qi]}^\gamma \widetilde{w}_{[qi]} + t_{[qi]}^\gamma (\beta_i \widetilde{w}_{[qi]} + (1-\beta_i)\widetilde{w}_{[qi]+1})\right) \quad (25)$$

$$= 2Lh\sum_{k=1}^{[qi]-1} t_k^\gamma \widetilde{w}_k + (2Lht_{[qi]}^\gamma + L\frac{h}{2}\beta_i t_{[qi]}^\gamma)\widetilde{w}_{[qi]} + (L\frac{h}{2} t_i^\gamma + L\frac{h}{2} t_{[qi]}^\gamma (1-\beta_i))\widetilde{w}_{[qi]+1}.$$

By letting h be so small that $(L\frac{h}{2} t_i^\gamma + L\frac{h}{2} t_{[qi]}^\gamma(1-\beta_i)) \leq \frac{1}{2}$, we can easily derive

$$\widetilde{w}_i \leq 4Lh\sum_{k=1}^{[qi]-1} t_k^\gamma w_k + (4Lht_{[qi]}^\gamma + Lh\beta_i t_{[qi]}^\gamma)\widetilde{w}_{[qi]} = h\sum_{k=1}^{i-1} B_k \widetilde{w}_k,$$

where

$$B_k = \begin{cases} 4Lt_k^\gamma, & j = 1, \cdots, [qi]-1, \\ 4Lt_{[qi]}^\gamma + L\beta_i t_{[qi]}^\gamma, & j = [qi]. \end{cases}$$

According to Lemma 4 with $A = 0$, we have $w_i = 0$, and the solution of Equation (21) is unique.

(2) The second situation is $[qi] + 1 < i$ (i.e., when $i > \frac{1}{1-q}$). Then, (24) can imply

$$\widetilde{w}_i \leq Lh \sum_{k=1}^{[qi]-1} t_k^\gamma \widetilde{w}_k + Lh t_{[qi]}^\gamma \widetilde{w}_{[qi]} + Lh t_{[qi]+1}^\gamma \widetilde{w}_{[qi]+1} + Lh \sum_{k=[qi]+2}^{i-1} t_k^\gamma \widetilde{w}_k + L\frac{h}{2} t_i^\gamma \widetilde{w}_i$$

$$+ Lh \sum_{k=1}^{[qi]-1} t_k^\gamma \widetilde{w}_k + L\frac{h}{2} t_{[qi]}^\gamma \widetilde{w}_{[qi]} + L\frac{h}{2} \left(t_{[qi]}^\gamma \widetilde{w}_{[qi]} + t_{[qi]}^\gamma (\beta_i \widetilde{w}_{[qi]} + (1-\beta_i) \widetilde{w}_{[qi]+1}) \right) \quad (26)$$

$$-2Lh \sum_{k=1}^{[qi]-1} t_k^\gamma \widetilde{w}_k + \left(2Lh t_{[qi]}^\gamma + L\frac{h}{2} \beta_i t_{[qi]}^\gamma \right) \widetilde{w}_{[qi]} + \left(Lh t_{[qi]+1}^\gamma + L\frac{h}{2} t_{[qi]}^\gamma (1-\beta_i) \right) \widetilde{w}_{[qi]+1}$$

$$+ Lh \sum_{k=[qi]+2}^{i-1} t_k^\gamma \widetilde{w}_k + L\frac{h}{2} t_i^\gamma \widetilde{w}_i.$$

Letting h be so small that $L\frac{h}{2} t_i^\gamma \leq \frac{1}{2}$, then

$$\widetilde{w}_i \leq 4Lh \sum_{k=1}^{[qi]-1} t_k^\gamma \widetilde{w}_k + (4Lh t_{[qi]}^\gamma + Lh\beta_i t_{[qi]}^\gamma) \widetilde{w}_{[qi]} + (2Lh t_{[qi]+1}^\gamma + Lh t_{[qi]}^\gamma (1-\beta_i)) \widetilde{w}_{[qi]+1} + 2Lh \sum_{k=[qi]+2}^{i-1} t_k^\gamma \widetilde{w}_k$$

$$= h \sum_{k=1}^{n-1} \widetilde{B}_k \widetilde{w}_k,$$

where

$$\widetilde{B}_k = \begin{cases} 4Lt_k^\gamma, & j = 1, \cdots, [qi]-1, \\ 4Lt_{[qi]}^\gamma + L\beta_i t_{[qi]}^\gamma, & j = [qi], \\ 2Lt_{[qi]+1}^\gamma + Lt_{[qi]}^\gamma (1-\beta_i), & j = [qi]+1, \\ 2Lt_k^\gamma, & j = [qi]+2, \cdots, i-1. \end{cases}$$

According to Lemma 4 with $A = 0$, we have $\widetilde{w}_i = 0$, i.e., $y_i = \widetilde{x}_i$, the solution of Equation (21) is unique. Combining the above situations, the proof of Theorem 2 is completed. □

5. Convergence Analysis

In this section, we will discuss errors caused by the process of obtaining discrete equations using a quadrature formula and interpolation technique and the errors caused by solving the discrete equation using iterative algorithms. According to the quadrature rule, Equation (12) can be expressed as

$$y(t_0) = f(t_0),$$

$$y(t_i) = f(t_i) - \zeta(-\lambda) k_1(t_i, t_0; y(t_0)) h^{1+\lambda} + h \sum_{k=1}^{i-1} t_k^\lambda k_1(t_i, t_k; y(t_k)) + \frac{h}{2} t_i^\lambda k_1(t_i, t_i; y(t_i)) + E_{1,i}$$

$$- \zeta(-\mu) h^{1+\mu} k_2(t_i, t_0; y(t_0)) + h \sum_{k=1}^{[qi]-1} t_k^\mu k_2(t_i, t_k; y(t_k)) + \frac{h}{2} t_{[qi]}^\mu k_2(t_i, t_{[qi]}; y(t_{[qi]})) + E_{2,i} \quad (27)$$

$$+ \frac{q t_i - t_{[qi]}}{2} \left(t_{[qi]}^\mu k_2(t_i, t_{[qi]}; y(t_{[qi]})) + (q t_i)^\mu k_2(t_i, q t_i; \beta_i y(t_{[qi]}) + (1-\beta_i) y(t_{[qi]+1})) \right) + E_{3,i}.$$

From Lemmas 2 and 3, the remainders are

$$E_{1,i} = [k_1(t_i, s; y(s))]'|_{s=0} \zeta(-\lambda - 1) h^{2+\lambda} + \frac{[k_1(t_i, s; y(s))]'|_{s=0}}{2!} \zeta(-\lambda - 2) h^{3+\lambda} + O(h^{4+\lambda})$$

$$= T_1(t_i) h^{2+\lambda} + O(h^{3+\lambda}),$$

$$E_{2,i} = [k_2(t_i,s;y(s))]'|_{s=0}\zeta(-\mu-1)h^{2+\gamma} + \frac{[k_2(t_i,s;y(s))]''|_{s=0}}{2!}\zeta(-\mu-2)h^{3+\mu} + O(h^{4+\mu})$$
$$= T_2(t_i)h^{2+\mu} + O(h^{3+\mu}),$$

$$E_{3,i} = -\frac{\beta(1-\beta)}{2}h^2 y''(qt_i)(qt_i)^\gamma k_2\left(t_i,qt_i;(\beta_i y(t_{[qi]}) + (1-\beta_i)y(t_{[qi]+1}))\right)$$
$$+ \frac{(qt_i - t_{[qi]})^2}{12}\int_{t_{[qi]}}^{qt_i}\frac{\partial^2}{\partial s^2}\left(k_2(t_i,s;y(s))s^\mu\right)ds + O(h^3)$$
$$= T_3(t_i)h^2 + \frac{(qt_i - t_{[qi]})^2 - h^2}{12}\int_{t_{[qi]}}^{qt_i}\frac{\partial^2}{\partial s^2}\left(k_2(t_i,s;y(s))s^\mu\right)ds + O(h^3)$$
$$= T_3(t_i)h^2 + O(h^3),$$

where

$$T_1(t_i) = [k_1(t_i,s;y(s))]'|_{s=0}\zeta(-\lambda-1),$$
$$T_2(t_i) = [k_2(t_i,s;y(s))]'|_{s=0}\zeta(-\mu-1),$$
$$T_3(t_i) = -\frac{\beta(1-\beta)}{2}u''(qt_i)(qt_i)^\mu k_2\left(t_i,qt_i;(\beta_i y(t_{[qi]}) + (1-\beta_i)y(t_{[qi]+1}))\right) + \frac{1}{12}\int_{t_{[qi]}}^{qt_i}\frac{\partial^2}{\partial s^2}k_2(t_i,s;y(s))s^\mu ds.$$

In order to investigate the error between the exact solution and the approximate solution of Equation (1), we first give the following theorem.

Theorem 3. *Under the conditions of Theorem 2, $y(t_i)$ is the exact solution of Equation (1) when $t = t_i$ and y_i is the solution of discrete Equation (19) at t_i. Assume that h is sufficiently small, then, the absolute error denote by $e_{1,i} = |y(t_i) - y_i|$ has the estimate*

$$\max_{1\leq i\leq N} |e_{1,i}| \leq O(h^{2+\gamma}).$$

Proof. Subtracting (19) from (27),

$$|e_{1,0}| = 0,$$

$$|e_{1,i}| = -\zeta(-\lambda)|k_1(t_i,t_0;y(t_0)) - k_1(t_i,t_0;y_0)|h^{1+\lambda} + h\sum_{k=1}^{i-1}t_k^\lambda|k_1(t_i,t_k;y(t_k)) - k_1(t_i,t_k;y_k)|$$
$$+ \frac{h}{2}t_i^\lambda|k_1(t_i,t_i;y(t_i)) - k_1(t_i,t_i;y_i)| - \zeta(-\mu)h^{1+\mu}|k_2(t_i,t_0;y(t_0)) - k_2(t_i,t_0;y_0)|$$
$$+ h\sum_{k=1}^{[qi]-1}t_k^\mu|k_2(t_i,t_k;y(t_k)) - k_2(t_i,t_k;y_k)| + \frac{h}{2}t_{[qi]}^\mu|k_2(t_i,t_{[qi]};y(t_{[qi]})) - k_2(t_i,t_{[qi]};y_{[qi]})|$$
$$+ \frac{qt_i - t_{[qi]}}{2}\left(t_{[qi]}^\mu|k_2(t_i,t_{[qi]};y(t_{[qi]})) - k_2(t_i,t_{[qi]};y_{[qi]})|\right.$$
$$+ (qt_i)^\mu|k_2(t_i,qt_i;\beta_i y(t_{[qi]}) + (1-\beta_i)y(t_{[qi]+1})) - k_2(t_i,qt_i;\beta_i y_{[qi]} + (1-\beta_i)y_{[qi]+1})|\right)$$
$$+ T_1(t_i)h^{2+\lambda} + T_2(t_i)h^{2+\mu} + T_3(t_i)h^2 + O(h^{3+\gamma})$$
$$= h\sum_{k=1}^{i-1}t_k^\lambda L_1|e_{1,k}| + \frac{h}{2}t_i^\lambda L_1|e_{1,i}| + h\sum_{k=1}^{[qi]-1}t_k^\mu L_2|e_{1,k}| + \frac{h}{2}t_{[qi]}^\mu L_2|e_{1,[qi]}|$$
$$+ \frac{qt_i - t_{[qi]}}{2}\left(t_{[qi]}^\mu L_2|e_{1,[qi]}| + (qt_i)^\mu L_2|\beta_i e_{1,[qi]} + (1-\beta_i)e_{1,[qi]+1}|\right)$$
$$+ T_1(t_i)h^{2+\lambda} + T_2(t_i)h^{2+\mu} + T_3(t_i)h^2 + O(h^{3+\gamma}). \tag{28}$$

Letting h be so small, that $\frac{h}{2}t_i^\lambda L_1 \leq \frac{1}{2}$, it is easy to derive

$$|e_{1,i}| \leq A + h\sum_{j=1}^{i-1} B_j |e_{1,j}|, \qquad 0 \leq i \leq N,$$

where

$$A = 2|T_1(t_i)|h^{2+\lambda} + T_2(t_i)h^{2+\mu} + T_3(t_i)h^2 + O(h^{3+\gamma}) = O(h^{2+\gamma}).$$

By Lemma 4, we have

$$\max_{1 \leq i \leq N} |e_{1,i}| \leq O(h^{2+\gamma}).$$

The proof is complete. □

Next, we evaluate the error arising from the iterative process.

Theorem 4. *Under the conditions of Theorem 2, y_i is the solution of Equation (19) and $\tilde{y}_i$ is the approximate solution of Equation (1), and $\tilde{y}_i$ is defined by (21). The absolute error is denoted by $e_{2,i} = |y_i - \tilde{y}_i|$. Assume that h is sufficiently small, then, there exist two positive constants, C_1 and C_2, which are independent of $h = \frac{T}{N}$, such that*

$$v_i \leq \begin{cases} C_1 h\epsilon, & [qi]+1 = i, \\ C_2 h\epsilon, & [qi]+1 \leq i. \end{cases}$$

Proof. Subtracting (21) from (19), we have $e_{2,0} = 0$. We consider two cases.

(1) The first case is $[qi]+1 = i$ (i.e., when $i \leq \frac{1}{1-q}$). Then, we have

$$\begin{aligned}
e_{2,i} =& h\sum_{k=1}^{i-1} t_k^\lambda L_1 e_{2,k} + \frac{h}{2}t_i^\lambda L_1 \epsilon + h\sum_{k=1}^{[qi]-1} t_k^\mu L_2 e_{2,k} + \frac{h}{2}t_{[qi]}^\mu L_2 e_{2,[qi]} \\
& + \frac{qt_i - t_{[qi]}}{2}(t_{[qi]}^\mu L_2 e_{2,[qi]} + (qt_i)^\mu L_2(\beta_i e_{2,[qi]} + (1-\beta_i)\epsilon)) \\
\leq& h\sum_{k=1}^{i-1} t_k^\lambda Le_{2,k} + h\sum_{k=1}^{[qi]-1} t_k^\mu Le_{2,k} + \frac{h}{2}t_{[qi]}^\mu Le_{2,[qi]} \qquad (29) \\
& + \frac{h}{2}(t_{[qi]}^\mu L + (qt_i)^\mu \beta_i)e_{2,[qi]} + (\frac{h}{2}(qt_i)^\mu L(1-\beta_i) + \frac{h}{2}t_i^\lambda L)\epsilon \\
=& h\sum_{k=1}^{i-1} B_k e_{2,k} + (\frac{1}{2}(qt_i)^\mu L(1-\beta_i) + \frac{1}{2}t_i^\lambda L)h\epsilon.
\end{aligned}$$

According to Lemma 4, we have $e_{2,i} \leq C_1 h\epsilon$.

(2) The second case is $[qi]+1 \leq i$ (i.e., when $i > \frac{1}{1-q}$). Then, we obtain

$$\begin{aligned}
e_{2,i} =& h\sum_{k=1}^{i-1} t_k^\lambda L_1 e_{2,k} + \frac{h}{2}t_i^\lambda L_1 \epsilon + h\sum_{k=1}^{[qi]-1} t_k^\mu L_2 e_{2,k} + \frac{h}{2}t_{[qi]}^\mu L_2 e_{2,[qi]} \\
& + \frac{qt_i - t_{[qi]}}{2}(t_{[qi]}^\mu L_2 e_{2,[qi]} + (qt_i)^\mu L_2(\beta_i e_{2,[qi]} + (1-\beta_i)e_{2,[qi]+1})) \\
\leq& h\sum_{k=1}^{i-1} t_k^\lambda Le_{2,k} + \frac{h}{2}t_i^\lambda L\epsilon + h\sum_{k=1}^{[qi]-1} t_k^\mu Le_{2,k} + \frac{h}{2}t_{[qi]}^\mu Le_{2,[qi]} \qquad (30) \\
& + \frac{h}{2}(t_{[qi]}^\mu Le_{2,[qi]} + (qt_i)^\mu L(\beta_i e_{2,[qi]} + (1-\beta_i)e_{2,[qi]+1})) \\
=& h\sum_{k=1}^{i-1} B_k e_{2,k} + \frac{1}{2}t_i^\lambda Lh\epsilon.
\end{aligned}$$

According to Lemma 4, we have $e_{2,i} \leq C_2 h \epsilon$. □

Theorem 5. *Under the conditions of Theorem 2, $y(t_i)$ is the exact solution of Equation (1), $\tilde{y}_i$ is the approximate solution of Equation (1) when $t = t_i$, we have*

$$|y(t_i) - \tilde{y}_i| \leq \begin{cases} C_1 h \epsilon + O(h^{2+\gamma}), & [qi] + 1 = i, \\ C_2 h \epsilon + O(h^{2+\gamma}), & [qi] + 1 \leq i. \end{cases}$$

Proof. By Theorems 3 and 4, the absolute error between $y(t_i)$ and $\tilde{y}_i$ has the expression

$$\begin{aligned} |y(t_i) - \tilde{y}_i| &= |y(t_i) - y_i + y_i - \tilde{y}_i| \\ &\leq |y(t_i) - y_i| + |y_i - \tilde{y}_i|. \end{aligned} \quad (31)$$

We obtain the conclusion of Theorem 5. □

6. Extrapolation Method

In this section, we first describe the asymptotic error expansion and then present an extrapolation technique for achieving high precision. Finally, a posterior error estimate is derived.

Theorem 6. *Let $f(t)$, $k_1(t, s; y(s))$, $k_2(t, s; y(s))$ are four times continuously differentiable on I, $D \times \mathbf{R}$, $D_\theta \times \mathbf{R}$, respectively. Additionally, $y(t)$ has continuous partial derivatives up to 3 on I and $k_i(t, s; y(s))$ $(i = 1, 2)$ satisfy Lipschitz conditions (2). There exist functions $\hat{W}_i(t)$ $(i = 1, 2, 3)$ independent of h, such that we have the following asymptotic expansions:*

$$y_i = y(t_i) + \hat{W}_1(t_i) h^{2+\lambda} + \hat{W}_2(t_i) h^{2+\mu} + \hat{W}_3(t_i) h^2 + O(h^{3+\gamma}), \quad -1 < \lambda < 0, \quad -1 < \mu \leq 0. \quad (32)$$

Proof. Assume that $\{\hat{W}_k(t), k = 1, 2, 3\}$ satisfy the auxiliary delay equations

$$\hat{W}_k(t) = W_k(t) + \int_0^t s^\lambda k_1(t, s; y(s)) \hat{W}_k(s) ds + \int_0^{qt} s^\mu k_2(t, s; y(s)) \hat{W}_k(s) ds,$$

and $\hat{W}_k(t_i), i = 1, \cdots, N$ satisfy the approximation equations

$$\begin{aligned} \hat{W}_k(t_i) =& -\zeta(-\lambda) h^{1+\lambda} k_1(t_i, t_0; y(t_0)) \hat{W}_k(t_0) + h \sum_{k=1}^{i-1} t_k^\lambda k_1(t_i, t_k; y(t_k)) \hat{W}_k(t_k) \\ &+ \frac{h}{2} t_i^\lambda k_1(t_i, t_i; y(t_i)) \hat{W}_k(t_i) - \zeta(-\mu) h^{1+\mu} k_2(t_i, t_0; y(t_0)) \hat{W}_k(t_0) \\ &+ h \sum_{k=1}^{[qi]-1} t_k^\mu k_2(t_i, t_k; y(t_k)) \hat{W}_k(t_k) + \frac{h}{2} t_{[qi]}^\mu k_2(t_i, t_{[qi]}; y(t_{[qi]})) \hat{W}_k(t_i) \\ &+ \frac{qt_i - t_{[qi]}}{2} \Big(t_{[qi]}^\mu k_2(t_i, t_{[qi]}; y(t_{[qi]})) \hat{W}_k(t_{[qi]}) + (qt_i)^\mu k_2(t_i, qt_i; \beta_i y(t_{[qi]})) \hat{W}_k(t_{[qi]}) \\ &+ (1 - \beta_i) y(t_{[qi]+1}) \hat{W}_k(t_{[qi]+1}) \Big) + W_k(t_i). \end{aligned} \quad (33)$$

The analysis procedure is similar to the proof of Theorem 3. We obtain

$$\max_{1 \leq i \leq N} |\hat{W}_k(t_i) - W(t_i)| \leq L h^{2+\gamma}.$$

Let

$$E_i = e_i - \Big(W_1(t_i) h^{2+\lambda} + W_2(t_i) h^{2+\mu} + W_3(t_i) \Big) h^2.$$

Then, we obtain

$$E_i = -\zeta(-\lambda)h^{1+\lambda}k_1(t_i,t_0;y(t_0))E_0 + h\sum_{k=1}^{i-1}t_k^\lambda k_1(t_i,t_k;y(t_k))E_k + \frac{h}{2}t_i^\lambda k_1(t_i,t_i;y(t_i))E_i$$

$$-\zeta(-\mu)h^{1+\mu}k_2(t_i,t_0;y(t_0))E_0 + h\sum_{k=1}^{[qi]-1}t_k^\mu k_2(t_i,t_k;y(t_k))E_k + \frac{h}{2}t_{[qi]}^\mu k_2(t_i,t_{[qi]};y(t_{[qi]}))E_{[qi]}$$

$$+\frac{qt_i-t_{[qi]}}{2}\Big(t_{[qi]}^\mu k_2(t_i,t_{[qi]};y(t_{[qi]}))E_{[qi]} + (qt_i)^\mu k_2(t_i,qt_i;\beta_i y(t_{[qi]})E_{[qi]} + (1-\beta_i)y(t_{[qi]+1})E_{[qi]+1})\Big).$$

According to Lemma 4, there exists a constant d such that

$$\max_{1\leq i\leq N}|E_i| \leq dh^{3+\gamma}.$$

The asymptotic expansion is

$$\widetilde{y}_i = y(t_i) + \widehat{W}_1(t_i)h^{2+\lambda} + \widehat{W}_2(t_i)h^{2+\mu} + \widehat{W}_3(t_i)h^2 + O(h^{3+\gamma}).$$

□

From Theorem 6, we consider the Richardson extrapolation method to achieve higher accuracy.

Extrapolation algorithm

Step 1. Assume $\gamma = \min(\lambda,\mu) = \lambda$, and halve the step length to obtain

$$\widetilde{y}_i^{\frac{h}{2}} = y(t_i) + \widehat{W}_1(t_i)\left(\frac{h}{2}\right)^{2+\lambda} + \widehat{W}_2(t_i)\left(\frac{h}{2}\right)^{2+\mu} + \widehat{W}_3(t_i)\left(\frac{h}{2}\right)^2 + O\left(\left(\frac{h}{2}\right)^{3+\lambda}\right). \tag{34}$$

Then, the term $\widehat{W}_1(t_i)h^{2+\lambda}$ can be removed.

$$\widetilde{y}_i^{1,h} = \frac{2^{2+\lambda}\widetilde{y}_i^{\frac{h}{2}} - \widetilde{y}_i^h}{2^{2+\lambda}-1} = y(t_i) + \widehat{W}_2(t_i)h^{2+\mu} + \widehat{W}_3(t_i)h^2 + O(h^{3+\lambda}). \tag{35}$$

Step 2. To eliminate $\widehat{W}_2(t_i)h^{2+\mu}$, we apply Richardson $h^{2+\mu}$ extrapolation:

$$\widetilde{y}_i^{1,\frac{h}{2}} = y(t_i) + \widehat{W}_2(t_i)\left(\frac{h}{2}\right)^{2+\mu} + \widehat{W}_3(t_i)\left(\frac{h}{2}\right)^2 + O\left(\left(\frac{h}{2}\right)^{3+\lambda}\right). \tag{36}$$

Combining (35) and (36), we have

$$\widetilde{y}_i^{2,h} = \frac{2^{2+\mu}\widetilde{y}_i^{1,\frac{h}{2}} - \widetilde{y}_i^{1,h}}{2^{2+\mu}-1} = y(t_i) + \widehat{W}_3(t_i)h^2 + O(h^{3+\lambda}). \tag{37}$$

A posteriori asymptotic error estimate is

$$\left|\widetilde{y}_i^{\frac{h}{2}} - y(t_i)\right| = \left|\frac{2^{2+\lambda}\widetilde{y}_i^{\frac{h}{2}} - \widetilde{y}_i^h}{2^{2+\lambda}-1} - y(t_i) + \frac{\widetilde{y}_i^h - \widetilde{y}_i^{\frac{h}{2}}}{2^{2+\lambda}-1}\right| \leq \left|\frac{2^{2+\lambda}\widetilde{y}_i^{\frac{h}{2}} - \widetilde{y}_i^h}{2^{2+\lambda}-1} - y(t_i)\right| + \left|\frac{\widetilde{y}_i^h - \widetilde{y}_i^{\frac{h}{2}}}{2^{2+\lambda}-1}\right|$$

$$= \left|\widetilde{y}_i^{1,h} - y(t_i)\right| + \left|\frac{\widetilde{y}_i^h - \widetilde{y}_i^{\frac{h}{2}}}{2^{2+\lambda}-1}\right| + O(h^2) \tag{38}$$

The error $\widetilde{y}_i^{\frac{h}{2}} - y(t_i)$ is bounded by $\frac{\widetilde{y}_i^h - \widetilde{y}_i^{\frac{h}{2}}}{2^{2+\lambda}-1}$, which is important for constructing adaptable algorithms.

7. Numerical Experiments

In this section, we illustrate the performance and accuracy of the quadrature method using the improved trapezoid formula. For ease of notation, we define

$$E_h = |y(t_i) - \hat{y}_i^h|, \quad E_{k,i} = |y(t_i) - \hat{y}_i^{k,h}| \; (k = 1, 2), \quad \text{Rate} = \log_2\left(\frac{E_h}{E_{\frac{h}{2}}}\right),$$

where $\hat{y}_i^h$ is the approximate solution of Equation (1), $\hat{y}_i^{k,h}$ is the approximate solution of k-th extrapolation, $E_{k,i}$ is the absolute error between the exact solution and the approximate solution of k-th extrapolation when $t = t_i$. The procedure was implemented in MATLAB.

Example 1. *Consider the following equation*

$$y(t) = f(t) - \int_0^t s^\lambda \sin(y(s))ds + \int_0^{qt}(t+s)\sin(y(s))ds, \qquad t \in [0,T], \qquad (39)$$

with $T = 1$, $\lambda = -\frac{1}{2}$, and $q = 0.95$. The exact solution is given by $y(t) = t$ and $f(t)$ is determined by the exact solution.

Applying the algorithm with $N = 2^4, 2^5, 2^6, 2^7, 2^8$, the numerical results at $t = 0.4$ are presented in Table 1, the CPU time(s) are 0.34, 0.55, 0.98, 1.62, and 3.01 s, respectively. By comparing E_h and $E_{1,i}$, we can observe that the accuracy was improved and the extrapolation algorithm was effective. In the third column, the rate values show that the convergence order was consistent with the theoretical analysis.

Table 1. Numerical results at $t = 0.4$ of Example 1.

N	E_h	Rate	$E_{1,i}$	Posteriori Errors
2^4	3.32×10^{-4}	—	—	—
2^5	1.18×10^{-4}	$2^{1.50}$	4.70×10^{-6}	1.17×10^{-4}
2^6	4.01×10^{-5}	$2^{1.55}$	2.04×10^{-6}	4.21×10^{-5}
2^7	1.35×10^{-5}	$2^{1.57}$	9.90×10^{-7}	1.46×10^{-5}
2^8	4.51×10^{-6}	$2^{1.58}$	4.21×10^{-7}	4.92×10^{-6}

Example 2. *Consider the following equation*

$$y(t) = f(t) - \int_0^t s^\lambda(t^2+s)(y(s))^2 ds + \int_0^{qt} s^\mu \sin(y(s))ds, \qquad t \in [0,T], \qquad (40)$$

where $T = 1$, $\lambda = \mu = -\frac{1}{2}$, $q = 0.8$ and the analytical solution is $y(t) = t$. Then, $f(t)$ is determined by the exact solution.

By applying the numerical method for $N = 2^4, 2^5, 2^6, 2^7, 2^8$, the obtained results at $t = 0.2$ are shown in Table 2. By comparing E_h and $E_{1,i}$, we can observe that the accuracy was improved, proving that the extrapolation algorithm is effective. The results verified the theoretic convergence order, which is $O(h^{1.5})$.

Table 2. Numerical results at $t = 0.2$ of Example 2.

N	E_h	Rate	$E_{1,i}$	Posteriori Errors
2^4	6.57×10^{-4}	—	—	—
2^5	2.30×10^{-4}	$2^{1.51}$	3.13×10^{-6}	2.33×10^{-4}
2^6	8.03×10^{-5}	$2^{1.52}$	1.58×10^{-6}	8.19×10^{-5}
2^7	2.81×10^{-5}	$2^{1.52}$	5.38×10^{-7}	2.86×10^{-5}
2^8	9.82×10^{-6}	$2^{1.52}$	1.56×10^{-7}	9.97×10^{-6}

Example 3. We consider the following equation

$$y(t) = f(t) - \int_0^t s^\lambda (t+s) \sin(y(s))ds + \int_0^{qt} s^\mu (t+s)(y(s))^2 ds, \quad t \in [0, T], \quad (41)$$

where $T = 1, \lambda = -\frac{1}{3}, \mu = -\frac{1}{4}, q = 0.9$, and the analytical solution is $y(t) = t$. Then, $f(t)$ is determined by the exact solution.

By applying the numerical method for $N = 2^4, 2^5, 2^6, 2^7$, and 2^8, the obtained results at $t = 0.4$ are shown in Table 3. As λ was not equal to μ, we first applied the Richardson $h^{2+\lambda}$ extrapolation, and then adopted the Richardson $h^{2+\mu}$ extrapolation. By comparing $E_h, E_{1,i}$ and $E_{2,i}$, these results verify the theoretical results, and we can see that the extrapolation improved the accuracy dramatically. When N = 8, 16, 32, 64, 128, the CPU time(s) are 1.43, 2.41, 3.99, 17.46, and 21.36 s, respectively. The exact solution and the approximation when N=8 are plotted in Figure 1.

Table 3. Numerical results at $t = 0.4$ of Example 3.

N	E_h	Rate	$E_{1,i}$	$E_{2,i}$	Posteriori Errors
2^4	9.36×10^{-5}	—	—	—	—
2^5	3.23×10^{-5}	$2^{1.53}$	4.12×10^{-6}	—	2.82×10^{-5}
2^6	1.06×10^{-5}	$2^{1.61}$	6.00×10^{-7}	8.89×10^{-7}	9.99×10^{-6}
2^7	3.41×10^{-6}	$2^{1.63}$	1.17×10^{-7}	8.70×10^{-8}	3.30×10^{-6}
2^8	1.10×10^{-6}	$2^{1.65}$	2.31×10^{-8}	1.68×10^{-8}	1.07×10^{-6}

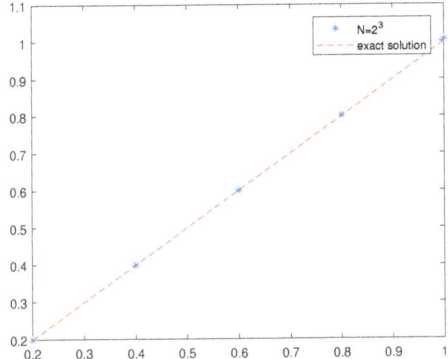

Figure 1. The absolute errors and the approximations when N = 2^3.

8. Conclusions

In this paper, by using the improved trapezoidal quadrature formula and linear interpolation, we obtained the approximate equation for non-linear Volterra integral equations with vanishing delay and weak singular kernels. The approximate solutions were obtained by an iterative algorithm, which possessed a high accuracy order $O(h^{2+\gamma})$. Additionally, we analyzed the existence and uniqueness of both the exact and approximate solutions. The significance of this work was that it demonstrated the efficiency and reliability of the Richardson extrapolation. The computational findings were compared with the exact solution: we found that our methods possess high accuracy and low computational complexity, and the results showed good agreement with the theoretical analysis. For future work, we can apply this method for solving two-dimensional delay integral equations.

Author Contributions: Conceptualization, J.H. and L.Z.; methodology, J.H. and L.Z.; validation, J.H. and H.L.; writing—review and editing, L.Z. and Y.W. All authors have read and agreed to the published version of the manuscript.

Funding: This research was funded by the Program of Chengdu Normal University, grant number CS18ZDZ02.

Institutional Review Board Statement: Not applicable.

Informed Consent Statement: Not applicable.

Data Availability Statement: Not applicable.

Acknowledgments: The authors would like to thank the editor and referees for their careful comments and fruitful suggestions.

Conflicts of Interest: The authors declare no conflict of interest.

References

1. Avaji, M.; Hafshejani, J.; Dehcheshmeh, S.; Ghahfarokhi, D. Solution of delay Volterra integral equations using the Variational iteration method. *J. Appl. Sci.* **2012**, *12*, 196–200. [CrossRef]
2. Williams, L.R.; Leggett, R.W. Nonzero Solutions of Nonlinear Integral Equations Modeling Infectious Disease. *Siam J. Math. Anal.* **1982**, *13*, 121. [CrossRef]
3. Volterra, V. On some questions of the inversion of definite integrals. (Sopra alcune questioni di inversione di integrali definiti). *Ann. Mat. Pura Appl.* **1897**, *25*, 139–178. [CrossRef]
4. Yang, K.; Zhang, R. Analysis of continuous collocation solutions for a kind of Volterra functional integral equations with proportional delay. *J. Comput. Appl. Math.* **2011**, *236*, 743–752. [CrossRef]
5. Xie, H.; Zhang, R.; Brunner, H. Collocation methods for general Volterra functional integral equations with vanishing delays. *SIAM J. Sci. Comput.* **2011**, *33*, 3303–3332. [CrossRef]
6. Ming, W.; Huang, C.; Zhao, L. Optimal superconvergence results for Volterra functional integral equations with proportional vanishing delays. *Appl. Math. Comput.* **2018**, *320*, 292–301. [CrossRef]
7. Mokhtary, P.; Moghaddam, B.P.; Lopes, A.M.; Machado, J.A.T. A computational approach for the non-smooth solution of non-linear weakly singular Volterra integral equation with proportional delay. *Numer. Algorithms* **2019**, *83*, 987–1006. [CrossRef]
8. Gu, Z.; Chen, Y. Chebyshev spectral-collocation method for a class of weakly singular Volterra integral equations with proportional delay. *J. Numer. Math.* **2014**, *22*, 311–342. [CrossRef]
9. Zhang, R.; Zhu, B.; Xie, H. Spectral methods for weakly singular Volterra integral equations with pantograph delays. *Front. Math. China* **2014**, *8*, 281–299. [CrossRef]
10. Brunner, H. *Collocation Methods for Volterra Integral and Related Functional Differential Equations*; Cambridge University Press: Cambridge, UK, 2004.
11. Zhang, G.; Song, M. Impulsive continuous Runge—Kutta methods for impulsive delay differential equations. *Appl. Math. Comput.* **2019**, *341*, 160–173. [CrossRef]
12. Shu, H.; Xu, W.; Wang, X.; Wu, J. Complex dynamics in a delay differential equation with two delays in tick growth with diapause. *J. Differ. Equ.* **2020**, *269*, 10937–10963. [CrossRef]
13. Fang, J.; Zhan, R. High order explicit exponential Runge—Kutta methods for semilinear delay differential equations. *J. Comput. Appl. Math.* **2021**, *388*, 113279. [CrossRef]
14. Song, H.; Xiao, Y.; Chen, M. Collocation methods for third-kind Volterra integral equations with proportional delays. *Appl. Math. Comput.* **2021**, *388*, 125509.
15. Brunner, H. The numerical solution of weakly singular Volterra functional integro-differential equations with variable delays. *Commun. Pure Appl. Anal.* **2006**, *5*, 261–276. [CrossRef]
16. Huang, C. Stability of linear multistep methods for delay integro-differential equations. *Comput. Math. Appl.* **2008**, *55*, 2830–2838. [CrossRef]
17. Sheng, C.; Wang, Z.; Guo, B. An h_p-spectral collocation method for nonlinear Volterra functional integro-differential equations with delays. *Appl. Numer. Math.* **2016**, *105*, 1–24. [CrossRef]
18. Abdi, A.; Berrut, J.P.; Hosseini, S.A. The Linear Barycentric Rational Method for a Class of Delay Volterra Integro-Differential Equations. *J. Sci. Comput.* **2018**, *75*, 1757–1775. [CrossRef]
19. Yaghoobi, S.; Moghaddam, B.P.; Ivaz, K. An efficient cubic spline approximation for variable-order fractional differential equations with time delay. *Nonlinear Dyn.* **2017**, *87*, 815–826. [CrossRef]
20. Rahimkhani, P.; Ordokhani, Y.; Babolian, E. A new operational matrix based on Bernoulli wavelets for solving fractional delay differential equations. *Numer. Algorithms* **2017**, *74*, 223–245. [CrossRef]
21. Rakhshan, S.A.; Effati, S. A generalized Legendre—Gauss collocation method for solving nonlinear fractional differential equations with time varying delays. *Appl. Numer. Math.* **2019**, *146*, 342–360. [CrossRef]
22. Zuniga-Aguilar, C.J.; Gomez-Aguilar, J.F.; Escobar-Jimenez, R.F.; Romero-Ugalde, H.M. A novel method to solve variable-order fractional delay differential equations based in lagrange interpolations. *Chaos Solitons Fractals* **2019**, *126*, 266–282. [CrossRef]
23. Xu, X.; Huang, Q. Superconvergence of discontinuous Galerkin methods for nonlinear delay differential equations with vanishing delay. *J. Comput. Appl. Math.* **2019**, *348*, 314–327. [CrossRef]

24. Bellour, A.; Bousselsal, M. A Taylor collocation method for solving delay integral equations. *Numer. Algorithms* **2014**, *65*, 843–857. [CrossRef]
25. Darania, P.; Sotoudehmaram, F. Numerical analysis of a high order method for nonlinear delay integral equations. *J. Comput. Appl. Math.* **2020**, *374*, 112738. [CrossRef]
26. Khasi, M.; Ghoreishi, F.; Hadizadeh, M. Numerical analysis of a high order method for state-dependent delay integral equations. *Numer. Algorithms* **2014**, *66*, 177–201. [CrossRef]
27. Bica, A.M.; Popescu, C. Numerical solutions of the nonlinear fuzzy Hammerstein-Volterra delay integral equations. *Inf. Sci.* **2013**, *223*, 236–255. [CrossRef]
28. Mosleh, M.; Otadi, M. Least squares approximation method for the solution of Hammerstein-Volterra delay integral equations. *Appl. Math. Comput.* **2015**, *258*, 105–110. [CrossRef]
29. Zhang, X. A new strategy for the numerical solution of nonlinear Volterra integral equations with vanishing delays. *Appl. Math. Comput.* **2020**, *365*, 124608.
30. Lima, P.; Diogo, T. Numerical solution of a nonuniquely solvable Volterra integral equation using extrapolation. *J. Comput. Appl. Math.* **2002**, *140*, 537–557. [CrossRef]
31. Sidi, A. *Practical Extrapolation Methods*; Cambridge University Press: Cambridge, UK, 2003.
32. Tao, L.; Jin, H. *High Precision Algorithm for Integral Equations*; China Science Press: Beijing, China, 2013.
33. Tao, L.; Yong, H. Extrapolation method for solving weakly singular nonlinear Volterra integral equations of the second kind. *J. Math. Anal. Appl.* **2006**, *324*, 225–237. [CrossRef]
34. Navot, J. A Further Extension of the Euler-Maclaurin Summation Formula. *J. Math. Phys.* **1962**, *41*, 155–163. [CrossRef]
35. Tao, L.; Yong, H. A generalization of Gronwall inequality and its application to weakly singular Volterra integral equation of the second kind. *J. Math. Anal. Appl.* **2003**, *282*, 56–62. [CrossRef]
36. Qin, Y. *Integral and Discrete Inequalities and Their Applications*; Springer International Publishing: Berlin/Heidelberg, Germany, 2016.

Article

An Iterative Algorithm for Approximating the Fixed Point of a Contractive Affine Operator

María Isabel Berenguer [1,2,*,†] and Manuel Ruiz Galán [1,2,†]

1. Department of Applied Mathematics, E.T.S. Ingeniería de Edificación, University of Granada, 18071 Granada, Spain; mruizg@ugr.es
2. Institute of Mathematics (IMAG), University of Granada, 18071 Granada, Spain
* Correspondence: maribel@ugr.es
† These authors contributed equally to this work.

Abstract: First of all, in this paper we obtain a perturbed version of the geometric series theorem, which allows us to present an iterative numerical method to approximate the fixed point of a contractive affine operator. This result requires some approximations that we obtain using the projections associated with certain Schauder bases. Next, an algorithm is designed to approximate the solution of Fredholm's linear integral equation, and we illustrate the behavior of the method with some numerical examples.

Keywords: iterative numerical methods; Schauder bases; Fredholm integral equation

MSC: 65R20; 46B15; 45B05

1. Introduction

The idea of iterative numerical methods is, given a complete metric space X (typically a Banach space) and a contractive operator $T : X \longrightarrow X$, or at least one which guarantees the convergence of the Picard iterates, to construct a sequence of approximations of the fixed point of that operator $x_0 = T(x_0)$. The calculation of the Picard iterates is not generally easy or even feasible, so several methods which allow us to approximate the elements of the Picard sequence have been proposed. Therefore, a part of the Picard-type iterative algorithms are focused on determining, for an element $x \in X$, a value close to $T(x)$ and in this way, successively approximating the iterates. The numerical techniques used are very diverse, and the resulting algorithms have numerous applications. Proof of all this are the recent references [1–16].

However, our approach here is completely different: given x, instead of approximating successively $T(x), T^2(x), T^3(x), \ldots$, which necessarily involves an accumulation of errors, in this paper we approximate directly $T^n(x)$ by means of the use of suitable Schauder bases, transforming it into a simple calculation which, for example, does not involve the resolution of systems of algebraic equations or the use of any quadrature formulae because simply linear combinations of certain values associated with the operator are calculated. What is more, motivated by its application for the numerical resolution of the linear Fredholm integral equation, the operator T is considered to be affine and continuous. This affine and continuous nature means that, instead of using a fixed-point language, we opted for resorting to an equivalent version using the geometric series theorem, and more specifically, our first contribution is to obtain a perturbed version of the same which is susceptible to presenting approximations by means of certain Schauder bases related to the operator. Such an approximation will imply a low computational cost as mentioned above. Thus, we are going to design an iterative-type algorithm which allows the approximation of the fixed point of a suitable continuous affine operator.

As we have mentioned, the application that we are presenting consists of a numerical algorithm to solve the linear Fredholm integral equation, which is chosen for its great versatility.

Citation: Berenguer, M.I.; Ruiz Galán, M. An Iterative Algorithm for Approximating the Fixed Point of a Contractive Affine Operator. *Mathematics* **2022**, *10*, 1012. https://doi.org/10.3390/math10071012

Academic Editor: Ioannis K. Argyros

Received: 27 February 2022
Accepted: 10 March 2022
Published: 22 March 2022

Publisher's Note: MDPI stays neutral with regard to jurisdictional claims in published maps and institutional affiliations.

Copyright: © 2022 by the authors. Licensee MDPI, Basel, Switzerland. This article is an open access article distributed under the terms and conditions of the Creative Commons Attribution (CC BY) license (https://creativecommons.org/licenses/by/4.0/).

The structure of this paper is as follows. In Section 2 we establish an analytical–numerical result, which provides us with an approximation of the fixed point of a suitable continuous affine operator in a Banach space. To continue, Section 3 interprets the previous result in terms of an algorithm when a Schauder basis is introduced into the considered space. Section 4 derives a specific algorithm in the case of the linear Fredholm integral equation in two distinct contexts. Next, Section 5 shows some illustrative examples of equations or a classic model of electrostatics (Love's equation), and finally, Section 6 rounds up with some conclusions.

2. Approximating Fixed Points of Affine Operators

The following result provides us with an approximation of the fixed point of a suitable continuous affine operator, as well as an estimation of the error. It addresses a version of the geometric series theorem, which we can label as perturbed: it presents the possibility of converting the precise calculations into approximate ones, in exchange for making the calculations possible.

Before establishing this, we present some standard notation. Given a (real) Banach space X, $L(X)$ will denote the Banach space (usual operator norm) of those bounded and linear operators from X to X. For $T \in L(X)$ and $n \in \mathbb{N}$, T^n denotes the power operator $T \circ \overbrace{\cdots}^{n \text{ times}} \circ T$, while $T^0 = I$, the identity map on X.

Theorem 1. *Let X be a Banach space, $y \in X$ and $L \in L(X)$ with $\|L\| < 1$, and consider the continuous affine operator $A : X \longrightarrow X$ defined by*

$$Ax := y + Lx, \quad (x \in X).$$

Let $y_0 \in X$, $n \in \mathbb{N}$ and $L_0, L_1, \ldots, L_n \in L(X)$. Then, the equation $Ax = x$ has a unique solution $x^\bullet \in X$ and

$$\left\| \sum_{j=0}^{n} L_j y_0 - x^\bullet \right\| \leq \sum_{j=0}^{n} \|L_j y_0 - L^j y_0\| + \left(\frac{1 - \|L\|^{n+1}}{1 - \|L\|} \right) \|y_0 - y\| + \frac{\|L\|^{n+1}}{1 - \|L\|} \|y\|.$$

Proof. Let us first observe that, according to the geometric series theorem, there exists a unique solution $x^\bullet \in X$ for the equation $Ax = x$,

$$x^\bullet = (I - L)^{-1} y,$$

which satisfies for any $k \in \mathbb{N}$,

$$\left\| \sum_{j=0}^{k} L^j y - x^\bullet \right\| \leq \frac{\|L\|^{k+1}}{1 - \|L\|} \|y\|.$$

Therefore,

$$\left\| \sum_{j=0}^{n} L_j y_0 - x^\bullet \right\| \leq \left\| \sum_{j=0}^{n} L_j y_0 - \sum_{j=0}^{n} L^j y_0 \right\| + \left\| \sum_{j=0}^{n} L^j y_0 - \sum_{j=0}^{n} L^j y \right\| + \left\| \sum_{j=0}^{n} L^j y - x^\bullet \right\|$$

$$\leq \sum_{j=0}^{n} \|L_j y_0 - L^j y_0\| + \sum_{j=0}^{n} \|L\|^j \|y_0 - y\| + \frac{\|L\|^{n+1}}{1 - \|L\|} \|y\|$$

$$= \sum_{j=0}^{n} \|L_j y_0 - L^j y_0\| + \left(\frac{1 - \|L\|^{n+1}}{1 - \|L\|} \right) \|y_0 - y\| + \frac{\|L\|^{n+1}}{1 - \|L\|} \|y\|,$$

as announced. □

It is worth mentioning that when $y_0 = y$ and for all $j = 0, 1, \ldots, m$, we have that $L_j = L^j$, and we recover a well-known algorithm associated with the geometric series theorem. However, iterative procedures such as this, used to involve difficult and even impossible calculations from a practical perspective, so the idea behind this theorem is to choose the operators $L_0, L_1, \ldots, L_n$ in such a way that $L_0 y_0, L_1 y_0, L_n y_0$ are not only calculable, but also have a low computational cost. In addition, if y_0 represents an approximation of y—normally due to a certain type of error—the previous result shows how y_0 influences the final approximation. Finally, we can obtain an approximation for $x^\bullet$ for some adequate $n \in \mathbb{N}$, and for each $j = 0, 1, \ldots, n$, $L_j y_0$ is close to $L^j y_0$. More specifically:

Corollary 1. *Suppose that X is a Banach space, $L \in \mathcal{L}(X)$ and $\|L\| < 1$, $y \in X$, and that $A : X \longrightarrow X$ is the continuous and affine operator $A(\cdot) := y + L(\cdot)$, whose unique fixed point is denoted by $x^\bullet \in X$. Additionally, assume that for some $y_0 \in X$, $n \in \mathbb{N}$, $L_0, L_1, \ldots, L_n \in \mathcal{L}(X)$ and $\varepsilon, \varepsilon_0, \varepsilon_n > 0$, we have that*

$$\sum_{j=0}^{n} \varepsilon_j < \frac{\varepsilon}{2},$$

$$j = 0, \ldots, n \Rightarrow \|L_j y_0 - L^j y_0\| < \varepsilon_j, \tag{1}$$

and that

$$\left(\frac{1 - \|L\|^{n+1}}{1 - \|L\|} \right) \|y_0 - y\| + \frac{\|L\|^{n+1}}{1 - \|L\|} \|y\| < \frac{\varepsilon}{2}. \tag{2}$$

Then

$$\left\| \sum_{j=0}^{n} L_j y_0 - x^\bullet \right\| < \varepsilon.$$

Obviously, (2) is valid as soon as n is large enough and $\|y_0 - y\|$ is small. For condition (1), we present some analytical tools in the next section.

3. Numerical Ideas behind the Algorithm for the Equation $y + Lx = x$

In view of Corollary 2.2 and under its hypotheses, we can approximate the fixed point $x^\bullet$ of A by a series close to the geometric one:

$$y_0 \in X \rightsquigarrow \begin{vmatrix} y_0 & Ly_0 & L^2 y_0 & \cdots & L^n y_0 & \rightsquigarrow & \sum_{j=0}^{n} L^j y_0 & \xrightarrow[(n \to \infty)]{} & x^\bullet \\ L_0 y_0 & L_1 y_0 & L_2 y_0 & \cdots & L_n y_0 & \rightsquigarrow & \sum_{j=0}^{n} L_j y_0 & \approx & \sum_{j=0}^{n} L^j y_0 \end{vmatrix}$$

In order to derive

$$\sum_{j=0}^{n} L_j y_0 \approx \sum_{j=0}^{n} L^j y_0$$

an approximation as that given in (1) is required. To this end, a possible tool appears provided by the Schauder bases, since they give an explicit linear approximation of any element of a Banach space by means of the associated projections, which is compatible with the continuity and affinity of the operator. What is more, in the case of classic bases, we easily obtain approximations of (the linear part of) A and its powers.

Thus, before continuing, we revise some of the basic notions of Schauder bases that we are going to need in the design of our algorithm. A sequence $\{e_j\}_{j \in \mathbb{N}}$ in a Banach space X is a *Schauder basis* if all the element $x \in X$ can be uniquely represented as

$$x = \sum_{j=1}^{\infty} \alpha_j e_j,$$

for a sequence of real $\{\alpha_j\}_{j\in\mathbb{N}}$. If we define for each $j \in \mathbb{N}$ the linear operator $P_j : X \longrightarrow X$, known as the *j-th projection* associated with the basis, as

$$P_j x := \sum_{k=0}^{j} \alpha_k e_k,$$

for such an x, it is easy to prove, as a consequence of the Baire lemma, that it is a continuous operator and, in view of the representation of x in terms of the elements of the basis,

$$\lim_{j\to\infty} \|P_j x - x\| = 0.$$

With the aid of a Schauder basis, we can approximate Lx with $L(P_j x)$ which, on occasion, is easy to calculate. To summarize all of this, we focus on a type of affine equation, linear Fredholm integral equations, although this is the objective of the following section.

4. Algorithm to Approximate the Solution of a Linear Fredholm Integral Equation

In the rest of this paper, we focus our efforts on realizing everything that we explained thus far in order to address the study of a specific problem, the numerical resolution of a linear Fredholm integral equation, in two distinct settings.

Let $X = C[a, b]$ or $X = L^p[a, b]$, $(1 < p < \infty)$, $k \in C[a, b]^2$ or $k \in L^\infty[a, b]^2$, respectively, and $y \in X$. Then we consider the corresponding linear Fredhlom integral equation

$$x(t) = y(t) + \int_a^b k(t, s) x(s) ds, \tag{3}$$

where $x \in X$ is the unknown function. In view of the previous results, we consider the continuous and linear operator $L : X \longrightarrow X$ defined at each $y_0 \in X$ as

$$L y_0 := \int_a^b k(\cdot, s) y_0(s) ds.$$

Then, given $j \in \mathbb{N}$,

$$L^j y_0 = \int_a^b \left(\cdots \int_a^b k(\cdot, t_1) k(t_1, t_2) \cdots k(t_{j-1}, t_j) y_0(t_j) dt_j \right) \cdots dt_1.$$

From now on, in both cases ($X = C[a, b]$ or $X = L^p[a, b]$), we assume that

$$\|k\|(b - a) < 1,$$

since such a condition is sufficient for the validity of $\|L\| < 1$ and it is very easy to check. Furthermore, for each $d \in \mathbb{N}$, we fix a Schauder basis $\{e_j^{(d)}\}_{j\in\mathbb{N}}$ in $C[a, b]^d$ (if $X = C[a, b]$) or in $L^p[a, b]^d$ (if $X = L^p[a, b]$) and we denote the projections in this basis as $\{P_j^{(d)}\}_{j\in\mathbb{N}}$.

With all of this, we are now ready to define the approximate operators L_j: for each $x \in X$ and $j \in \mathbb{N}$, we take

$$\Phi_j(x)(t, t_1, \ldots, t_j) := k(\cdot, t_1) k(t_1, t_2) \cdots k(t_{j-1}, t_j) y_0(t_j)$$

and fixed on $r_j \in \mathbb{N}$, thus $L_j : X \longrightarrow X$ is given as

$$L_j y_0 := \int_a^b \left(\cdots \int_a^b P_{r_j}^{(j+1)} (\Phi_j(y_0)) (\cdot, t_1, \ldots, t_j) dt_j \right) \cdots dt_1. \tag{4}$$

Now we can apply the corollary 1 since without going any further, each r_j is big enough, $\|L_j x - L^j x\| < \varepsilon_j$.

Corollary 2. For any $\varepsilon > 0$ and $y_0 \in X$, there are natural numbers n and $r_0, \ldots, r_n$ in such a way that if $x^\bullet$ is the unique solution to the linear Fredholm integral Equation (3), then

$$\left\| \sum_{j=0}^{n} L_j y_0 - x^\bullet \right\| < \varepsilon,$$

where $L_0 = I$ and for each $j \geq 1$, the operator L_j is defined by (4).

Thus, we have established the following (Algorithm 1)

Algorithm 1: Algorithm for approximating the solution of the linear Fredholm integral equation.

Choose $y_0, k, n, \varepsilon, \varepsilon_0, \ldots, \varepsilon_n, r_0, \ldots, r_n \in \mathbb{N}$, and $\{e_i^{(d)}\}_{i \in \mathbb{N}}, d = 1, \ldots, n+1$;
$L_0 \leftarrow I$;
$j \leftarrow 1$;
while $\left\| \sum_{j=0}^{n} L_j y_0 - x^\bullet \right\| \geq \varepsilon$ and $j \leq n$

$\quad \Phi_j(y_0)(t, t_1, \ldots, t_j) \leftarrow k(\cdot, t_1) k(t_1, t_2) \cdots k(t_{j-1}, t_j) y_0(t_j)$;
$\quad L_j y_0 \leftarrow \int_a^b \left(\cdots \int_a^b P_{r_j}^{(j+1)}(\Phi_j(y_0)(\cdot, t_1, \ldots, t_j) dt_j \right) \cdots dt_1$;
$\quad j \leftarrow j+1$; **end (while)**

sol_approx $\leftarrow \sum_{j=0}^{n} L_j y_0$.

Observe that

$$\|\text{sol\_approx} - x^\bullet\| < \varepsilon$$

and that for an appropriate choice of the bases $\{e_j^{(d)}\}_{j \in \mathbb{N}}$, the calculations are immediate, as justified below.

Returning to the considered spaces in order to study the linear Fredholm integral equation, $X = C[a, b]$ or $X = L^p[a, b]$, we remember how it is possible to tensorially construct bases $\{e_j^{(d)}\}_{j \in \mathbb{N}}$ in $X = C[a, b]^d$ or $X = L^p[a, b]^d$, respectively, from a basis $\{e_j^{(1)}\}_{j \in \mathbb{N}}$ in the aforementioned spaces.

Specifically, given $d \in \mathbb{N}$, $d \geq 2$, we consider in $\mathbb{N}^d$ the square ordering introduced in [17] in a inductive form: for $d \geq 2$, $(1,1), (1,2), (2,2), (2,1), (1,3), (2,3), (3,3), (3,2), \ldots$, and given the ordering $o_1, o_2, \ldots$ of $\mathbb{N}^{d-1}$, the order in $\mathbb{N}^d$ is $(o_1, 1), (o_1, 2), (o_2, 2), (o_2, 1)$, $(o_1, 3), (o_2, 3), (o_3, 3), \ldots$. Graphically,

$$\begin{array}{cccc}
(o_1,1) \longrightarrow (o_1,2) & (o_1,3) & (o_1,4) \\
\downarrow & \downarrow & \downarrow \\
(o_2,1) \longleftarrow (o_2,2) & (o_2,3) & (o_2,4) \\
& & \downarrow & \downarrow \\
(o_3,1) \longleftarrow (o_3,2) \longleftarrow (o_3,3) & (o_3,4) \\
& & & \downarrow \\
\cdots \longleftarrow (o_4,3) \longleftarrow (o_4,4)
\end{array}$$

Thus, we establish a bijection $\tau : \mathbb{N} \longrightarrow \mathbb{N}^d$, that for each $j \in \mathbb{N}$ a d-upla is assigned in the form

$$\tau(j) = (\alpha_1, \ldots, \alpha_d)$$

and for such a j, we define

$$e_j^{(d)}(t_1,\ldots,t_d) := e_{\alpha_1}(t_1)\cdots e_{\alpha_d}(t_d), \qquad ((t_1,\ldots,t_d)\in [a,b]^d). \tag{5}$$

The usual Schauder basis in $C[a,b]$ is the Faber–Schauder system, and in $L^p[a,b]$ is the Haar system [18]. More specifically, and assuming without loss of generality that $a=0$ and $b=1$, for the Faber–Schauder system, we start from the nodes $\{t_j\}_{j\in\mathbb{N}}$, which are the points of $[a,b]$ arranged dyadically, and the basis functions $\{e_j^{(1)}\}_{j\in\mathbb{N}}$ are continuous piecewise linear functions, the so-called *hat functions*, satisfying for each $j \in \mathbb{N}$

$$e_j^{(1)}(t_j) = 1$$

and

$$1 \le k < n \Rightarrow e_k^{(1)}(t_j) = 0.$$

On the other hand, if A is a non-empty subset of $[0,1]$ and $\delta_A : [0,1] \longrightarrow \mathbb{R}$ is the function defined in each $0 \le t \le 1$ as

$$\delta_A(t) := \begin{cases} 1, & \text{if } t \in A \\ 0, & \text{if } t \notin A \end{cases}$$

and $\varphi : [0,1] \longrightarrow \mathbb{R}$ is the function such that in each $0 \le t \le 1$

$$\varphi(t) := \delta_{[0,0.5)}(t) - \delta_{[0.5,1]}(t),$$

then the Haar system is given by

$$e_1^{(1)} := 1$$

and for $j \ge 2$, written uniquely as $j = 2^k + r + 1$, with $k = 0, 1, \ldots$ and $r = 0, 1, \ldots, 2^k - 1$,

$$e_j^{(1)}(\cdot) := \varphi(2^k(\cdot) - r).$$

In both cases, the tensorial sequences defined as (5) constitute Schauder bases in their respective spaces, $C[a,b]^d$ and $L^p[a,b]^d$ [17,19]. However, what really makes these bases useful when they are used in our Algorithm 1 is precisely that the calculation of the approximate operators L_j is very easy, since the basis functions $e_j^{(d)}$ are of separate variables and each factor is immediately integrable. Let us mention that these Schauder bases allow us to preserve the linearity of the convergence that it is guaranteed by the series geometric theorem.

5. Numerical Examples

We now show the numerical results obtained in several specific examples. Beforehand, let us mention that the reordering of a finite number of Schauder basis elements produces another new Schauder basis, which could be interesting from a computational point of view. Thus, for each $r \in \mathbb{N}$, we reordered the bases of $C[a,b]^d$ and $L^p[a,b]^d$ so that the r^d first elements correspond to $(\alpha_1, \alpha_2, \ldots, \alpha_d)$ being $1 \le \alpha_i \le r$. For these reordered bases, we maintain the same previous notation, $\{e_j^{(d)}\}_{j\in\mathbb{N}^d}$ for the basis and $\{P_j^{(d)}\}_{j\in\mathbb{N}}$ for the sequence of projections. Furthermore, given $n, r \in \mathbb{N}$, we write

$$x^{(n,r)} := \sum_{j=0}^{n} L_j y_0,$$

where the indices r_j involved in the definition of L_j are given by $\tau(r_j) = (\overbrace{r,\ldots,r}^{j+1 \text{ times}})$.

In each example, we consider $y_0 = y$ since another choice of y_0 is rather more theoretical, and since as we have indicated previously, it addresses the function y when some kind of error is produced in this function. Calculations were obtained by means of the Mathematica 12 software.

Example 1. We consider the equation of the Example 1 in [10]:

$$x(t) = \frac{30\pi t - \sin(\pi t)}{15} + \frac{1}{15}\int_0^1 t\cos(\pi t s^2)x(s)\,ds$$

whose solution is $x^{\bullet}(t) = 2\pi t$.

The errors obtained with our method are comparable to the order of those obtained in the reference taking $m = 4$ and $p = 2$, as shown in Table 1. The advantage in our case is that it is not necessary to start with an approximate solution "close enough" to the exact solution and it is not necessary either solve any system of linear equations.

Table 1. $\|x^{\bullet} - x^{(n,r)}\|$ for Example 1 using the usual basis in $C[0, 1]$.

n	r = 9	r = 17	r = 33
1	0.00435474	0.00216401	0.00162257
2	0.00300495	0.000773636	0.000210816
3	0.00298439	0.000752736	0.00018924
4	0.00298394	0.000752272	0.000188771

Example 2. The following equation is also extracted from the same reference (Example 2, [10]):

$$x(t) = t^2 - t + 1 + \frac{1}{4}\int_0^1 e^{ts}x(s)\,ds.$$

As in the referenced paper, since the solution of this equation is not known, we consider the operator $F : C[0,1] \to C[0,1]$ given by

$$F(x)(t) = x(t) - t^2 + t - 1 - \frac{1}{4}\int_0^1 e^{ts}x(s)\,ds$$

and we show $\|F(x^{(n,r)})\|$ for different values of n and r in Table 2.

The errors obtained are similar to those reported in Table 2 of [10] but with the same advantage mentioned above.

Table 2. $\|F(x^{(n,r)})\|$ for Example 2 using the usual basis in $C[0, 1]$.

n	r = 9	r = 17	r = 33
1	0.122201	0.123111	0.123339
2	0.0399626	0.0413395	0.0416839
3	0.0120328	0.0136133	0.0140084
4	0.00258589	0.00422851	0.0046442

Example 3. The following equation,

$$x(t) = \frac{2t^2 - 1}{3} + \frac{2}{3}e^t(t-1) + \frac{1}{3}\int_0^1 t^3 e^{ts}x(s)\,ds,$$

is taken from [20], Example 3. Its solution is $x^{\bullet}(t) = t^2 - 1$. See Table 3 for the error generated by Algorithm 1.

Table 3. $\|x^\bullet - x^{(n,r)}\|$ for Example 3 using the usual basis in $C[0,1]$.

n	$r = 9$	$r = 17$	$r = 33$
1	0.0627248	0.0593289	0.0584785
2	0.0133747	0.0104771	0.00975651
3	0.00503508	0.00242016	0.00156699
4	0.00362812	0.00109348	0.000463489

Example 4. *This is a standard test problem, and it arises in electrostatics (see [21]) where it is called Love's equation.*

$$x(t) = y(t) + \frac{\delta}{\pi} \int_0^1 \frac{x(s)}{\delta^2 + (t-s)^2} ds.$$

We consider $\delta = -1$ and $y(t) = 1 + \frac{1}{\pi}(\arctg(1-t) + \arctg(t))$ as in Example 3.2 of [22]. In this case, the exact solution is $x^\bullet(t) = 1$.

The errors—see Tables 4 nad 5—are similar to those obtained by the Haar wavelet method and rationalized Haar functions method (see Table 1 in [22]), although their computation requires to solve some high-order systems of linear equations.

Table 4. $\|x^\bullet - x^{(n,r)}\|$ for Example 4 using the usual basis in $C[0,1]$.

n	$r = 9$	$r = 17$	$r = 33$
1	0.0819571	0.0825347	0.0826789
2	0.0241024	0.0234044	0.023227
3	0.0059927	0.00634808	0.00645712
4	0.00299427	0.00211501	0.0018917

Table 5. $\|x^\bullet - x^{(n,r)}\|$ for Example 4 using the usual basis in $L_2[0,1]$.

n	$r = 8$	$r = 16$	$r = 32$
1	0.0785242	0.0785241	0.0785217
2	0.0235324	0.0235323	0.0235264
3	0.0101296	0.0101295	0.0101140
4	0.0083851	0.0083850	0.0083669

Example 5. *Now considering Example 2 of [23] which has solution $x^\bullet(t) = \sin(2\pi t)$*

$$x(t) = \sin(2\pi t) + \int_0^1 (t^2 - t - s^2 - s)x(s) ds.$$

We observe that the numerical results obtained with our method (Table 6) significantly improve those obtained in the reference.

Table 6. $\|x^\bullet - x^{(n,r)}\|$ for Example 5 using the usual basis in $L_2[0,1]$.

n	$r = 8$	$r = 16$	$r = 32$
4	3.17949×10^{-11}	4.33093×10^{-11}	4.28502×10^{-9}

6. Conclusions

In this paper, we present an algorithm for iteratively approximating the fixed point of a continuous coercive affine operator. Its design is based on a perturbed version of the classic geometric series theorem, the error control that this provides, and the use of certain Schauder bases. All of this is illustrated for a wide group of affine problems, the linear Fredholm integral equations. The low computational cost that our algorithm entails makes it particularly efficient. All of this is illustrated by several examples. We consider that future research could be focused on extending the algorithm to solve different types of integral and even integro-differential equations.

Author Contributions: Conceptualization, M.I.B. and M.R.G.; methodology, M.I.B. and M.R.G.; software M.I.B. and M.R.G.; validation, M.I.B. and M.R.G.; formal analysis, M.I.B. and M.R.G.; investigation, M.I.B. and M.R.G.; writing—original draft preparation, M.I.B. and M.R.G.; writing—review and editing, M.I.B. and M.R.G.; supervision, M.I.B. and M.R.G. All authors have read and agreed to the published version of the manuscript.

Funding: This research was partially supported by Junta de Andalucía, Project "Convex and numerical analysis", reference FQM359, and by the "María de Maeztu" Excellence Unit IMAG, reference CEX2020-001105-M, funded by MCIN/AEI/10.13039/501100011033/.

Institutional Review Board Statement: Not applicable.

Informed Consent Statement: Not applicable.

Data Availability Statement: Not applicable.

Conflicts of Interest: The authors declare no conflict of interest.

References

1. Alguliyev, R.M.; Sukhostat, L.V. Efficient algorithm for big data clustering on single machine. *CAAI Trans. Intell. Technol.* **2020**, *5*, 9–14. [CrossRef]
2. Alipour, S.; Mirzaee, F. An iterative algorithm for solving two dimensional nonlinear stochastic integral equations: A combined successive approximations method with bilinear spline interpolation. *Appl. Math. Comput.* **2020**, *371*, 124947. [CrossRef]
3. Asgari, Z.; Toutounian, F.; Babolian, E.; Tohidi, E. LSMR iterative method for solving one- and two-dimensional linear Fredholm integral equations. *Comput. Appl. Math.* **2019**, *38*, 135. [CrossRef]
4. Berenguer, M.I.; Gámez, D. Projected Iterations of Fixed-Point Type to Solve Nonlinear Partial Volterra Integro-Differential Equations. *Bull. Malays. Math. Sci. Soc.* **2020**, *43*, 4431–4442. [CrossRef]
5. Berenguer, M.I.; Garralda-Guillem, A.I.; Ruiz Galán, M. An approximation method for solving systems of Volterra integro-differential equations. *Appl. Numer. Math.* **2013**, *67*, 126–135. [CrossRef]
6. Cominola, A.; Giuliania, M.; Pigab, D.; Castellettia, A.; Rizzoli, A.E. A Hybrid Signature-based Iterative Disaggregation algorithm for Non-Intrusive Load Monitoring. *Appl. Energy* **2017**, *185*, 331–344. [CrossRef]
7. Derviskadic, A.; Romano, P.; Paolone, M. Iterative-Interpolated DFT for Synchrophasor Estimation: A Single Algorithm for P- and M-Class Compliant PMUs. *IEEE Trans. Instrum. Meas.* **2018**, *67*, 547–558. [CrossRef]
8. Ding, F.; Wang, F.; Xua, L.; Wu, M. Decomposition based least squares iterative identification algorithm for multivariate pseudo-linear ARMA systems using the data filtering. *J. Frankl. Inst.* **2017**, *354*, 1321–1339. [CrossRef]
9. Muthuvalu, M.S.; Sulaiman, J. Half-Sweep Arithmetic Mean method with composite trapezoidal scheme for solving linear Fredholm integral equations. *Appl. Math. Comput.* **2011**, *217*, 5442–5448. [CrossRef]
10. Gutiérrez, J.M.; Hernández-Verón, M.A.; Martínez, E. Improved iterative solution of linear fredholm integral equations of second kind via inverse-free iterative schemes. *Mathematics* **2020**, *8*, 1747. [CrossRef]
11. Karimi, S.; Jozi, M. A new iterative method for solving linear Fredholm integral equations using the least squares method. *Appl. Math. Comput.* **2015**, *250*, 744–758. [CrossRef]
12. Qin, X.; Cho, S.Y.; Wang, L. Strong convergence of an iterative algorithm involving nonlinear mappings of nonexpansive and accretive type. *Optimization* **2018**, *67*, 1377–1388. [CrossRef]
13. Rabbani, M.; Das, A.; Hazarika, B.; Arab, R. Existence of solution for two dimensional nonlinear fractional integral equation by measure of noncompactness and iterative algorithm to solve it. *J. Comput. Appl. Math.* **2020**, *370*, 112654. [CrossRef]
14. Ray, S.S.; Sahu, P.K. Numerical Methods for Solving Fredholm Integral Equations of Second Kind. *Abstr. Appl. Anal.* **2013**, *2013*, 426916. [CrossRef]
15. Yao, Y.; Postolache, M.; Yao, J.C. An iterative algorithm for solving generalized variational inequalities and fixed points problems. *Mathematics* **2019**, *7*, 61. [CrossRef]
16. Qin, X.; Petruşel, A.; Yao, J.C. CQ iterative algorithms for fixed points of nonexpansive mappings and split feasibility problems in Hilbert spaces. *J. Nonlinear Convex Anal.* **2018**, *19*, 157–165.
17. Gelbaum, B.; de Lamadrid, J.G. Bases of tensor products of Banach spaces. *Pac. J. Math.* **1961**, *11*, 1281–1286. [CrossRef]
18. Lindenstrauss, J.; Tzafriri, L. *Classical Banach Spaces*; Lecture Notes in Mathematics 338; Springer: Berlin/Heidelberg, Germany; New York, NY, USA, 1973.
19. Pap, E. (Ed.) *Handbook of Measure Theory*; Elsevier: Amsterdam, The Netherland, 2002; Volume II.
20. Gutiérrez, J.M.; Hernández-Verón, M.A. A Picard-Type Iterative Scheme for Fredholm Integral Equations of the Second Kind. *Mathematics* **2021**, *9*, 83. [CrossRef]
21. Love, E. The electrostatic field of two equal circular conducting disks. *Q. J. Mech. Appl. Math.* **1949**, *2*, 420–451. [CrossRef]

22. Amiri, S.; Hajipour, M.; Baleanu, D. On accurate solution of the Fredholm integral equations of the second kind. *Appl. Numer. Math.* **2020**, *150*, 478–490. [CrossRef]
23. Maleknejad, K.; Yousefi, M. Numerical solution of the integral equation of the second kind by using wavelet bases of Hermite cubic splines. *Appl. Math. Comput.* **2006**, *183*, 134–141. [CrossRef]

Article

Gradient-Based Optimization Algorithm for Solving Sylvester Matrix Equation

Juan Zhang [1,*] and Xiao Luo [2]

[1] Key Laboratory of Intelligent Computing and Information Processing of Ministry of Education, Xiangtan University, Xiangtan 411105, China
[2] Hunan Key Laboratory for Computation and Simulation in Science and Engineering, Xiangtan University, Xiangtan 411105, China; lxxiangtandaxue@163.com
* Correspondence: zhangjuan@xtu.edu.cn; Tel.: +86-131-0722-4973

Abstract: In this paper, we transform the problem of solving the Sylvester matrix equation into an optimization problem through the Kronecker product primarily. We utilize the adaptive accelerated proximal gradient and Newton accelerated proximal gradient methods to solve the constrained non-convex minimization problem. Their convergent properties are analyzed. Finally, we offer numerical examples to illustrate the effectiveness of the derived algorithms.

Keywords: Sylvester matrix equation; Kronecker product; adaptive accelerated proximal gradient method; Newton-accelerated proximal gradient method

MSC: 15A24; 65F45

1. Introduction

Matrix equations are ubiquitous in signal processing [1], control theory [2], and linear systems [3]. Most time-dependent models accounting for the prediction, simulation, and control of real-world phenomena may be represented as linear or nonlinear dynamical systems. Therefore, the relevance of matrix equations within engineering applications largely explains the great effort put forth by the scientific community into their numerical solution. Linear matrix equations have an important role in the stability analysis of linear dynamical systems and the theoretical development of the nonlinear system. The Sylvester matrix equation was first proposed by Sylvester and produced from the research of relevant fields in applied mathematical cybernetics. It is a famous matrix equation that occurs in linear and generalized eigenvalue problems for the computation of invariant subspaces using Riccati equations [4–6]. The Sylvester matrix equation takes part in linear algebra [7–9], image processing [10], model reduction [11], and numerical methods for differential equations [12,13].

We consider the Sylvester matrix equation of the form

$$AX + XB = C, \qquad (1)$$

where $A \in \mathbb{R}^{m \times m}, B \in \mathbb{R}^{n \times n}, C \in \mathbb{R}^{m \times n}$ are given matrices, and $X \in \mathbb{R}^{m \times n}$ is an unknown matrix to be solved. We discuss a special form of the Sylvester matrix equation, in which A and B are symmetric positive definite.

Recently, there has been a lot of discussion on the solution and numerical calculation of the Sylvester matrix equation. The standard methods for solving this equation are the Bartels–Stewart method [14] and the Hessenberg–Schur method [15], which are efficient for small and dense system matrices. When system matrices are small, the block Krylov subspace methods [16,17] and global Krylov subspace methods [18] are proposed. These methods use the global Arnoldi process, block Arnoldi process, or nonsymmetric block

Lanczos process to produce low-dimensional Sylvester matrix equations. More feasible methods for solving large and sparse problems are iterative methods. When system matrices are large, there are some effective methods such as the alternating direction implicit (ADI) method [19], global full orthogonalization method, global generalized minimum residual method [20], gradient-based iterative method [21], and global Hessenberg and changing minimal residual with Hessenberg process method [22]. When system matrices are low-rank, the ADI method [23], block Arnoldi method [17], preconditioned block Arnoldi method [24], and extended block Arnoldi method [25] and its variants [26,27], including the global Arnoldi method [28,29] and extended global Arnoldi method [25], are proposed to obtain the low-rank solution.

The adaptive accelerated proximal gradient (A-APG) method [30] is an efficient numerical method for calculating the steady states of the minimization problem, motivated by the accelerated proximal gradient (APG) method [31], which has wide applications in image processing and machine learning. In each iteration, the A-APG method takes the step size by using a line search initialized with the Barzilai–Borwein (BB) step [32] to accelerate the numerical speed. Moreover, as the traditional APG method is proposed for the convex problem and its oscillation phenomenon slows down the convergence, the restart scheme has been used for speeding up the convergence. For more details, one can refer to [30] and the references therein.

The main contribution is to study gradient-based optimization methods such as the A-APG and Newton-APG methods for solving the Sylvester matrix equation through transforming this equation into an optimization problem by using Kronecker product. The A-APG and Newton-APG methods are theoretically guaranteed to converge to a global solution from an arbitrary initial point and achieve high precision. These methods are especially efficient for large and sparse coefficient matrices.

The rest of this paper is organized as follows. In Section 2, we transform this equation into an optimization problem by using the Kronecker product. In Section 3, we apply A-APG and Newton-APG algorithms to solve the optimization problem and compare them with other methods. In Section 4, we focus on the convergence analysis of the A-APG method. In Section 5, the computational complexity of these algorithms is analyzed exhaustively. In Section 6, we offer corresponding numerical examples to illustrate the effectiveness of the derived methods.

Throughout this paper, let $\mathbb{R}^{n \times m}$ be the set of all $n \times m$ real matrices. I_n is the identity matrix of order n. If $A \in \mathbb{R}^{n \times n}$, the symbols A^T, A^{-1}, $\|A\|$ and $tr(A)$ express the transpose, the inverse, the 2-norm, and the trace of A, respectively. The inner product in matrix space $\mathbb{E}$ is $\langle x, y \rangle = tr(x,y), \forall x, y \in \mathbb{E}$.

2. The Variant of an Optimization Problem

In this section, we transform the Sylvester equation into an optimization problem. We recall some definitions and lemmas.

Definition 1. *Let $Y = (y_{ij}) \in \mathbb{R}^{m \times n}, Z \in \mathbb{R}^{p \times q}$, the Kronecker product of Y and Z be defined by*

$$Y \otimes Z = \begin{bmatrix} y_{11}Z & y_{12}Z & \cdots & y_{1n}Z \\ y_{21}Z & y_{22}Z & \cdots & y_{2n}Z \\ \vdots & \vdots & \vdots & \vdots \\ y_{m1}Z & y_{m2}Z & \cdots & y_{mn}Z \end{bmatrix}.$$

Definition 2. *If $Y \in \mathbb{R}^{m \times n}$, then the straightening operator $vec : \mathbb{R}^{m \times n} \longrightarrow \mathbb{R}^{mn}$ of Y is*

$$vec(Y) = (y_1^T, y_2^T, \ldots, y_n^T)^T.$$

Lemma 1. Let $Y \in \mathbb{R}^{l \times m}, Z \in \mathbb{R}^{m \times n}, W \in \mathbb{R}^{n \times k}$, then

$$vec(YZW) = (W^T \otimes Y)vec(Z).$$

From Lemma 1, the Sylvester Equation (1) can be rewritten as

$$(I_n \otimes A + B^T \otimes I_m)vec(X) = vec(C). \quad (2)$$

Lemma 2. Let A be a symmetric positive matrix; solving the equation $Ax = b$ is equivalent to obtaining the minimum of $\varphi(x) = x^T Ax - 2b^T x$.

According to Lemma 2 and Equation (2), define

$$\tilde{A} = (I_n \otimes A + B^T \otimes I_m), \ \tilde{x} = vec(X), \ \tilde{b} = vec(C).$$

Therefore, Equation (2) should be $\tilde{A}\tilde{x} = \tilde{b}$. Obviously, if A and B are symmetric positive, then $\tilde{A}$ is symmetric positive. The variant of the Sylvester Equation (2) reduces to the optimization problem:

$$\begin{aligned}
\min \varphi(x) &= \min\left\{\tilde{x}^T \tilde{A} \tilde{x} - 2\tilde{b}^T \tilde{x}\right\} \\
&= \min\left\{vec(X)^T(I_n \otimes A + B^T \otimes I_m)vec(X) - 2vec(X)^T vec(C)\right\} \\
&= \min\left\{vec(X)^T \cdot vec(AX) + vec(X)^T \cdot vec(XB) - 2vec(X)^T \cdot vec(C)\right\} \\
&= \min\left\{tr(X^T AX) + tr(X^T XB) - 2tr(X^T C)\right\}.
\end{aligned} \quad (3)$$

Using the calculation of the matrix differential from [33], we have the following propositions immediately.

Proposition 1. If $A = (a_{ij}) \in \mathbb{R}^{m \times n}, X = (x_{ij}) \in \mathbb{R}^{m \times n}$, then $\frac{\partial tr(A^T X)}{\partial X} = \frac{\partial tr(X^T A)}{\partial X} = A$.

Proposition 2. If $A = (a_{ij}) \in \mathbb{R}^{m \times m}, X = (x_{ij}) \in \mathbb{R}^{m \times n}$, then $\frac{\partial tr(X^T AX)}{\partial X} = AX + A^T X$.

Proposition 3. If $B = (b_{ij}) \in \mathbb{R}^{n \times n}, X = (x_{ij}) \in \mathbb{R}^{m \times n}$, then $\frac{\partial tr(XX^T B)}{\partial X} = XB + XB^T$.

Using Propositions 2 and 3, the gradient of the objective function (3) is

$$\nabla \varphi(X) = AX + XB + A^T X + XB^T - 2C. \quad (4)$$

By (4), the Hessian matrix is

$$\nabla^2 \varphi(X) = A + A^T + B + B^T. \quad (5)$$

3. Iterative Methods

In this section, we will introduce the adaptive accelerated proximal gradient (A-APG) method and the Newton-APG method to solve the Sylvester equation. Moreover, we compare the A-APG and Newton-APG methods with other existing methods.

3.1. APG Method

The traditional APG method [31] is designed for solving the composite convex problem:

$$\min_{x \in \mathbb{H}} H(x) = g(x) + f(x),$$

where $\mathbb{H}$ is the finite-dimensional Hilbert space equipped with the inner product $<\cdot,\cdot>$, g and f are both continuously convex, and ∇f has a Lipschitz constant L. Given initializations $x_1 = x_0$ and $t_0 = 1$, the APG method is

$$t_k = (\sqrt{4(t-k-1)^2 + 1} + 1)/2,$$
$$Y_k = X_k + \frac{t_{k-1} - 1}{t_k}(X_k - X_{k-1}),$$
$$X_{k+1} = \text{Prox}_g^\alpha(Y_k - \alpha \nabla f(Y_k)),$$

where $\alpha \in (0, L]$ and the mapping $\text{Prox}_g^\alpha(\cdot) : \mathbb{R}^n \mapsto \mathbb{R}^n$ is defined as

$$\text{Prox}_g^\alpha(x) = \underset{y}{\text{argmin}}\left\{g(y) + \frac{1}{2\alpha}\|y - x\|^2\right\}.$$

Since our minimization problem is linear, we choose the explicit scheme. The explicit scheme is a simple but effective approach for the minimization problem. Given an initial value Y_0 and the step α_k, the explicit scheme is

$$Y_{k+1} = Y_k - \alpha_k \nabla \varphi(Y_k), \tag{6}$$

where Y_k is the approximation solution. The explicit scheme satisfies the sufficient decrease property using the gradient descent (GD) method.

Let X_k and X_{k-1} be the current and previous states and the extrapolation weight be w_k. Using the explicit method (6), the APG iterative scheme is

$$w_k = k - 2/k + 1,$$
$$Y_k = (1 + w_k)X_k - wX_{k-1}, \tag{7}$$
$$Y_{k+1} = Y_k - \alpha_k \nabla \varphi(Y_k).$$

Together with the standard backtracking, we adopt the step size α_k when the following condition holds:

$$\varphi(Y_k) - \varphi(Y_{k+1}) \geq \eta\|Y_{k+1} - Y_k\|^2, \tag{8}$$

for some $\eta > 0$.

Combining (7) and (8), the APG algorithm is summarized in Algorithm 1.

Algorithm 1 APG algorithm.

Require: $X_0, tol, \alpha_0, \eta > 0, \beta \in (0,1)$, and $k = 1$.
1: **while** the stop condition is not satisfied **do**
2:     Update Y_k via Equation (7);
3:     **if** Equation (8) holds **then**
4:         break
5:     **else**
6:         $\alpha_k = \beta \alpha_k$;
7:     Calculate Y_{k+1} via (7);
8:     $k = k + 1$.

3.2. Restart APG Method

Recently, an efficient and convergent numerical algorithm has been developed for solving a discretized phase-field model by combining the APG method with the restart technique [30]. Unlike the APG method, the restart technique involves choosing $X_{k+1} = Y_{k+1}$ whenever the following condition holds:

$$\varphi(X_k) - \varphi(Y_{k+1}) \geq \gamma\|X_k - Y_{k+1}\|^2, \tag{9}$$

for some $\gamma > 0$. If the condition is not met, we restart the APG by setting $w_k = 0$. The restart APG method (RAPG) is summarized in Algorithm 2.

Algorithm 2 RAPG algorithm.

Require: $X_0, tol, \alpha_0, \eta > 0, \gamma > 0, \beta \in (0,1)$, and $k = 1$.
1: **while** the stop condition is not satisfied **do**
2:     Calculate Y_{k+1} by APG Algorithm 1;
3:     **if** Equation (9) holds **then**
4:         $X_{k+1} = Y_{k+1}$ and update w_{k+1};
5:     **else**
6:         $X_{k+1} = X_k$ and reset $w_{k+1} = 0$;
7:     $k = k + 1$.

3.3. A-APG Method

In RAPG Algorithm 2, we can adaptively estimate the step size α_k by using the line search technique. Define

$$s_k := X_k - X_{k-1}, g_k := \nabla\varphi(X_k) - \nabla\varphi(X_{k-1}).$$

We initialize the search step by the Barzilai–Borwein (BB) method, i.e.,

$$\alpha_k = \frac{tr(s_k^T s_k)}{tr(s_k^T g_k)} \text{ or } \frac{tr(g_k^T s_k)}{tr(g_k^T g_k)}. \tag{10}$$

Therefore, we obtain the A-APG algorithm summarized in Algorithm 3.

Algorithm 3 A-APG algorithm.

Require: $X_0, tol, \alpha_0, \eta > 0, \gamma > 0, \beta \in (0,1)$, and $k = 1$.
1: **while** the stop condition is not satisfied **do**
2:     Initialize α_k by BB step Equation (10);
3:     Update X_{k+1} by RAPG Algorithm 2.

3.4. Newton-APG Method

Despite the fast initial convergence speed of the gradient-based methods, the tail convergence speed becomes slow. Therefore, we use a practical Newton method to solve the minimization problem. We obtain the initial value from A-APG Algorithm 3, and then choose the Newton direction as the gradient in the explicit scheme in RAPG Algorithm 2. Then we have the Newton-APG method shown in Algorithm 4.

Algorithm 4 Newton-APG algorithm.

Require: $X0, \alpha 0, \gamma > 0, \eta > 0, \beta \in (0,1), \epsilon, tol$ and $k = 1$.
1: Obtain the initial value from A-APG Algorithm 3 by the precision ϵ;
2: **while** the stop condition is not satisfied **do**
3:     Initialize α_k by BB step Equation (10);
4:     Update X_{k+1} by RAPG Algorithm 2 using Newton direction.

3.5. Gradient Descent (GD) and Line Search (LGD) Methods

Moreover, we show gradient descent (GD) and line search (LGD) methods for comparing with the A-APG and Newton-APG methods. The GD and line search LGD methods are summarized in Algorithm 5.

Algorithm 5 GD and LGD algorithms.

Require: $X_0, tol, \alpha_0, \eta > 0, \beta \in (0,1)$, and $k = 1$.
1: **while** the stop condition is not satisfied **do**
2:     **if** the step size is fixed **then**
3:         Calculate X_{k+1} via $X_{k+1} = X_k - \alpha \nabla \varphi(X_k)$ using GD;
4:     **else**
5:         Initialize α_k by BB step Equation (10);
6:         **if** Equation (8) holds **then**
7:             break
8:         **else**
9:             $\alpha_k = \beta \alpha_k$;
10:        Calculate X_{k+1} via X_{k+1} via $X_{k+1} = X_k - \alpha \nabla \varphi(X_k)$ using LGD;
11:     $k = k + 1$.

3.6. Computational Complexity Analysis

Further, we analyze the computational complexity of each iteration of the derived algorithms.

The computation of APG is mainly controlled by matrix multiplication and addition operations in three main parts. The iterative scheme needs $4m^2n + 4mn^2 + O(mn)$ computational complexity. The backtracking linear search needs $14m^2n + 20n^2m + 6n^3 + O(mn) + O(n^2)$ computational complexity defined by Equation (8). The extrapolation needs $O(mn)$ computational complexity defined by the Equation (7). The total computational complexity is $18m^2n + 24n^2m + 6n^3 + O(mn) + O(n^2)$ in Algorithm 1.

The computation of RAPG is mainly controlled by matrix multiplication and addition operations in four main parts. The iterative scheme needs $4m^2n + 4mn^2 + O(mn)$ computational complexity. The backtracking linear search defined by Equation (8) needs $14m^2n + 20n^2m + 6n^3 + O(mn) + O(n^2)$ computational complexity. The extrapolation defined by Equation (7) needs $O(mn)$ computational complexity. The restart defined by Equation (9) needs $4m^2n + 14n^2m + 4n^3 + O(mn) + O(n^2)$ computational complexity. The total computational complexity is $22m^2n + 38n^2m + 10n^3 + O(mn) + O(n^2)$ in Algorithm 2.

The computation of A-APG is mainly controlled by matrix multiplication and addition operations in four main parts. The iterative scheme needs $4m^2n + 4mn^2 + O(mn)$ computational complexity. The BB step and the backtracking linear search defined by Equations (8) and (10) need mn, $4m^2n + 4mn^2 + 6mn$, $2n^2(2m-1) + 2n$, and $14m^2n + 20n^2m + 6n^3 + O(mn) + O(n^2)$ computational complexity. The extrapolation defined by Equation (7) needs $O(mn)$ computational complexity. The restart defined by Equation (9) needs $4m^2n + 14n^2m + 4n^3 + O(mn) + O(n^2)$ computational complexity. The total computational complexity is $26m^2n + 46n^2m + 10n^3 + O(mn) + O(n^2)$ in Algorithm 3.

The computation of Newton-APG is mainly controlled by matrix multiplication and addition operations in four main parts, different from the A-APG method. The iterative scheme needs $8n^3 + 3n^2 + O(n^2) + O(n^3)$ computational complexity. The BB step and the backtracking linear search defined by Equations (8) and (10) need n^2, $8n^3 + 6n^2$, $2n^2(2n-1) + 2n$, and $10n^2(2n-1) + 8n^3 + 3n^2 + O(n^3) + O(n^2)$ computational complexity. The extrapolation defined by Equation (7) needs $O(n^2)$ computational complexity. The restart defined by Equation (9) needs $5n^2(2n-1) + n^2 + O(n^3)$ computational complexity. The total computational complexity is $50n^3 - 10n^2 + 2n + O(n^2) + O(n^3)$ in Algorithm 4.

The computation of GD is mainly controlled by matrix multiplication and addition operations in Equations (4) and (6). It requires $mn(2m-1)$, $mn(2n-1)$, $mn(2m-1)$, $mn(2n-1)$ computational complexity to compute AX, XB, $A^T X$, XB^T. The total computational complexity is $4m^2n + 4mn^2 + O(mn)$ in Algorithm 5 using GD.

The computation of LGD is mainly controlled by matrix multiplication and addition operations in the calculation of s, g defined by Equation (8) and (10), and the calculation of GD, which require mn, $4m^2n + 4mn^2 + 6mn$, $2n^2(2m-1) + 2n$, $14m^2n + 20n^2m +$

$6n^3 + O(mn) + O(n^2)$, and $4m^2n + 4mn^2 + O(mn)$, respectively. The total computational complexity is $22m^2n + 32n^2m + 6n^3 + O(mn) + O(n^2)$ in Algorithm 5 using GD.

4. Convergent Analysis

In this section, we focus on the convergence analysis of A-APG Algorithm 3. The following proposition is required.

Proposition 4. Let M be a bounded region that contains $\{\varphi \leqslant \varphi(X_0)\}$ in $\mathbb{R}^{n \times n}$, then $\nabla \varphi(X)$ satisfies the Lipschitz condition in M, i.e., there exists $L_M > 0$ such that

$$\|\nabla \varphi(X) - \nabla \varphi(Y)\| \leqslant L_M \|X - Y\| \text{ for } X, Y \in M.$$

Proof. Using the continuity of $\nabla \varphi(X)$, note that

$$\left\|\nabla^2 \varphi(X)\right\| = \left\|(A + A^T) + (B + B^T)\right\|$$

defined by (5) is bounded. Then $\nabla \varphi(X)$ satisfies the Lipschitz condition in M. □

In recent years, the proximal method based on the Bregman distance has been applied for solving optimization problems. The proximal operator is

$$\text{Prox}_{\varphi}^{\alpha}(y) := \underset{y}{\text{argmin}}\{\varphi(y) + \frac{1}{2\alpha}\|X - X_k\|^2\}.$$

Basically, given the current estimation X_k and step size $\alpha_k > 0$, update X_{k+1} via

$$X_{k+1} = \text{Prox}_0^{\alpha}(X_k - \alpha_k \nabla \varphi(X_k)) = \underset{X}{\text{argmin}}\{\frac{1}{2\alpha_k}\|X - (X_k - \alpha_k \nabla \varphi(X_k))\|^2\}. \quad (11)$$

Thus we obtain

$$\frac{1}{2\alpha_k}(X_{k+1} - (X_k - \alpha_k \nabla \varphi(X_k))) = 0,$$

which implies that

$$X_{k+1} = X_k - \alpha_k \nabla \varphi(X_k).$$

This is exactly the explicit scheme in our algorithm.

4.1. Linear Search Is Well-Defined

Using the optimization from Equation (11), it is evident that

$$X_{k+1} = \underset{X}{\text{argmin}}\{\frac{1}{2\alpha_k}\|X - (X_k - \alpha_k \nabla \varphi(X_k))\|^2\}$$

$$= \underset{X}{\text{argmin}}\{\frac{1}{2\alpha_k}\|X - X_k\|^2 + \langle X - X_k, \nabla \varphi(X_k)\rangle\}$$

$$= \underset{X}{\text{argmin}}\{\frac{1}{2\alpha_k}\|X - X_k\|^2 + \langle X - X_k, \nabla \varphi(X_k)\rangle + \varphi(X_k)\}.$$

Then we obtain

$$\varphi(X_k) \geqslant \frac{1}{2\alpha_k}\|X_{k+1} - X_k\|^2 + \langle X_{k+1} - X_k, \nabla \varphi(X_k)\rangle + \varphi(X_k)$$

$$\geqslant \varphi(X_{k+1}) + \frac{1}{2\alpha_k}\|X_k - X_{k+1}\|^2 - \frac{\|\nabla^2 \varphi(X)\|}{2}\|X_k - X_{k+1}\|^2 \quad (12)$$

$$\geqslant \varphi(X_{k+1}) + (\frac{1}{2\alpha_k} - \frac{L_M}{2})\|X_k - X_{k+1}\|^2,$$

where the second inequality follows from Taylor expansion of $\varphi(X_{k+1})$. By Equation (12), set

$$0 < \alpha_k < \bar{\alpha} := \min\{\frac{1}{L_M + 2\eta}, \frac{1}{L_M + 2\gamma}\}, \tag{13}$$

the conditions in linear search Equation (8) and non-restart Equation (9) are both satisfied. Therefore, the backtracking linear search is well-defined.

4.2. Sufficient Decrease Property

In this section, we show the sufficient decrease property of the sequence generated by A-APG Algorithm 3. If α_k satisfies the condition Equation (13), then

$$\varphi(X_k) - \varphi(Y_{k+1}) \geq \rho_1 \|X_k - Y_{k+1}\|^2,$$

where $\rho_1 = \min\{\eta, \gamma\} > 0$. Since φ is a bounded function, then there exists φ^* such that $\varphi(X_k) \geq \varphi^*$ and $\varphi(X_k) \to \varphi^*$ as $k \to +\infty$. This implies

$$\rho_1 \sum_{k=0}^{\infty} \|X_{k+1} - X_k\|^2 \leq \varphi(X_0) - \varphi^* < +\infty,$$

which shows that

$$\lim_{k \to +\infty} \|X_{k+1} - X_k\| = 0.$$

4.3. Bounded Gradient

Define two sets $\Omega_2 = \{k : k = 2\}$ and $\Omega_1 = N \setminus \Omega_2$. Let $w_k = k - 2/k + 1$, for any $k \in \Omega_2$, then $X_{k+1} = Y_{k+1}$ when $w_k = 0$. There exists $\bar{w} = k_{max} - 2/k_{max} + 1 \in [0, 1)$ such that $w_k \leq \bar{w}$ as k increases. If $k \in \Omega_1$, since

$$Y_{k+1} = \underset{X}{\operatorname{argmin}}\{\frac{1}{2\alpha_k}\|X - (Y_k - \alpha_k \nabla \varphi(Y_k))\|^2\},$$

we have

$$0 = \nabla \varphi(Y_k) + \frac{1}{\alpha_k}(Y_{k+1} - Y_k).$$

Thus,

$$\nabla \varphi(Y_k) = \frac{1}{\alpha_k}(Y_k - Y_{k+1}).$$

Note that $Y_k = (1 + w_k)X_k - w_k X_{k-1}$, then

$$\begin{aligned}
\|\nabla \varphi(Y_k)\| &= \frac{1}{\alpha_k}\|(1 + w_k)X_k - w_k X_{k-1} - X_{k+1}\| \\
&= \frac{1}{\alpha_k}\|w_k(X_k - X_{k-1}) + (X_k - X_{k+1})\| \\
&\leq \frac{1}{\alpha_{min}}(\bar{w}\|X_k - X_{k-1}\| + \|X_k - X_{k+1}\|) \\
&= c_1(\|X_{k+1} - X_k\| + \bar{w}\|X_k - X_{k-1}\|),
\end{aligned} \tag{14}$$

where $c_1 = \frac{1}{\alpha_{min}} > 0$.
If $k \in \Omega_2$, then

$$X_{k+1} = \underset{X}{\operatorname{argmin}}\{\frac{1}{2\alpha_k}\|X - (X_k - \alpha_k \nabla \varphi(X_k))\|^2\},$$

which implies that

$$0 = \nabla \varphi(X_k) + \frac{1}{\alpha_k}(X_{k+1} - X_k).$$

Thus

$$\|\nabla\varphi(X_k)\| = \frac{1}{\alpha_k}\|X_k - X_{k+1}\| \leqslant \frac{1}{\alpha_{min}}\|X_k - X_{k+1}\| = c_1(\|X_k - X_{k+1}\|), \quad (15)$$

Combining Equations (14) and (15), it follows that

$$\|\nabla\varphi(X_k)\| \leqslant c_1(\|X_{k+1} - X_k\| + \overline{w}\|X_k - X_{k-1}\|).$$

4.4. Subsequence Convergence

As $\{X_k\} \in M$ is compact, there exists a subsequence $\{X_{k_j}\} \subset M$ and $X^* \in M$ such that $\lim_{j \to +\infty} X_{k_j} = X^*$. Then φ is bounded, i.e., $\varphi(X) > -\infty$ and φ keeps decreasing. Hence, there exists φ^* such that $\lim_{k \to +\infty} \varphi(X_k) = \varphi^*$. Note that

$$\varphi(X_k) - \varphi(X_{k+1}) \geqslant c_0 \|X_k - X_{k+1}\|^2, \quad k = 1, 2, \ldots \quad (16)$$

Summation over k yields

$$c_0 \sum_{k=0}^{\infty} \|X_k - X_{k+1}\|^2 \leqslant \varphi(X_0) - \varphi^* < +\infty.$$

Therefore,

$$\lim_{k \to +\infty} \|X_k - X_{k+1}\| = 0.$$

Due to the property of the gradient, thus

$$\lim_{j \to +\infty} \left\|\nabla\varphi(X_{k_j})\right\| = 0.$$

Considering the continuity of φ and $\nabla\varphi$, we have

$$\lim_{j \to +\infty} \varphi(X_{k_j}) = \varphi(X^*), \lim_{j \to +\infty} \nabla\varphi(X_{k_j}) = \nabla\varphi(X^*) = 0,$$

which implies that $\nabla\varphi(X^*) = 0$.

4.5. Sequence Convergence

In this section, the subsequence convergence can be strengthened by using the Kurdyka–Lojasiewicz property.

Proposition 5. *For $\overline{x} \in \text{dom } \partial\varphi := \{x : \partial\varphi(x) \neq \varnothing\}$, there exists $\eta > 0$, an ϵ neighborhood of $\overline{x}$, and $\psi \in \Psi_\eta = \{\psi \subset C[0,\eta) \cap C'(0,\eta)$, where ψ is concave, $\psi(0) = 0, \psi' > 0$ on $(0,\eta)\}$ such that for all $x \in \Gamma_\eta(\overline{x}, \epsilon) : U \cap \{x : \varphi(\overline{x}) < \varphi(x) < \varphi(\overline{x}) + \eta\}$, we have*

$$\psi'(\varphi(x) - \varphi(\overline{x}))\|\nabla\varphi(x)\| \geqslant 1.$$

Then we say $\varphi(x)$ satisfies the Kurdyka–Lojasiewicz property.

Theorem 1. *Assume that Propositions 4 and 5 are met. Let $\{X_k\}$ be the sequence generated by A-APG Algorithm 3. Then, there exists a point $X^* \in M$ so that $\lim_{k \to +\infty} X_k = X^*$ and $\nabla\varphi(X^*) = 0$.*

Proof. Let $\omega(X_0)$ be the set of limiting points of the sequence $\{X_k\}$. Based on the boundedness of $\{X_k\}$ and the fact that $\omega(X_0) = \cap_{q \in \mathbb{N}} \cup_{k > q} \{X_k\}$, it follows that $\omega(X_0)$ is a non-empty and compact set. In addition, by Equation (16), we know that $\varphi(X)$ is a constant on $\omega(X_0)$, denoted by φ^*. If there exists some k_0 such that $\varphi(X_{k_0}) = \varphi^*$, then for $\forall k > k_0$, we have $\varphi(X_k) = \varphi^*$. Next, we assume that $\forall k, \varphi(X_k) > \varphi^*$. Therefore, for

$\forall \epsilon, \eta > 0, \exists l > 0$, for $\forall k > l$ we have $dist(\omega(X_0), X_k) \leqslant \epsilon$ and $\varphi^* < \varphi(X_k) < \varphi^* + \eta$ i.e., for $\forall X^* \in \omega(X_0), X \in \Gamma_\eta(X^*, \epsilon)$. Applying Proposition 5, for $\forall k > l$, we have

$$\psi'(\varphi(X_k) - \varphi^*)\|\nabla\varphi(X_k)\| \geqslant 1.$$

Then

$$\psi'(\varphi(X_k) - \varphi^*) \geqslant \frac{1}{c_1(\|X_k - X_{k-1}\| + \overline{w}\|X_{k-1} - X_{k-2}\|)}. \quad (17)$$

By the convexity of ψ, it is obvious that

$$\psi(\varphi(X_k) - \varphi^*) - \psi(\varphi(X_{k+1}) - \varphi^*) \geqslant \psi'(\varphi(X_k) - \varphi^*)(\varphi(X_k) - \varphi(X_{k+1})). \quad (18)$$

Define

$$\triangle_{p,q} = \psi(\varphi(X_p) - \varphi^*) - \psi(\varphi(X_q) - \varphi^*), \quad c = (1 + \overline{w})c_1/c_0 > 0.$$

Combining with Equations (16)–(18), for $\forall k > l$, we obtain

$$\triangle_{k,k+1} \geqslant \frac{c_0\|X_{k+1} - X_k\|^2}{c_1(\|X_k - X_{k-1}\| + \overline{w}\|X_{k-1} - X_{k-2}\|)} \geqslant \frac{\|X_{k+1} - X_k\|^2}{c(\|X_k - X_{k-1}\| + \|X_{k-1} - X_{k-2}\|)}. \quad (19)$$

Applying the geometric inequality to Equation (19), thus

$$2\|X_{k+1} - X_k\| \leqslant \frac{1}{2}(\|X_k - X_{k-1}\| + \|X_{k-1} - X_{k-2}\|) + 2c\triangle_{k,k+1}.$$

Therefore, for $\forall k > l$, summing up the above inequality for $i = l+1, \ldots, k$, we obtain

$$2\sum_{i=l+1}^{k}\|X_{i+1} - X_i\| \leqslant \frac{1}{2}\sum_{i=l+1}^{k}(\|X_i - X_{i-1}\| + \|X_{i-1} - X_{i-2}\|) + 2c\sum_{i=l+1}^{k}\triangle_{i,i+1}$$

$$\leqslant \sum_{i=l+1}^{k}\|X_{i+1} - X_i\| + \|X_{l+1} - X_l\| + \frac{1}{2}\|X_l - X_{l-1}\|$$

$$+ 2c\triangle_{l+1,k+1}.$$

For $\forall k > l, \psi \geqslant 0$, it is evident that

$$\sum_{i=l+1}^{k}\|X_{i+1} - X_i\| \leqslant \|X_{l+1} - X_l\| + \frac{1}{2}\|X_l - X_{l-1}\| + 2c\psi(\varphi(X_l) - \varphi^*),$$

which implies that

$$\sum_{k=1}^{\infty}\|X_{k+1} - X_k\| < \infty.$$

In the end, we have $\lim_{k \to +\infty} X_k = X^*$. □

5. Numerical Results

In this section, we offer two corresponding numerical examples to illustrate the efficiency of the derived algorithms. All code is written in Python language. Denote iteration and error by the iteration step and error of the objective function. We take the matrix order "n" as 128, 1024, 2048, and 4096.

Example 1. Let

$$A_1 = \begin{pmatrix} 2 & -1 & & & \\ -1 & 2 & -1 & & \\ & \ddots & \ddots & \ddots & \\ & & \ddots & \ddots & -1 \\ & & & -1 & 2 \end{pmatrix}, B_1 = \begin{pmatrix} 1 & 0.5 & & & \\ 0.5 & 1 & 0.5 & & \\ & \ddots & \ddots & \ddots & \\ & & \ddots & \ddots & 0.5 \\ & & & 0.5 & 1 \end{pmatrix}$$

be tridiagonal matrices in the Sylvester Equation (1). Set the matrix C_1 as the identity matrix. The initial step size is 0.01, which is small enough to iterate. The parameters are $\eta_1 = 0.25, \omega_1 = 0.2$ taken from (0,1) randomly. Table 1 and Figure 1 show the numerical results of Algorithms 1–5. It can be seen that the LGD, A-APG, and Newton-APG Algorithms are more efficient than other methods. Moreover, the iteration step does not increase when the matrix order increases due to the same initial value. The A-APG method has higher error accuracy compared with other methods. The Newton-APG method takes more CPU time and fewer iteration steps than the A-APG method. The Newton method needs to calculate the inverse of the matrix, while it has quadratic convergence. From Figure 1, the error curves of the LGD, A-APG, and Newton-APG algorithms are hard to distinguish. We offer another example below.

Table 1. Numerical results for Example 1.

Algorithm	n	Iteration	Error	Time(s)
GD	128	356	1.13687×10^{-13}	3.30
LGD	128	15	1.26477×10^{-12}	0.27
APG	128	374	1.4353×10^{-12}	4.31
RAPG	128	69	1.4353×10^{-12}	1.45
A-APG	128	19	3.55271×10^{-14}	0.38
Newton-APG	128	18	9.47438×10^{-11}	0.48
CG	128	19	3.49364×10^{-14}	0.42
GD	1024	356	1.02318×10^{-12}	806
LGD	1024	15	1.06866×10^{-11}	69
APG	1024	374	1.18803×10^{-11}	1261
RAPG	1024	69	2.59774×10^{-11}	367
A-APG	1024	19	2.84217×10^{-13}	113
Newton-APG	1024	18	8.95682×10^{-10}	144
CG	1024	19	3.37046×10^{-14}	71
GD	2048	356	2.04636×10^{-12}	6315
LGD	2048	15	2.13731×10^{-11}	569
APG	2048	374	2.38742×10^{-11}	9752
RAPG	2048	69	5.20686×10^{-11}	2994
A-APG	2048	19	6.82121×10^{-13}	926
Newton-APG	2048	18	8.95682×10^{-10}	1015
CG	2048	19	3.34616×10^{-14}	521
GD	4096	356	4.09273×10^{-12}	66,155
LGD	4096	15	4.27463×10^{-11}	4199
APG	4096	374	4.77485×10^{-11}	71,636
RAPG	4096	69	1.04365×10^{-10}	21,596
A-APG	4096	19	1.81899×10^{-12}	6829
Newton-APG	4096	18	3.64571×10^{-9}	7037
CG	4096	19	3.33322×10^{-14}	3553

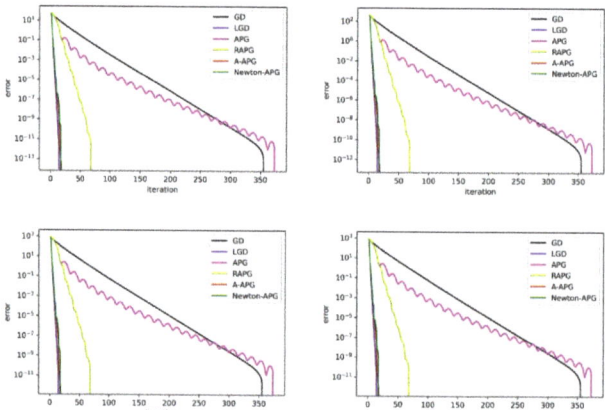

Figure 1. The error curves when n = 128, 1024, 2048, 4096 for Example 1.

Example 2. Let $A_2 = A_1 A_1^T, B_2 = B_1 B_1^T$ be positive semi-definite matrices in the Sylvester Equation (1). Set the matrix C_2 as the identity matrix. The initial step size is 0.009. The parameters are $\eta_2 = 0.28, \omega_2 = 0.25$ taken from (0,1) randomly. Table 2 and Figure 2 show the numerical results of Algorithms 1–5. It can be seen that the LGD, A-APG, and Newton-APG algorithms take less CPU time compared with other methods. Additionally, we can observe the different error curves of the LGD, A-APG, and Newton-APG algorithms from Figure 2.

Remark 1. The difference of the iteration step in Examples 1 and 2 emerges due to the given different initial values. It can be seen that the LGD, A-APG, and Newton-APG algorithms have fewer iteration steps. Whether the A-APG method or Newton-APG yields fewer iteration steps varies from problem to problem. From Examples 1 and 2, we observe that the A-APG method has higher accuracy, although it takes more time and more iteration steps than the LGD method.

Remark 2. Moreover, we compare the performance of our methods with other methods such as the conjugate gradient method (CG) in Tables 1 and 2. We take the same initial values and set the error to 1×10^{-14}. From Tables 1 and 2, it can be seen that the LGD and A-APG methods are more efficient for solving the Sylvester matrix equation when the order n is small. When n is large, the LGD and A-APG methods nearly have a convergence rate with the CG method.

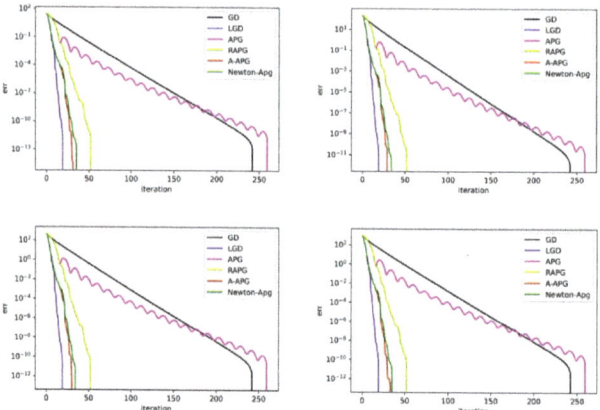

Figure 2. The error curves when n = 128, 1024, 2048, 4096 for Example 2.

Table 2. Numerical results for Example 2.

Algorithm	n	Iteration	Error	Time(s)
GD	128	243	1.63425×10^{-13}	2.38
LGD	128	20	2.45137×10^{-12}	0.47
APG	128	260	1.58096×10^{-12}	4.51
RAPG	128	53	1.90781×10^{-12}	1.46
A-APG	128	32	3.55271×10^{-15}	0.78
Newton-APG	128	36	2.30926×10^{-13}	1.26
CG	128	34	4.13025×10^{-14}	0.79
GD	1024	243	1.3074×10^{-12}	516
LGD	1024	20	1.89573×10^{-11}	95
APG	1024	260	1.25056×10^{-11}	835
RAPG	1024	53	1.51772×10^{-11}	267
A-APG	1024	32	4.61569×10^{-14}	181
Newton-APG	1024	36	4.20641×10^{-12}	214
CG	1024	34	4.29936×10^{-14}	92
GD	2048	243	2.6148×10^{-12}	4129
LGD	2048	20	3.78577×10^{-11}	814
APG	2048	260	2.48974×10^{-11}	6507
RAPG	2048	53	3.03544×10^{-11}	2193
A-APG	2048	32	2.27374×10^{-13}	1622
Newton-APG	2048	36	8.52651×10^{-12}	2125
CG	2048	34	4.22694×10^{-14}	797
GD	4096	243	5.22959×10^{-12}	29,859
LGD	4096	20	7.54881×10^{-11}	6023
APG	4096	260	4.97948×10^{-11}	48,238
RAPG	4096	53	6.07088×10^{-11}	16,482
A-APG	4096	32	2.27374×10^{-13}	12,896
Newton-APG	4096	36	7.95808×10^{-12}	14,901
CG	4096	34	4.18275×10^{-14}	5337

6. Conclusions

In this paper, we have introduced the A-APG and Newton-APG methods for solving the Sylvester matrix equation. The key idea is to change the Sylvester matrix equation to an optimization problem by using the Kronecker product. Moreover, we have analyzed the computation complexity and proved the convergence of the A-APG method. Convergence results and preliminary numerical examples have shown that the schemes are promising in solving the Sylvester matrix equation.

Author Contributions: J.Z. (methodology, review, and editing); X.L. (software, visualization, data curation). All authors have read and agreed to the published version of the manuscript.

Funding: The work was supported in part by the National Natural Science Foundation of China (12171412, 11771370), Natural Science Foundation for Distinguished Young Scholars of Hunan Province (2021JJ10037), Hunan Youth Science and Technology Innovation Talents Project (2021RC3110), the Key Project of the Education Department of Hunan Province (19A500, 21A0116).

Institutional Review Board Statement: Not applicable.

Informed Consent Statement: Not applicable.

Data Availability Statement: Not applicable.

Conflicts of Interest: The authors declare no conflict of interest.

References

1. Dooren, P.M.V. *Structured Linear Algebra Problems in Digital Signal Processing*; Springer: Berlin/Heidelberg, Germany, 1991.
2. Gajic, Z.; Qureshi, M.T.J. *Lyapunov Matrix Equation in System Stability and Control*; Courier Corporation: Chicago, IL, USA, 2008.
3. Corless, M.J.; Frazho, A. *Linear Systems and Control: An Operator Perspective*; CRC Press: Boca Raton, FL, USA, 2003.
4. Stewart, G.W.; Sun, J. *Matrix Perturbation Theory*; Academic Press: London, UK, 1990.
5. Simoncini, V.; Sadkane, M. Arnoldi-Riccati method for large eigenvalue problems. *BIT Numer. Math.* **1996**, *36*, 579–594.
6. Demmel, J.W. Three methods for refining estimates of invariant subspaces. *Computing* **1987**, *38*, 43–57.
7. Chen, T.W.; Francis, B.A. *Optimal Sampled-Data Control Systems*; Springer: London, UK, 1995.
8. Datta, B. *Numerical Methods for Linear Control Systems*; Elsevier Inc.: Amsterdam, The Netherlands, 2004.
9. Lord, N. Matrix computations. *Math. Gaz.* **1999**, *83*, 556–557.
10. Zhao, X.L.; Wang, F.; Huang, T.Z. Deblurring and sparse unmixing for hyperspectral images. *IEEE Trans. Geosci. Remote Sens.* **2013**, *51*, 4045–4058.
11. Obinata, G.; Anderson, B.D.O. *Model Reduction for Control System Design*; Springer Science & Business Media: London, UK, 2001.
12. Bouhamidi, A.; Jbilou, K. A note on the numerical approximate solutions for generalized Sylvester matrix equations with applications. *Appl. Math. Comput.* **2008**, *206*, 687–694.
13. Bai, Z.Z.; Benzi, M.; Chen, F. Modified HSS iteration methods for a class of complex symmetric linear systems. *Computing* **2010**, *87*, 93–111.
14. Bartels, R.H.; Stewart, G.W. Solution of the matrix equation $AX + XB = C$. *Commun. ACM* **1972**, *15*, 820–826.
15. Golub, G.H. *A Hessenberg-Schur Method for the Problem $AX + XB = C$*; Cornell University: Ithaca, NY, USA, 1978.
16. Robbé, M.; Sadkane, M. A convergence analysis of GMRES and FOM methods for Sylvester equations. *Numer. Algorithms* **2002**, *30*, 71–89.
17. Guennouni, A.E.; Jbilou, K.; Riquet, A.J. Block Krylov subspace methods for solving large Sylvester equations. *Numer. Algorithms* **2002**, *29*, 75–96.
18. Salkuyeh, D.K.; Toutounian, F. New approaches for solving large Sylvester equations. *Appl. Math. Comput.* **2005**, *173*, 9–18.
19. Wachspress, E.L. Iterative solution of the Lyapunov matrix equation. *Appl. Math. Lett.* **1988**, *1*, 87–90.
20. Jbilou, K.; Messaoudi, A.; Sadok, H. Global FOM and GMRES algorithms for matrix equations. *Appl. Numer. Math.* **1999**, *31*, 49–63.
21. Feng, D.; Chen, T. Gradient Based Iterative Algorithms for Solving a Class of Matrix Equations. *IEEE Trans. Autom. Control* **2005**, *50*, 1216–1221.
22. Heyouni, M.; Movahed, F.S.; Tajaddini, A. On global Hessenberg based methods for solving Sylvester matrix equations. *Comput. Math. Appl.* **2019**, *77*, 77–92.
23. Benner, P.; Kürschner, P. Computing real low-rank solutions of Sylvester equations by the factored ADI method. *Comput. Math. Appl.* **2014**, *67*, 1656–1672.
24. Bouhamidi, A.; Hached, M.; Heyouni, M.J.; Bilou, K. A preconditioned block Arnoldi method for large Sylvester matrix equations. *Numer. Linear Algebra Appl.* **2013**, *20*, 208–219.
25. Heyouni, M. Extended Arnoldi methods for large low-rank Sylvester matrix equations. *Appl. Numer. Math.* **2010**, *60*, 1171–1182.
26. Agoujil, S.; Bentbib, A.H.; Jbilou, K.; Sadek, E.M. A minimal residual norm method for large-scale Sylvester matrix equations. *Electron. Trans. Numer. Anal. Etna* **2014**, *43*, 45–59.
27. Abdaoui, I.; Elbouyahyaoui, L.; Heyouni, M. An alternative extended block Arnoldi method for solving low-rank Sylvester equations. *Comput. Math. Appl.* **2019**, *78*, 2817–2830.
28. Jbilou, K. Low rank approximate solutions to large Sylvester matrix equations. *Appl. Math. Comput.* **2005**, *177*, 365–376.
29. Liang, B.; Lin, Y.Q.; Wei, Y.M. A new projection method for solving large Sylvester equations. *Appl. Numer. Math.* **2006**, *57*, 521–532.
30. Jiang, K.; Si, W.; Chen, C.; Bao, C. Efficient numerical methods for computing the stationary states of phase-field crystal models. *SIAM J. Sci. Comput.* **2020**, *42*, B1350–B1377.
31. Beck, A.; Teboulle, M. A Fast Iterative Shrinkage-Thresholding Algorithm for Linear Inverse Problems. *SIAM J. Imaging Sci.* **2009**, *2*, 183–202.
32. Bao, C.; Barbastathis, G.; Ji, H.; Shen, Z.; Zhang, Z. Coherence retrieval using trace regularization. *SIAM J. Imaging Sci.* **2018**, *11*, 679–706.
33. Magnus, J.R.; Neudecker, H. *Matrix Differential Calculus*; John Willey & Sons: Hoboken, NJ, USA, 1999.

Article

Generalized Three-Step Numerical Methods for Solving Equations in Banach Spaces

Michael I. Argyros [1], Ioannis K. Argyros [2,*], Samundra Regmi [3,*] and Santhosh George [4]

1. Department of Computer Science, University of Oklahoma, Norman, OK 73019, USA; michael.i.argyros-1@ou.edu
2. Department of Mathematical Sciences, Cameron University, Lawton, OK 73505, USA
3. Department of Mathematics, University of Houston, Houston, TX 77204, USA
4. Department of Mathematical and Computational Sciences, National Institute of Technology Karnataka, Mangaluru 575 025, India; sgeorge@nitk.edu.in
* Correspondence: iargyros@cameron.edu (I.K.A.); sregmi5@uh.edu (S.R.)

Abstract: In this article, we propose a new methodology to construct and study generalized three-step numerical methods for solving nonlinear equations in Banach spaces. These methods are very general and include other methods already in the literature as special cases. The convergence analysis of the specialized methods is been given by assuming the existence of high-order derivatives which are not shown in these methods. Therefore, these constraints limit the applicability of the methods to equations involving operators that are sufficiently many times differentiable although the methods may converge. Moreover, the convergence is shown under a different set of conditions. Motivated by the optimization considerations and the above concerns, we present a unified convergence analysis for the generalized numerical methods relying on conditions involving only the operators appearing in the method. This is the novelty of the article. Special cases and examples are presented to conclude this article.

Keywords: generalized three-step numerical method; convergence; Banach space

MSC: 49M15; 47H17; 65J15; 65G99; 47H17; 41A25; 49M15

1. Introduction

A plethora of applications from diverse disciplines of computational sciences are converted to nonlinear equations such as

$$F(x) = 0 \qquad (1)$$

using modeling (mathematical) [1–4]. The nonlinear operator F is defined on an open and convex subset Ω of a Banach space X with values in X. The solution of the equation is denoted by x_*. Numerical methods are mainly used to find x_*. This is the case since the analytic form of the solution x_* is obtained in special cases.

Researchers, as well as practitioners, have proposed numerous numerical methods under a different set of convergence conditions using high-order derivatives, which are not present in the methods.

Let us consider an example.

Example 1. *Define the function F on $X = [-0.5, 1.5]$ by*

$$F(t) = \begin{cases} t^3 \ln t^2 + t^5 - t^4, & t \neq 0 \\ 0, & t = 0 \end{cases}$$

Clearly, the point $t_* = 1$ solves the equation $F(t) = 0$. It follows that

$$F'''(t) = 6\ln t^2 + 60t^2 - 24t + 22.$$

Then, the function F does not have a bounded third derivative in X.

Hence, many high convergence methods (although they may converge) cannot apply to show convergence. In order to address these concerns, we propose a unified approach for dealing with the convergence of these numerical methods that take into account only the operators appearing on them. Hence, the usage of these methods becomes possible and under weaker conditions.

Let $x_0 \in \Omega$ be a starting point. Define the generalized numerical method $\forall n = 0, 1, 2, \ldots$ by

$$\begin{aligned} y_n &= a_n = a(x_n) \\ z_n &= b_n = b(x_n, y_n) \\ x_{n+1} &= c_n = c(x_n, y_n, z_n), \end{aligned} \quad (2)$$

where $a : \Omega \longrightarrow X$, $b : \Omega \times \Omega \longrightarrow X$ and $c : \Omega \times \Omega \times \Omega \longrightarrow X$ are given operators chosen so that $\lim_{n \to \infty} x_n = x_*$.

The specialization of (2) is

$$\begin{aligned} y_n &= x_n + \alpha_n F(x_n) \\ z_n &= u_n + \beta_n F(x_n) + \gamma_n F(y_n) \\ x_{n+1} &= v_n + \delta_n F(x_n) + \epsilon_n F(y_n) + \theta_n F(z_n), \end{aligned} \quad (3)$$

where $u_n = x_n$ or $u_n = y_n$, $v_n = x_n$ or $v_n = y_n$ or $v_n = z_n$, and $\alpha_n, \beta_n, \gamma_n, \delta_n, \epsilon_n, \theta_n$ are linear operators on Ω, $\Omega \times \Omega$ and $\Omega \times \Omega \times \Omega$, with values in X, respectively. By choosing some of the linear operators equal to the O linear operators in (3), we obtain the methods studied in [5]. Moreover, if $X = \mathbb{R}^k$, then we obtain the methods studied in [6,7]. In particular, the methods in [5] are of the special form

$$\begin{aligned} y_n &= x_n - \mathcal{O}_{1,n}^{-1} F(x_n) \\ z_n &= y_n - \mathcal{O}_{2,n}^{-1} F(y_n) \\ x_{n+1} &= z_n - \mathcal{O}_{3,n}^{-1} F(z_n), \end{aligned} \quad (4)$$

$$\begin{aligned} y_n &= x_n - sF'(x_n)^{-1} F(x_n) \\ z_n &= x_n - \mathcal{O}_{4,n} F(x_n) \\ x_{n+1} &= z_n - \mathcal{O}_{5,n} F(z_n), \end{aligned} \quad (5)$$

where they, as the methods in [7,8], are of the form

$$\begin{aligned} y_n &= x_n - F'(x_n)^{-1} F(x_n) \\ z_n &= y_n - \mathcal{O}_{6,n} F'(x_n)^{-1} F(y_n) \\ x_{n+1} &= z_n - \mathcal{O}_{7,n} F'(x_n)^{-1} F(z_n), \end{aligned} \quad (6)$$

where $s \in \mathbb{R}$ is a given parameter, and $\mathcal{O}_{k,n}$, $k = 1, 2, \ldots, 7$ are linear operators acting between Ω and X. In particular, operators must have a special form to obtain the fourth, seventh or eighth order of convergence.

Further specifications of operators "$\mathcal{O}$" lead to well-studied methods, a few of which are listed below (other choices can be found in [6,7,9,10]):

Newton method (second order) [1,4,11,12]:

$$y_n = x_n - F'(x_n)^{-1} F(x_n). \quad (7)$$

Jarrat method (second order) [13]:

$$y_n = x_n - \frac{2}{3}F'(x_n)^{-1}F(x_n). \tag{8}$$

Traub-type method (fifth order) [14]:

$$\begin{aligned} y_n &= x_n - F'(x_n)^{-1}F(x_n) \\ z_n &= x_n - F'(x_n)^{-1}F(y_n) \\ x_{n+1} &= x_n - F'(x_n)^{-1}F(z_n). \end{aligned} \tag{9}$$

Homeir method (third order) [15]:

$$\begin{aligned} y_n &= x_n - \frac{1}{2}F'(x_n)^{-1}F(x_n) \\ x_{n+1} &= y_n - F'(x_n)^{-1}F(y_n). \end{aligned} \tag{10}$$

Cordero–Torregrosa (third Order) [2]:

$$\begin{aligned} y_n &= x_n - F'(x_n)^{-1}F(x_n) \\ x_{n+1} &= x_n - 6\left(F'(x_n) + 4F'(\frac{x_n+y_n}{2})\right)F'(y_n)^{-1}F(x_n). \end{aligned} \tag{11}$$

or

$$\begin{aligned} y_n &= x_n - F'(x_n)^{-1}F(x_n) \\ x_{n+1} &= x_n - 2\left[2F'(\frac{3x_n+y_n}{4}) - F'(\frac{x_n+y_n}{2}) + 2F'(\frac{x_n+3y_n}{4})\right]^{-1}F(x_n). \end{aligned} \tag{12}$$

Noor–Wasseem method (third order) [3]:

$$\begin{aligned} y_n &= x_n - F'(x_n)^{-1}F(x_n) \\ x_{n+1} &= x_n - 4\left[3F'(\frac{2x_n+y_n}{3}) + F'(y_n)\right]^{-1}F(x_n). \end{aligned} \tag{13}$$

Xiao–Yin method (third order) [16]:

$$\begin{aligned} y_n &= x_n - F'(x_n)^{-1}F(x_n) \\ x_{n+1} &= x_n - \frac{2}{3}\left[(3F'(y_n) - F'(x_n))^{-1} + F'(x_n)^{-1}\right]F(x_n). \end{aligned} \tag{14}$$

Corder–Torregrosa method (fifth order) [2]:

$$\begin{aligned} y_n &= x_n - \frac{2}{3}F'(x_n)^{-1}F(x_n) \\ z_n &= x_n - \frac{1}{2}(3F'(y_n) - F'(x_n))^{-1}(3F'(y_n) + F'(x_n))F'(x_n)^{-1}F(x_n) \\ x_{n+1} &= z_n - (\frac{1}{2}F'(y_n) + \frac{1}{2}F'(x_n))^{-1}F(z_n). \end{aligned} \tag{15}$$

or

$$\begin{aligned} y_n &= x_n - F'(x_n)^{-1}F(x_n) \\ z_n &= x_n - 2(F'(y_n) + F'(x_n))^{-1}F(x_n) \\ x_{n+1} &= z_n - F'(y_n)^{-1}F(z_n). \end{aligned} \tag{16}$$

Sharma–Arora method (fifth order) [17,18]:

$$\begin{aligned} y_n &= x_n - F'(x_n)^{-1} F(x_n) \\ x_{n+1} &= x_n - (2F'(y_n)^{-1} - F'(x_n)^{-1}) F(x_n). \end{aligned} \quad (17)$$

Xiao–Yin method (fifth order) [16]:

$$\begin{aligned} y_n &= x_n - \frac{2}{3} F'(x_n)^{-1} F(x_n) \\ z_n &= x_n - \frac{1}{4}(3F'(y_n)^{-1} + F'(x_n)^{-1}) F(x_n) \\ x_{n+1} &= x_n - \frac{1}{3}\left[(3F'(y_n) - F'(x_n))^{-1}\right] F(x_n). \end{aligned} \quad (18)$$

Traub-type method (second order) [14]:

$$\begin{aligned} y_n &= x_n - [w_n, x_n; F]^{-1} F(x_n) \\ w_n &= x_n + dF(x_n), \end{aligned} \quad (19)$$

where $[.,.; F] : \Omega \times \Omega \longrightarrow L(X, X)$ is a divided difference of order one.

Moccari–Lofti method (fourth order) [19]:

$$\begin{aligned} y_n &= x_n - [x_n, w_n; F]^{-1} F(x_n) \\ x_{n+1} &= y_n - ([y_n, w_n; F] + [y_n, x_n; F] - [x_n, w_n; F])^{-1} F(y_n). \end{aligned} \quad (20)$$

Wang–Zang method (seventh order) [8,16,20]:

$$\begin{aligned} y_n &= x_n - [w_n, x_n; F]^{-1} F(x_n) \\ z_n &= M_8(x_n, y_n) \\ x_{n+1} &= z_n - ([z_n, x_n; F] + [z_n, y_n; F] - [y_n, x_n; F])^{-1} F(z_n), \end{aligned} \quad (21)$$

where M_8 is any fourth-order Steffensen-type iteration method.

Sharma–Arora method (seventh order) [17]:

$$\begin{aligned} y_n &= x_n - [w_n, x_n; F]^{-1} F(x_n) \\ z_n &= y_n - (3I - [w_n, x_n; F]^{(}[y_n, x_n; F] + [y_n, w_n; F])) \\ & \quad [w_n, x_n; F]^{-1}) F(y_n) \\ x_{n+1} &= z_n - [z_n, y_n; F]^{-1}([w_n, x_n; F] \\ & \quad +[y_n, x_n; F] - [z_n, x_n; F])[w_n, x_n; F]^{-1} F(z_n). \end{aligned} \quad (22)$$

The local, as well as the semi-local, convergence for methods (4) and (5), were presented in [17], respectively, using hypotheses relating only to the operators on these methods. However, the local convergence analysis of method (6) requires the usage of derivatives or divided differences of higher than two orders, which do not appear in method (6). These high-order derivatives restrict the applicability of method (6) to equations whose operator F has high-order derivatives, although method (6) may converge (see Example 1).

Similar restrictions exist for the convergence of the aforementioned methods of order three or above.

It is also worth noticing that the fifth convergence order method by Sharma [18]

$$\begin{aligned} y_n &= x_n - F'(x_n)^{-1} F(x_n) \\ z_n &= y_n - 5F'(x_n)^{-1} F(y_n) \\ x_{n+1} &= y_n - \frac{1}{5}[9F'(x_n)^{-1} F(y_n) + F'(x_n)^{-1} F(z_n)] \end{aligned} \quad (23)$$

cannot be handled with the analyses given previously [5–7] for method (4), method (5), or method (6).

Based on all of the above, clearly, it is important to study the convergence of method (2) and its specialization method (3) with the approach employed for method (4) or (5). This way, the resulting unified convergence criteria can apply to their specialized methods listed or not listed previously. Hence, this is the motivation as well as the novelty of the article.

There are two important types of convergence: the semi-local and the local. The semi-local uses information involving the initial point to provide criteria, assuring the convergence of the numerical method, while the local one is based on the information about the solution to find the radii of the convergence balls.

The local convergence results are vital, although the solution is unknown in general since the convergence order of the numerical method can be found. This kind of result also demonstrates the degree of difficulty in selecting starting points. There are cases when the radius of convergence of the numerical method can be determined without the knowledge of the solution.

As an example, let $X = \mathbb{R}$. Suppose function F satisfies an autonomous differential [5,21] equation of the form

$$H(F(t)) = F'(t),$$

where H is a continuous function. Notice that $H(F(t_*)) = F'(t_*)$ or $F'(t_*) = H(0)$. In the case of $F(t) = e^t - 1$, we can choose $H(t) = t + 1$ (see also the numerical section).

Moreover, the local results can apply to projection numerical methods, such as Arnoldi's, the generalized minimum residual numerical method (GMRES), the generalized conjugate numerical method (GCS) for combined Newton/finite projection numerical methods, and in relation to the mesh independence principle to develop the cheapest and most efficient mesh refinement techniques [1,5,11,21].

In this article, we introduce a majorant sequence and use our idea of recurrent functions to extend the applicability of the numerical method (2). Our analysis includes error bounds and results on the uniqueness of x_* based on computable Lipschitz constants not given before in [5,13,21–24] and in other similar studies using the Taylor series. This idea is very general. Hence, it applies also to other numerical methods [10,14,22,25].

The convergence analysis of method (2) and method (3) is given in Section 2. Moreover, the special choices of operators appear in the method in Sections 3 and 4. Concluding remarks, open problems, and future work complete this article.

2. Convergence Analysis of Method

The local is followed by the semi-local convergence analysis. Let $S = [0, \infty)$ and $S_0 = [0, \rho_0)$ for some $\rho_0 > 0$. Consider functions $h_1 : S_0 \longrightarrow \mathbb{R}$, $h_2 : S_0 \times S_0 \longrightarrow \mathbb{R}$ and $h_3 : S_0 \times S_0 \times S_0 \longrightarrow \mathbb{R}$ be continuous and nondecreasing in each variable.

Suppose that equations

$$h_i(t) - 1 = 0, \ i = 1, 2, 3 \quad (24)$$

have the smallest solutions, $\rho_i \in S - \{0\}$. The parameter ρ defined by

$$\rho = \min\{\rho_i\} \quad (25)$$

shall be shown to be a radius of convergence for method (2). Let $S_1 = [0, \rho)$. It follows by the definition of radius ρ that for all $t \in S_1$

$$0 \leq h_i(t) < 1. \quad (26)$$

The notation $U(x, \varsigma)$ denotes an open ball with center $x \in X$ and of radius $\varsigma > 0$. By $U[x, \varsigma]$, we denote the closure of $U(x, \varsigma)$.

The following conditions are used in the local convergence analysis of the method (2). Suppose the following:

(H1) Equation $F(x) = 0$ has a solution $x_* \in \Omega$.
(H2) $\|a(x) - x_*\| \leq h_1(\|x - x_*\|)\|x - x_*\|$,

$$\|b(x,y) - x_*\| \leq h_2(\|x - x_*\|, \|y - x_*\|)\|x - x_*\|$$

and

$$\|c(x,y,z) - x_*\| \leq h_3(\|x - x_*\|, \|y - x_*\|, \|z - x_*\|)\|x - x_*\|$$

for all $x, y, z \in \Omega_0 = \Omega \cap U(x_*, \rho_0)$.
(H3) Equations (24) have smallest solutions $\rho_i \in S_0 - \{0\}$;
(H4) $U[x_*, \rho] \subset \Omega$, where the radius ρ is given by Formula (25).

Next, the main local convergence analysis is presented for method (2).

Theorem 1. *Suppose that the conditions (H1)–(H4) hold and $x_0 \in U(x_*, r) - \{x_*\}$. Then, the sequence $\{x_n\}$ generated by method (2) is well defined and converges to x_*. Moreover, the following estimates hold $\forall\, n = 0, 1, 2, \ldots$*

$$\|y_n - x_*\| \leq h_1(\|x_n - x_*\|)\|x_n - x_*\| \leq \|x_n - x_*\| < \rho \tag{27}$$

$$\|z_n - x_*\| \leq h_2(\|x_n - x_*\|, \|y_n - x_*\|)\|x_n - x_*\| \leq \|x_n - x_*\| \tag{28}$$

and

$$\|x_{n+1} - x_*\| \leq h_3(\|x_n - x_*\|, \|y_n - x_*\|, \|z_n - x_*\|)\|x_n - x_*\| \leq \|x_n - x_*\|. \tag{29}$$

Proof. Let $x_0 \in U(x_*, \rho_0)$. Then, it follows from the first condition in (H1) the definition of ρ, (26) (for $i = 1$) and the first substep of method (2) for $n = 0$ that

$$\|y_0 - x_*\| \leq h_1(\|x_0 - x_*\|)\|x_0 - x_*\| \leq \|x_0 - x_*\| < \rho, \tag{30}$$

showing estimate (27) for $n = 0$ and the iterate $y_0 \in U(x_*, \rho)$. Similarly,

$$\begin{aligned}
\|z_0 - x_*\| &\leq h_2(\|x_0 - x_*\|, \|y_0 - x_*\|)\|x_0 - x_*\| \\
&\leq h_2(\|x_0 - x_*\|, \|y_0 - x_*\|) \\
&\leq h_2(\|x_0 - x_*\|, \|x_0 - x_*\|)\|x_0 - x_*\| \leq \|x_0 - x_*\|
\end{aligned} \tag{31}$$

and

$$\begin{aligned}
\|x_1 - x_*\| &\leq h_3(\|x_0 - x_*\|, \|y_0 - x_*\|, \|z_0 - x_*\|)\|x_0 - x_*\| \\
&\leq h_3(\|x_0 - x_*\|, \|x_0 - x_*\|, \|x_0 - x_*\|)\|x_0 - x_*\| \\
&\leq \|x_0 - x_*\|,
\end{aligned}$$

showing estimates (28), (29), respectively and the iterates $z_0, x_1 \in U(x_*, \rho)$. By simply replacing x_0, y_0, z_0, x_1 by x_k, y_k, z_k, x_{k+1} in the preceding calculations, the induction for estimates (27)–(29) is terminated. Then, from the estimate

$$\|x_{k+1} - x_*\| \leq d\|x_k - x_*\| < \rho,$$

where

$$d = h_3(\|x_0 - x_*\|, \|x_0 - x_*\|, \|x_0 - x_*\|) \in [0, 1) \tag{32}$$

we conclude $x_{k+1} \in U[x_*, \rho]$ and $\lim_{k \to \infty} x_k = x_*$. □

Remark 1. *It follows from the proof of Theorem 1 that y, z can be chosen in particular as $y_n = a(x_n)$ and $z_n = b(x_n, y_n)$. Thus, the condition (H2) should hold for all $x, a(x), b(x,y) \in \Omega_0$ and not $x, y, z \in \Omega_0$. Clearly, in this case, the resulting functions $\bar{h}_i$ are at least as tight as the functions h_i, leading to an at least as large radius of convergence $\bar{\rho}$ as ρ (see the numerical section).*

Concerning the semi-local convergence of method (2), let us introduce scalar sequences $\{t_n\}, \{s_n\}$ and $\{u_n\}$ defined for $t_0 = 0, s_0 = \eta \geq 0$ and the rest of the iterates, depending on operators a, b, c and F (see how in the next section). These sequences shall be shown to be majorizing for method (2). However, first, a convergence result for these sequence is needed.

Lemma 1. *Suppose that* $\forall n = 0, 1, 2, \ldots$

$$t_n \leq s_n \leq u_n \leq t_{n+1} \tag{33}$$

and

$$t_n \leq \lambda \tag{34}$$

for some $\lambda \geq 0$. *Then, the sequence* $\{t_n\}$ *is convergent to its unique least upper bound* $t_* \in [0, \lambda]$.

Proof. It follows from conditions (33) and (34) that sequence $\{t_n\}$ is nondecreasing and bounded from above by λ, and as such, it converges to t_*. □

Theorem 2. *Suppose the following:*
(H5) Iterates $\{x_n\}, \{y_n\}, \{z_n\}$ *generated by method (2) exist, belong in* $U(x_0, t_*)$ *and satisfy the conditions of Lemma 1 for all* $n = 0, 1, 2, \ldots$
(H6) $\|a(x_n) - x_n\| \leq s_n - t_n$,

$$\|b(x_n, y_n) - y_n\| \leq u_n - s_n$$

and

$$\|c(x_n, y_n, z_n) - z_n\| \leq t_{n+1} - u_n$$

for all $n = 0, 1, 2, \ldots$ *and*
(H7) $U[x_0, t_*] \subset \Omega$.
Then, there exists $x_* \in U[x_0, t_*]$ *such that* $\lim_{n \to \infty} x_n = x_*$.

Proof. It follows by condition (H5) that sequence $\{t_n\}$ is complete as convergent. Thus, by condition (H6), sequence $\{x_n\}$ is also complete in a Banach space X, and as such, it converges to some $x_* \in U[x_0, t_*]$ (since $U[x_0, t_*]$ is a closed set). □

Remark 2. *(i) Additional conditions are needed to show* $F(x_*) = 0$. *The same is true for the results on the uniqueness of the solution.*
(ii) The limit point t_* *is not given in the closed form. So, it can be replaced by* λ *in Theorem 2.*

3. Special Cases I

The iterates of method (3) are assumed to exist, and operator F has a divided difference of order one.

Local Convergence

Three possibilities are presented for the local cases based on different estimates for the determination of the functions h_i. It follows by method (3) that

(P1) $y_n - x_* = x_n - x_* + \alpha_n F(x_n) = (I + \alpha_n [x_n, x_*; F])(x_n - x_*)$,

$$\begin{aligned} z_n - x_* &= (I + \gamma_n [y_n, x_*; F])(y_n - x_*) + \beta_n [x_n, x_*; F](x_n - x_*) \\ &= [(I + \gamma_n [y_n, x_*; F])(I + \alpha_n [x_n, x_*; F]) + \beta_n [x_n, x_*; F]](x_n - x_*) \end{aligned}$$

and

$$x_{n+1} - x_* = (I + \theta_n[z_n, x_*; F])(z_n - x_*) + \delta_n[x_n, x_*; F](x_n - x_*)$$
$$+ \epsilon_n[y_n, x_*; F](y_n - x_*)$$
$$= [(I + \theta_n[z_n, x_*; F])(I + \gamma_n[y_n, x_*; F])(I + \beta_n[x_n, x_*; F])$$
$$+ \delta_n[x_n, x_*; F] + \epsilon_n[y_n, x_*; F](I + \alpha_n[x_n, x_*; F])](x_n - x_*)$$

Hence, the functions h_i are selected to satisfy $\forall x_n, y_n, z_n \in \Omega$

$$\|I + \alpha_n[x_n, x_*; F]\| \leq h_1(\|x_n - x_*\|),$$

$$\|(I + \gamma_n[y_n, x_*; F])(I + \alpha_n[x_n, x_*; F]) + \beta_n[x_n, x_*; F]\| \leq h_2(\|x_n - x_*\|, \|y_n - x_*\|)$$

$$\|(I + \theta_n[z_n, x_*; F])(I + \gamma_n[y_n, x_*; F])(I + \beta_n[x_n, x_*; F])$$
$$+ \delta_n[x_n, x_*; F] + \epsilon_n[y_n, x_*; F](I + \alpha_n[x_n, x_*; F])\|$$
$$\leq h_3(\|x_n - x_*\|, \|y_n - x_*\|, \|z_n - x_*\|).$$

A practical non-discrete choice for the function h_1 is given by

$$\|I + \alpha(x)[x, x_*; F]\| \leq h_1(\|x - x_*\|) \ \forall x \in \Omega.$$

Another choice is given by

$$h_1(t) = \sup_{x \in \Omega, \|x - x_*\| \leq t} \|I + \alpha(x)[x, x_*; F]\|.$$

The choices of functions h_2 and h_3 can follow similarly.

(P2) Let $M^i : \Omega \longrightarrow X$ be a linear operator. By M_n^i we denote $M^i(x_n) \ \forall n = 0, 1, 2, \ldots$. Then, it follows from method (3)

$$y_n - x_* = x_n - x_* - M_n^1 F(x_n) + (\alpha_n + M_n) F(x_n)$$
$$= (I - M_n^2[x_n, x_*; F]) + (\alpha_n + M_n^2)[x_n, x_*; F])(x_n - x_*),$$
$$z_n - x_* = ((I - M_n^2[y_n, x_*; F]) + (\gamma_n + M_n^2)[y_n, x_*; F])(y_n - x_*)$$

and

$$x_{n+1} - x_* = ((I - M_n^3[z_n, x_*; F]) + (\theta_n + M_n^3)[z_n, x_*; F])(z_n - x_*).$$

Thus, the functions h_i must satisfy

$$\|I + \alpha_n\| \leq h_1(\|x_n - x_*\|),$$

$$(I + \gamma_n)(I + \alpha_n)\| \leq h_2(\|x_n - x_*\|, \|y_n - x_*\|)$$

and

$$\|x_{n+1} - x_*\| \leq \|(I + \theta_n)(I + \gamma_n)(I + \alpha_n)\| \leq h_3(\|x_n - x_*\|, \|y_n - x_*\|, \|z_n - x_*\|).$$

Clearly, the function h_1 can be chosen again as in case (P1). The functions h_2 and h_3 can be defined similarly.

(P3) Assume $\exists$ function $\varphi_0 : [0, \infty) \longrightarrow \mathbb{R}$ continuous and non-decreasing such that

$$\|F'(x_*)^{-1}(F'(x) - F'(x_*))\| \leq \varphi_0(\|x - x_*\|) \ \forall x \in \Omega.$$

Then, we can write

$$F(x_n) = F(x_n) - F(x_*) = \int_0^1 F'(x_* + \theta(x_n - x_*)) d\theta (x_n - x_*)$$

leading to
$$\|F'(x_*)^{-1}F(x_n)\| \leq \int_0^1 \varphi_0(\theta\|x_n - x_*\|)d\theta \|x_n - x_*\|.$$

Then, by method (3) we obtain, in turn, that

$$\begin{aligned}y_n - x_* &= [I + \alpha_n F'(x_*)F'(x_*)^{-1} \\ &\quad \times \left(\int_0^1 F'(x_* + \theta(x_n - x_*))d\theta - F'(x_*) + F'(x_*)\right)](x_n - x_*),\end{aligned}$$

so, the function h_1 must satisfy

$$\|I + \alpha_n \int_0^1 F'(x_* + \theta(x_n - x_*))d\theta\| \leq h_1(\|x_n - x_*\|)$$

or

$$\|h_1(t)\| = \sup_{\|x - x_*\| \leq t, x \in \Omega} \|I + \alpha(x) \int_0^1 F'(x_* + \theta(x_n - x_*))d\theta\|$$

or

$$\|I + \alpha_n F'(x_*)\|(1 + \int_0^1 \varphi_0(\theta\|x_n - x_*\|)d\theta) \leq h_1(\|x_n - x_*\|)$$

or

$$h_1(t) = \sup_{\|x - x_*\| \leq t, x \in \Omega} \|I + \alpha(x)F'(x_*)\|(1 + \int_0^1 \varphi_0(\theta\|x_n - x_*\|)d\theta).$$

Similarly, for the other two steps, we obtain in the last choice

$$\begin{aligned}\|z_n - x_*\| &\leq \|I + \gamma_n F'(x_*)\|(1 + \int_0^1 \varphi_0(\theta\|y_n - x_*\|)d\theta)\|y_n - x_*\| \\ &\quad + \|\beta_n F'(x_*)\|(1 + \int_0^1 \varphi_0(\theta\|x_n - x_*\|)d\theta)\|x_n - x_*\|\end{aligned}$$

and

$$\begin{aligned}\|x_{n+1} - x_*\| &\leq \|I + \theta_n F'(x_*)\|(1 + \int_0^1 \varphi_0(\theta\|z_n - x_*\|)d\theta)\|z_n - x_*\| \\ &\quad + \|\delta_n F'(x_*)\|(1 + \int_0^1 \varphi_0(\theta\|x_n - x_*\|)d\theta)\|x_n - x_*\| \\ &\quad + \|\epsilon_n F'(x_*)\|(1 + \int_0^1 \varphi_0(\theta\|y_n - x_*\|)d\theta)\|y_n - x_*\|.\end{aligned}$$

Thus, the function h_2 satisfies

$$\begin{aligned}&\|I + \gamma_n F'(x_*)\|(1 + \int_0^1 \varphi_0(\theta\|y_n - x_*\|)d\theta)\|y_n - x_*\| \\ &\quad + \|\beta_n F'(x_*)\|(1 + \int_0^1 \varphi_0(\theta\|x_n - x_*\|)d\theta) \\ &\leq h_2(\|x_n - x_*\|, \|y_n - x_*\|)\end{aligned}$$

or

$$\begin{aligned}h_2(s, t) &= \sup_{\|x - x_*\| \leq s, \|y - x_*\| \leq t} [\|I + \gamma(x)F'(x_*)\| \\ &\quad \times (1 + \int_0^1 \varphi_0(\theta t)d\theta)t) \\ &\quad + \|\beta(x)F'(x_*)\|(1 + \int_0^1 \varphi_0(\theta s)d\theta)].\end{aligned}$$

Finally, concerning the choice of the function h_3, by the third substep of method (3)

$$\|x_{n+1} - x_*\| \leq \|I + \theta_n F'(x_*)\|(1 + \int_0^1 \varphi_0(\theta\|z_n - x_*\|)d\theta)\|z_n - x_*\|$$
$$+ \|\delta_n F'(x_*)\|(1 + \int_0^1 \varphi_0(\theta\|x_n - x_*\|)d\theta)\|x_n - x_*\|$$
$$+ \|\epsilon_n F'(x_*)\|(1 + \int_0^1 \varphi_0(\theta\|y_n - x_*\|)d\theta)\|y_n - x_*\|,$$

so the function h_3 must satisfy

$$\|I + \theta_n F'(x_*)\|(1 + \int_0^1 \varphi_0(\theta\|y_n - x_*\|)d\theta)h_2(\|x_n - x_*\|, \|y_n - x_*\|)$$
$$+ \|\delta_n F'(x_*)\|(1 + \int_0^1 \varphi_0(\theta\|x_n - x_*\|)d\theta)$$
$$+ \|\epsilon_n F'(x_*)\|(1 + \int_0^1 \varphi_0(\theta\|y_n - x_*\|)d\theta)h_1(\|x_n - x_*\|)$$
$$\leq h_3(\|x_n - x_*\|, \|y_n - x_*\|, \|z_n - x_*\|)$$

or

$$h(x, s, t, u) = \sup_{\|x-x_*\|\leq s, \|y-x_*\|\leq t, \|z-x_*\|\leq u} \mu(x, s, t, u),$$

where

$$\mu(x, s, t, u) = \|I + \theta(x)F'(x_*)\|$$
$$\times (1 + \int_0^1 \varphi_0(\theta u)d\theta)h_2(t, s)$$
$$+ \|\delta(x)F'(x_*)\|(1 + \int_0^1 \varphi_0(\theta s)d\theta)$$
$$+ \|\epsilon(x)F'(x_*)\|(1 + \int_0^1 \varphi_0((\theta t)d\theta)h_1(s)].$$

The functions h_2 and h_3 can also be defined with the other two choices as those of function h_1 given previously.

Semi-local Convergence

Concerning this case, we can have instead of the conditions of Theorem 2 (see (H6)) but for method (3)

$$\|\alpha_n F(x_n)\| \leq s_n - t_n,$$
$$\|\beta_n F(x_n) + \gamma_n F(y_n)\| \leq u_n - s_n$$

and

$$\|\delta_n F(x_n) + \epsilon_n F(y_n) + \theta_n F(z_n)\| \leq t_{n+1} - u_n \ \forall n = 0, 1, 2, \ldots.$$

Notice that under these choices,

$$\|y_n - x_n\| \leq s_n - t_n$$
$$\|z_n - y_n\| \leq u_n - s_n$$

and

$$\|x_{n+1} - z_n\| \leq t_{n+1} - u_n.$$

Then, the conclusions of Theorem 2 hold for method (3). Even more specialized choices of linear operators appearing on these methods as well as function h_i can be found in the Introduction, the next section, or in [1,2,11,21] and the references therein.

4. Special Cases II

The section contains even more specialized cases of method (2) and method (3). In particular, we study the local and semi-local convergence first of method (22) and second of method (20). Notice that to obtain method (22), we set in method (3)

$$\alpha_n = -F'(x_n)^{-1}, u_n = y_n, \beta_n = O, \gamma_n = -5F'(x_n)^{-1},$$
$$v_n = y_n, \delta_n = O, \epsilon_n = -\frac{9}{5}F'(x_n)^{-1} \text{ and } \theta_n = -\frac{1}{5}F'(x_n). \tag{35}$$

Moreover, for method (20), we let

$$\alpha_n = -[x_n, w_n; F]^{-1}, u_n = y_n, \beta_n = O, z_n = x_{n+1},$$
$$\gamma_n = ([y_n, w_n; F] + [y_n, x_n; F] - [x_n, w_n; F])^{-1}, \delta_n = \epsilon_n = \theta_n = O \tag{36}$$

and $v_n = z_n$.

5. Local Convergence of Method

The local convergence analysis of method (23) utilizes some functions parameters. Let $S = [0, \infty)$.

Suppose the following:

(i) ∃ function $w_0 : S \longrightarrow \mathbb{R}$ continuous and non-decreasing such that equation

$$w_0(t) - 1 = 0$$

has a smallest solution $\rho_0 \in S - \{0\}$. Let $S_0 = [0, \rho_0)$.

(ii) ∃ function $w : S_0 \longrightarrow \mathbb{R}$ continuous and non-decreasing such that equation

$$h_1(t) - 1 = 0$$

has a smallest solution $\rho_1 \in S_0 - \{0\}$, where the function $h_1 : S_0 \longrightarrow \mathbb{R}$ defined by

$$h_1(t) = \frac{\int_0^1 w((1-\theta)t)d\theta}{1 - w_0(t)}.$$

(iii) Equation

$$w_0(h_1(t)t) - 1 = 0$$

has a smallest solution $\bar{\rho}_1 \in S_0 - \{0\}$. Let

$$\bar{\rho}_0 = \min\{\rho_0, \bar{\rho}_1\}$$

and $\tilde{S}_1 = [0, \bar{\rho}_0)$.

(iv) Equation

$$h_2(t) - 1 = 0$$

has a smallest solution $\rho_2 \in \tilde{S}_1 - \{0\}$, where the function $h_2 : \tilde{S}_1 \longrightarrow \mathbb{R}$ is defined as

$$h_2(t) = \left[\frac{\int_0^1 w((1-\theta)h_1(t)t)d\theta}{1 - w_0(h_1(t)t)} \right.$$
$$+ \frac{w((1+h_1(t))t)(1+\int_0^1 w_0(\theta h_1(t)t)d\theta)}{(1-w_0(t))(1-w_0(h_1(t)t))}$$
$$\left.+ \frac{4(1+\int_0^1 w_0(\theta h_1(t)t)d\theta)}{1-w_0(t)}\right]h_1(t).$$

(v) Equation
$$h_3(t) - 1 = 0$$
has a smallest solution $\rho_3 \in \tilde{S}_1 - \{0\}$, where the function $h_3 : \tilde{S}_1 \longrightarrow \mathbb{R}$ is defined by

$$\begin{aligned} h_3(t) &= h_1(t) + \frac{1}{5}[\frac{9(1+\int_0^1 w_0(\theta h_1(t)t)d\theta)h_1(t)}{1-w_0(t)} \\ &\quad (1+\int_0^1 w_0(\theta h_2(t)t)d\theta)h_2(t)]. \end{aligned}$$

The parameter ρ defined by

$$\rho = \min\{\rho_j\} \quad j = 1, 2, 3 \tag{37}$$

is proven to be a radius of convergence for method (2) in Theorem 3. Let $S_1 = [0, \rho)$. Then, it follows by these definitions that $\forall\, t \in S_2$

$$0 \le w_0(t) < 1 \tag{38}$$

$$0 \le w_0(h_1(t)t) < 1 \tag{39}$$

and

$$0 \le h_i(t) < 1. \tag{40}$$

The conditions required are as follows:
(C1) Equation $F(x) = 0$ has a simple solution $x_* \in \Omega$.
(C2) $\|F'(x_*)^{-1}(F'(x) - F'(x_*))\| \le w_0(\|x - x_*\|) \; \forall\, x \in \Omega$.
Set $\Omega_1 = U(x_*, \rho_0) \cap \Omega$.
(C3) $\|F'(x_*)^{-1}(F'(y) - F'(x))\| \le w(\|y - x\|) \; \forall\, x, y \in \Omega_1$
and
(C4) $U[x_0, \rho] \subset \Omega$.
Next, the main local convergence result follows for method (23).

Theorem 3. *Suppose that conditions (C1)–(C4) hold and $x_0 \in U(x_*, \rho) - \{x_*\}$. Then, the sequence $\{x_n\}$ generated by method (23) is well defined in $U(x_*, \rho)$, remains in $U(x_*, \rho)$ $\forall\, n = 0, 1, 2, \ldots$ and is convergent to x_*. Moreover, the following assertions hold:*

$$\|y_n - x_*\| \le h_1(\|x_n - x_*\|)\|x_n - x_*\| \le \|x_n - x_*\| < \rho, \tag{41}$$

$$\|z_n - x_*\| \le h_2(\|x_n - x_*\|)\|x_n - x_*\| \le \|x_n - x_*\|, \tag{42}$$

and

$$\|x_{n+1} - x_*\| \le h_3(\|x_n - x_*\|)\|x_n - x_*\| \le \|x_n - x_*\|, \tag{43}$$

where functions h_i are defined previously and the radius ρ is given by Formula (37).

Proof. Let $u \in U(x_*, \rho) - \{x_*\}$. By using conditions (C1), (C2) and (37), we have that

$$\|F'(x_*)^{-1}(F'(u) - F'(x_*))\| \le w_0(\|x_0 - x_*\|) \le w_0(r) < 1. \tag{44}$$

It follows by (44) and the Banach lemma on invertible operators [11,15] that $F'(u)^{-1} \in L(X, X)$ and

$$\|F'(u)^{-1}F'(x_*)\| \le \frac{1}{1 - w_0(\|x_0 - x_*\|)}. \tag{45}$$

If $u = x_0$, then the iterate y_0 is well defined by the first substep of method (23) and we can write

$$
\begin{aligned}
y_0 - x_* &= x_0 - x_* - F'(x_0)^{-1}F(x_0) \\
&= F'(x_0)^{-1}\int_0^1 (F'(x_* + \theta(x_0 - x_*))d\theta - F'(x_0))(x_0 - x_*). \quad (46)
\end{aligned}
$$

In view of (C1)–(C3), (45) (for $u = x_0$), (40) (for $i = 1$) and (46), we obtain in turn that

$$
\begin{aligned}
\|y_0 - x_*\| &\le \frac{\int_0^1 w((1-\theta)\|x_0 - x_*\|)d\theta \|x_0 - x_*\|}{1 - w_0(\|x_0 - x_*\|)} \\
&\le h_1(\|x_0 - x_*\|)\|x_0 - x_*\| < \|x_0 - x_*\| < \rho. \quad (47)
\end{aligned}
$$

Thus, the iterate $y_0 \in U(x_*, r)$ and (41) holds for $n = 0$. The iterate z_0 is well defined by the second substep of method (23), so we can write

$$
\begin{aligned}
z_0 - x_* &= y_0 - x_0 - 5F'(x_0)^{-1}F(y_0) \\
&= y_0 - x_* - F'(y_0)^{-1}F(y_0) \\
&\quad + F'(y_0)^{-1}(F'(x_0) - F'(y_0))F'(x_0)^{-1}F(y_0) \\
&\quad - 4F'(x_0)^{-1}F(y_0). \quad (48)
\end{aligned}
$$

Notice that linear operator $F'(y_0)^{-1}$ exists by (45) (for $u = y_0$). It follows by (37), (40) (for $j = 1$), (C3), (45) (for $u = x_0, y_0$), in turn that

$$
\begin{aligned}
\|z_0 - x_*\| &\le \Bigg[\frac{\int_0^1 w((1-\theta)\|y_0 - x_*\|)d\theta}{1 - w_0(\|y_0 - x_*\|)} \\
&\quad + \frac{w(\|y_0 - x_0\|)(1 + \int_0^1 w_0(\theta\|y_0 - x_*\|)d\theta)}{(1 - w_0(\|x_0 - x_*\|))(1 - w_0(\|y_0 - x_*\|))} \\
&\quad + \frac{4(1 + \int_0^1 w_0(\theta\|y_0 - x_*\|)d\theta)}{1 - w_0(\|x_0 - x_*\|)}\Bigg]\|y_0 - x_*\| \\
&\le h_2(\|x_0 - x_*\|)\|x_0 - x_*\| \le \|x_0 - x_*\|. \quad (49)
\end{aligned}
$$

Thus, the iterate $z_0 \in U(x_*, \rho)$ and (42) holds for $n = 0$, where we also used (C1) and (C2) to obtain the estimate

$$
\begin{aligned}
\|F'(x_*)^{-1}F(y_0)\| &= \|F'(x_*)^{-1}[\int_0^1 F'(x_* + \theta(y_0 - x_*))d\theta - F'(x_*) \\
&\quad + F'(x_*)](y_0 - x_*)\| \\
&\le (1 + \int_0^1 w_0(\theta\|y_0 - x_*\|)d\theta)\|y_0 - x_*\|.
\end{aligned}
$$

Moreover, the iterate x_1 is well defined by the third substep of method (23), so we can have

$$
x_1 - x_* = y_0 - x_* - \frac{1}{5}F'(x_0)^{-1}(9F(y_0) + F(z_0)),
$$

leading to

$$
\begin{aligned}
\|x_1 - x_*\| &\le \|y_0 - x_*\| + \frac{1}{5}\Bigg(\frac{9(1 + \int_0^1 w_0(\theta\|y_0 - x_*\|)d\theta)\|y_0 - x_*\|}{1 - w_0(\|y_0 - x_*\|)} \\
&\quad + (1 + \int_0^1 w_0(\theta\|z_0 - x_*\|)d\theta)\|z_0 - x_*\|\Bigg) \\
&\le h_3(\|x_0 - x_*\|)\|x_0 - x_*\| \le \|x_0 - x_*\| < \rho. \quad (50)
\end{aligned}
$$

Therefore, the iterate $x_1 \in U(x_*, \rho)$ and (43) holds for $n = 0$.

Switch x_0, y_0, z_0, x_1 by x_m, y_m, z_m, x_{m+1} $\forall m = 0, 1, 2 \ldots$ in the preceding calculations to complete the induction for the estimates (41)–(43). Then, by the estimate

$$\|x_{m+1} - x_*\| \le d\|x_m - x_*\| < \rho, \tag{51}$$

where $d = h_3(\|x_0 - x_*\|) \in [0, 1)$, we obtain that $x_{m+1} \in U(x_*, \rho)$ and $\lim_{m \to \infty} x_m = x_*$. □

The uniqueness of the solution result for method (23) follows.

Proposition 1. *Suppose the following:*
(i) Equation $F(x) = 0$ has a simple solution $x_* \in U(x_*, r) \subset \Omega$ for some $r > 0$.
(ii) Condition (C2) holds.
(iii) There exists $r_1 \ge r$ such that

$$\int_0^1 w_0(\theta r_1) d\theta < 1. \tag{52}$$

Set $\Omega_2 = U[x_*, r_1] \cap \Omega$. Then, the only solution of equation $F(x) = 0$ in the set Ω_2 is x_*.

Proof. Let $y_* \in D_2$ be such that $F(y_*) = 0$. Define the linear operator $J = \int_0^1 h(x_* + \theta(y_* - x_*)) d\theta$. It then follows by (ii) and (52) that

$$\|h(x_*)^{-1}(J - F'(x_*))\| \le \int_0^1 w_0(\theta \|y_* - x_*\|) d\theta$$

$$\le \int_0^1 w_0(\theta r_1) d\theta < 1.$$

Hence, we deduce $x_* = y_*$ by the invertibility of J and the estimate $J(x_* - y_*) = F(x_*) - F(y_*) = 0$. □

Remark 3. *Under all conditions of Theorem 3, we can set $\rho = r$.*

Example 2. *Consider the motion system*

$$F_1'(v_1) = e^{v_1}, \quad F_2'(v_2) = (e-1)v_2 + 1, \quad F_3'(v_3) = 1$$

with $F_1(0) = F_2(0) = F_3(0) = 0$. Let $F = (F_1, F_2, F_3)^{tr}$. Let $X = \mathbb{R}^3, \Omega = U[0, 1], x_* = (0, 0, 0)^{tr}$. Let function F on Ω for $v = (v_1, v_2, v_3)^{tr}$ given as

$$F(v) = (e^{v_1} - 1, \frac{e-1}{2} v_2^2 + v_2, v_3)^{tr}.$$

Using this definition, we obtain the derivative as

$$F'(v) = \begin{bmatrix} e^{v_1} & 0 & 0 \\ 0 & (e-1)v_2 + 1 & 0 \\ 0 & 0 & 1 \end{bmatrix}.$$

Hence, $F'(x_*) = I$. Let $v \in \mathbb{R}^3$ with $v = (v_1, v_2, v_3)^{tr}$. Moreover, the nor for $N \in \mathbb{R}^3 \times \mathbb{R}^3$ is

$$\|N\| = \max_{1 \le j \le 3} \sum_{i=1}^3 \|n_{j,i}\|.$$

Conditions (C1)–(C3) are verified for $w_0(t) = (e-1)t$ and $w(t) = 2(1 + \frac{1}{e-1})t$. Then, the radii are

$$\rho_1 = 0.3030, \, \rho_2 = 0.1033 = \rho \text{ and } \rho_3 = 0.1461.$$

Example 3. If $X = C[0,1]$ is equipped with the max-norm, $\Omega = U[0,1]$, consider $G : \Omega \longrightarrow E_1$ given as

$$G(\lambda)(x) = \varphi(x) - 6\int_0^1 x\tau \lambda(\tau)^3 d\tau. \tag{53}$$

We obtain

$$G'(\lambda(\xi))(x) = \xi(x) - 18\int_0^1 x\tau \lambda(\tau)^2 \xi(\tau) d\tau, \text{ for each } \xi \in D.$$

Clearly, $x_* = 0$ and the conditions (C1)–(C3) hold for $w_0(t) = 9t$ and $w(t) = 18t$. Then, the radii are

$$\rho_1 = 0.0556, \ \rho_2 = 0.0089 = \rho \text{ and } \rho_3 = 0.0206.$$

6. Semi-Local Convergence of Method

As in the local case, we use some functions and parameters for the method (23).
Suppose:
There exists function $v_0 : S \longrightarrow \mathbb{R}$ that is continuous and non-decreasing such that equation

$$v_0(t) - 1 = 0$$

has a smallest solution $\tau_0 \in S - \{0\}$. Consider function $v : S_0 \longrightarrow \mathbb{R}$ to be continuous and non-decreasing. Define the scalar sequences for $\eta \geq 0$ and $\forall n = 0, 1, 2, \ldots$ by

$$
\begin{aligned}
t_0 &= 0, \ s_0 = \eta \\
u_n &= s_n + \frac{5\int_0^1 v(\theta(s_n - t_n)) d\theta(s_n - t_n)}{1 - v_0(t_n)}, \\
t_{n+1} &= u_n + \frac{1}{1 - v_0(t_n)}[(1 + \int_0^1 v_0(u_n + \theta(u_n - s_n)) d\theta(u_n - s_n) \\
&\quad + 3\int_0^1 v(\theta(s_n - t_n)) d\theta(s_n - t_n)] \\
s_{n+1} &= t_{n+1} + \frac{1}{1 - v_0(t_{n+1})}[\int_0^1 v(\theta(t_{n+1} - t_n)) d\theta(t_{n+1} - t_n) \\
&\quad + (1 + \int_0^1 v_0(\theta t_n) d\theta(t_{n+1} - s_n)].
\end{aligned}
\tag{54}
$$

This sequence is proven to be majorizing for method (23) in Theorem 4. However, first, we provide a general convergence result for sequence (54).

Lemma 2. Suppose that $\forall n = 0, 1, 2, \ldots$

$$v_0(t_n) < 1 \tag{55}$$

and there exists $\tau \in [0, \tau_0)$ such that

$$t_n \leq \tau. \tag{56}$$

Then, sequence $\{t_n\}$ converges to some $t_* \in [0, \tau]$.

Proof. It follows by (54)–(56) that sequence $\{t_n\}$ is non-decreasing and bounded from above by τ. Hence, it converges to its unique least upper bound t_*. □

Next, the operator F is related to the scalar functions.
Suppose the following:
(h1) There exists $x_0 \in \Omega$, $\eta \geq 0$ such that $F'(x_0)^{-1}L(B_2, B_1)$ and $\|F'(x_0)^{-1}F(x_0)\| \leq \eta$.
(h2) $\|F'(x_0)^{-1}(F'(x) - F'(x_0))\| \leq v_0(\|x - x_0\|)$ for all $x \in \Omega$.
Set $\Omega_3 = \Omega \cap U(x_0, \tau_0)$.
(h3) $\|F'(x_0)^{-1}(F'(y) - F'(x))\| \leq v(\|y - x\|)$ for all $x, y \in \Omega_3$.

(h4) Conditions of Lemma 2 hold.
and
(h5) $U[x_0, t_*] \subset \Omega$.

We present the semi-local convergence result for the method (23).

Theorem 4. *Suppose that conditions (h1)–(h5) hold. Then, sequence $\{x_n\}$ given by method (23) is well defined, remains in $U[x_0, t_*]$ and converges to a solution $x_* \in U[x_0, t_*]$ of equation $F(x) = 0$. Moreover, the following assertions hold:*

$$\|y_n - x_n\| \leq s_n - t_n, \tag{57}$$

$$\|z_n - y_n\| \leq u_n - s_n \tag{58}$$

and

$$\|x_{n+1} - z_n\| \leq t_{n+1} - u_n. \tag{59}$$

Proof. Mathematical induction is utilized to show estimates (57)–(59). Using (h1) and method (23) for $n = 0$

$$\|y_0 - x_0\| = \|F'(x_0)^{-1} F(x_0)\| \leq \eta = s_0 - t_0 \leq t_*.$$

Thus, the iterate $y_0 \in U[x_0, t_*]$ and (57) holds for $n = 0$.
Let $u \in U[x_0, t_*]$. Then, as in Theorem 3, we get

$$\|F'(u)^{-1} F'(x_0)\| \leq \frac{1}{1 - v_0(\|u - x_0\|)}. \tag{60}$$

Hence, if we set $u = x_0$, iterates y_0, z_0 and x_1 are well defined by method (23) for $n = 0$. Suppose iterates x_k, y_k, z_k, x_{k+1} also exist for all integer values k smaller than n. Then, we have the estimates

$$\begin{aligned}
\|z_n - y_n\| &= 5\|F'(x_n)^{-1} F(y_n)\| \\
&\leq \frac{5 \int_0^1 v(\theta \|y_n - x_n\|) d\theta \|y_n - x_n\|}{1 - v_0(\|x_n - x_0\|)} \\
&\leq \frac{5 \int_0^1 v(\theta \|s_n - t_n\|) d\theta (s_n - t_n)}{1 - v_0(t_n)} = u_n - s_n,
\end{aligned}$$

$$\begin{aligned}
\|x_{n+1} - z_n\| &= \left\| \frac{1}{5} F'(x_n)^{-1}(F(y_n) - F(z_n)) + 3 F'(x_n)^{-1} F(y_n) \right\| \\
&\leq \frac{1}{1 - v_0(\|x_n - x_0\|)} [(1 + \frac{1}{5} \int_0^1 v_0(\|z_n - x_0\| + \theta \|z_n - y_n\|) d\theta) \|y_n - x_n\| \\
&\quad + 3 \int_0^1 v(\theta \|y_n - x_n\|) d\theta \|y_n - x_n\|] \\
&\leq t_{n+1} - u_n
\end{aligned}$$

and

$$\begin{aligned}
\|y_{n+1} - x_{n+1}\| &= \|F'(x_{n+1})^{-1} F(x_{n+1})\| \\
&\leq \|F'(x_{n+1})^{-1} F'(x_0)\| \|F'(x_0)^{-1} F(x_{n+1})\| \\
&\leq \frac{1}{1 - v_0(\|x_{n+1} - x_0\|)} [\int_0^1 v(\theta \|x_{n+1} - x_n\|) d\theta \|x_{n+1} - x_n\| \\
&\quad + (1 + \int_0^1 v_0(\theta \|x_n - x_0\|) d\theta) \|x_{n+1} - y_n\|] \\
&\leq s_{n+1} - t_{n+1},
\end{aligned}$$

where we also used

$$F(y_n) = F(y_n) - F(x_n) - F'(x_n)(y_n - x_n)$$
$$= \int_0^1 [F'(x_n + \theta(y_n - x_n))d\theta - F'(x_n)](y_n - x_n),$$

so

$$\|F'(x_0)^{-1}F(y_n)\| \leq \int_0^1 v(\theta\|y_n - x_n\|)d\theta\|y_n - x_n\|$$

and

$$F(x_{n+1}) = F(x_{n+1}) - F(x_n) - F'(x_n)(y_n - x_n)$$
$$- F'(x_n)(x_{n+1} - x_n) + F'(x_n)(x_{n+1} - x_n)$$
$$= F(x_{n+1}) - F(x_n) - F'(x_n)(x_{n+1} - x_n) + F'(x_n)(x_{n+1} - y_n),$$

so

$$\begin{aligned}
\|F'(x_0)^{-1}F(x_{n+1})\| &\leq \int_0^1 v(\theta\|x_{n+1} - x_n\|)d\theta\|x_{n+1} - x_n\| \\
&\quad + (1 + v_0(\|x_n - x_0\|))\|x_{n+1} - y_n\| \\
&\leq \int_0^1 v(\theta(t_{n+1} - t_n))d\theta(t_{n+1} - t_n) \\
&\quad + (1 + v_0(t_n))(t_{n+1} - s_n), \quad (61) \\
\|z_n - x_0\| &\leq \|z_n - y_n\| + \|y_n - x_0\| \\
&\leq u_n - s_n + s_n - t_0 \leq t_*
\end{aligned}$$

and

$$\begin{aligned}
\|x_{n+1} - x_0\| &\leq \|x_{n+1} - z_n\| + \|z_n - x_0\| \\
&\leq t_{n+1} - u_n + u_n - t_0 \leq t_*.
\end{aligned}$$

Hence, sequence $\{t_n\}$ is majorizing for method (2) and iterates $\{x_n\}, \{y_n\}, \{z_n\}$ belong in $U[x_0, t_*]$. The sequence $\{x_n\}$ is complete in Banach space X and as such, it converges to some $x_* \in U[x_0, t_*]$. By using the continuity of F and letting $n \longrightarrow \infty$ in (61), we deduce $F(x_*) = 0$. □

Proposition 2. *Suppose:*
(i) There exists a solution $x_* \in U(x_0, \rho_2)$ of equation $F(x) = 0$ for some $\rho_2 > 0$.
(ii) Condition (h2) holds.
(iii) There exists $\rho_3 \geq \rho_2$ such that

$$\int_0^1 v_0((1-\theta)\rho_2 + \theta\rho_3)d\theta < 1. \quad (62)$$

Set $\Omega_4 = \Omega \cap U[x_0, \rho_3]$. Then, x_* is the only solution of equation $F(x) = 0$ in the region Ω_4.

Proof. Let $y_* \in \Omega_4$ with $F(y_*) = 0$. Define the linear operator $Q = \int_0^1 F'(x_* + \theta(y_* - x_*))d\theta$. Then, by (h2) and (62), we obtain in turn that

$$\begin{aligned}
\|F'(x_0)^{-1}(Q - F'(x_0))\| &\leq \int_0^1 v_0((1-\theta)\|x_0 - y_*\| + \theta\|x_0 - x_*\|)d\theta \\
&\leq \int_0^1 v_0((1-\theta)\rho_2 + \theta\rho_3)d\rho < 1.
\end{aligned}$$

Thus, $x_* = y_*$. □

The next two examples show how to choose the functions v_0, v, and the parameter η.

Example 4. Set $X = \mathbb{R}$. Let us consider a scalar function F defined on the set $\Omega = U[x_0, 1 - \mu]$ for $\mu \in (0, 1)$ by
$$F(x) = x^3 - \mu.$$

Choose $x_0 = 1$. Then, the conditions (h1)–(h3) are verified for $\eta = \frac{1-\mu}{3}, v_0(t) = (3-\mu)t$ and $v(t) = 2(1 + \frac{1}{3-\mu})t$.

Example 5. Consider $X = C[0, 1]$ and $\Omega = U[0, 1]$. Then the problem [5]
$$\Xi(0) = 0, \Xi(1) = 1,$$
$$\Xi'' = -\Xi - \iota\Xi^2$$
is also given as integral equation of the form
$$\Xi(q_2) = q_2 + \int_0^1 \Theta(q_2, q_1)(\Xi^3(q_1) + \iota\Xi^2(q_1))dq_1$$
where ι is a constant and $\Theta(q_2, q_1)$ is the Green's function
$$\Theta(q_2, q_1) = \begin{cases} q_1(1-q_2), & q_1 \leq q_2 \\ q_2(1-q_1), & q_2 < q_1. \end{cases}$$

Consider $F : \Omega \longrightarrow X$ as
$$[F(x)](q_2) = x(q_2) - q_2 - \int_0^1 \Theta(q_2, q_1)(x^3(q_1) + \iota x^2(q_1))dq_1.$$

Choose $\Xi_0(q_2) = q_2$ and $\Omega = U(\Xi_0, \epsilon_0)$. Then, clearly $U(\Xi_0, \epsilon_0) \subset U(0, \epsilon_0 + 1)$, since $\|\Xi_0\| = 1$. If $2\iota < 5$. Then, conditions (C1)–(C3) are satisfied for
$$w_0(t) = \frac{2\iota + 3\rho_0 + 6}{8}t, \quad w(t) = \frac{\iota + 6\rho_0 + 3}{4}t.$$

Hence, $w_0(t) \leq w(t)$.

7. Local Convergence of Method

The local analysis is using on certain parameters and real functions. Let L_0, L and α be positive parameters. Set $T_1 = [0, \frac{1}{(2+\alpha)L_0}]$ provided that $(2+\alpha)L_0 < 1$.
Define the function $h_1 : T_1 \longrightarrow \mathbb{R}$ by
$$h_1(t) = \frac{(1+\alpha)Lt}{1-(2+\alpha)L_0 t}.$$

Notice that parameter ρ
$$\rho = \frac{1}{(1+\alpha)L + (2+\alpha)L_0}$$
is the only solution of equation
$$h_1(t) - 1 = 0$$
in the set T_1.
Define the parameter ρ_0 by
$$\rho_0 = \frac{1}{(2+\alpha)(L_0 + L)}.$$

Notice that $\rho_0 < \rho$. Set $T_0 = [0, \rho_0]$.
Define the function $h_2 : T_0 \longrightarrow \mathbb{R}$ by

$$h_2(t) = \frac{(2 + 2\alpha + h_1(t))Lh_1(t)t}{1 - (2 + \alpha)(L_0 + L)t}.$$

The equation

$$h_2(t) - 1 = 0$$

has a smallest solution $\rho \in T_0 - \{0\}$ by the intermediate value theorem, since $h_2(0) - 1 = -1$ and $h_2(t) \longrightarrow \infty$ as $y \longrightarrow \rho_0^-$. It shall be shown that R is a radius of convergence for method (20). It follows by these definitions that $\forall t \in T_0$

$$0 \leq (L_0 + L)(2 + \alpha)t < 1 \tag{63}$$

$$0 \leq h_1(t) < 1 \tag{64}$$

and

$$0 \leq h_2(t) < 1. \tag{65}$$

The following conditions are used:
(C1) There exists a solution $x_* \in \Omega$ of equation $F(x) = 0$ such that $F'(x_*)^{-1} \in L(X, X)$.
(C2) There exist positive parameters L_0 and α such that $\forall v, z \in \Omega$

$$\|F'(x_*)^{-1}([v, z; F] - F'(x_*))\| \leq L_0(\|v - x_*\| + \|z - x_*\|)$$

and

$$\|F(x)\| \leq \alpha \|x - x_*\|.$$

Set $\Omega_1 = U(x_*, \rho) \cap \Omega$.
(C3) There exists a positive constant $L > 0$ such that $\forall x, y, v, z \in \Omega_1$

$$\|F'(x_*)^{-1}([x, y; F] - [v, z; F])\| \leq L(\|x - v\| + \|y - z\|)$$

and
(C4) $U[x_0, \rho] \subset \Omega$.

Next, the local convergence of method (20) is presented using the preceding terminology and conditions.

Theorem 5. *Under conditions (C1)–(C4), further suppose that $x_0 \in U(x_*, \rho)$. Then, the sequence $\{x_n\}$ generated by method (20) is well defined in $U(x_*, \rho)$, stays in $U(x_*, \rho)$ $\forall n = 0, 1, 2, \ldots$ and is convergent to x_* so that*

$$\|y_n - x_*\| \leq h_1(\|x_n - x_*\|)\|x_n - x_*\| \leq \|x_n - x_*\| < \Omega \tag{66}$$

and

$$\|x_{n+1} - x_*\| \leq h_2(\|x_n - x_*\|)\|x_n - x_*\| \leq \|x_n - x_*\|, \tag{67}$$

where the functions h_1, h_2 and the radius ρ are defined previously.

Proof. It follows by method (20), (C1), (C2) and $x_0 \in U(x_*, \rho)$ in turn that

$$\begin{aligned}
\|F'(x_*)^{-1}(A_0 - F'(x_*))\| &= \|F'(x_*)^{-1}([x_0, x_0 + F(x_0); F] - F'(x_*))\| \\
&\leq L_0(2\|x_0 - x_*\| + \|F(x_0) - F(x_*)\|) \\
&\leq L_0(2 + \alpha)\|x_0 - x_*\| \\
&< L_0(2 + \alpha)\rho. \tag{68}
\end{aligned}$$

It follows by (68) and the Banach lemma on invertible operators [24] that $A_0^{-1} \in L(X, X)$ and

$$\|A_0^{-1}F'(x_*)\| \leq \frac{1}{1-(2+\alpha)L_0\|x_0-x_*\|}. \tag{69}$$

Hence, the iterate y_0 exists by the first substep of method (20) for $n=0$. It follows from the first substep of method (20), (C2) and (C3), that

$$\begin{aligned}
\|y_0 - x_*\| &\leq \|x_0 - x_* - A_0^{-1}F(x_0)\| \\
&\quad \|A_0^{-1}F'(x_*)F'(x_*)^{-1}(A_0 - (F(x_0) - F(x_*)))(x - 0 - x_*)\| \\
&\leq \|A_0^{-1}F'(x_*)\|\|F'(x_*)^{-1}(A_0 - (F(x_0) - F(x_*)))\|\|x_0 - x_*\| \\
&\leq \frac{L(\|x_0 - x_*\| + \|F(x_0) - F(x_*)\|)}{1 - L_0(2+\alpha)\|x_0 - x_*\|} \tag{70} \\
&\leq h_1(\|x_0 - x_*\|)\|x_0 - x_*\| \leq \|x_0 - x_*\| < \rho.
\end{aligned}$$

Thus, the iterate $y_0 \in U(x_*, \rho)$ and (66) holds for $n = 0$. Similarly, by the second substep of method (20), we have

$$\begin{aligned}
\|F'(x_*)^{-1}(B_0 - F'(x_*))\| &= \|F'(x_*)^{-1}([y_0, w_0; F] \\
&\quad -[y_0, x_0; F] - [x_0, w_0; F] - [x_*, x_*; F])\| \\
&\leq L\|y_0 - w_0\| + L_0(\|y_0 - x_*\| + \|w_0 - x_*\|) \\
&\leq L(\|y_0 - x_*\| + \|w_0 - x_*\|) + L_0(\|y_0 - x_*\| + \|w_0 - x_*\|) \\
&\leq (L+L_0)(2+\alpha)\rho \leq \frac{L+L_0}{L+L_0} = 1. \tag{71}
\end{aligned}$$

Hence, $B_0^{-1} \in L(X,X)$ and

$$\|B_0^{-1}F'(x_*)\| \leq \frac{1}{1-(L+L_0)(2+\alpha)\|x_0-x_*\|}. \tag{72}$$

Thus, the iterate x_1 exists by the second sub-step of method (20). Then, as in (70) we obtain in turn that

$$\begin{aligned}
\|x_1 - x_*\| &\leq \|y_0 - x_* - B_0^{-1}F(y_0)\| \\
&\leq \|B_0^{-1}F'(x_*)\|\|F'(x_*)^{-1}(B_0 - (F(y_0) - F(x_*)))\|\|y_0 - x_*\| \\
&\leq \frac{\|F'(x_*)^{-1}([y_0, w_0; F] + [y_0, x_0; F] - [x_0, w_0; F] - [y_0, x_* : F])\|}{1-(L+L_0)(2+\alpha)\|x_0 - x_*\|} \\
&\quad \|y_0 - x_*\| \\
&\leq \frac{L(2 + 2\alpha + h_2(\|x_0 - x_*\|))\|x_0 - x_*\|}{1-(L+L_0)(2+\alpha)\|x_0 - x_*\|} h_1(\|x_0 - x_*\|) \\
&\quad \|x_0 - x_*\| \tag{73} \\
&\leq h_2(\|x_0 - x_*\|)\|x_0 - x_*\| \leq \|x_0 - x_*\| < \rho.
\end{aligned}$$

Therefore, the iterate $x_1 \in U(x_*, \rho)$ and (67) holds for $n=0$.
Simply replace x_0, y_0, x_1 by x_m, y_m, x_{m+1} $\forall m = 0, 1, 2 \ldots$ in the preceding calculations to complete the induction for (66) and (67). It then follows from the estimate

$$\|x_{m+1} - x_*\| \leq \mu\|x_m - x_*\| < \rho, \tag{74}$$

where, $\mu = h_2(\|x_0 - x_*\|) \in [0,1)$ leading to $x_{m+1} \in U(x_*, \rho)$ and $\lim_{m \to \infty} x_m = x_*$. □

Concerning the uniqueness of the solution x_* (not given in [9]), we provide the result.

Proposition 3. *Suppose:*
(i) The point x_* is a simple solution $x_* \in U(x_*, r) \subset \Omega$ for some $r > 0$ of equation $F(x) = 0$.
(ii) There exists positive parameter L_1 such that $\forall y \in \Omega$

$$\|F'(x_*)^{-1}([x_*, y; F] - F'(x_*))\| \leq L_1 \|y - x_*\| \tag{75}$$

(iii) There exists $r_1 \geq r$ such that
$$L_1 r_1 < 1. \tag{76}$$

Set $\Omega_2 = U[x_*, r_1] \cap \Omega$. Then, x_* is the only solution of equation $F(x) = 0$ in the set Ω_2.

Proof. Set $P = [x_*, y_*; F]$ for some $y_* \in D_2$ with $F(y_*) = 0$. It follows by (i), (75) and (76) that

$$\|F'(x_*)^{-1}(P - F'(x_*))\| \leq L_1 \|y_* - x_*\|) < 1.$$

Thus, we conclude $x_* = y_*$ by the invertability of P and identity $P(x_* - y_*) = F(x_*) - F(y_*) = 0$. □

Remark 4. *(i) Notice that not all conditions of Theorem 5 are used in Proposition 3. If they were, then we can set $r_1 = \rho$.*
(ii) By the definition of set Ω_1 we have

$$\Omega_1 \subset \Omega. \tag{77}$$

Therefore, the parameter
$$L \leq L_2, \tag{78}$$

where L_2 is the corresponding Lipschitz constant in [1,3,9,19] appearing in the condition $\forall x, y, z \in \Omega$

$$\|F'(x_*)^{-1}([x, y; F] - [v, z; F])\| \leq L_2(\|x - v\| + \|y - z\|). \tag{79}$$

Thus, the radius of convergence R_0 in [1,7,8,20] uses L_2 instead of L. That is by (78)

$$R_0 \leq \rho. \tag{80}$$

Examples where (77), (78) and (80) are strict can be found in [2,5,11–13,15,21–24].

8. Majorizing Sequences for Method

Let K_0, K, be given positive parameters and $\delta \in [0, 1)$, $K_0 \leq K$, $\eta \geq 0$, and $T = [0, 1)$. Consider recurrent polynomials defined on the interval T for $n = 1, 2, \ldots$ by

$$
\begin{aligned}
f_n^{(1)}(t) &= Kt^{2n}\eta + Kt^{2n-1}\eta + 2K_0(1 + t + \ldots + t^{2n+1})\eta \\
&\quad + K_0(t^{2n+1} + 2t^{2n})t^{2n+1}\eta + \delta - 1, \\
f_n^{(2)}(t) &= Kt^{2n+1}\eta + K(t^{2n+1} + 2t^{2n})t^{2n}\eta \\
&\quad + 2K_0(1 + t + \ldots + t^{2n+2})\eta + \delta - 1, \\
g_n^{(1)}(t) &= Kt^3 + Kt^2 - Kt - K + 2K_0(t^3 + t^4) \\
&\quad + K_0(t^{2n+3} + 2t^{n+2})t^4\eta - K_0(t^{2n+1} + 2t^{2n})t^2\eta, \\
g_n^{(2)}(t) &= Kt^3 + K(t^3 + 2t^2)t^{2n+2}\eta \\
&\quad + 2K_0(t^3 + t^4) - Kt - K(t + 2)t^{2n}\eta, \\
h_{n+1}^{(1)}(t) &= g_{n+1}^{(1)}(t) - g_n^{(1)}(t), \\
h_{n+1}^{(2)}(t) &= g_{n+1}^{(2)}(t) - g_n^{(2)}(t),
\end{aligned}
$$

and polynomials

$$g_\infty^{(1)}(t) = g_1(t) = Kt^3 + Kt^2 - Kt - K + 2K_0(t^3 + t^4),$$

$$g_\infty^{(2)}(t) = g_2(t) = Kt^3 + 2K_0(t^3 + t^4) - Kt = g_3(t)t$$

and

$$g(t) = (t-1)^2(t^5 + 4t^4 + 6t^3 + 6t^2 + 5t + 2).$$

Then, the following auxiliary result connecting these polynomials can be shown.

Lemma 3. *The following assertions hold:*

$$f_{n+1}^{(1)}(t) = f_n^{(1)}(t) + g_n^{(1)}(t)t^{2n-1}\eta, \tag{81}$$

$$f_{n+1}^{(2)}(t) = f_n^{(2)}(t) + g_n^{(2)}(t)t^{2n}\eta, \tag{82}$$

$$h_{n+1}^{(1)}(t) = g(t)K_0 t^{2n+2}\eta, \tag{83}$$

$$h_{n+1}^{(2)}(t) = g(t)Kt^{2n}\eta, \tag{84}$$

polynomials g_1 and g_2 have smallest zeros in the interval $T - \{0\}$ denoted by ξ_1 and α_2, respectively,

$$h_{n+1}^{(1)}(t) \geq 0 \ \forall t \in [0, \xi_1) \tag{85}$$

and

$$h_{n+1}^{(2)}(t) \geq 0 \ \forall \ t \in [0, \xi_2). \tag{86}$$

Moreover, define functions on the interval T by

$$g_\infty^{(1)}(t) = \lim_{n \to \infty} g_n^{(1)}(t) \tag{87}$$

and

$$g_\infty^{(2)}(t) = \lim_{n \to \infty} g_n^{(2)}(t). \tag{88}$$

Then,

$$g_\infty^{(1)}(t) = g_1(t) \ \forall t \in [0, \alpha_1), \tag{89}$$

$$g_\infty^{(2)}(t) = g_2(t) \ \forall \ t \in [0, \alpha_2), \tag{90}$$

$$f_{n+1}^{(1)}(t) \leq f_n^{(1)}(t) + g_1(t)t^{2n-1}\eta \ \forall \ t \in [0, \xi_1), \tag{91}$$

$$f_{n+1}^{(2)}(t) \leq f_n^{(2)}(t) + g_2(t)t^{2n}\eta \ \forall \ t \in [0, \xi_2), \tag{92}$$

$$f_{n+1}^{(1)}(\xi_1) \leq f_n^{(1)}(\xi_1), \tag{93}$$

and

$$f_{n+1}^{(2)}(\xi_2) \leq f_n^{(2)}(\xi_2). \tag{94}$$

Proof. Assertions (81)–(84) hold by the definition of these functions and basic algebra. By the intermediate value theorem polynomials g_1 and g_3 have zeros in the interval $T - \{0\}$, since $g_1(0) = -K$, $g_1(1) = 4K_0$, $g_2(0) = -K$ and $g_2(1) = 4K_0$. Then, assertions (85) and (86) follow by the definition of these polynomials and zeros ξ_1 and ξ_2. Next, assertions (91) and (94) also follow from (87), (88) and the definition of these polynomials. □

The preceding result is connected to the scalar sequence defined $\forall n = 0, 1, 2, \ldots$ by $t_0 = 0, s_0 = \eta$,

$$\begin{aligned} t_1 &= s_0 + \frac{K(\eta + \delta)\eta}{1 - K_0(2\eta + \delta)}, \\ s_{n+1} &= t_{n+1} + \frac{K(t_{n+1} - t_n + s_n - t_n)(t_{n+1} - s_n)}{1 - K_0(2t_{n+1} + \gamma_n + \delta)} \\ t_{n+2} &= s_{n+1} + \frac{K(s_{n+1} - t_{n+1} + \gamma_n)(s_{n+1} - t_{n+1})}{1 - K_0(2s_{n+1} + \delta)}, \end{aligned} \quad (95)$$

where $\gamma_n = K(t_{n+1} - t_n + s_n - t_n)(t_{n+1} - s_n)$, $\delta \geq \gamma_0$.

Moreover, define parameters $\xi_1 = \frac{K(s_1 - t_1 + \gamma_0)}{1 - K_0(2s_1 + \delta)}$, $\xi_2 = \frac{K(t_1 + s_0)}{1 - K_0(2t_1 + \gamma_0 + \delta)}$ and $a = \max\{\xi_1, \xi_2\}$,
Then, the first convergence result for sequence $\{t_n\}$ follows.

Lemma 4. *Suppose*

$$K\eta \leq 1, \; 0 < \xi_1, \; 0 < \xi_2, \; a < \xi < 1, \quad (96)$$

$$f_1^{(1)}(\xi_1) \leq 0 \quad (97)$$

and

$$f_2^{(1)}(\xi_2) \leq 0. \quad (98)$$

Then, scalar sequence $\{t_n\}$ is non-decreasing, bounded from above by $t_{**} = \frac{\eta}{1-\xi}$, and converges to its unique least upper bound $t_* \in [0, t_{**}]$. Moreover, the following error bounds hold

$$0 < t_{n+1} - s_n \leq \xi(s_n - t_n) \leq \xi^{2n+1}\eta, \quad (99)$$

$$0 < s_n - t_n \leq \xi(t_n - s_{n-1}) \leq \xi^{2n}\eta \quad (100)$$

and

$$\gamma_{n+1} \leq \gamma_n \leq \gamma_0. \quad (101)$$

Proof. Assertions (99)–(101) hold if we show using induction that

$$0 < \frac{K(t_{n+1} - t_n + s_n - t_n)}{1 - K_0(2t_{n+1} + \gamma_n + \delta)} \leq \xi_1, \quad (102)$$

$$0 < \frac{K(s_{n+1} - t_{n+1} + \gamma_n)}{1 - K_0(2s_{n+1} + \delta)} \leq \xi_2, \quad (103)$$

and

$$t_n \leq s_n \leq t_{n+1}. \quad (104)$$

By the definition of t_1, we obtain

$$\frac{t_1}{s_0} = \frac{1 - K\eta}{1 - K_0(2\eta + \delta)} > 1,$$

so $s_0 < t_1$, and (103) holds for $n = 0$. Suppose assertions (101)–(103) hold for each $m = 0, 1, 2, 3, \ldots, n$. By (99) and (100) we have

$$\begin{aligned} s_m &\leq t_m + \xi^{2m}\eta \leq s_{m-1} + \xi^{2m-1}\eta + \xi^{2m}\eta \\ &\leq \eta + \xi\eta + \ldots + \xi^{2m}\eta \\ &= \frac{1 - \xi^{2m+1}}{1 - \xi}\eta \leq t_{**} \end{aligned} \quad (105)$$

and

$$
\begin{aligned}
t_{m+1} &\leq s_m + \xi^{2m+1}\eta \leq t_m + \xi^{2m+1}\eta + \xi^{2m}\eta \\
&\leq \eta + \xi\eta + \ldots + \xi^{2m+1}\eta \\
&= \frac{1-\xi^{2m+2}}{1-\xi}\eta \leq t_{**}.
\end{aligned}
\qquad (106)
$$

By the induction hypotheses sequences $\{t_m\}, \{s_m\}$ are increasing. Evidently, estimate (101) holds if

$$K\xi^{2m+1}\eta + K\xi^{2m}\eta + 2K_0\xi\frac{1-\xi^{2m+2}}{1-\xi}\eta$$
$$+K_0\xi\delta + \xi\gamma_m K_0 - \xi \leq 0$$

or

$$f_m^{(1)}(t) \leq 0 \text{ at } t = \xi_1, \qquad (107)$$

where $\gamma_m \leq K(\xi^{2m+1} + 2\xi^{2m})\xi^{2m+1}\eta^2$. By (91), (93), and (98) estimate (107) holds.

Similarly, assertion (103) holds if

$$K\xi^{2m+2}\eta + K^2(\xi^{2m+1}\eta + 2\xi^{2m}\eta)\xi^{2m+1}\eta$$
$$+2\xi K_0(1+\xi+\ldots+\xi^{2m+2})\eta + \delta\xi - \xi \leq 0$$

or

$$f_m^{(2)}(t) \leq 0 \text{ at } t = \xi_2. \qquad (108)$$

By (92) and (94), assertion (108) holds. Hence, (100) and (103) also hold. Notice that γ_n can be written as $\gamma_n = K(E_n + E_n^1)E_n^2$, where $E_n = t_{n+1} - t_n > 0$, $E_n^1 = s_n - t_n$, and $E_n^2 = t_{n+1} - s_n > 0$. Hence, we get

$$E_{n+1} - E_n = t_{n+2} - 2t_{n+1} + t_n \leq \xi^{2n}(\xi^2 - 1)(\xi+1)\eta < 0,$$

$$E_{n+1}^1 - E_n^1 = s_{n+1} - t_{n+1} - (s_n - t_n) \leq \xi^{2n}(\xi^2 - 1)\eta < 0,$$

and

$$E_{n+1}^2 - E_n^2 = t_{n+2} - s_{n+1} - (t_{n+1} - s_n) \leq \xi^{2n+1}(\xi^2 - 1)\eta < 0,$$

so

$$\gamma_{n+1} \leq \gamma_n \leq \gamma_0.$$

It follows that sequence $\{t_n\}$ is non-decreasing, bounded from above by t_{**}. Thus, it converges to t_*. □

Next, a second convergence result for sequence (95) is presented but the sufficient criteria are weaker but more difficult to verify than those of Lemma 4.

Lemma 5. *Suppose*

$$K_0\delta < 1, \qquad (109)$$

$$K_0(2t_{n+1} + \gamma_n + \delta) < 1, \qquad (110)$$

and

$$K_0(2s_{n+1} + \delta) < 1 \qquad (111)$$

hold. Then, sequence $\{t_n\}$ is increasing and bounded from above by $t_1^{**} = \frac{1-K_0\delta}{2K_0}$, so it converges to its unique least upper bound $t_1^* \in [0, t_1^{**}]$.

Proof. It follows from the definition of sequence (95), and conditions (109)–(111). □

9. Semi-Local Convergence of Method

The conditions (C) shall be used in the semi-local convergence analysis of method (20).

Suppose

(C1) There exist $x_0 \in \Omega, \eta \geq 0, \delta \in [0,1)$ such that $A_0^{-1} \in L(X,X)$, $\|A_0^{-1}F(x_0)\| \leq \eta$, and $\|F(x_0)\| \leq \delta$.

(C2) There exists $K_0 > 0$ such that for all $u, v \in \Omega$

$$\|A_0^{-1}([u,v;F] - A_0)\| \leq K_0(\|u - x_0\| + \|v - w_0\|).$$

Set $\Omega_0 = U(x_0, \frac{1-K_0\delta}{2K_0}) \cap \Omega$ for $K_0\delta < 1$.

(C3) There exists $K > 0$ such that for all $u, v, \bar{u}, \bar{v} \in \Omega_0$

$$\|A_0^{-1}([u,v;F] - [\bar{u}, \bar{v}; F])\| \leq K(\|u - \bar{u}\| + \|v - \bar{v}\|).$$

(C4) $U[x_0, \rho + \delta] \subset \Omega$, where $\rho = \begin{cases} t_* + \gamma_0 \text{ or } t_{**}, & \text{if conditions of Lemma 4 hold} \\ t_1^* + \gamma_0 \text{ or } t_1^{**}, & \text{if conditions of Lemma 5 hold.} \end{cases}$

Remark 5. *The results in [19] are given in the non-affine form. The benefits of using affine invariant results over non-affine are well-known [1,5,11,21]. In particular, they assumed $\|A_0^{-1}\| \leq \beta$ and (C3)' $\|[x,y;F] - [\bar{x}, \bar{y}; F]\| \leq \bar{K}(\|x - \bar{x}\| + \|y - \bar{y}\|)$ holds for all $x, y, \bar{x}, \bar{y} \in \Omega$. By the definition of the set Ω_0, we get*

$$\Omega_0 \subset \Omega, \tag{112}$$

so

$$K_0 \leq \beta\bar{K} \tag{113}$$

and

$$K \leq \beta\bar{K}. \tag{114}$$

Hence, K can replace $\beta\bar{K}$ in the results in [19]. Notice also that using (C3)' they estimated

$$\|B_{n+1}^{-1}A_0\| \leq \frac{1}{1 - \beta\bar{K}(2\bar{s}_{n+1} + \delta)} \tag{115}$$

and

$$\|A_0^{-1}(A_{n+1} - A_0)\| \leq \frac{1}{1 - \beta\bar{K}(\bar{t}_{n+1} - \bar{t}_0) + \tilde{\gamma}_n + \delta)}, \tag{116}$$

where $\{\bar{t}_n\}$, $\{\bar{s}_n\}$ are defined for $n = 0, 1, 2, \ldots$ by $\bar{t}_0 = 0$, $\bar{s}_0 = \eta$,

$$\begin{aligned} \bar{t}_1 &= \bar{s}_0 + \frac{\beta\bar{K}(\eta + \delta)\eta}{1 - \beta\bar{K}(2\bar{s}_0 + \delta)}, \\ \bar{s}_{n+1} &= \bar{t}_{n+1} + \frac{\beta\tilde{\gamma}}{1 - \beta\bar{K}(2\bar{t}_{n+1} + \tilde{\gamma}_n + \delta)} \\ \bar{t}_{n+2} &= \bar{s}_{n+1} + \frac{\beta\bar{K}(\bar{s}_{n+1} - \bar{t}_{n+1} + \tilde{\gamma}_n)(\bar{s}_{n+1} - \bar{t}_{n+1})}{1 - \beta\bar{K}(2\bar{s}_{n+1} + \delta)}, \end{aligned} \tag{117}$$

where $\tilde{\gamma}_n = \bar{K}(\bar{t}_{n+1} - \bar{t}_n + \bar{s}_n - \bar{t}_n)(\bar{t}_{n+1} - \bar{s}_n)$, $\delta \geq \tilde{\gamma}_0$. But using the weaker condition (C2) we obtain respectively,

$$\|B_{n+1}^{-1}A_0\| \leq \frac{1}{1 - K_0(2s_{n+1} + \delta)} \tag{118}$$

and

$$\|A_0^{-1}(A_{n+1} - A_0)\| \leq \frac{1}{1 - K_0(t_{n+1} - t_0 + \gamma_n + \delta)} \tag{119}$$

which are tighter estimates than (115) and (116), respectively. Hence, K_0, K can replace $\beta\bar{K}, \beta, \bar{K}$ and (118), (119) can replace (115), (116), respectively, in the proof of Theorem 3 in [19]. Examples where (112)–(114) are strict can be found in [1,5,11,21]. Simple induction shows that

$$0 < s_n - t_n \leq \bar{s}_n - \bar{t}_n \tag{120}$$

$$0 < t_{n+1} - s_n \leq \bar{t}_{n+1} - \bar{s}_n \tag{121}$$

and

$$t_* \leq \bar{t}^* = \lim_{n \to \infty} \bar{t}_n. \tag{122}$$

These estimates justify the claims made at the introduction of this work along the same lines. The local results in [19] can also be extended using our technique.

Next, we present the semi-local convergence result for the method (20).

Theorem 6. *Suppose that conditions (C) hold. Then, iteration $\{x_n\}$ generated by method (20) exists in $U[x_0, t_*]$, remains in $U[x_0, t_*]$ and $\lim_{n \to \infty} x_n = x_* \in U[x_0, t_*]$ with $F(x_*) = 0$, so that*

$$\|x_n - x_*\| \leq t_* - t_n.$$

Proof. It follows from the comment above Theorem 6. □

Next, we present the uniqueness of the solution result, where conditions (C) are not necessarily utilized.

Proposition 4. *Suppose the following:*
(i) There exists a simple solution $x_* \in U(x_0, r) \subset \Omega$ for some $r > 0$.
(ii) Condition (C2) holds
and
(iii) There exists $r^* \geq r$ such that $K_0(r + r^* + \delta) < 1$.

Set $\Omega_1 = U(x_0, \frac{1 - K_0(\delta + r)}{K_0}) \cap \Omega$. Then, the element x_* is the only solution of equation $F(x) = 0$ in the region Ω_1.

Proof. Let $z^* \in \Omega_1$ with $F(z^*) = 0$. Define $Q = [x_*, z^*; F]$. Then, in view of (ii) and (iii),

$$\|A_0^{-1}(Q - A_0)\| \leq K_0(\|x_* - x_0\| + \|z^* - w_0\|) \leq K_0(r + r^* + \delta) < 1.$$

Therefore, we conclude $z^* = x_*$ is a consequence of the invertibility of Q and the identity $Q(x_* - z^*) = F(x_*) - F(z^*) = 0$. □

Remark 6. *(i) Notice that r can be chosen to be t_*.*
(ii) The results can be extended further as follows. Replace
$(C3)''$ $\|A_0^{-1}([u, v; F] - [\bar{u}, \bar{v}; F])\| \leq \tilde{K}(\|u - \bar{u}\| + \|v - \bar{v}\|), \forall u, \bar{u} \in \Omega_0, v = u - A(u)^{-1}F(u)$ and $\bar{v} = A(\bar{u})^{-1}F(\bar{u})$. Then, we have
(iii) $\tilde{K} \leq K$.

Another way is if we define the set $\Omega_2 = U(x_1, \frac{1 - K_0(\delta + \gamma_0)}{2K_0} - \eta)$ provided that $K_0(\delta + \gamma_0) < 1$. Moreover, suppose $\Omega_2 \subset \Omega$. Then, we have $\Omega_2 \subset \Omega_0$ if condition $(C3)''$ on Ω_2, say, with constant $\tilde{K}_0$. Then, we have that

$$\tilde{K}_0 \leq K$$

also holds. Hence, tighter $\tilde{K}$ or $\tilde{K}_0$ can replace K in Theorem 6.

10. Conclusions

The convergence analysis is developed for generalized three-step numerical methods. The advantages of the new approach include weaker convergence criteria and a uniform set of conditions utilizing information on these methods in contrast to earlier works on special cases of these methods, where the existence of high-order derivatives is assumed to prove convergence. The methodology is very general and does not depend on the methods.

That is why it can be applied to multi-step and other numerical methods that shall be the topic of future work.

The weak point of this methodology is the observation that the computation of the majorant functions "*h*" at this generality is hard in general. Notice that this is not the case for the special cases of method (2) or method (3) given below them (see, for example, Examples 4 and 5). As far as we know, there is no other methodology that can be compared to the one introduced in this article to handle the semi-local or the local convergence of method (2) or method (3) at this generality.

Author Contributions: Conceptualization, M.I.A., I.K.A., S.R. and S.G.; methodology, M.I.A., I.K.A., S.R. and S.G.; software, M.I.A., I.K.A., S.R. and S.G.; validation, M.I.A., I.K.A., S.R. and S.G.; formal analysis, M.I.A., I.K.A., S.R. and S.G.; investigation, M.I.A., I.K.A., S.R. and S.G.; resources, M.I.A., I.K.A., S.R. and S.G.; data curation, M.I.A., I.K.A., S.R. and S.G.; writing—original draft preparation, M.I.A., I.K.A., S.R. and S.G.; writing—review and editing, M.I.A., I.K.A., S.R. and S.G.; visualization, M.I.A., I.K.A., S.R. and S.G.; supervision, M.I.A., I.K.A., S.R. and S.G.; project administration, M.I.A., I.K.A., S.R. and S.G.; funding acquisition, M.I.A., I.K.A., S.R. and S.G. All authors have read and agreed to the published version of the manuscript.

Funding: This research received no external funding.

Institutional Review Board Statement: Not applicable.

Informed Consent Statement: Not applicable.

Data Availability Statement: Not applicable.

Conflicts of Interest: The authors declare no conflict of interest.

References

1. Appell, J.; DePascale, E.; Lysenko, J.V.; Zabrejko, P.P. New results on Newton-Kantorovich approximations with applications to nonlinear integral equations. *Numer. Funct. Anal. Optim.* **1997**, *18*, 1–17. [CrossRef]
2. Ezquerro, J.A.; Hernandez, M.A. *Newton's Method: An Updated Approach of Kantorovich's Theory*; Birkhäuser: Cham Switzerland, 2018.
3. Proinov, P.D. New general convergence theory for iterative processes and its applications to Newton-Kantorovich type theorems. *J. Complex.* **2010**, *26*, 3–42. [CrossRef]
4. Regmi, S.; Argyros, I.K.; George, S.; Argyros, C. Numerical Processes for Approximating Solutions of Nonlinear Equations. *Axioms* **2022**, *11*, 307. [CrossRef]
5. Argyros, I.K. *The Theory and Applications of Iteration Methods*, 2nd ed.; Engineering Series; CRC Press: Boca Raton, FL, USA; Taylor and Francis Group: Abingdon, UK, 2022.
6. Zhanlav, K.H.; Otgondorj, K.H.; Sauul, L. A unified approach to the construction of higher-order derivative-free iterative methods for solving systems of nonlinear equations. *Int. J. Comput. Math.* **2021**.
7. Zhanlav, T.; Chun, C.; Otgondorj, K.H.; Ulziibayar, V. High order iterations for systems of nonlinear equations. *Int. J. Comput. Math.* **2020**, *97*, 1704–1724. [CrossRef]
8. Wang, X. An Ostrowski-type method with memory using a novel self-accelerating parameters. *J. Comput. Appl. Math.* **2018**, *330*, 710–720. [CrossRef]
9. Moccari, M.; Lofti, T. On a two-step optimal Steffensen-type method: Relaxed local and semi-local convergence analysis and dynamical stability. *J. Math. Anal. Appl.* **2018**, *468*, 240–269. [CrossRef]
10. Shakhno, S.M.; Gnatyshyn, O.P. On an iterative Method of order 1.839... for solving nonlinear least squares problems. *Appl. Math. Comput.* **2005**, *161*, 253–264.
11. Argyros, I.K. Unified Convergence Criteria for Iterative Banach Space Valued Methods with Applications. *Mathematics* **2021**, *9*, 1942. [CrossRef]
12. Potra, F.-A.; Pták, V. *Nondiscrete Induction and Iterative Processes*; Pitman Publishing: Boston, MA, USA, 1984.
13. Cordero, A.; Torregrosa, J.R. Variants of Newton's method using fifth-order quadrature formulas. *Appl. Math. Comput.* **2007**, *190*, 686–698. [CrossRef]
14. Traub, J.F. *Iterative Methods for the Solution of Equations*; Prentice Hall: Hoboken, NJ, USA, 1964.
15. Kantorovich, L.V.; Akilov, G.P. *Functional Analysis*; Pergamon Press: Oxford, UK, 1982.
16. Xiao, X.; Yin, H. Achieving higher order of convergence for solving systems of nonlinear equations. *Appl. Math. Comput.* **2017**, *311*, 251–261. [CrossRef]
17. Sharma, J.R.; Arora, H. Efficient derivative-free numerical methods for solving systems of nonlinear equations. *Comput. Appl. Math.* **2016**, *35*, 269–284. [CrossRef]

18. Sharma, J.R.; Guha, R.K. Simple yet efficient Newton-like method for systems of nonlinear equations. *Calcolo* **2016**, *53*, 451–473. [CrossRef]
19. Noor, M.A.; Waseem, M. Some iterative methods for solving a system of nonlinear equations. *Comput. Math. Appl.* **2009**, *57*, 101–106. [CrossRef]
20. Wang, X.; Zhang, T. A family of Steffensen type methods with seventh-order convergence. *Numer. Algor.* **2013**, *62*, 429–444. [CrossRef]
21. Argyros, I.K.; Magréñan, A.A. *A Contemporary Study of Iterative Methods*; Elsevier: Amsterdam, The Netherlands; Academic Press: New York, NY, USA, 2018.
22. Grau-Sanchez, M.; Grau, A.; Noguera, M. Ostrowski type methods for solving system of nonlinear equations. *Appl. Math. Comput.* **2011**, *218*, 2377–2385. [CrossRef]
23. Homeier, H.H.H. A modified Newton method with cubic convergence: The multivariate case. *J. Comput. Appl. Math.* **2004**, *169*, 161–169. [CrossRef]
24. Kou, J.; Wang, X.; Li, Y. Some eight order root finding three-step methods. *Commun. Nonlinear Sci. Numer. Simul.* **2010**, *15*, 536–544. [CrossRef]
25. Verma, R. *New Trends in Fractional Programming*; Nova Science Publisher: New York, NY, USA, 2019.

Article

A Methodology for Obtaining the Different Convergence Orders of Numerical Method under Weaker Conditions

Ioannis K. Argyros [1], Samundra Regmi [2], Stepan Shakhno [3,*] and Halyna Yarmola [4]

[1] Department of Mathematical Sciences, Cameron University, Lawton, OK 73505, USA
[2] Department of Mathematics, University of Houston, Houston, TX 77204, USA
[3] Department of Theory of Optimal Processes, Ivan Franko National University of Lviv, Universytetska Str. 1, 79000 Lviv, Ukraine
[4] Department of Computational Mathematics, Ivan Franko National University of Lviv, Universytetska Str. 1, 79000 Lviv, Ukraine
* Correspondence: stepan.shakhno@lnu.edu.ua

Abstract: A process for solving an algebraic equation was presented by Newton in 1669 and later by Raphson in 1690. This technique is called Newton's method or Newton–Raphson method and is even today a popular technique for solving nonlinear equations in abstract spaces. The objective of this article is to update developments in the convergence of this method. In particular, it is shown that the Kantorovich theory for solving nonlinear equations using Newton's method can be replaced by a finer one with no additional and even weaker conditions. Moreover, the convergence order two is proven under these conditions. Furthermore, the new ratio of convergence is at least as small. The same methodology can be used to extend the applicability of other numerical methods. Numerical experiments complement this study.

Keywords: nonlinear equation; criterion; integral equation; convergence

MSC: 49M15; 47H17; 65G99; 65H10; 65N12; 58C15

Citation: Argyros, I.K.; Regmi, S.; Shakhno, S.; Yarmola, H. A Methodology for Obtaining the Different Convergence Orders of Numerical Method under Weaker Conditions. *Mathematics* **2022**, *10*, 2931. https://doi.org/10.3390/math10162931

Academic Editors: Maria Isabel Berenguer and Manuel Ruiz Galán

Received: 22 July 2022
Accepted: 10 August 2022
Published: 14 August 2022

Publisher's Note: MDPI stays neutral with regard to jurisdictional claims in published maps and institutional affiliations.

Copyright: © 2022 by the authors. Licensee MDPI, Basel, Switzerland. This article is an open access article distributed under the terms and conditions of the Creative Commons Attribution (CC BY) license (https://creativecommons.org/licenses/by/4.0/).

1. Introduction

Given Banach spaces $\mathcal{U}, \mathcal{V}$. Let $L(\mathcal{U}, \mathcal{V})$ stand for the space of all continuous linear operators mapping $\mathcal{U}$ into $\mathcal{V}$. Consider differentiable as per Fréchet operator $\mathcal{L} : D \subseteq \mathcal{U} \longrightarrow \mathcal{V}$ and its corresponding nonlinear equation

$$\mathcal{L}(x) = 0, \qquad (1)$$

with D denoting a nonempty open set. The task of determining a solution $x^* \in D$ is very challenging but important, since applications from numerous computational disciplines are brought in form (1) [1,2]. The analytic form of x^* is rarely attainable. That is why mainly numerical methods are used generating approximations to solution x^*. Most of them are based on Newton's method [3–7]. Moreover, authors developed efficient high-order and multi-step algorithms with derivative [8–13] and divided differences [14–18].

Among these processes the most widely used is Newton's and its variants. In particular, Newton's Method (NM) is developed as

$$x_0 \in D, \; x_{n+1} = x_n - \mathcal{L}'(x_n)^{-1}\mathcal{L}(x_n) \; \forall \; n = 0, 1, 2, \ldots. \qquad (2)$$

There exists a plethora of results related to the study of NM [3,5–7,19–21]. These papers are based on the theory inaugurated by Kantorovich and its variants [21]. Basically, the conditions (K) are used in non-affine or affine invariant form. Suppose (K1) ∃ point $x_0 \in D$ and parameter $s \geq 0 : \mathcal{L}'(x_0)^{-1} \in L(\mathcal{V}, \mathcal{U})$, and

$$\|\mathcal{L}'(x_0)^{-1}\mathcal{L}(x_0)\| \leq s,$$

(K2) $\exists$ parameter $M_1 > 0$: Lipschitz condition

$$\|\mathcal{L}'(x_0)^{-1}(\mathcal{L}'(w_1) - \mathcal{L}'(w_2))\| \leq M_1\|w_1 - w_2\|$$

holds $\forall w_1 \in D$ and $w_2 \in D$,
(K3)

$$s \leq \frac{1}{2M_1}$$

and
(K4) $B[x_0, \rho] \subset D$, where parameter $\rho > 0$ is given later.

Denote $B[x_0, r] := \{x \in D : \|x - x_0\| \leq r\}$ for $r > 0$. Set $\rho = r_1 = \dfrac{1 - \sqrt{1 - 2M_1 s}}{M_1}$.

There are many variants of Kantorovich's convergence result for NM. One of these results follows [4,7,20].

Theorem 1. *Under conditions (K) for $\rho = r_1$; NM is contained in $B(x_0, r_1)$, convergent to a solution $x^* \in B[x_0, r_1]$ of Equation (1), and*

$$\|x_{n+1} - x_n\| \leq u_{n+1} - u_n.$$

Moreover, the convergence is linear if $s = \dfrac{1}{2M_1}$ and quadratic if $s < \dfrac{1}{2M_1}$. Furthermore, the solution is unique $B[x_0, r_1]$ in the first case and in $B(x_0, r_2)$ in the second case where $r_2 = \dfrac{1 + \sqrt{1 - 2M_1 s}}{M_1}$ and scalar sequence $\{u_n\}$ is given as

$$u_0 = 0,\ u_1 = s,\ u_{n+1} = u_n + \frac{M_1(u_n - u_{n-1})^2}{2(1 - M_1 u_n)}.$$

A plethora of studies have used conditions (K) [3–5,19,21–23].

Example 1. *Consider the cubic polynomial*

$$c(x) = x^3 - a$$

for $D = B(x_0, 1 - a)$ and parameter $a \in (0, \dfrac{1}{2})$. Select initial point $x_0 = 1$. Conditions (K) give $s = \dfrac{1-a}{3}$ and $M_1 = 2(2-a)$. It follows that estimate

$$\frac{1-a}{3} > \frac{1}{4(2-a)}$$

holds $\forall a \in (0, \dfrac{1}{2})$. That is condition (K3) is not satisfied. Therefore convergence is not assured by this theorem. However, NM may converge. Hence, clearly, there is a need to improve the results based on the conditions K.

By looking at the crucial sufficient condition (K3) for the convergence, (K4) and the majorizing sequence given by Kantorovich in the preceding Theorem 1 one sees that if the Lipschitz constants M_1 is replaced by a smaller one, say $L > 0$, than the convergence domain will be extended, the error distances $\|x_{n+1} - x_n\|$, $\|x_n - x^*\|$ will be tighter and the location of the solution more accurate. This replacement will also lead to fewer Newton iterates to reach a certain predecided accuracy (see the numerical Section). That is why with the new methodology, a new domain is obtained inside D that also contains the Newton iterates. However, then, L can replace M_1 in Theorem 1 to obtain the aforementioned extensions and benefits.

In this paper several avenues are presented for achieving this goal. The idea is to replace Lipschitz parameter M_1 by smaller ones.

(K5) Consider the center Lipschitz condition

$$\|\mathcal{L}'(x_0)^{-1}(\mathcal{L}'(w_1) - \mathcal{L}'(x_0))\| \leq M_0 \|w_1 - x_0\| \quad \forall w_1 \in D,$$

the set $D_0 = B[x_0, \frac{1}{M_0}] \cap D$ and the Lipschitz-2 condition

(K6)

$$\|\mathcal{L}'(x_0)^{-1}(\mathcal{L}'(w_1) - \mathcal{L}'(w_2))\| \leq M \|w_1 - w_2\| \quad \forall w_1, w_2 \in D_0.$$

These Lipschitz parameters are related as

$$M_0 \leq M_1, \tag{3}$$

$$M \leq M_1 \tag{4}$$

since

$$D_0 \subset D. \tag{5}$$

Notice also since parameters M_0 and M are specializations of parameter M_1, $M_1 = M_1(D)$, $M_0 = M_0(D)$, but $M = M(D_0)$. Therefore, no additional work is required to find M_0 and M (see also [22,23]). Moreover the ratio $\frac{M_0}{M}$ can be very small (arbitrarily). Indeed,

Example 2. *Define scalar function*

$$F(t) = b_0 t + b_1 + b_2 \sin e^{b_3 t},$$

for $t_0 = 0$, where b_j, $j = 0, 1, 2, 3$ are real parameters. It follows by this definition that for b_3 sufficiently large and b_2 sufficiently small, $\frac{M_0}{M_1}$ can be small (arbitrarily), i.e., $\frac{M_0}{M_1} \to 0$.

Then, clearly there can be a significant extension if parameters M_1 and M_0 or M and M_0 can be replace M_1 in condition (K3). Looking at this direction the following replacements are presented in a series of papers [19,22,23], respectively

(N2): $$s \leq \frac{1}{q_2},$$

(N3): $$s \leq \frac{1}{q_3},$$

and

(N4): $$s \leq \frac{1}{q_4},$$

where $q_1 = 2M_1$, $q_2 = M_1 + M_0$, $q_3 = \frac{1}{4}(4M_0 + M_1 + \sqrt{M_1^2 + 8M_1 M_0})$ and $q_4 = \frac{1}{4}(4M_0 + \sqrt{M_1^2 + 8M_0 M_1} + \sqrt{M_1 M_0})$. These items are related as follows:

$$q_4 \leq q_3 \leq q_2 \leq q_1,$$

$$(N2) \Rightarrow (N3) \Rightarrow (N4),$$

and as relation $\frac{M_0}{M_1} \to 0$,

$$\frac{q_2}{q_1} \to \frac{1}{2}, \frac{q_3}{q_2} \to \frac{1}{4}, \frac{q_4}{q_3} \to 0$$

and

$$\frac{q_4}{q_2} \longrightarrow 0.$$

Preceding items indicate the times (at most) one is improving the other. These are the extensions given in this aforementioned references. However, it turns out that parameter L can replace M_1 in these papers (see Section 3). Denote by $\tilde{N}, \tilde{q}$ the corresponding items. It follows

$$\frac{\tilde{q}_1}{q_1} = \frac{M}{M_1} \longrightarrow 0, \frac{\tilde{q}_2}{q_2} \longrightarrow 0, \frac{\tilde{q}_3}{q_3} \longrightarrow 0$$

for $\frac{M_0}{M_1} \longrightarrow 0$ and $\frac{M}{M_1} \longrightarrow 0$. Hence, the new results also extend the ones in the aforementioned references. Other extensions involve tighter majorizing sequences for NM (see Section 2) and improved uniqueness report for solution x^* (Section 3). The applications appear in Section 4 followed by conclusions in Section 5.

2. Majorizations

Let K_0, M_0, K, M be given positive parameters and s be a positive variable. The real sequence $\{t_n\}$ defined for $t_0 = 0$, $t_1 = s$, $t_2 = t_1 + \frac{K(t_1 - t_0)^2}{2(1 - K_0 t_1)}$ and $\forall n = 0, 1, 2, \ldots$ by

$$t_{n+2} = t_{n+1} + \frac{M(t_{n+1} - t_n)^2}{2(1 - M_0 t_{n+1})} \tag{6}$$

plays an important role in the study of NM, we adopted the notation $t_n(s) = t_n$ $\forall n = 1, 2, \ldots$. That is why some convergence results for it are listed in what follows next in this study.

Lemma 1. *Suppose conditions*

$$K_0 t_1 < 1 \text{ and } t_{n+1} < \frac{1}{M_0} \tag{7}$$

hold $\forall n = 1, 2, \ldots$. *Then, the following assertions hold*

$$t_n < t_{n+1} < \frac{1}{M_0} \tag{8}$$

and $\exists t^* \in [s, \frac{1}{M_0}]$ *such that* $\lim_{n \to \infty} t_n = t^*$.

Proof. The definition of sequence $\{t_n\}$ and the condition (7) implies (8). Moreover, increasing sequence $\{t_n\}$ has $\frac{1}{M_0}$ as an upper bound. Hence, it is convergent to its (unique) least upper bound t^*. □

Next, stronger convergence criteria are presented. However, these criteria are easier to verify than conditions of Lemma 1. Define parameter δ by

$$\delta = \frac{2M}{M + \sqrt{M^2 + 8M_0 M}}. \tag{9}$$

This parameter plays a role in the following results.
Case: $K_0 = M_0$ and $K = M$.
Part (i) of the next auxiliary result relates to the Lemma in [19].

Lemma 2. *Suppose condition*

$$s \leq \frac{1}{2M_2} \tag{10}$$

holds, where
$$M_2 = \frac{1}{4}(M + 4M_0 + \sqrt{M^2 + 8M_0 M}). \tag{11}$$

Then, the following assertions hold

(i) Estimates
$$t_{n+1} - t_n \leq \delta(t_n - t_{n-1}) \tag{12}$$
$$t_n < \frac{1 - \delta^{n+1}}{1 - \delta} s < \frac{s}{1 - \delta} \tag{13}$$

hold. Moreover, conclusions of Lemma 1 are true for sequence $\{t_n\}$. The sequence, $\{t_n\}$ converges linearly to $t^* \in (0, \frac{s}{1-\delta}]$. Furthermore, if for some $\mu > 0$
$$s < \frac{\mu}{(1+\mu)M_2}. \tag{14}$$

Then, the following assertions hold

(ii)
$$t_{n+1} - t_n \leq \frac{M}{2}(1+\mu)(t_n - t_{n-1})^2 \tag{15}$$

and
$$t_{n+1} - t_n \leq \frac{1}{\alpha}(\alpha s)^{2^n}, \tag{16}$$

where $\alpha = \frac{M}{2}(1+\mu)$ and the conclusions of Lemma 1 for sequence $\{t_n\}$ are true. The sequence, $\{t_n\}$ converges quadratically to t^*.

Proof. (i) It is given in [19].
(ii) Notice that condition (14) implies (11) by the choice of parameter μ. Assertion (15) holds if estimate
$$0 < \frac{M}{2(1 - M_0 t_{n+1})} \leq \frac{M}{2}(1+\mu) \tag{17}$$

is true. This estimate is true for $n = 1$, since it is equivalent to $M_0 s \leq \frac{\mu}{1+\mu}$. But this is true by $M_0 \leq 2M_2$, condition (11) and inequality $\frac{\mu M_0}{(1+\mu)2M_2} \leq \frac{\mu}{1+\mu}$. Then, in view of estimate (13), estimate (17) certainly holds provided that
$$(1+\mu)M_0(1 + \delta + \ldots + \delta^{n+1})s - \mu \leq 0. \tag{18}$$

This estimate motivates the introduction of recurrent polynomials p_n which are defined by
$$p_n(t) = (1+\mu)M_0(1 + t + \ldots + t^{n+1})s - \mu, \tag{19}$$

$\forall t \in [0,1)$. In view of polynomial p_n assertion (18) holds if
$$p_n(t) \leq 0 \text{ at } t = \delta. \tag{20}$$

The polynomials p_n are connected:
$$p_{n+1}(t) - p_n(t) = (1+\mu)M_0 t^{n+2} s > 0,$$

so
$$p_n(t) < p_{n+1}(t) \, \forall \, t \in [0,1). \tag{21}$$

Define function $p_\infty : [0,1) \longrightarrow \mathbb{R}$ by

$$p_\infty(t) = \lim_{n\to\infty} p_n(t). \tag{22}$$

It follows by definitions (19) and (20) that

$$p_\infty(t) = \frac{(1+\mu)M_0 s}{1-t} - \mu. \tag{23}$$

Hence, assertion (20) holds if

$$p_\infty(t) \leq 0 \text{ at } t = \delta, \tag{24}$$

or equivalently

$$M_0 s \leq \frac{\mu}{1+\mu} \frac{\sqrt{M^2 + 8M_0 M} - M}{\sqrt{M^2 + 8M_0 M} + M},$$

which can be rewritten as condition (14). Therefore, the induction for assertion (17) is completed. That is assertion (15) holds by the definition of sequence $\{t_n\}$ and estimate (15). It follows that

$$\begin{aligned}
\alpha(t_{n+1} - t_n) &\leq \alpha^2(t_n - t_{n-1}) = (\alpha(t_n - t_{n-1}))^2, \\
&\leq \alpha^2(\alpha(t_{n-1} - t_{n-2}))^2 \\
&\leq \alpha^2 \alpha^2 (t_{n-1} - t_{n-2})^{2^2} \\
&\leq \alpha^2 \alpha^2 \alpha^2 (t_{n-2} - t_{n-3})^{2^3} \\
&\vdots
\end{aligned}$$

so

$$\begin{aligned}
t_{n+1} - t_n &\leq \alpha^{1+2+2^2+\ldots+2^{n-1}} s^{2^n} \\
&= \frac{1}{\alpha}(\alpha s)^{2^n}.
\end{aligned}$$

Notice also that $M\mu < 4M_2$, then $\frac{\mu}{(1+\mu)M_1} < \frac{2}{M(1+\mu)}$, so $\alpha s < \mu$. □

Remark 1. (1) The technique of recurrent polynomials in part (i) is used: to produce convergence condition (11) and a closed form upper bound on sequence $\{t_n\}$ (see estimate (13)) other than $\frac{1}{M_0}$ and t^* (which is not given in closed form). This way we also established the linear convergence of sequence $\{t_n\}$. By considering condition (14) but being able to use estimate (13) we establish the quadratic convergence of sequence $\{t_n\}$ in part (ii) of Lemma 2.
(2) If $\mu = 1$, then (14) is the strict version of condition (10).
(3) Sequence $\{t_n\}$ is tighter than the Kantorovich sequence $\{u_n\}$ since $M_0 \leq M_1$ and $M \leq M_1$. Concerning the ration of convergence αs this is also smaller than $r = \frac{2M_1 s}{(1-\sqrt{1-2M_1 s})^2}$ given in the Kantorovich Theorem [19]. Indeed, by these definitions $\alpha s < r$ provided that $\mu \in (0, \mu_1)$, where $\mu_1 = \frac{4M_1}{M(1+\sqrt{1-2M_1 s})^2} - 1$. Notice that

$$(1 + \sqrt{1-2M_1 s})^2 < (1+1)^2 = 4 \leq \frac{4M_1}{M},$$

so $\mu_1 > 0$.

Part (i) of the next auxiliary result relates to a Lemma in [19]. The case $M_0 = M$ has been studied in the introduction. So, in the next Lemma we assume $M_0 \neq M$ in part (ii).

Lemma 3. *Suppose condition*

$$s \leq \frac{1}{2M_3} \qquad (25)$$

holds, where

$$M_3 = \frac{1}{8}(4M_0 + \sqrt{M_0 M + 8M_0^2} + \sqrt{M_0 M}).$$

Then, the following assertions hold

(i)
$$t_{n+1} - t_n \leq \delta(t_n - t_{n-1}) \leq \frac{\delta^{n-1} M_0 s^2}{2(1 - M_0 s)} \qquad (26)$$

and

$$t_{n+2} \leq s + \frac{1 - \delta^{n+1}}{1 - \delta}(t_2 - t_1) < t^{**} = s + \frac{t_2 - t_1}{1 - \delta} s, \quad \forall n = 1, 2, \ldots. \qquad (27)$$

Moreover, conclusions of Lemma 1 are true for sequence $\{t_n\}$. *The sequence* $\{t_n\}$ *converges linearly to* $t^* \in (0, t^{**}]$. *Define parameters* h_0 *by*

$$h_0 = \frac{2(\sqrt{M_0 M + 8M_0^2} + \sqrt{M_0 M})}{M(\sqrt{M_0 M + 8M_0^2} + \sqrt{M_0 M} + 4M_0)}, \quad \bar{M}_3 = \frac{h_0}{2},$$

$$\gamma = 1 + \mu, \ \beta = \frac{\mu}{1 + \mu}, \ d = 2(1 - \delta)$$

and

$$\mu = \frac{M_0}{2M_3 - M_0}.$$

(ii) *Suppose*

$$M_0 < M \leq \frac{M_0}{\theta} \qquad (28)$$

and (25) hold, where $\theta \approx 0.6478$ *is the smallest solution of scalar equation* $2z^4 + z - 1 = 0$. *Then, the conclusions of Lemma 2 also hold for sequence* $\{t_n\}$. *The sequence converges quadratically to* $t^* \in (0, t^{**}]$.

(iii) *Suppose*

$$M \geq \frac{1}{\theta} M_0 \text{ and } s < \frac{1}{2\bar{M}_3} \qquad (29)$$

hold. Then, the conclusions of Lemma 2 are true for sequence $\{t_n\}$. *The sequence* $\{t_n\}$ *converges quadratically to* $t^* \in (0, t^{**}]$.

(iv) $M_0 > M$ *and (25) hold. Then,* $\bar{M}_3 \leq M_3$ *and the conclusions of Lemma 2 are true for sequence* $\{t_n\}$. *The sequence* $\{t_n\}$ *converges quadratically to* $t^* \in (0, t^{**}]$.

Proof. (i) It is given in Lemma 2.1 in [23].
(ii) As in Lemma 2 but using estimate (27) instead of (13) to show

$$\frac{M}{2(1 - M_0 t_{n+1})} \leq \frac{M\gamma}{2}.$$

It suffices

$$\gamma M_0 \left(s + \frac{1 - \delta^n}{1 - \delta}(t_2 - t_1) \right) + 1 - \gamma \leq 0$$

or
$$p_n(t) \leq 0 \text{ at } t = \delta, \tag{30}$$
where
$$p_n(t) = \gamma M_0(1 + t + \ldots + t^{n-1})(t_2 - t_1) + \gamma M_0 s + 1 - \gamma.$$
Notice that
$$p_{n+1}(t) - p_n(t) = \gamma M_0 t^n (t_2 - t_1) > 0.$$
Define function $p_\infty : [0, 1) \longrightarrow \mathbb{R}$ by
$$p_\infty(t) = \lim_{n \to \infty} p_n(t).$$
It follows that
$$p_\infty(t) = \frac{\gamma M_0(t_2 - t_1)}{1 - t} + \gamma M_0 s + 1 - \gamma.$$
So, (30) holds provided that
$$p_\infty(t) \leq 0 \text{ at } t = \delta. \tag{31}$$
By the definition of parameters γ, d, β and for $M_0 s = x$, (31) holds if
$$\frac{x^2}{2(1-x)(1-\delta)} + x \leq \beta$$
or
$$(d-1)x^2 + (1+\beta)x - \beta \leq 0$$
or
$$x \leq \frac{1 + \beta - \sqrt{(1-\beta)^2 + 4\beta d}}{2(1-d)}$$
or
$$s \leq \frac{1 + \beta - \sqrt{(1-\beta)^2 + 4\beta d}}{2(1-d)}. \tag{32}$$

Claim. The right hand side of assertion (31) equals $\frac{1}{M_2}$. Indeed, this is true if
$$1 + \beta - \sqrt{(1-\beta)^2 + 4\beta d} = \frac{2M_0(1-d)}{M_2}$$
or
$$1 + \beta - \frac{2M_0(1-d)}{2M_3} = \sqrt{(1-\beta)^2 + 4\beta d}$$
or by squaring both sides
$$1 + \beta^2 + \frac{4M_0^2(1-d)^2}{4M_3^2} + 2\beta - \frac{4M_0(1-d)}{2M_3} - \frac{4\beta M_0(1-d)}{2M_3} = 1 + \beta^2 - 2\beta + 4\beta d$$
or
$$\beta \left(1 - \frac{M_0(1-d)}{2M_3} - d\right) = \frac{M_0(1-d)}{2M_3}\left(1 - \frac{M_0}{2M_3}\right)$$
or

$$\beta\left(1 - \frac{M_0}{2M_3}\right)(1-d) = \left(1 - \frac{M_0}{2M_3}\right)(1-d)\frac{M_0}{2M_3}$$

or

$$\beta = \frac{M_0}{2M_3}$$

or

$$\frac{\mu}{1+\mu} = \frac{M_0}{2M_3}$$

or

$$\mu = \frac{M_0}{2M_3 - M_0},$$

which is true. Notice also that

$$\begin{aligned} 2M_3 - M_0 &= \frac{1}{4}(4M_0 + \sqrt{M_0 M} + \sqrt{M_0 M + 8M_0^2}) \\ &= \frac{1}{4}(\sqrt{M_0 M} + \sqrt{M_0 M + 8M_0^2}) > 0 \end{aligned}$$

and $2M_3 - 2M_0 > 0$, since $2M_3 - M_0 = \dfrac{\sqrt{M_0 M} + \sqrt{M_0 M + 8M_0^2} - 4M_0}{4}$, $M_0 < \sqrt{M_0 M}$ and $3M_0 < \sqrt{M_0 M + 8M_0^2}$ (by condition (25)). Thus, $\mu \in (0,1)$. It remains to show

$$\alpha = \frac{M}{2}(1+\mu)s < 1$$

or by the choice of μ and M_2

$$\frac{M_2}{2}\left(1 + \frac{M_0}{2M_3 - M_0}\right)s < 1$$

or

$$s < \frac{1}{2\tilde{M}_3}. \tag{33}$$

Claim. $\tilde{M}_3 \leq M_3$. By the definition of parameters M_2 and $\tilde{M}_3$ it must be shown that

$$\frac{M(\sqrt{M_0 M} + \sqrt{M_0 M + 8M_0^2} + 4M_0)}{2(\sqrt{M_0 M} + \sqrt{M_0 M + 8M_0^2})} \leq \frac{\sqrt{M_0 M} + \sqrt{M_0 M + 8M_0^2} + 4M_0}{4}$$

or if for $y = \dfrac{M_0}{M}$

$$2 - \sqrt{y} \leq \sqrt{y + 8y^2}. \tag{34}$$

By (28) $2 - \sqrt{y} > 0$, so estimate (34) holds if $2y^2 + \sqrt{y} - 1 \geq 0$ or

$$2z^4 + z - 1 \geq 0 \text{ for } z = \sqrt{y}.$$

However, the last inequality holds by (28). The claimed is justified. So, estimate (33) holds by (25) and this claim.

(iii) It follows from the proof in part (ii). However, this time $M_2 \leq \tilde{M}_2$ follows from (29). Notice also that according to part (ii) condition (25) implies (29). Moreover, according to part (iii) condition (29) implies (25).

(iv) As in case (ii) estimate (34) must be satisfied. If $M_0 \geq 4M$, then the estimate (34) holds, since $2 - \sqrt{y} \leq 0$. If $M < M_0 < 4M$ then again $M_0 > \theta M$, so estimate (34) or equivalently $2z^2 + z - 1 > 0$ holds. □

Comments similar to Remark 1 can follow for Lemma 3.

Case. Parameters K_0 and K are not equal to M_0. Comments similar to Remark 1 can follow for Lemma 3.

It is convenient to define parameter δ_0 by

$$\delta_0 = \frac{K(t_2 - t_1)}{2(1 - K_0 t_2)}$$

and the quadratic polynomial φ by

$$\varphi(t) = (MK + 2\delta M_0(K - 2K_0))t^2 + 4\delta(M_0 + K_0)t - 4\delta.$$

The discriminant $\triangle$ of polynomial q can be written as

$$\triangle = 16\delta(\delta(M_0 - K_0))^2 + (M + 2\delta M_0)K > 0.$$

It follows that the root $\frac{1}{h_1}$ given by the quadratic formula can be written as

$$\frac{1}{2h_1} = \frac{2}{\delta(M_0 + K_0) + \sqrt{(\delta(M_0 + K_0))^2 + \delta(MK + 2\delta M_0)(K - 2K_0)}}.$$

Denote by $\frac{1}{h_2}$ the unique positive zero of equation

$$M_0(K - 2K_0)t^2 + 2M_0 t - 1 = 0.$$

This root can be written as

$$\frac{1}{2h_2} = \frac{1}{M_0 + \sqrt{M^2 + M_0(K - 2K_0)}}.$$

Define parameter M_4 by

$$\frac{1}{M_4} = \min\left\{\frac{1}{h_1}, \frac{1}{h_2}\right\}. \tag{35}$$

Part (i) of the next auxiliary result relates to Lemma 2.1 in [22].

Lemma 4. *Suppose*

$$s \leq \frac{1}{2M_4} \tag{36}$$

holds, where parameter M_4 is given by Formula (35). Then, the following assertions hold

(i) Estimates

$$t_{n+2} - t_{n+1} \leq \delta_0 \delta^{n-1} \frac{Ks^2}{2(1 - K_0 s)},$$

and

$$t_{n+2} \leq s + \left(1 + \delta_0 \frac{1 - \delta^n}{1 - \delta}\right)(t_2 - t_1) \leq \bar{t} = s + \left(1 + \frac{\delta_0}{1 - \delta}\right)(t_2 - t_1).$$

Moreover, conclusions of Lemma 2 are true for sequence $\{t_n\}$. The sequence $\{t_n\}$ converges linearly to $t^* \in (0, \bar{t}]$.

(ii) Suppose
$$M_0\left(\frac{\delta_0(t_2-t_1)}{1-\delta}+s\right)\leq \beta, \qquad (37)$$
$$s < \frac{2}{(1+\mu)M} \qquad (38)$$
and (36) hold for some $\mu > 0$. Then, the conclusions of Lemma 3 are true for sequence $\{t_n\}$. The sequence $\{t_n\}$ converges quadratically to $t^* \in (0, \bar{t}]$.

Proof. (i) It is given in Lemma 2.1 in [22].
(ii) Define polynomial p_n by
$$p_n(t) = \gamma M_0 \delta_0(1+t+\ldots+t^{n-1})(t_2-t-1) + \gamma M_0 s + 1 - \gamma.$$
By this definition it follows
$$p_{n+1}(t) - p_n(t) = \gamma M_0 \delta_0 (t_2 - t_1) t^n > 0.$$
As in the proof of Lemma 3 (ii), estimate
$$\frac{M}{2(1-M_0 t_{n+1})} \leq \frac{M}{2}\gamma$$
holds provided that
$$p_n(t) \leq 0 \text{ at } t = \delta. \qquad (39)$$
Define function $p_\infty : [0,1) \longrightarrow \mathbb{R}$ by
$$p_\infty(t) = \lim_{n \to \infty} p_n(t).$$
It follows by the definition of function p_∞ and polynomial p_n that
$$p_\infty(t) = \frac{\gamma M_0 \delta_0 (t_2 - t_1)}{1-t} + \gamma M_0 s - \gamma.$$
Hence, estimate (39) holds provided that
$$p_\infty(t) \leq 0 \text{ at } t = \delta.$$
However, this assertion holds, since $\mu \in (0,1)$. Moreover, the definition of α and condition (38) of the Lemma 4 imply
$$\alpha s = \frac{M}{2}(1+\mu).$$
Hence, the sequence $\{t_n\}$ converges quadratically to t^*. □

Remark 2. Conditions (36)–(38) can be condensed and a specific choice for μ can be given as follows: Define function $f : \left[0, \frac{1}{K_0}\right) \longrightarrow \mathbb{R}$ by
$$f(t) = 1 - M_0\left(\frac{\delta_0(t)(t_2(t)-t_1(t))}{1-\delta}+t\right).$$
It follows by this definition
$$f(0) = 1 > 0, \ f(t) \longrightarrow -\infty \text{ as } t \longrightarrow \frac{1}{K_0}^-.$$

Denote by μ_2 the smallest solution of equation $f(t) = 0$ in $\left(0, \dfrac{1}{K_0}\right)$. Then, by choosing $\mu = \mu_2$ conditions (37) holds as equality. Then, if follows that if we solve the first condition in (37) for "s", then conditions (36)–(38) can be condensed as

$$s \leq s_1 \min\left\{\frac{1}{M_4}, \frac{2}{(2+\mu_2)M}\right\}. \tag{40}$$

If $s_1 = \dfrac{2}{(2+\mu_2)M}$, then condition (40) should hold as a strict inequality to show quadratic convergence.

3. Semi-Local Convergence

Sequence $\{t_n\}$ given by (6) was shown to be majorizing for $\{x_n\}$ and tighter than $\{u_n\}$ under conditions of Lemmas in [19,22,23], respectively. These Lemmas correspond to part (i) of Lemma 1, Lemma 3 and Lemma 4, respectively. However, by asking the initial approximation s to be bounded above by a slightly larger bound the quadratic order of convergence is recovered. Hence, the preceding Lemmas can replace the order ones, respectively in the semi-local proofs for NM in these references. The parameter K_0 and K are connected to x_0 and $\mathcal{L}'$ as follows

(K7) $\exists$ parameter $K_0 > 0$ such that for $x_1 = x_0 - \mathcal{L}'(x_0)^{-1}\mathcal{L}(x_0)$

$$\|\mathcal{L}'(x_0)^{-1}(\mathcal{L}'(x_1) - \mathcal{L}'(x_0))\| \leq K_0 \|x_1 - x_0\|,$$

(K8) $\exists$ parameter K such that $\forall \xi \in [0,1]$, $\forall x, y \in D_0$,

$$\left\|\int_0^1 \mathcal{L}'(x_0)^{-1}(\mathcal{L}'(x + \xi(y-x)) - \mathcal{L}'(x))d\xi\right\| \leq \frac{K}{2}\|y - x\|.$$

Note that $K_0 \leq M_0$ and $K \leq M$. The convergence criteria in Lemmas 1, 3 and 4 do not necessarily imply each other in each case. That is why we do not only rely on Lemma 4 to show the semi-local convergence of NM. Consider the following three sets of conditions:

(A1): (K1), (K4), (K5), (K6) and conditions of Lemma 1 hold for $\rho = t^*$, or
(A2): (K1), (K4) (K5), (K6), conditions of Lemma 2 hold with $\rho = t^*$, or
(A3): (K1), (K4) (K5), (K6), conditions of Lemma 3 hold with $\rho = t^*$, or
(A4): (K1), (K4) (K5), (K6), conditions of Lemma 4 hold with $\rho = t^*$.

The upper bounds of the limit point given in the Lemmas and in closed form can replace ρ in condition (K4). The proof are omitted in the presentation of the semi-local convergence of NM since the proof is given in the aforementioned references [19,20,22,23] with the exception of quadratic convergence given in part (ii) of the presented Lemmas.

Theorem 2. *Suppose any of conditions Ai, $i = 1, 2, 3, 4$ hold. Then, sequence $\{x_n\}$ generated by NM is well defined in $B[x_0, \rho]$, remains in $B[x_0, \rho]$ $\forall n = 0, 1, 2, \ldots$ and converges to a solution $x^* \in B[x_0, \rho]$ of equation $\mathcal{L}(x) = 0$. Moreover, the following assertion hold $\forall n = 0, 1, 2, \ldots$*

$$\|x_{n+1} - x_n\| \leq t_{n+1} - t_n$$

and

$$\|x^* - x_n\| \leq t^* - t_n.$$

The convergence ball is given next. Notice, however that we do not use all conditions Ai.

Proposition 1. *Suppose: there exists a solution $x^* \in B(x_0, \rho_0)$ of equation $\mathcal{L}(x) = 0$ for some $\rho_0 > 0$; condition (K5) holds and $\exists \rho_1 \geq \rho_0$ such that*

$$\frac{M_0}{2}(\rho_0 + \rho_1) < 1. \tag{41}$$

Set $D_1 = D \cap B[x_0, \rho_1]$. Then, the only solution of equation $\mathcal{L}(x) = 0$ in the set D_1 is x^*.

Proof. Let $x_* \in D_1$ be a solution of equation $\mathcal{L}(x) = 0$. Define linear operator $J = \int_0^1 \mathcal{L}'(x^* + \tau(x_* - x^*))d\tau$. Then, using (K5) and (41)

$$\|\mathcal{L}'(x_0)^{-1}(\mathcal{L}'(x_0) - J)\| \leq M_0 \int_0^1 ((1-\tau)\|x_0 - x^*\| + \tau\|x_0 - x_*\|)d\tau$$

$$\leq \frac{M_0}{2}(\rho_0 + \rho_1) < 1. \qquad (42)$$

Therefore, $x^* = x_*$ is implied by the invertability of J and

$$J(x^* - x_*) = \mathcal{L}(x^*) - \mathcal{L}(x_*) = 0.$$

If conditions of Theorem 2 hold, set $\rho_0 = \rho$. □

4. Numerical Experiments

Two experiments are presented in this Section.

Example 3. *Recall Example 1 (with $\mathcal{L}(x) = c(x)$). Then, the parameters are $s = \frac{1-a}{3}$, $K_0 = \frac{a+5}{3}$, $M_0 = 3 - a$, $M_1 = 2(2-a)$. It also follows $D_0 = B(1, 1-a) \cap B\left[1, \frac{1}{M_0}\right] = B\left[1, \frac{1}{M_0}\right]$, so $K = M = 2\left(1 + \frac{1}{3-a}\right)$. Denote by $T_i, i = 1, 2, 3, 4$ the set of values a for which conditions (K3), (N2) − N4) are satisfied. Then, by solving these inequalities for a : $T_1 = \emptyset$, $T_2 = [0.4648, 0.5)$, $T_3 = [0.4503, 0.5)$, and $T_4 = [0.4272, 0.5)$, respectively.*

The domain can be further extended. Choose $a = 0.4$, then, $\frac{1}{M_0} = 0.3846$. The following Table 1 shows, that the conditions of Lemma 1, since $K_0 t < 1$ and $M_0 t_{n+1} < 1 \,\forall n = 1, 2, \ldots$.

Table 1. Sequence (6) for Example 1.

n	1	2	3	4	5	6	7	8
t_n	0.2000	0.2865	0.3272	0.3425	0.3455	0.3456	0.3456	0.3456

Example 4. *Let $\mathcal{U} = \mathcal{V} = \mathbb{R}^3$, $D = B(x_0, 0.5)$ and*

$$\mathcal{L}(x) = \left(e^{x_1} - 1, \, x_2^3 + x_2, \, x_3\right)^T.$$

The equation $\mathcal{L}(x) = 0$ has the solution $x^* = (0,0,0)^T$ and $\mathcal{L}'(x) = diag(e^{x_1}, 3x_2^2 + 1, 1)$. Let $x_0 = (0.1, 0.1, 0.1)^T$. Then $s = \|\mathcal{L}'(x_0)^{-1}\mathcal{L}(x_0)\|_\infty \approx 0.1569$,

$$M_0 = \max\left\{\frac{e^{0.6}}{e^{0.1}}, \frac{3(0.6 + 0.1)}{1.03}\right\} \approx 2.7183,$$

$$M_1 = \max\left\{\frac{e^{0.6}}{e^{0.1}}, \frac{3(0.6 + 0.6)}{1.03}\right\} \approx 3.49513.$$

It also follows that $\frac{1}{M_0} \approx 0.3679$, $D_0 = D \cap B[x_0, \frac{1}{M_0}] = B[0.1, 0.3679]$ and

$$K_0 = \max\left\{\frac{e^{p_1}}{e^{0.1}}, \frac{3(p_2 + 0.1)}{1.03}\right\} \approx 2.3819,$$

$$M = K = \max\left\{\frac{e^{p_1}}{e^{0.1}}, \frac{6p_1}{1.03}\right\} \approx 2.7255,$$

where $p_1 = 0.1 + \frac{1}{M_0} \approx 0.4679$, $p_2 \approx 0.0019$.

Notice that $M_0 < M_1$ and $M < M_1$. The Kantorovich convergence condition (K3) is not fulfilled, since $2M_1 s \approx 1.0968 > 1$. Hence, convergence of converge NM is not assured by the Kantorovich criterion. However, the new conditions (N2)–(N4) are fulfilled, since $q_2 s \approx 0.9749 < 1$, $q_3 s \approx 0.9320 < 1$, $q_4 s \approx 0.8723 < 1$.

The following Table 2 shows, that the conditions of Lemma 1 are fulfilled, since $K_0 t < 1$ and $M_0 t_{n+1} < 1 \,\forall n = 1, 2, \ldots$.

Table 2. Sequence (6) for Example 4.

n	1	2	3	4	5	6
t_n	0.1569	0.2154	0.2266	0.2271	0.2271	0.2271

Example 5. *Let* $\mathcal{U} = \mathcal{V} = C[0,1]$ *be the domain of continuous real functions defined on the interval* $[0,1]$. *Set* $D = B[x_0, 3]$, *and define operator* $\mathcal{L}$ *on D as*

$$\mathcal{L}(v)(v_1) = v(v_1) - y(v_1) - \int_0^1 N(v_1, t) v^3(t) dt, \ v \in C[0,1], v_1 \in [0,1], \quad (43)$$

where y is given in $C[0,1]$, *and N is a kernel given by Green's function as*

$$N(v_1, t) = \begin{cases} (1 - v_1) t, & t \leq v_1 \\ v_1 (1 - t), & v_1 \leq t. \end{cases} \quad (44)$$

By applying this definition the derivative of $\mathcal{L}$ *is*

$$[\mathcal{L}'(v)(z)](v_1) = z(v_1) - 3 \int_0^1 N(v_1, t) v^2(t) z(t) dt \quad (45)$$

$z \in C[0,1], v_1 \in [0,1]$. Pick $x_0(v_1) = y(v_1) = 1$. The norm-max is used. It then follows from (43)–(45) that $\mathcal{L}'(x_0)^{-1} \in L(B_2, B_1)$,

$$\|I - \mathcal{L}'(x_0)\| < 0.375, \ \|\mathcal{L}'(x_0)^{-1}\| \leq 1.6,$$
$$s = 0.2, M_0 = 2.4, M_1 = 3.6,$$

and $D_0 = B(x_0, 3) \cap B[x_0, 0.4167] = B[x_0, 0.4167]$, so $M = 1.5$. Notice that $M_0 < M_1$ and $M < M_1$. Choose $K_0 = K = M_0$. The Kantorovich convergence condition (K3) is not fulfilled, since $2M_1 s = 1.44 > 1$. Hence, convergence of converge NM is not assured by the Kantorovich criterion. However, new condition (36) is fulfilled, since $2M_4 s = 0.6 < 1$.

Example 6. *Let* $\mathcal{U} = \mathcal{V} = \mathbb{R}$, $D = (-1, 1)$ *and*

$$\mathcal{L}(x) = e^x + 2x - 1.$$

The equation $\mathcal{L}(x) = 0$ *has the solution* $x^* = 0$. *The parameters are* $s = \left| \frac{e^{x_0} + 2x_0 - 1}{e^{x_0} + 2} \right|$, $M_0 = M_1 = e$, $K_0 = K = M = e^{x_0 + \frac{1}{e}}$ *and*

$$D_0 = (-1, 1) \cap \left[x_0 - \frac{1}{e}, x_0 + \frac{1}{e} \right] = \left[x_0 - \frac{1}{e}, x_0 + \frac{1}{e} \right].$$

Let us choose $x_0 = 0.15$. Then, $s \approx 0.1461$. Conditions (K3) and (N2) are fulfilled. The majorizing sequences $\{t_n\}$ (6) and $\{u_n\}$ from Theorem 1 are:

$$\{t_n\} = \{0, 0.1461, 0.1698, 0.1707, 0.1707, 0.1707, 0.1707\},$$

$$\{u_n\} = \{0, 0.1461, 0.1942, 0.2008, 0.2009, 0.2009, 0.2009, 0.2009\}.$$

In Table 3, there are error bounds. Notice that the new error bounds are tighter, than the ones in Theorem 1.

Table 3. Results for $x_0 = 0.15$ for Example 6.

n	$|x_{n+1} - x_n|$	$|t_{n+1} - t_n|$	$|u_{n+1} - u_n|$
0	1.4607×10^{-1}	1.4607×10^{-1}	1.4607×10^{-1}
1	3.9321×10^{-3}	2.3721×10^{-2}	4.8092×10^{-2}
2	2.5837×10^{-6}	8.7693×10^{-4}	6.6568×10^{-3}
3	1.1126×10^{-12}	1.2039×10^{-6}	1.3262×10^{-4}
4	0	2.2688×10^{-12}	5.2681×10^{-8}

Let us choose $x_0 = 0.2$. Then, $s \approx 0.1929$. In this case condition (K3) is not held, but (N2) holds. The majorizing sequence $\{t_n\}$ (6) is:

$$\{t_n\} = \{0, 0.1929, 0.2427, 0.2491, 0.2492, 0.2492, 0.2492\}.$$

Table 4 shows the error bounds from Theorem 2.

Table 4. Results for $x_0 = 0.2$ for Example 6.

n	$|x_{n+1} - x_n|$	$|t_{n+1} - t_n|$
0	1.929×10^{-1}	1.929×10^{-1}
1	7.0934×10^{-3}	4.9769×10^{-2}
2	8.4258×10^{-6}	6.4204×10^{-3}
3	1.1832×10^{-11}	1.1263×10^{-4}
4	0	3.4690×10^{-8}

5. Conclusions

We developed a comparison between results on the semi-local convergence of NM. There exists an extensive literature on the convergence analysis of NM. Most convergence results are based on recurrent relations, where the Lipschitz conditions are given in affine or non-affine invariant forms. The new methodology uses recurrent functions. The idea is to construct a domain included in the one used before which also contains the Newton iterates. That is important, since the new results do not require additional conditions. This way the new sufficient convergence conditions are weaker in the Lipschitz case, since they rely on smaller constants. Other benefits include tighter error bounds and more precise uniqueness of the solution results. The new constants are special cases of earlier ones. The methodology is very general making it suitable to extend the usage of other numerical methods under Hölder or more generalized majorant conditions. This will be the topic of our future work.

Author Contributions: Conceptualization I.K.A.; Methodology I.K.A.; Investigation S.R., I.K.A., S.S. and H.Y. All authors have read and agreed to the published version of the manuscript.

Funding: This research received no external funding.

Institutional Review Board Statement: Not applicable.

Informed Consent Statement: Not applicable.

Data Availability Statement: Not applicable.

Conflicts of Interest: The authors declare no conflict of interest.

References

1. Appell, J.; DePascale, E.; Lysenko, J.V.; Zabrejko, P.P. New results on Newton-Kantorovich approximations with applications to nonlinear integral equations. *Numer. Funct. Anal. Optim.* **1997**, *18*, 1–17. [CrossRef]
2. Traub, J.F. *Iterative Methods for the Solution of Equations*; Prentice Hall: Hoboken, NJ, USA, 1964.
3. Ezquerro, J.A.; Hernández-Verón, M.A. *Newton's Method: An Updated Approach of Kantorovich's Theory. Frontiers in Mathematics*; Birkhäuser/Springer: Cham, Switzerland, 2017.
4. Kantorovich, L.V.; Akilov, G.P. *Functional Analysis*; Pergamon Press: Oxford, UK, 1982.

5. Potra, F.A.; Pták, V. Nondiscrete induction and iterative processes. In *Research Notes in Mathematics*; Pitman (Advanced Publishing Program): Boston, MA, USA, 1984; Volume 103.
6. Verma, R. *New Trends in Fractional Programming*; Nova Science Publisher: New York, NY, USA, 2019.
7. Yamamoto, T. Historical developments in convergence analysis for Newton's and Newton-like methods. *J. Comput. Appl. Math.* **2000**, *124*, 1–23. [CrossRef]
8. Zhanlav, T.; Chun, C.; Otgondorj, K.H.; Ulziibayar, V. High order iterations for systems of nonlinear equations. *Int. J. Comput. Math.* **2020**, *97*, 1704–1724. [CrossRef]
9. Sharma, J.R.; Guha, R.K. Simple yet efficient Newton-like method for systems of nonlinear equations. *Calcolo* **2016**, *53*, 451–473. [CrossRef]
10. Grau-Sanchez, M.; Grau, A.; Noguera, M. Ostrowski type methods for solving system of nonlinear equations. *Appl. Math. Comput.* **2011**, *218*, 2377–2385. [CrossRef]
11. Homeier, H.H.H. A modified Newton method with cubic convergence: The multivariate case. *J. Comput. Appl. Math.* **2004**, *169*, 161–169. [CrossRef]
12. Kou, J.; Wang, X.; Li, Y. Some eight order root finding three-step methods. *Commun. Nonlinear Sci. Numer. Simul.* **2010**, *15*, 536–544. [CrossRef]
13. Nashed, M.Z.; Chen, X. Convergence of Newton-like methods for singular operator equations using outer inverses. *Numer. Math.* **1993**, *66*, 235–257. [CrossRef]
14. Wang, X. An Ostrowski-type method with memory using a novel self-accelerating parameters. *J. Comput. Appl. Math.* **2018**, *330*, 710–720. [CrossRef]
15. Moccari, M.; Lofti, T. On a two-step optimal Steffensen-type method: Relaxed local and semi-local convergence analysis and dynamical stability. *J. Math. Anal. Appl.* **2018**, *468*, 240–269. [CrossRef]
16. Sharma, J.R.; Arora, H. Efficient derivative-free numerical methods for solving systems of nonlinear equations. *Comput. Appl. Math.* **2016**, *35*, 269–284. [CrossRef]
17. Noor, M.A.; Waseem, M. Some iterative methods for solving a system of nonlinear equations. *Comput. Math. Appl.* **2009**, *57*, 101–106. [CrossRef]
18. Shakhno, S.M. On a two-step iterative process under generalized Lipschitz conditions for first-order divided differences. *J. Math. Sci.* **2010**, *168*, 576–584. [CrossRef]
19. Argyros, I.K. On the Newton-Kantorovich hypothesis for solving equations. *J. Comput. Math.* **2004**, *169*, 315–332. [CrossRef]
20. Argyros, I.K. Unified Convergence Criteria for Iterative Banach Space Valued Methods with Applications. *Mathematics* **2021**, *9*, 1942. [CrossRef]
21. Proinov, P.D. New general convergence theory for iterative processes and its applications to Newton-Kantorovich type theorems. *J. Complex.* **2010**, *26*, 3–42. [CrossRef]
22. Argyros, I.K.; Hilout, S. On an improved convergence analysis of Newton's scheme. *Appl. Math. Comput.* **2013**, *225*, 372–386.
23. Argyros, I.K.; Hilout, S. Weaker conditions for the convergence of Newton's scheme. *J. Complex.* **2012**, *28*, 364–387. [CrossRef]

Article

Constructing a Class of Frozen Jacobian Multi-Step Iterative Solvers for Systems of Nonlinear Equations

R. H. Al-Obaidi and M. T. Darvishi *

Department of Mathematics, Faculty of Science, Razi University, Kermanshah 67149, Iran
* Correspondence: darvishi@razi.ac.ir

Abstract: In this paper, in order to solve systems of nonlinear equations, a new class of frozen Jacobian multi-step iterative methods is presented. Our proposed algorithms are characterized by a highly convergent order and an excellent efficiency index. The theoretical analysis is presented in detail. Finally, numerical experiments are presented for showing the performance of the proposed methods, when compared with known algorithms taken from the literature.

Keywords: iterative method; frozen Jacobian multi-step iterative method; system of nonlinear equations; high-order convergence

MSC: 65Hxx

1. Introduction

Approximating a locally unique solution α of the nonlinear system

$$F(\mathbf{x}) = 0 \tag{1}$$

has many applications in engineering and mathematics [1–4]. In (1), we have n equations with n variables. In fact, F is a vector-valued function with n variables. Several problems arising from the different areas in natural and applied sciences take the form of systems of nonlinear Equation (1) that need to be solved, where $F(\mathbf{x}) = (f_1(\mathbf{x}), f_2(\mathbf{x}), \cdots, f_n(\mathbf{x}))$ such that for all $k = 1, 2, \cdots, n$, f_k is a scalar nonlinear function. Additionally, there are many real life problems for which, in the process of finding their solutions, one needs to solve a system of nonlinear equations, see for example [5–9]. It is known that finding an exact solution $\alpha^t = (\alpha_1, \alpha_2, \cdots, \alpha_n)$ of the nonlinear system (1) is not an easy task, especially when the equation contains terms consisting of logarithms, trigonometric and exponential functions, or a combination of transcendental terms. Hence, in general, one cannot find the solution of Equation (1) analytically, therefore, we have to use iterative methods. Any iterative method starts from one approximation and constructs a sequence such that it converges to the solution of the Equation (1) (for more details, see [10]).

The most commonly used iterative method to solve (1) is the classical Newton method, given by

$$\mathbf{x}^{(k+1)} = \mathbf{x}^{(k)} - J_F(\mathbf{x}^{(k)})^{-1} F(\mathbf{x}^{(k)}),$$

where $J_F(\mathbf{x})$ (or $F'(\mathbf{x})$) is the Jacobian matrix of function F, and $\mathbf{x}^{(k)}$ is the k-th approximation of the root of (1) with the initial guess $\mathbf{x}^{(0)}$. It is well known that Newton's method is a quadratic convergence method with the efficiency index $\sqrt{2}$ [11]. The third and higher-order methods such as the Halley and Chebyshev methods [12] have little practical value because of the evaluation of the second Frechèt-derivative. However, third and higher-order multi-step methods can be good substitutes because they require the evaluation of the function and its first derivative at different points.

In the recent decades, many authors tried to design iterative procedures with better efficiency and higher order of convergence than the Newton scheme, see, for example, ref. [13–24] and references therein. However, the accuracy of solutions is highly dependent on the efficiency of the utilized algorithm. Furthermore, at each step of any iterative method, we must find the exact solution of an obtained linear system which is expensive in actual applications, especially when the system size n is very large. However, the proposed higher-order iterative methods are futile unless they have high-order convergence. Therefore, the important aim in developing any new algorithm is to achieve high convergence order with requiring as small as possible the evaluations of functions, derivatives and matrix inversions. Thus, here, we focus on the technique of the frozen Jacobian multi-step iterative algorithms. It is shown that this idea is computationally attractive and economical for constructing iterative solvers because the inversion of the Jacobian matrix (regarding LU-decomposition) is performed once. Many researchers have reduced the computational cost of these algorithms by frozen Jacobian multi-step iterative techniques [25–28].

In this work, we construct a new class of frozen Jacobian multi-step iterative methods for solving the nonlinear systems of equations. This is a high-order convergent algorithm with an excellent efficiency index. The theoretical analysis is presented completely. Further, by solving some nonlinear systems, the ability of the methods is compared with some known algorithms.

The rest of this paper is organized as follows. In the following section, we present our new methods with obtaining of their order of convergence. Additionally, their computational efficiency are discussed in general. Some numerical examples are considered in Sections 3 and 4 to show the asymptotic behavior of these methods. Finally, a brief concluding remark is presented in Section 5.

2. Constructing New Methods

In this section, two high-order frozen Jacobian multi-step iterative methods to solve systems of nonlinear equations are presented. These come by increasing the convergence in Newton's method and simultaneously decreasing its computational costs. The framework of these Frozen Jacobian multi-step iterative Algorithms (FJA) can be described as

$$\begin{cases} \text{No. of steps} &= m > 1, \\ \text{Order of convergence} &= m+1, \\ \text{Function evaluations} &= m, \\ \text{Jacobian evaluations} &= 1, \\ \text{No. of } LU \text{ decomposition} &= 1; \end{cases} \quad \text{FJA}: \begin{cases} \mathbf{y}_0 = \text{initial guess} \\ \mathbf{y}_1 = \mathbf{y}_0 - J_F(\mathbf{y}_0)^{-1} F(\mathbf{y}_0) \\ \text{for } i=1:m-1 \\ \quad \mathcal{E}_i = J_F(\mathbf{y}_0)^{-1}(F(\mathbf{y}_i) + F(\mathbf{y}_{i-1})) \\ \quad \mathbf{y}_{i+1} = \mathbf{y}_{i-1} - \mathcal{E}_i \\ \text{end} \\ \mathbf{y}_0 = \mathbf{y}_m. \end{cases} \quad (2)$$

In (2), for an m-step method ($m > 1$), one needs m function evaluations and only one Jacobian evaluation. Further, the number of LU decompositions is one. The order of convergence for such FJA method is $m+1$. In the right-hand side column of (2), the algorithm is briefy described.

In the following subsections, by choosing two different values for m, a third- and a fourth-order frozen Jacobian multi-step iterative algorithm are presented.

2.1. The Third-Order FJA

First, we investigate case $m=2$, that is,

$$\mathbf{y}^{(k)} = \mathbf{x}^{(k)} - J_F(\mathbf{x}^{(k)})^{-1} F(\mathbf{x}^{(k)}),$$

$$\mathbf{x}^{(k+1)} = \mathbf{x}^{(k)} - J_F(\mathbf{x}^{(k)})^{-1} (F(\mathbf{y}^{(k)}) + F(\mathbf{x}^{(k)})),$$
(3)

we denote this by M_3.

2.1.1. Convergence Analysis

In this part, we prove that the order of convergence of method (3) is three. First, we need to definition of the Frechèt derivative.

Definition 1 ([29]). *Let F be an operator which maps a Banach space X into a Banach space Y. If there exists a bounded linear operator T from X into Y such that*

$$\lim_{y \to 0} \frac{\|F(x+y) - F(x) - T(y)\|}{\|y\|} = 0,$$

then F is said to be Frechèt differentiable and $F'(x_0) = T(x_0)$.

For more details on the Frechèt differentiability and Frechèt derivative, we refer the interested readers to a review article by Emmanuel [30] and references therein.

Theorem 1. *Let $F : I \subseteq \mathbb{R}^n \to \mathbb{R}^n$ be a Frechèt differentiable function at each point of an open convex neighborhood I of α, the solution of system $F(x) = 0$. Suppose that $J_F(x^{(k)})$ is continuous and nonsingular in α, then, the sequence $\{x^{(k)}\}_{(k \geq 0)}$ obtained using the iterative method (3) converges to α and its rate of convergence is three.*

Proof. Suppose that $E_n = x^{(n)} - \alpha$, using Taylor's expansion [31], we obtain

$$F(x^{(n)}) = F(\alpha) + F'(\alpha)E_n + \frac{1}{2!}F''(\alpha)E_n^2 + \frac{1}{3!}F'''(\alpha)E_n^3 + \frac{1}{4!}F''''(\alpha)E_n^4 + \ldots$$

as α is the root of F so $F(\alpha) = 0$. As a matter of fact, one may yield the following equations of $F(x^{(n)})$ and $F'(x^{(n)})$ in a neighborhood of α by using Taylor's series expansions [32],

$$F(x^{(n)}) = F'(\alpha)\left[E_n + C_2 E_n^2 + C_3 E_n^3 + C_4 E_n^4 + C_5 E_n^5 + O\|E_n^6\|\right], \tag{4}$$

$$F'(x^{(n)}) = F'(\alpha)\left[I + 2C_2 E_n + 3C_3 E_n^2 + 4C_4 E_n^3 + 5C_5 E_n^4 + 6C_6 E_n^5 + O\|E_n^6\|\right], \tag{5}$$

wherein $C_n = \frac{[F'(\alpha)]^{-1} F^{(n)}(\alpha)}{n!}$ and I is the identity matrix whose order is the same as the order of the Jacobian matrix. Note that $iC_i E_n^{i-1} \in \mathcal{L}(\mathbb{R}^n)$. Using (4) and (5) we obtain

$$F'(x^{(n)})^{-1} F(x^{(n)}) = E_n - C_2 E_n^2 + (2C_2^2 - 2C_3)E_n^3 + (-4C_2^3 + 7C_2 C_3 - 3C_4)E_n^4$$
$$+ (-32C_2^5 + 8C_2^4 - 20C_2^2 C_3 + 10C_2 C_4 + 6C_3^2 - 4C_5)E_n^5 + O\|E_n^6\|.$$

Since $y^{(n)} = x^{(n)} - F'(x^{(n)})^{-1} F(x^{(n)})$, we find

$$y^{(n)} = \alpha + C_2 E_n^2 + (-2C_2^2 + 2C_3)E_n^3 + (4C_2^3 - 7C_2 C_3 + 3C_4)E_n^4$$
$$+ (32C_2^5 - 8C_2^4 + 20C_2^2 C_3 - 10C_2 C_4 - 6C_3^2 + 4C_5)E_n^5 + O\|E_n^6\|. \tag{6}$$

By the definition of error term E_n, the error term of $y^{(n)}$ as an approximation of α, that is, $y^{(n)} - \alpha$ is obtained from the second term of the right-hand side of Equation (6). Similarly, the Taylor's expansion of the function $F(y^{(n)})$ is

$$F(y^{(n)}) = F'(\alpha)\left[C_2 E_n^2 + (-2C_2^2 + 2C_3)E_n^3 + (5C_2^3 - 7C_2 C_3 + 3C_4)E_n^4 + \right.$$
$$\left. (32C_2^5 - 12C_2^4 + 24C_2^2 C_3 - 10C_2 C_4 - 6C_3^2 + 4C_5)E_n^5 + O\|E_n^6\|\right]. \tag{7}$$

From (4) and (7), we obtain

$$(F(\mathbf{x}^{(n)}) + F(\mathbf{y}^{(n)})) = F'(\alpha)\Big[E_n + 2C_2E_n^2 + (-2C_2^2 + 3C_3)E_n^3 + (5C_2^3 - 7C_2C_3 + 4C_4)E_n^4 + (32C_2^5 - 12C_2^4 + 24C_2^2 - 10C_2C_4 - 6C_3^2 + 6C_5)E_n^5] + O||E_n^6||\Big].$$

Thus,

$$F'(\mathbf{x}^{(n)})^{-1}(F(\mathbf{x}^{(n)}) + F(\mathbf{y}^{(n)})) = E_n - (2C_2^2)E_n^3 + (9C_2^3 - 7C_2C_3)E_n^4$$
$$+ (-30C_2^4 + 44C_2^2C_3 - 10C_2C_4 - 6C_3^2 + C_5)E_n^5 + O||E_n^6||.$$

Finally, since

$$\mathbf{x}^{(n+1)} = \mathbf{x}^{(n)} - J_F(\mathbf{x}^{(n)})^{-1}(F(\mathbf{x}^{(n)}) + F(\mathbf{y}^{(n)})),$$

we have

$$\mathbf{x}^{(n+1)} = \alpha - (2C_2^2)E_n^3 - (9C_2^3 - 7C_2C_3)E_n^4 - (-30C_2^4 + 44C_2^2C_3 - 10C_2C_4 + \cdots - 6C_3^2 + C_5)E_n^5 + O||E_n^6||. \quad (8)$$

Clearly, the error Equation (8) shows that the order of convergence of the frozen Jacobian multi-step iterative method (3) is three. This completes the proof. □

2.1.2. The Computational Efficiency

In this section, we compare the computational efficiency of our third-order scheme (3), denoted as M_3, with some existing third-order methods. We will assess the efficiency index of our new frozen Jacobian multi-step iterative method in contrast with the existing methods for systems of nonlinear equations, using two famous efficiency indices. The first one is the classical efficiency index [33] as

$$IE = p^{\frac{1}{c}}$$

where p is the rate of convergence and c stands for the total computational cost per iteration in terms of the number of functional evaluations, such that $c = (rn + mn^2)$ where r refers to the number of function evaluations needed per iteration and m is the number of Jacobian matrix evaluations needed per iteration.

It is well known that the computation of LU factorization by any of the existing methods in the literature normally needs $2n^3/3$ flops in floating point operations, while the floating point operations to solve two triangular systems needs $2n^2$ flops.

The second criterion is the flops-like efficiency index ($FLEI$) which was defined by Montazeri et al. [34] as

$$FLEI = p^{\frac{1}{c}}$$

where p is the order of convergence of the method, c denotes the total computational cost per loop in terms of the number of functional evaluations, as well as the cost of LU factorization for solving two triangular systems (based on the flops).

As the first comparison, we compare M_3 with the third-order method given by Darvishi [35], which is denoted as $M_{3,1}$

$$\mathbf{y}^{(k)} = \mathbf{x}^{(k)} - J_F(\mathbf{x}^{(k)})^{-1}F(\mathbf{x}^{(k)}),$$
$$\mathbf{x}^{(k+1)} = \mathbf{x}^{(k)} - 2(J_F(\mathbf{x}^{(k)}) + J_F(\mathbf{y}^{(k)}))^{-1}F(\mathbf{x}^{(k)}).$$

The second iterative method shown by $M_{3,2}$ is the following third-order method introduced by Hernández [36]

$$\mathbf{y}^{(k)} = \mathbf{x}^{(k)} - \tfrac{1}{2}J_F(\mathbf{x}^{(k)})^{-1}F(\mathbf{x}^{(k)}),$$
$$\mathbf{x}^{(k+1)} = \mathbf{x}^{(k)} + J_F(\mathbf{x}^{(k)})^{-1}(J_F(\mathbf{y}^{(k)}) - 2J_F(\mathbf{x}^{(k)})) \times J_F(\mathbf{x}^{(k)})^{-1}F(\mathbf{x}^{(k)}).$$

Another method is the following third-order iterative method given by Babajee et al. [37], $M_{3,3}$,

$$\mathbf{y}^{(k)} = \mathbf{x}^{(k)} - J_F(\mathbf{x}^{(k)})^{-1}F(\mathbf{x}^{(k)}),$$
$$\mathbf{x}^{(k+1)} = \mathbf{x}^{(k)} + \tfrac{1}{2}J_F(\mathbf{x}^{(k)})^{-1}(J_F(\mathbf{y}^{(k)}) - 3J_F(\mathbf{x}^{(k)})) \times J_F(\mathbf{x}^{(k)})^{-1}F(\mathbf{x}^{(k)}).$$

Finally, the following third-order iterative method, $M_{3,4}$, ref. [38] is considered

$$\mathbf{y}^{(k)} = \mathbf{x}^{(k)} - \tfrac{2}{3}J_F(\mathbf{x}^{(k)})^{-1}F(\mathbf{x}^{(k)}),$$
$$\mathbf{x}^{(k+1)} = \mathbf{x}^{(k)} - 4(J_F(\mathbf{x}^{(k)}) + 3J_F(\mathbf{y}^{(k)}))^{-1}F(\mathbf{x}^{(k)}).$$

The computational efficiency of our third-order method revealed that our method, M_3, is the best one in respect with methods $M_{3,1}$, $M_{3,2}$, $M_{3,3}$ and $M_{3,4}$, as presented in Table 1, and Figures 1 and 2.

Table 1. Comparison of efficiency indices between M_3 and other third-order methods.

Methods	M_3	$M_{3,1}$	$M_{3,2}$	$M_{3,3}$	$M_{3,4}$
No. of steps	2	2	2	2	2
Order of convergence	3	3	3	3	3
Functional evaluations	$2n+n^2$	$n+2n^2$	$n+2n^2$	$n+2n^2$	$n+2n^2$
The classical efficiency index (IE)	$3^{1/(2n+n^2)}$	$3^{1/(n+2n^2)}$	$3^{1/(n+2n^2)}$	$3^{1/(n+2n^2)}$	$3^{1/(n+2n^2)}$
No. of LU decompositions	1	2	1	1	2
Cost of LU decompositions	$\frac{2n^3}{3}$	$\frac{4n^3}{3}$	$\frac{2n^3}{3}$	$\frac{2n^3}{3}$	$\frac{4n^3}{3}$
Cost of linear systems (based on flops)	$\frac{2n^3}{3}+4n^2$	$\frac{4n^3}{3}+4n^2$	$\frac{5n^3}{3}+2n^2$	$\frac{5n^3}{3}+2n^2$	$\frac{4n^3}{3}+4n^2$
Flops-like efficiency index (FLEI)	$3^{1/(\frac{2n^3}{3}+5n^2+2n)}$	$3^{1/(\frac{4n^3}{3}+6n^2+n)}$	$3^{1/(\frac{5n^3}{3}+4n^2+n)}$	$3^{1/(\frac{5n^3}{3}+4n^2+n)}$	$3^{1/(\frac{4n^3}{3}+6n^2+n)}$

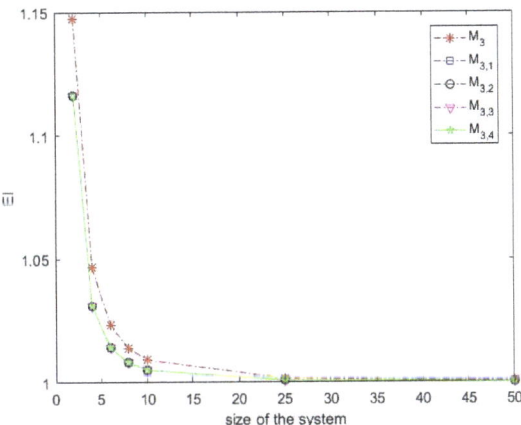

Figure 1. The classical efficiency index for methods M_3, $M_{3,1}$, $M_{3,2}$, $M_{3,3}$ and $M_{3,4}$.

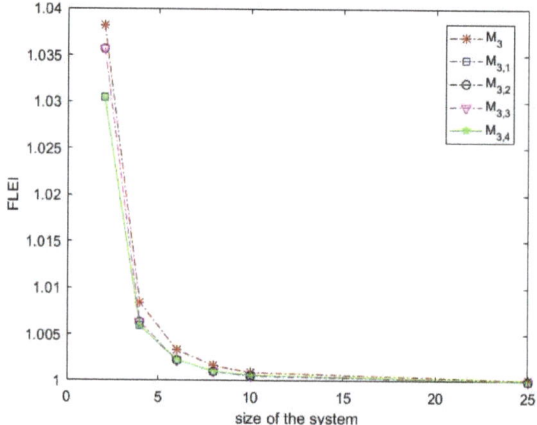

Figure 2. The flops-like efficiency index for methods M_3, $M_{3,1}$, $M_{3,2}$, $M_{3,3}$ and $M_{3,4}$.

2.2. The Fourth-Order FJA

By setting $m = 3$ in FJA, the following three-step algorithm is deduced

$$\begin{aligned} \mathbf{y}^{(k)} &= \mathbf{x}^{(k)} - J_F(\mathbf{x}^{(k)})^{-1} F(\mathbf{x}^{(k)}), \\ \mathbf{z}^{(k)} &= \mathbf{x}^{(k)} - J_F(\mathbf{x}^{(k)})^{-1} (F(\mathbf{y}^{(k)}) + F(\mathbf{x}^{(k)})), \\ \mathbf{x}^{(k+1)} &= \mathbf{y}^{(k)} - J_F(\mathbf{x}^{(k)})^{-1} (F(\mathbf{z}^{(k)}) + F(\mathbf{y}^{(k)})). \end{aligned} \qquad (9)$$

In the following subsections, the order of convergence and efficiency indices are obtained for the method described in (9).

2.2.1. Convergence Analysis

The frozen Jacobian three-step iterative process (9) has the rate of convergence order four by using three evaluations of function F and one first-order Frechèt derivative F per full iterations. To avoid any repetition, we take a sketch of proof on this subject. Similar to the proof of Theorem 1, by setting $\mathbf{z}^{(k)} = \mathbf{x}^{(k+1)}$ in (8) we obtain

$$F(\mathbf{z}^{(k)}) = F'(\alpha)[2C_2^2 E_n^3 + (-9C_2^3 + 7C_2 C_3) E_n^4 + (30C_2^4 - 44C_2^2 C_3 + \\ \ldots + 10C_2 C_4 - C_5) E_n^5 + O||E_n^6||].$$

Hence,

$$(F(\mathbf{z}^{(k)}) + F(\mathbf{y}^{(k)})) = F'(\alpha)\Big[C_2 E_n^2 + 2C_3 E_n^3 + (-4C_2^3 + 3C_4) E_n^4 \\ + (32C_2^5 + 18C_2^4 - 20C_2^2 C_3 + 3C_5) E_n^5 + O||E_n^6||\Big]. \qquad (10)$$

Therefore, from (5) and (10), we find

$$F'(\mathbf{x}^{(k)})^{-1}(F(\mathbf{z}^{(k)}) + F(\mathbf{y}^{(k)})) = \Big[C_2 E_n^2 + (-2C_2^2 + 2C_3) E_n^3 + (-7C_2 C_3 + \ldots \\ + 3C_4) E_n^4 + (18C_2^4 - 10C_2 C_4 - 6C_3^2 + 3C_5) E_n^5 + O||E_n^6||\Big]. \qquad (11)$$

Since we have $x^{(k+1)} = y^{(k)} - J_F(x^{(k)}))^{-1}(F(z^{(k)}) + F(y^{(k)}))$ from (6) and (11), the following result is obtained

$$x^{(k+1)} = \alpha + (4C_2^3)E_n^4 + (32C_2^5 - 26C_2^4 + 20C_2^2C_3 + C_5)E_n^5 + O||E_n^6||. \tag{12}$$

This completes the proof, since error Equation (12) shows that the order of convergence of the frozen Jacobian multi-step iterative method (9) is four.

2.2.2. The Computational of Efficiency

Now, we compare the computational efficiency of our fourth-order scheme (9), called by M_4, with some existing fourth-order methods. The considered methods are: the third-order method $M_{4,1}$ given by Sharma et al. [39],

$$y^{(k)} = \tfrac{2}{3}x^{(k)} - J_F(x^{(k)})^{-1}F(x^{(k)}),$$
$$x^{(k+1)} = x^{(k)} - \tfrac{1}{2}\left[-I + \tfrac{9}{4}J_F(y^{(k)})^{-1}J_F(x^{(k)}) + \tfrac{3}{4}J_F(x^{(k)})^{-1}J_F(y^{(k)})\right]$$
$$\times J_F(x^{(k)})^{-1}F(x^{(k)}),$$

the fourth-order iterative method $M_{4,2}$ given by Darvishi and Barati [40],

$$y^{(k)} = x^{(k)} - J_F(x^{(k)})^{-1}F(x^{(k)}),$$
$$z^{(k)} = x^{(k)} - J_F(x^{(k)})^{-1}\left(F(y^{(k)}) + F(x^{(k)})\right),$$
$$x^{(k+1)} = x^{(k)} - \left[\tfrac{1}{6}J_F(x^{(k)}) + \tfrac{2}{3}J_F(\tfrac{(x^{(k)}+z^{(k)})}{2}) + \tfrac{1}{6}J_F(z^{(k)})\right]^{-1}F(x^{(k)}),$$

the fourth-order iterative method $M_{4,3}$ given by Soleymani et al. [34,41],

$$y^{(k)} = \tfrac{2}{3}x^{(k)} - J_F(x^{(k)})^{-1}F(x^{(k)}),$$
$$x^{(k+1)} = x^{(k)} - \left[I - \tfrac{3}{8}\left(I - (J_F(y^{(k)})^{-1}J_F(x^{(k)}))^2\right)\right]J_F(x^{(k)})^{-1}F(x^{(k)}),$$

and the following Jarratt fourth-order method $M_{4,4}$ [42],

$$y^{(k)} = \tfrac{2}{3}x^{(k)} - J_F(x^{(k)})^{-1}F(x^{(k)}),$$
$$x^{(k+1)} = x^{(k)} - \tfrac{1}{2}(3J_F(y^{(k)}) - J_F(x^{(k)}))^{-1}(3J_F(y^{(k)}) + J_F(x^{(k)}))$$
$$\times J_F(x^{(k)})^{-1}F(x^{(k)}).$$

The computational efficiency of our fourth-order method showed that our method M_4 is better than methods $M_{4,1}$, $M_{4,2}$, $M_{4,3}$ and $M_{4,4}$ as the comparison results are presented in Table 2, and Figures 3 and 4. As we can see from Table 2, the indices of our method M_4 are better than similar ones in methods $M_{4,1}$, $M_{4,2}$, $M_{4,3}$ and $M_{4,4}$. Furthermore, Figures 3 and 4 show the superiority of our method in respect with the another schemes.

Table 2. Comparison of efficiency indices between M_4 and other fourth-order methods.

Methods	M_4	$M_{4,1}$	$M_{4,2}$	$M_{4,3}$	$M_{4,4}$
No. of steps	3	2	3	2	2
Order of convergence	4	4	4	4	4
Functional evaluations	$3n + n^2$	$n + 2n^2$	$2n + 3n^2$	$n + 2n^2$	$n + 2n^2$
The classical efficiency index (IE)	$4^{1/(3n+n^2)}$	$4^{1/(n+2n^2)}$	$4^{1/(2n+3n^2)}$	$4^{1/(n+2n^2)}$	$4^{1/(n+2n^2)}$
No. of LU decompositions	1	2	2	2	2
Cost of LU decompositions	$\tfrac{2n^3}{3}$	$\tfrac{4n^3}{3}$	$\tfrac{4n^3}{3}$	$\tfrac{4n^3}{3}$	$\tfrac{4n^3}{3}$
Cost of linear systems (based on flops)	$\tfrac{2n^3}{3} + 6n^2$	$\tfrac{10n^3}{3} + 2n^2$	$\tfrac{4n^3}{3} + 6n^2$	$\tfrac{7n^3}{3} + 2n^2$	$\tfrac{7n^3}{3} + 2n^2$
Flops-like efficiency index (FLEI)	$4^{1/(\tfrac{2n^3}{3}+7n^2+3n)}$	$4^{1/(\tfrac{10n^3}{3}+4n^2+n)}$	$4^{1/(\tfrac{4n^3}{3}+9n^2+2n)}$	$4^{1/(\tfrac{7n^3}{3}+4n^2+n)}$	$4^{1/(\tfrac{7n^3}{3}+4n^2+n)}$

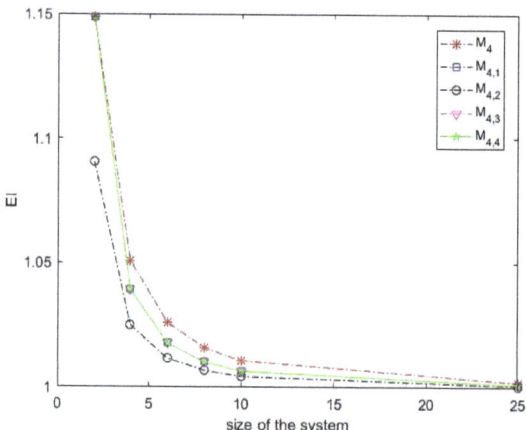

Figure 3. The classical efficiency index for methods M_4, $M_{4,1}$, $M_{4,2}$, $M_{4,3}$ and $M_{4,4}$.

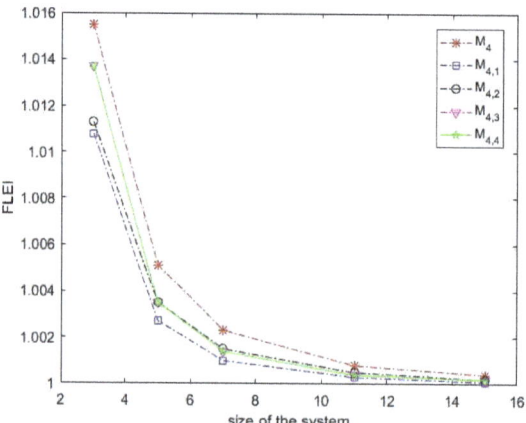

Figure 4. The Flops-like efficiency index for methods M_4, $M_{4,1}$, $M_{4,2}$, $M_{4,3}$ and $M_{4,4}$.

3. Numerical Results

In order to check the validity and efficiency of our proposed frozen Jacobian multi-step iterative methods, three test problems are considered to illustrate convergence and computation behaviors such as efficiency index and some another indices of the frozen Jacobian multi-step iterative methods. Numerical computations have been performed using variable precision arithmetic that uses floating point representation of 100 decimal digits of mantissa in MATLAB. The computer specifications are: Intel(R) Core(TM) i7-1065G7 CPU 1.30 GHz with 16.00 GB of RAM on Windows 10 pro.

Experiment 1. We begin with the following nonlinear system of n equations [43],

$$f_i(\mathbf{x}) = \cos(x_i) - 1, \quad i = 1, 2, \ldots, n. \tag{13}$$

The exact zero of $F(\mathbf{x}) = (f_1(\mathbf{x}), f_2(\mathbf{x}), \ldots, f_n(\mathbf{x}))^t = 0$ is $(0, 0, \ldots, 0)^t$. To solve (13), we set the initial guess as $(0.78, 0.78, \ldots, 0.78)^t$. The stopping criterion is selected as $\|f(\mathbf{x}^{(k)})\| \leq 10^{-3}$.

Experiment 2. The next test problem is the following system of nonlinear equations [44],

$$f_i(\mathbf{x}) = (1 - x_i^2) + x_i(1 + x_i x_{n-2} x_{n-1} x_n) - 2, \quad i = 1, 2, \ldots, n. \tag{14}$$

The exact root of $F(\mathbf{x}) = 0$ is $(1, 1, \ldots, 1)^t$. To solve (14), the initial guess is taken as $(2, 2, \ldots, 2)^t$. The stopping criterion is selected as $||f(\mathbf{x}^{(k)})|| \leq 10^{-8}$.

Experiment 3. The last test problem is the following nonlinear system [9],

$$\begin{aligned} f_i(\mathbf{x}) &= x_i^2 x_{i+1} - 1, \quad i = 1, 2, \ldots, n-1, \\ f_n(\mathbf{x}) &= x_n^2 x_1 - 1, \end{aligned} \tag{15}$$

with the exact solution $(1, 1, \ldots, 1)^t$. To solve (15), the initial guess and the stopping criterion are respectively considered as $(3, 3, \ldots, 3)^t$ and $||f(\mathbf{x}^{(k)})|| \leq 10^{-8}$.

Table 3 shows the comparison results between our third-order frozen Jacobian two-step iterative method M_3 and some third-order frozen Jacobian iterative methods, namely, $M_{3,1}$, $M_{3,2}$, $M_{3,3}$ and $M_{3,4}$. For all test problems, two different values for n are considered, namely, $n = 50, 100$. As this table shows, in all cases, our method works better than the others. Similarly, in Table 4, CPU time and number of iterations are presented for our fourth-order method, namely, M_4 and methods $M_{4,1}$, $M_{4,2}$, $M_{4,3}$ and $M_{4,4}$. Similar to M_3, the CPU time for M_4 is less than the CPU time for the other methods. These tables show superiority of our methods in respect with the other ones. In Tables 3 and 4, it shows the number of iterations.

Table 3. Comparison results between M_3 and other third-order methods.

Methods	Experiment 1			Experiment 2			Experiment 3		
	n	it	cpu	n	it	cpu	n	it	cpu
M_3	50	4	7.7344	50	5	10.6250	50	5	10.4844
	100	5	59.6406	100	5	59.8594	100	5	60.0313
$M_{3,1}$	50	4	11.0625	50	5	13.8125	50	5	14.1406
	100	4	69.4219	100	5	87.3594	100	5	87.4063
$M_{3,2}$	50	4	18.7188	50	5	24.9375	50	5	21.5469
	100	5	157.2344	100	5	143.7344	100	5	146.2656
$M_{3,3}$	50	4	20.7031	50	5	23.1563	50	5	24.2969
	100	5	153.1719	100	5	143.2969	100	5	145.4063
$M_{3,4}$	50	4	13.1719	50	5	13.2500	50	4	11.0156
	100	4	73.2500	100	5	88.2031	100	4	70.2500

Table 4. Comparison results between M_4 and other fourth order methods.

Methods	Experiment 1			Experiment 2			Experiment 3		
	n	it	cpu	n	it	cpu	n	it	cpu
M_4	50	4	12.2463	50	4	13.3218	50	4	11.5781
	100	4	78.1563	100	5	94.9063	100	4	74.2969
$M_{4,1}$	50	4	23.6875	50	4	21.9531	50	4	21.7969
	100	4	151.9844	100	4	144.7656	100	4	140.8438
$M_{4,2}$	50	3	15.3906	50	4	18.9531	50	4	18.6875
	100	4	121.6563	100	4	122.7344	100	4	118.5781
$M_{4,3}$	50	3	12.2188	50	4	17.8750	50	4	15.2656
	100	4	97.5469	100	4	99.0469	100	4	97.1250
$M_{4,4}$	50	3	16.4688	50	4	21.7344	50	4	20.7188
	100	3	109.1719	100	4	152.0156	100	4	140.2969

4. Another Comparison

In the previous parts, we presented some comparison results between our methods M_3 and M_4 with some another frozen Jacobian multi-step iterative methods from third- and fourth-order methods. In this section, we compare our presented methods with three other methods which are fourth- and fifth-order ones. As Tables 5 and 6 and Figures 5 and 6 show, our methods are also better than these methods.

First. The fourth-order method given by Qasim et al. [25], M_A,

$$\begin{aligned}
J_F(\mathbf{x}^{(k)})\theta_1 &= F(\mathbf{x}^{(k)}), \\
\mathbf{y}^{(k)} &= \mathbf{x}^{(k)} - \theta_1, \\
J_F(\mathbf{x}^{(k)})\theta_2 &= F(\mathbf{y}^{(k)}), \\
J_F(\mathbf{x}^{(k)})\theta_3 &= J_F(\mathbf{y}^{(k)})\theta_2, \\
\mathbf{x}^{(k+1)} &= \mathbf{y}^{(k)} - 2\theta_2 + \theta_3.
\end{aligned}$$

Second. The fourth-order Newton-like method by Amat et al. [26], M_B,

$$\begin{aligned}
\mathbf{y}^{(k)} &= \mathbf{x}^{(k)} - J_F(\mathbf{x}^{(k)})^{-1} F(\mathbf{x}^{(k)}), \\
\mathbf{z}^{(k)} &= \mathbf{y}^{(k)} - J_F(\mathbf{x}^{(k)})^{-1} F(\mathbf{y}^{(k)}), \\
\mathbf{x}^{(k+1)} &= \mathbf{z}^{(k)} - J_F(\mathbf{x}^{(k)})^{-1} F(\mathbf{z}^{(k)}).
\end{aligned}$$

Third. The fifth-order iterative method by Ahmad et al. [28], M_C,

$$\begin{aligned}
J_F(\mathbf{x}^{(k)})\theta_1 &= F(\mathbf{x}^{(k)}), \\
\mathbf{y}^{(k)} &= \mathbf{x}^{(k)} - \theta_1, \\
J_F(\mathbf{x}^{(k)})\theta_2 &= F(\mathbf{y}^{(k)}), \\
\mathbf{z}^{(k)} &= \mathbf{y}^{(k)} - 3\theta_2, \\
J_F(\mathbf{x}^{(k)})\theta_3 &= J_F(\mathbf{z}^{(k)})\theta_2, \\
J_F(\mathbf{x}^{(k)})\theta_4 &= J_F(\mathbf{z}^{(k)})\theta_3, \\
\mathbf{x}^{(k+1)} &= \mathbf{y}^{(k)} - \tfrac{7}{4}\theta_2 + \tfrac{1}{2}\theta_3 + \tfrac{1}{4}\theta_4.
\end{aligned}$$

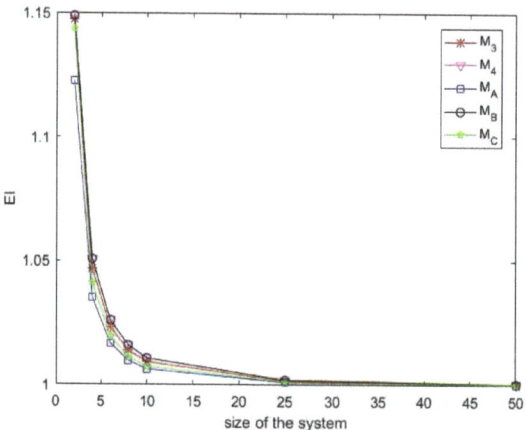

Figure 5. The classical efficiency index for M_3, M_4, M_A, M_B and M_C.

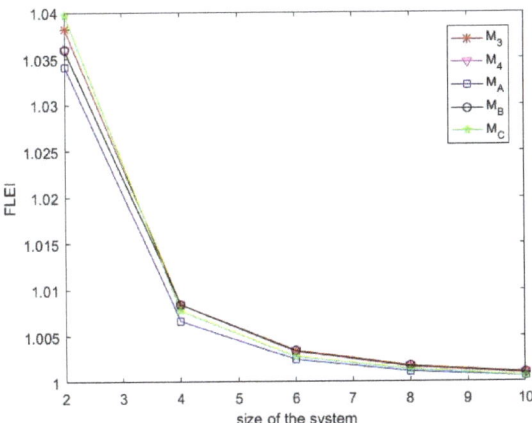

Figure 6. The Flops-like efficiency index for M_3, M_4, M_A, M_B and M_C.

Table 5. Numerical results for comparing of M_3 and M_4 with M_A, M_B and M_C.

Methods	M_3	M_4	M_A	M_B	M_C
No. of steps	2	3	2	3	3
Order of convergence	3	4	4	4	5
Functional evaluations	$2n+n^2$	$3n+n^2$	$2n+2n^2$	$3n+n^2$	$2n+2n^2$
The classical efficiency index (IE)	$3^{1/(2n+n^2)}$	$4^{1/(3n+n^2)}$	$4^{1/(2n+2n^2)}$	$4^{1/(3n+n^2)}$	$5^{1/(2n+2n^2)}$
No. of LU decompositions	1	1	1	1	1
Cost of LU decompositions	$\frac{2n^3}{3}$	$\frac{2n^3}{3}$	$\frac{2n^3}{3}$	$\frac{2n^3}{3}$	$\frac{2n^3}{3}$
Cost of linear systems (based on flops)	$\frac{2n^3}{3}+4n^2$	$\frac{2n^3}{3}+6n^2$	$\frac{5n^3}{3}+4n^2$	$\frac{2n^3}{3}+6n^2$	$\frac{5n^3}{3}+4n^2$
Flops-like efficiency index (FLEI)	$3^{1/(\frac{2n^3}{3}+5n^2+2n)}$	$4^{1/(\frac{2n^3}{3}+7n^2+3n)}$	$4^{1/(\frac{5n^3}{3}+6n^2+2n)}$	$4^{1/(\frac{2n^3}{3}+7n^2+3n)}$	$5^{1/(\frac{5n^3}{3}+6n^2+2n)}$

The comparison results of computational efficiency between our methods M_3 and M_4 with selected methods M_A, M_B and M_C are presented in Table 5. Additionally, Figures 5 and 6 show the graphical comparisons between these methods. Finally, Table 6 shows CPU time and number of iterations to solve our test problems by methods M_3, M_4, M_A, M_B and M_C. These numerical and graphical reports show the quality of our algorithms.

Table 6. Comparison results between M_3, M_4, M_A, M_B and M_C.

Methods	Experiment 1			Experiment 2			Experiment 3		
	n	it	CPU	n	it	CPU	n	it	CPU
M_3	50	4	7.7344	50	5	10.6250	50	5	10.4844
	100	5	59.6406	100	5	59.8594	100	5	60.0313
M_4	50	4	12.2463	50	4	13.3218	50	4	11.5781
	100	4	78.1563	100	5	94.9063	100	4	74.2969
M_A	50	6	23.1875	50	7	25.0625	50	6	25.4063
	100	6	139.5625	100	7	173.8125	100	6	150.8594
M_B	50	4	15.2509	50	4	12.1563	50	4	12.9219
	100	4	76.1406	100	5	91.1719	100	4	71.6406
M_C	50	4	23.4688	50	4	23.4854	50	4	22.1531
	100	4	139.9844	100	4	185.1406	100	4	138.4063

5. Conclusions

In this article, two new frozen Jacobian two- and three-step iterative methods to solve systems of nonlinear equations are presented. For the first method, we proved that the order of convergence is three, while for the second one, a fourth-order convergence is proved. By solving three different examples, one may see our methods work as well. Further, the CPU time of our methods is less than some selected frozen Jacobian multi-step iterative methods in the literature. Moreover, other indices of our methods such as number of steps, functional evaluations, the classical efficiency index, and so on, are better than these indices for other methods. This class of the frozen Jacobian multi-step iterative methods can be a pattern for new research on the frozen Jacobian iterative algorithms.

Author Contributions: Investigation, R.H.A.-O. and M.T.D.; Project administration, M.T.D.; Resources, R.H.A.-O.; Supervision, M.T.D.; Writing—original draft, M.T.D. All authors have read and agreed to the published version of the manuscript.

Funding: This research received no external funding.

Institutional Review Board Statement: Not applicable.

Informed Consent Statement: Not applicable.

Data Availability Statement: Not applicable.

Acknowledgments: The authors would like to thank the editor of the journal and three anonymous reviewers for their generous time in providing detailed comments and suggestions that helped us to improve the paper.

Conflicts of Interest: The authors declare no conflict of interest.

References

1. Fay, T.H.; Graham, S.D. Coupled spring equations. *Int. J. Math. Educ. Sci. Technol.* **2003**, *34*, 65–79. [CrossRef]
2. Petzold, L. Automatic selection of methods for solving stiff and non stiff systems of ordinary differential equations. *SIAM J. Sci. Stat. Comput.* **1983**, *4*, 136–148. [CrossRef]
3. Ehle, B.L. High order A-stable methods for the numerical solution of systems of D.E.'s. *BIT Numer. Math.* **1968**, *8*, 276–278. [CrossRef]
4. Wambecq, A. Rational Runge-Kutta methods for solving systems of ordinary differential equations. *Computing* **1978**, *20*, 333–342. [CrossRef]
5. Liang, H.; Liu, M.; Song, M. Extinction and permanence of the numerical solution of a two-prey one-predator system with impulsive effect. *Int. J. Comput. Math.* **2011**, *88*, 1305–1325. [CrossRef]
6. Harko, T.; Lobo, F.S.N.; Mak, M.K. Exact analytical solutions of the Susceptible-Infected-Recovered (SIR) epidemic model and of the SIR model with equal death and birth rates. *Appl. Math. Comput.* **2014**, *236*, 184–194. [CrossRef]
7. Zhao, J.; Wang, L.; Han, Z. Stability analysis of two new SIRs models with two viruses. *Int. J. Comput. Math.* **2018**, *95*, 2026–2035. [CrossRef]
8. Kröger, M.; Schlickeiser, R. Analytical solution of the SIR-model for the temporal evolution of epidemics, Part A: Time-independent reproduction factor. *J. Phys. A Math. Theor.* **2020**, *53*, 505601. [CrossRef]
9. Ullah, M.Z.; Behl, R.; Argyros, I.K. Some high-order iterative methods for nonlinear models originating from real life problems. *Mathematics* **2020**, *8*, 1249. [CrossRef]
10. Argyros, I.K. Concerning the "terra incognita" between convergence regions of two Newton methods. *Nonlinear Anal.* **2005**, *62*, 179–194. [CrossRef]
11. Drexler, M. Newton Method as a Global Solver for Non-Linear Problems. Ph.D Thesis, University of Oxford, Oxford, UK, 1997.
12. Guti'errez, J.M.; Hern'andez, M.A. A family of Chebyshev-Halley type methods in Banach spaces. *Bull. Aust. Math. Soc.* **1997**, *55*, 113–130. [CrossRef]
13. Cordero, A.; Jordán, C.; Sanabria, E.; Torregrosa, J.R. A new class of iterative processes for solving nonlinear systems by using one divided differences operator. *Mathematics* **2019**, *7*, 776. [CrossRef]
14. Stefanov, S.M. Numerical solution of systems of non linear equations defined by convex functions. *J. Interdiscip. Math.* **2022**, *25*, 951–962. [CrossRef]
15. Lee, M.Y.; Kim, Y.I.K. Development of a family of Jarratt-like sixth-order iterative methods for solving nonlinear systems with their basins of attraction. *Algorithms* **2020**, *13*, 303. [CrossRef]
16. Cordero, A.; Jordán, C.; Sanabria-Codesal, E.; Torregrosa, J.R. Design, convergence and stability of a fourth-order class of iterative methods for solving nonlinear vectorial problems. *Fractal Fract.* **2021**, *5*, 125. [CrossRef]

17. Amiri, A.; Cordero, A.; Darvishi, M.T.; Torregrosa, J.R. A fast algorithm to solve systems of nonlinear equations. *J. Comput. Appl. Math.* **2019**, *354*, 242–258. [CrossRef]
18. Argyros, I.K.; Sharma, D.; Argyros, C.I.; Parhi, S.K.; Sunanda, S.K. A family of fifth and sixth convergence order methods for nonlinear models. *Symmetry* **2021**, *13*, 715. [CrossRef]
19. Singh, A. An efficient fifth-order Steffensen-type method for solving systems of nonlinear equations. *Int. J. Comput. Sci. Math.* **2018**, *9*, 501–514. [CrossRef]
20. Ullah, M.Z.; Serra-Capizzano, S.; Ahmad, F. An efficient multi-step iterative method for computing the numerical solution of systems of nonlinear equations associated with ODEs. *Appl. Math. Comput.* **2015**, *250*, 249–259. [CrossRef]
21. Pacurar, M. Approximating common fixed points of Prešic-Kannan type operators by a multi-step iterative method. *An. St. Univ. Ovidius Constanta* **2009**, *17*, 153–168.
22. Rafiq, A.; Rafiullah, M. Some multi-step iterative methods for solving nonlinear equations. *Comput. Math. Appl.* **2009**, *58*, 1589–1597. [CrossRef]
23. Aremu, K.O.; Izuchukwu, C.; Ogwo, G.N.; Mewomo, O.T. Multi-step iterative algorithm for minimization and fixed point problems in p-uniformly convex metric spaces. *J. Ind. Manag. Optim.* **2021**, *17*, 2161. [CrossRef]
24. Soleymani, F.; Lotfi, T.; Bakhtiari, P. A multi-step class of iterative methods for nonlinear systems. *Optim. Lett.* **2014**, *8*, 1001–1015. [CrossRef]
25. Qasim, U.; Ali, Z.; Ahmad, F.; Serra-Capizzano, S.; Ullah, M.Z.; Asma, M. Constructing frozen Jacobian iterative methods for solving systems of nonlinear equations, associated with ODEs and PDEs using the homotopy method. *Algorithms* **2016**, *9*, 18. [CrossRef]
26. Amat, S.; Busquier, S.; Grau, À.; Grau-Sánchez, M. Maximum efficiency for a family of Newton-like methods with frozen derivatives and some applications. *Appl. Math. Comput.* **2013**, *219*, 7954–7963. [CrossRef]
27. Kouser, S.; Rehman, S.U.; Ahmad, F.; Serra-Capizzano, S.; Ullah, M.Z.; Alshomrani, A.S.; Aljahdali, H.M.; Ahmad, S.; Ahmad, S. Generalized Newton multi-step iterative methods $GMN_{p,m}$ for solving systems of nonlinear equations. *Int. J. Comput. Math.* **2018**, *95*, 881–897. [CrossRef]
28. Ahmad, F.; Tohidi, E.; Ullah, M.Z.; Carrasco, J.A. Higher order multi-step Jarratt-like method for solving systems of nonlinear equations: Application to PDEs and ODEs. *Comput. Math. Appl.* **2015**, *70*, 624–636. [CrossRef]
29. Kaplan, W.; Kaplan, W.A. *Ordinary Differential Equations*; Addison-Wesley Publishing Company: Boston, MA, USA, 1958.
30. Emmanuel, E.C. On the Frechet derivatives with applications to the inverse function theorem of ordinary differential equations. *Aian J. Math. Sci.* **2020**, *4*, 1–10.
31. Ortega, J.M.; Rheinboldt, W.C.; Werner, C. *Iterative Solution of Nonlinear Equations in Several Variables*; Society for Industrial and Applied Mathematics: Philadelphia, PA, USA, 2000.
32. Behl, R.; Bhalla, S.; Magre nán, A.A.; Kumar, S. An efficient high order iterative scheme for large nonlinear systems with dynamics. *J. Comput. Appl. Math.* **2022**, *404*, 113249. [CrossRef]
33. Ostrowski, A.M. *Solutions of the Equations and Systems of Equations*; Prentice-Hall: England Cliffs, NJ, USA; New York, NY, USA, 1964.
34. Montazeri, H.; Soleymani, F.; Shateyi, S.; Motsa, S.S. On a new method for computing the numerical solution of systems of nonlinear equations. *J. Appl. Math.* **2012**, *2012*, 751975. [CrossRef]
35. Darvishi, M.T. A two-step high order Newton-like method for solving systems of nonlinear equations. *Int. J. Pure Appl. Math.* **2009**, *57*, 543–555.
36. Hernández, M.A. Second-derivative-free variant of the Chebyshev method for nonlinear equations. *J. Optim. Theory Appl.* **2000**, *3*, 501–515. [CrossRef]
37. Babajee, D.K.R.; Dauhoo, M.Z.; Darvishi, M.T.; Karami, A.; Barati, A. Analysis of two Chebyshev-like third order methods free from second derivatives for solving systems of nonlinear equations. *J. Comput. Appl. Math.* **2010**, *233*, 2002–2012. [CrossRef]
38. Noor, M.S.; Waseem, M. Some iterative methods for solving a system of nonlinear equations. *Comput. Math. Appl.* **2009**, *57*, 101–106. [CrossRef]
39. Sharma, J.R.; Guha, R.K.; Sharma, R. An efficient fourth order weighted-Newton method for systems of nonlinear equations. *Numer. Algorithms* **2013**, *62*, 307–323. [CrossRef]
40. Darvishi, M.T.; Barati, A. A fourth-order method from quadrature formulae to solve systems of nonlinear equations. *Appl. Math. Comput.* **2007**, *188*, 257–261. [CrossRef]
41. Soleymani, F.,Regarding the accuracy of optimal eighth-order methods. *Math. Comput. Modell.* **2011**, *53*, 1351–1357. [CrossRef]
42. Cordero, A.; Hueso, J.L.; Martínez, E.; Torregrosa, J.R. A modified Newton-Jarratt's composition. *Numer. Algorithms* **2010**, *55*, 87–99. [CrossRef]
43. Shin, B.C.; Darvishi, M.T.; Kim, C.H.,A comparison of the Newton–Krylov method with high order Newton-like methods to solve nonlinear systems. *Appl. Math. Comput.* **2010**, *217*, 3190–3198. [CrossRef]
44. Waziri, M.Y.; Aisha, H.; Gambo, A.I. On performance analysis of diagonal variants of Newton's method for large-scale systems of nonlinear equations. *Int. J. Comput. Appl.* **2011**, *975*, 8887.

Article

Approximation of the Fixed Point of the Product of Two Operators in Banach Algebras with Applications to Some Functional Equations

Khaled Ben Amara [1], Maria Isabel Berenguer [2,3,*] and Aref Jeribi [1]

1. Department of Mathematics, Faculty of Sciences of Sfax, University of Sfax, Sfax 3000, Tunisia
2. Department of Applied Mathematics, E.T.S. de Ingeniería de Edificación, University of Granada, 18071 Granada, Spain
3. Institute of Mathematics (IMAG), University of Granada, 18071 Granada, Spain
* Correspondence: maribel@ugr.es

Abstract: Making use of the Boyd-Wong fixed point theorem, we establish a new existence and uniqueness result and an approximation process of the fixed point for the product of two nonlinear operators in Banach algebras. This provides an adequate tool for deriving the existence and uniqueness of solutions of two interesting type of nonlinear functional equations in Banach algebras, as well as for developing an approximation method of their solutions. In addition, to illustrate the applicability of our results we give some numerical examples.

Keywords: Banach algebras; fixed point theory; functional equations; Schauder bases

MSC: 65J15; 47J25; 46B15; 32A65

1. Introduction

Many phenomena in physics, chemistry, mechanics, electricity, and so as, can be formulated by using the following nonlinear differential equations with nonlocal initial condition of the form:

$$\begin{cases} \dfrac{d}{dt}\left(\dfrac{x(t)}{f(t,x(t))}\right) = g(t,x(t)), & t \in J := [0,\rho], \\ x(0) = \mu(x), \end{cases} \quad (1)$$

where $\rho > 0$ is a real constant, $f : J \times \mathbb{R} \to \mathbb{R} \setminus \{0\}$, $g : J \times \mathbb{R} \to \mathbb{R}$ are supposed to be $\mathcal{D}$-Lipschitzian with respect to the second variable, and the operator $\mu : C(J) \to \mathbb{R}$ represents the nonlocal initial condition, see [1,2]. Here, $C(J)$ is the space of all continuous functions from J into $\mathbb{R}$ endowed with the norm $\|\cdot\|_\infty = \sup_{t \in J}\|x(t)\|$.

The nonlocal condition $x(0) = \mu(x)$ can be more descriptive in physics with better effect than the classical initial condition $x(0) = x_0$, (see, e.g., [2–5]). In the last case, i.e., $x(0) = x_0$, the problem (1) has been studied by Dhage [6] and O'Regan [7]. Therefore it is of interest to discuss and to approximate the solution of (1) with a nonlocal initial condition.

Similarly another class of nonlinear equations is used frequently to describe many phenomena in different fields of applied sciences such as physics, control theory, chemistry, biology, and so forth (see [8–11]). This class is generated by the nonlinear integral equations of the form:

$$x(t) = f(t, x(\sigma(t))) \cdot \left[q(t) + \int_0^{\eta(t)} K(t,s, x(\tau(s)))ds\right], \quad t \in J := [0,\rho], \quad (2)$$

where $\rho > 0$ is a real constant, $\sigma, \tau, \eta : J \to J$ and $q : J \to \mathbb{R}$ are supposed to be continuous, and the functions $f : J \times \mathbb{R} \to \mathbb{R}$, $K : J \times J \times \mathbb{R} \to \mathbb{R}$ are supposed to be $\mathcal{D}$-Lipschizian with respect to the second and the third variable, respectively.

Both, (1) and (2), can be interpreted as fixed point problems in which the equation involved is a nonlinear hybrid equation on a Banach algebra E of the type

$$x = A(x) \cdot B(x), \qquad (3)$$

where A and B are nonlinear operators map a nonempty closed convex subset $\Omega \subset E$ into E.

A hybrid fixed point result to (3) was proved by Dhage in [12] and since then, several extensions and generalizations of this result have been achieved. See [13–15] and the references therein. These results can be used to achieves the existence of solutions. Although the explicit calculation of the fixed point is difficult in most cases, the previous cited results are regarded as one of the most powerful tools to give an approximation of the fixed point by a computational method and to develop numerical methods that allow us to approximate the solution of these equations.

In Banach spaces, several works deals with developing numerical techniques in order to approximate the solutions of integral and integro–differential equations, by using different methods such as the Chebyshev polynomial [16], the secant-like methods [17], using Schauder's basis [18,19], the parameterization method [20], the wavelet methods [21], a collocation method in combination with operational matrices of Berstein polynomials [22], the contraction principle and a suitable quadrature formula [23], the variational iteration method [24], etc.

Since the Banach algebras represents a practical framework for several equations such as (1) and (2), and in general (3), the purposes of this paper are twofold. Firstly, to present, under suitable conditions, a method to approximate the fixed point of a hybrid equation of type (3), by means of the product and composition of operators defined in a Banach algebra. Secondly, to set forth and apply the proposed method to obtain an approximation of the solutions of (1) and (2).

The structure of this work is as follows: in Section 2 we present some definitions and auxiliary results; in Section 3 we derive an approximation method for the fixed point of the hybrid Equation (3); in Sections 4 and 5, we apply our results to prove the existence and the uniqueness of solution of (1) and (2), we give an approximation method for these solutions and moreover, we establish some numerical examples to illustrate the applicability of our results. Finally, some conclusions are quoted in Section 6.

2. Analytical Tools

In this section, we provide some concepts and results that we will need in the following sections. The first analytical tool to be used comes from the theory of the fixed point. Let X be a Banach space with norm $\| \cdot \|$ and the zero element θ. We denote by $B(x, r)$ the closed ball centered at x with radius r. We write B_r to denote $B(\theta, r)$. For any bounded subset Ω of X, the symbol $\|\Omega\|$ denotes the norm of a set Ω, i.e., $\|\Omega\| = \sup\{\|x\|, x \in \Omega\}$.

Let us introduce the concept of $\mathcal{D}$-Lipschitzian mappings which will be used in the sequel.

Definition 1. *Let X be a Banach space. A mapping $A : X \longrightarrow X$ is said to be $\mathcal{D}$-Lipschitzian if*

$$\|Ax - Ay\| \leq \phi(\|x - y\|) \quad \forall x, y \in X$$

with $\phi : \mathbb{R}_+ \longrightarrow \mathbb{R}_+$ a continuous nondecreasing function such that $\phi(0) = 0$. The mapping ϕ is called the $\mathcal{D}$-function associate to A. When $\phi(r) < r$ for $r > 0$, the mapping A is called a nonlinear contraction on X.

The class of $\mathcal{D}$-Lipschitzian mappings on X contains the class of Lipschitzian mapping on X, indeed if $\phi(r) = \alpha r$, for some $\alpha > 0$, then A is called Lipschitzian mapping with Lipschitz constant α or an α-Lipschitzian mapping. When $0 \leq \alpha < 1$, we say that A is a contraction.

The Banach fixed point theorem ensures that every contraction operator A on a complete metric space X has a unique fixed point $\tilde{x} \in X$, and, for every $x_0 \in X$, the sequence $\{A^n(x_0)\}_{n \in \mathbb{N}}$ converges to $\tilde{x}$. Much attention has been paid to Banach principle and it was generalized in different works (we quote, for instance, [25,26]). In [25], Boyd and Wong established the following result.

Theorem 1. *Let (X, d) be a complete metric space, and let $A : X \to X$ be a mapping satisfying*

$$d(A(x), A(y)) \leq \varphi(d(x, y)), \quad \forall x, y \in X$$

where $\varphi : [0, \infty) \to [0, \infty)$ is a continuous function such that $\varphi(r) < r$ if $r > 0$. Then A has a unique fixed point $\tilde{x} \in X$ and for any $x_0 \in X$, the sequence $\{A^n(x_0)\}_{n \in \mathbb{N}}$ converges to $\tilde{x}$.

On the other hand, Schauder bases will constitute the second essential tool. We recall that a Schauder basis in a Banach space E is a sequence $\{e_n\}_{n \in \mathbb{N}} \subset E$ such that for every $x \in E$, there is a unique sequence $\{a_n\}_{n \in \mathbb{N}} \subset \mathbb{R}$ such that

$$x = \sum_{n \geq 1} a_n e_n.$$

This notion produces the concept of the sequence of projections $P_n : E \to E$, defined by the formula

$$P_n\left(\sum_{k \geq 1} a_k e_k\right) = \sum_{k=1}^{n} a_k e_k,$$

and the sequence of coordinate functionals $e_n^* \in E^*$ defined as

$$e_n^*\left(\sum_{k \geq 1} a_k e_k\right) = a_n.$$

Moreover, in view of the Baire category Theorem [27], that for all $n \geq 1$, e_n^* and P_n are continuous. This yields, in particular, that

$$\lim_{n \to \infty} \|P_n(x) - x\| = 0.$$

3. Existence, Uniqueness and Approximation of a Fixed Point of the Product of Two Operators in Banach Algebras

Based on the Boyd-Wong Theorem, we establish the following fixed point result for the product of two nonlinear operators in Banach algebras.

Theorem 2. *Let X be a nonempty closed convex subset of a Banach algebra E. Let $A, B : X \to E$ be two operators satisfying the following conditions:*

(i) *A and B are $\mathcal{D}$-lipschitzian with $\mathcal{D}$-functions φ and ψ respectively,*
(ii) *$A(X)$ and $B(X)$ are bounded,*
(iii) *$A(x) \cdot B(x) \in X$, for all $x \in X$.*

Then, if $\|A(X)\|\psi(r) + \|B(X)\|\varphi(r) < r$ when $r > 0$, there is a unique point $\tilde{x} \in X$ such that $A(\tilde{x}) \cdot B(\tilde{x}) = \tilde{x}$. In addition, for each $x_0 \in X$, the sequence $\{(A \cdot B)^n(x_0)\}_{n \in \mathbb{N}}$ converges to $\tilde{x}$.

Proof. Let $x, y \in X$. we have

$$\|A(x) \cdot B(x) - A(y) \cdot B(y)\| \leq \|A(x) \cdot (B(x) - B(y))\| + \|(A(x) - A(y)) \cdot B(y)\| \leq$$

$$\|A(x)\| \|B(x) - B(y)\| + \|B(y)\| \|A(x) - A(y)\| \leq \|A(X)\| \psi(\|x-y\|) + \|B(X)\| \varphi(\|x-y\|).$$

This implies that $A \cdot B$ defines a nonlinear contraction with $\mathcal{D}$-function

$$\phi(r) = \|A(X)\| \psi(r) + \|B(X)\| \varphi(r), \; r > 0.$$

Applying the cited Boyd-Wong's fixed point Theorem, we obtain the desired result. □

Boyd-Wong's fixed point Theorem expresses the fixed point of $A \cdot B$ as the limit of the sequence $\{(A \cdot B)^n(x_0)\}_{n \in \mathbb{N}}$ with $x_0 \in X$. If it is possible explicitly compute $(A \cdot B)^n(x_0)$, then for each n, the expression $(A \cdot B)^n(x_0)$ would be an approximation of the fixed point. But in the practice, this explicit calculation use to be not possible. For that, our aim is to propose another approximation of the fixed point which simple to calculate. We will need the following lemma.

Lemma 1. *Let X be a nonempty closed convex subset of a Banach algebra E. Let $A, B : X \to E$ be two $\mathcal{D}$-Lipschitzian operators with $\mathcal{D}$-functions φ and ψ, respectively, and $A \cdot B$ maps X into X. Moreover, suppose that*

$$\phi(r) < r, \; r > 0.$$

Let $\tilde{x}$ be the unique fixed point of $A \cdot B$ and $x_0 \in X$. Let $\varepsilon > 0$, $m \in \mathbb{N}$, and $T_0, T_1, \ldots, T_m : E \to E$, with $T_0 \equiv I$, I being the identity operator on E, such that

$$\|\tilde{x} - (A \cdot B)^m(x_0)\| \leq \frac{\varepsilon}{2} \quad (4)$$

and

$$\sum_{p=1}^{m-1} \phi^{m-p}(\|(A \cdot B) \circ T_{p-1} \circ \ldots \circ T_1(x_0) - T_p \circ \ldots \circ T_1(x_0)\|) +$$

$$\|(A \cdot B) \circ T_{m-1} \circ \ldots \circ T_1(x_0) - T_m \circ \ldots \circ T_1(x_0)\| \leq \frac{\varepsilon}{2}. \quad (5)$$

Then,

$$\|\tilde{x} - T_m \circ \ldots \circ T_1(x_0)\| \leq \varepsilon.$$

Proof. Arguing as in the proof of Theorem 2, it follows that $A \cdot B$ is a nonlinear contraction with $\mathcal{D}$-function ϕ, and by induction argument, it is easy to show that

$$\|(A \cdot B)^n(x) - (A \cdot B)^n(y)\| \leq \phi^n(\|x - y\|), \; x, y \in X. \quad (6)$$

By using the triangular inequality, we have

$$\|(A \cdot B)^m(x_0) - T_m \circ \ldots \circ T_1(x_0)\| \leq$$
$$\left\|(A \cdot B)^{m-1} \circ (A \cdot B)(x_0) - (A \cdot B)^{m-1} \circ T_1(x_0)\right\|$$
$$+ \left\|(A \cdot B)^{m-2} \circ (A \cdot B) \circ T_1(x_0) - (A \cdot B)^{m-2} \circ T_2 \circ T_1(x_0)\right\| + \cdots +$$
$$+ \|(A \cdot B) \circ (A \cdot B) \circ T_{m-2} \circ \ldots \circ T_1(x_0) - (A \cdot B) \circ T_{m-1} \circ \ldots \circ T_1(x_0)\|$$
$$+ \|(A \cdot B) \circ T_{m-1} \circ \ldots \circ T_1(x_0) - T_m \circ \ldots \circ T_1(x_0)\|.$$

Taking into account (6), we obtain

$$\|(A \cdot B)^m(x_0) - T_m \circ \ldots \circ T_1(x_0)\| \leq$$
$$\sum_{p=1}^{m-1} \phi^{m-p}(\|(A \cdot B) \circ T_{p-1} \circ \ldots \circ T_1(x_0) - T_p \circ \ldots \circ T_1(x_0)\|)$$
$$+ \|(A \cdot B) \circ T_{m-1} \circ \ldots \circ T_1(x_0) - T_m \circ \ldots \circ T_1(x_0)\|.$$

This implies, by using the Triangular inequality again, that

$$\|\tilde{x} - T_m \circ \ldots \circ T_1(x_0)\| \leq$$
$$\sum_{p=1}^{m-1} \phi^{m-p}\left(\|(A \cdot B) \circ T_{p-1} \circ \ldots \circ T_1(x_0) - T_p \circ \ldots \circ T_1(x_0)\|\right)$$
$$+ \|(A \cdot B) \circ T_{m-1} \circ \ldots \circ T_1(x_0) - T_m \circ \ldots \circ T_1(x_0)\| + \|\tilde{x} - (A \cdot B)^m(x_0)\| \leq \varepsilon. \quad (7)$$

□

Taking into account the above lemma, observe that, under the previous hypotheses,

$$x^* = T_m \circ \ldots \circ T_1(x_0) \approx \tilde{x}$$

In order to get the approximation $x^* = T_m \circ \ldots \circ T_1(x_0)$ of the fixed point $\tilde{x}$, it is evident that, given $\varepsilon > 0$, by Theorem 2, condition (4) is satisfied for m sufficiently large. So, we are interested in building $T_1, T_2, \ldots, T_m$ satisfying (5), i. e. with the idea that

$$(A \cdot B)^m(x_0) \approx T_m \circ \ldots \circ T_1(x_0).$$

Schauder bases are the tool we will use next to build such operators. Concretely, for the case of problems (1) and (2), which can be written as a fixed point problem $x = A(x) \cdot B(x)$, where B is given by an integral operator, we will choice to approximate only the power terms of the operator B which is difficult to compute in general, unlike operator A which is easy to calculate and does not need to approximate their power terms. For this reason, we specifically propose the following scheme, in which we will construct $S_1, S_2, \cdots, S_m$:

$$x_0$$
$$\downarrow$$
$$(A \cdot B)(x_0) \approx \quad\quad T_1(x_0) = A(x_0) \cdot S_1(x_0)$$
$$\downarrow \quad\quad\quad\quad\quad\quad\quad\quad \downarrow$$
$$(A \cdot B)^2(x_0) \approx \quad\quad T_2 \circ T_1 x_0 = (A \cdot S_2) \circ T_1(x_0)$$
$$\vdots \quad\quad \vdots \quad\quad\quad\quad\quad\quad \vdots$$
$$\vdots \quad\quad \vdots \quad\quad\quad\quad\quad\quad \vdots$$
$$\downarrow \quad\quad\quad\quad\quad\quad\quad\quad \downarrow$$
$$(A \cdot B)^m(x_0) \approx T_m \circ \ldots \circ T_1(x_0) = (A \cdot S_m) \circ T_{m-1} \circ \ldots \circ T_1(x_0) \approx \tilde{x}$$

Remark 1. *The above scheme is constructed as follows. In the first term, we approximate $B(x_0)$ by $S_1(x_0)$, then we obtain $T_1(x_0) := A(x_0) \cdot S_1(x_0)$ as an approximation of the first term of the Picard iterate, $A(x_0) \cdot B(x_0)$. In the second term of our scheme, we approximate the second term of the Picard iterate, $(A \cdot B)^2(x_0) = A((A \cdot B)(x_0)) \cdot B((A \cdot B)(x_0))$. So we obtain the second term of our scheme by combining the first term $T_1(x_0)$, with an approximation of the operator B, which denoted by S_2, and consequently we obtain a second term of our scheme $T_2 \circ T_1(x_0) = (A \cdot S_2)(T_1(x_0))$ which approximate $(A \cdot B)^2(x_0)$.*

4. Nonlinear Differential Equations with Nonlocal Initial Condition

In this section we focus our attention in the nonlinear differential equation with nonlocal initial condition (1). This equation will be studied when the mappings $f, g : J \times \mathbb{R} \to \mathbb{R}$ are such that:

(i) The partial mappings $t \mapsto f(t, x)$, $t \mapsto g(t, x)$ are continuous and the mapping $\mu : C(J) \to \mathbb{R}$ is L_μ-Lipschitzian.

(ii) There exist $r > 0$, $\alpha, \gamma : J \to \mathbb{R}$ two continuous functions and $\varphi, \psi : \mathbb{R}_+ \to \mathbb{R}_+$ two nondecreasing, continuous functions such that

$$|f(t,x) - f(t,y)| \leq \alpha(t)\varphi(|x-y|), t \in J, \text{ and } x, y \in \mathbb{R} \text{ with } |x|, |y| \leq r,$$

and

$$|g(t,x) - g(t,y)| \leq \gamma(t)\psi(|x-y|), t \in J \text{ and } x, y \in \mathbb{R} \text{ with } |x|, |y| \leq r.$$

(iii) There is a constant $\delta > 0$ such that $\sup_{x \in \mathbb{R}, |x| \leq r} |f(0,x)|^{-1} \leq \delta$.

Throughout this section, Ω will denote the closed ball B_r of $C(J)$, where r is defined in the above assumption (ii). Observe that Ω is a non-empty, closed, convex and bounded subset of $C(J)$.

4.1. Existence and Uniqueness of Solutions

In this subsection, we prove the existence and the uniqueness of a solution to the functional differential problem (1).

Theorem 3. *Assume that the assumptions (i), (ii) and (iii) hold. If*

$$M_A M_B \leq r \text{ and}$$

$$M_A \delta L_\mu t + \left(M_A \delta^2 |\alpha(0)| M_\mu + M_B \|\alpha\|_\infty \right) \varphi(t) + M_A \|\gamma(\cdot)\|_{L^1} \psi(t) < t, \; \forall t > 0,$$

where $M_A = \|\alpha\|_\infty \varphi(r) + \|f(\cdot, 0)\|_\infty$, $M_B = \delta M_\mu + \|\gamma\|_\infty \rho \psi(r) + \rho \|g(\cdot, 0)\|_\infty$ *and* $M_\mu = (L_\mu r + |\mu(0)|)$, *then the nonlinear differential problem (1) has a unique solution in* Ω.

Proof. Notice that the problem of the existence of a solution to (1) can be formulated in the following fixed point problem $x = A(x) \cdot B(x)$, where A, B are given for $x \in C(J)$ by

$$(A(x))(t) = f(t, x(t))$$

$$(B(x))(t) = \left[\frac{1}{f(0, x(0))} \mu(x) + \int_0^t g(s, x(s)) ds \right], t \in J. \tag{8}$$

Let $x \in \Omega$ and $t, t' \in J$. Since f is $\mathcal{D}$-lipschitzian with respect to the second variable and is continuous with respect to the first variable, then by using the inequality

$$|f(t, x(t)) - f(t', x(t'))| \leq |f(t, x(t)) - f(t', x(t))| + |f(t', x(t)) - f(t', x(t'))|,$$

we can show that A maps Ω into $C(J)$.

Now, let us claim that B maps Ω into $C(J)$. In fact, let $x \in \Omega$ and $t, t' \in J$ be arbitrary. Taking into account that $t \mapsto g(t, x)$ is a continuous mapping, it follows from assumption (ii) that

$$|(B(x))(t) - (B(x))(t')| \leq \int_{t'}^{t} |g(s, x(s)) - g(s, 0)| ds + (t - t') \|g(\cdot, 0)\|_\infty \leq$$

$$(t - t')(\|\gamma\|_\infty \psi(r) + \|g(\cdot, 0)\|_\infty).$$

This proves the claim. Our strategy is to apply Theorem 2 to show the existence and the uniqueness of a fixed point for the product $A \cdot B$ in Ω which in turn is a continuous solution for problem (1).

For this purpose, we will claim, first, that A and B are $\mathcal{D}$-lipschitzian mappings on Ω. The claim regarding A is clear in view of assumption (ii), that is A is $\mathcal{D}$-lipschitzian with $\mathcal{D}$-function Φ such that

$$\Phi(t) = \|\alpha\|_\infty \varphi(t), t \in J.$$

We corroborate now the claim for B. Let $x, y \in \Omega$, and let $t \in J$. By using our assumptions, we obtain

$$|(B(x))(t) - (B(y))(t)| =$$
$$\left| \frac{1}{f(0, x(0))} \mu(x) - \frac{1}{f(0, y(0))} \mu(y) + \int_0^t g(s, x(s)) - g(s, y(s)) ds \right| \leq$$
$$\frac{L_\mu}{|f(0, x(0))|} \|x - y\| + \frac{|\alpha(0)|}{|f(0, x(0)) f(0, y(0))|} (L_\mu r + |\mu(0)|) \varphi(\|x - y\|) +$$
$$\int_0^t |\gamma(s)| \psi(|x(s) - y(s)|) ds \leq$$
$$\delta L_\mu \|x - y\| + \delta^2 |\alpha(0)| (L_\mu r + |\mu(0)|) \varphi(\|x - y\|) + \|\gamma(\cdot)\|_{L^1} \psi(\|x - y\|).$$

Taking the supremum over t, we obtain that B is $\mathcal{D}$-lipschitzian with $\mathcal{D}$-function Ψ such that

$$\Psi(t) = \delta L_\mu t + \delta^2 |\alpha(0)| (L_\mu r + |\mu(0)|) \varphi(t) + \|\gamma(\cdot)\|_{L^1} \psi(t), t \in J.$$

On the other hand, bearing in mind assumption (i), by using the above discussion we can see that $A(\Omega)$ and $B(\Omega)$ are bounded with bounds M_A and M_B respectively. Taking into account the estimate $M_A M_B \leq r$, we obtain that $A \cdot B$ maps Ω into Ω.
Since

$$|(B(x))(t)| \leq \left| \frac{1}{f(0, x(0))} \mu(x) \right| + \int_0^t |g(s, x(s))| ds$$
$$\leq \delta(|\mu(x) - \mu(0)| + |\mu(0)|) + \int_0^t |g(s, x(s)) - g(s, 0)| ds + \int_0^t |g(s, 0)| ds$$
$$\leq \delta(L_\mu \|x\| + |\mu(0)|) + \int_0^t |\gamma(s)| \psi(|x(s)|) ds + \int_0^t |g(s, 0)| ds,$$

and using the fact that $|\gamma(s)| \psi(|x(s)|) \leq \|\gamma\|_\infty \psi(\|x\|) \leq \|\gamma\|_\infty \psi(r)$, we have that

$$\|B(x)\| \leq \delta(L_\mu \|x\| + |\mu(0)|) + \rho \|\gamma\|_\infty \psi(r) + \rho \|g(\cdot, 0)\|_\infty = M_B.$$

On the other hand, $\|A(x)\| \leq M_A$ since

$$|(A(x))(t)| = |f(t, x(t))| \leq |f(t, x(t)) - f(t, 0)| + |f(t, 0)| \leq$$
$$|\alpha(t)| \varphi(|x(t)|) + |f(t, 0)| \leq \|\alpha\|_\infty \varphi(r) + \|f(\cdot, 0)\|_\infty = M_A.$$

Taking into account that

$$\|(A \cdot B)(x) - (A \cdot B)(y)\| \leq \|A(x)\| \|B(x) - B(y)\| + \|B(y)\| \|A(x) - A(y)\|,$$

we can notice that $A \cdot B$ is a nonlinear contraction with $\mathcal{D}$-function $\Theta(\cdot) := M_A \Psi(\cdot) + M_B \Phi(\cdot)$, i.e.,

$$\|(A \cdot B)(x) - (A \cdot B)(y)\| \leq \Theta(\|x - y\|), \ x, y \in \Omega. \tag{9}$$

Now, applying Theorem 2, we infer that (1) has one and only one solution $\tilde{x}$ in Ω, and for each $x_0 \in \Omega$ we have

$$\lim_{n \to \infty} (A \cdot B)^n (x_0) = \tilde{x}. \tag{10}$$

□

In what follows we will assume that the hypotheses of the Theorem 3 are satisfied.

4.2. Numerical Method to Approximate the Solution

In this subsection we find a numerical approximation of the solution to the nonlinear Equation (1) using a Schauder basis $\{e_n\}_{n\geq 1}$ in $C(J)$ and the sequence of associated projections $\{P_n\}_{n\geq 1}$. Let $p \in \mathbb{N}$ and $n_p \in \mathbb{N}$. We consider

$$S_p : C(J) \longrightarrow C(J)$$
$$x \longmapsto S_p(x)$$

defined as

$$S_p(x)(t) = \frac{1}{f(0, x(0))} \mu(x) + \int_0^t P_{n_p}(U_0(x))(s)\,ds,$$

where $U_0 : C(J) \longrightarrow C(J)$ is given by $U_0(x)(s) = g(s, x(s))$.

Now consider the operator $T_p : C(J) \longrightarrow C(J)$ such that for each $x \in C(J)$, $T_p(x)$ is defined by

$$T_p(x)(t) = A(x)(t) S_p(x)(t), \quad t \in J, \tag{11}$$

with $A : C(J) \longrightarrow C(J)$, $A(x)(t) = f(t, x(t))$.

Remark 2. *For $p \geq 1$ and any $n_p \in \mathbb{N}$ that we use for defining T_p, the operator T_p maps Ω into Ω, since just keep in mind that for $x \in \Omega$, we have*

$$|T_p(x)(t)| = \left| A(x)(t) \left(\frac{1}{f(0, x(0))} \mu(x) + \int_0^t P_{n_p}(U_0(x))(s)\,ds \right) \right| \leq$$

$$|f(t, x(t))| \left(\delta|\mu(x)| + \int_0^t \left| P_{n_p}(U_0(x))(s) \right| ds \right),$$

and proceeding as in the above subsection and using the fact that P_{n_p} is a bounded linear operator on $C(J)$, we get

$$|T_p(x)(t)| \leq M_A \left[\delta|\mu(x)| + \rho \left\| P_{n_p}(U_0(x)) \right\| \right] \leq$$

$$M_A \left[\delta(L_\mu r + |\mu(0)|) + \rho \sup_{s \in J} |g(s, x(s))| \right] \leq M_A M_B < r.$$

In particular, for $m \geq 1$, the operator $T_m \circ \ldots \circ T_1$ maps Ω into Ω.

Our goal is to prove that we can chose $n_1, n_2, \ldots \in \mathbb{N}$ in order that $T_1, T_2, \ldots$, which are defined above, can be used to approximate the solution of (1).

Theorem 4. *Let $\tilde{x}$ be the unique solution to the nonlinear problem (1). Let $x_0 \in \Omega$ and $\varepsilon > 0$, then there exist $m \in \mathbb{N}$ and $n_i \in \mathbb{N}$ to construct T_i for $i = 1, \ldots, m$, in such a way that*

$$\|\tilde{x} - T_m \circ \ldots \circ T_1(x_0)\| \leq \varepsilon.$$

Proof. Let $x_0 \in \Omega$ and $\varepsilon > 0$. By using (10), there is $m \in \mathbb{N}$ such that

$$\|(A \cdot B)^m(x_0) - \tilde{x}\| \leq \varepsilon/2.$$

For that m, and for $p \in \{1, \ldots, m\}$, we define $U_p : C(J) \to C(J)$ by

$$U_p(x)(s) := g(s, T_p \circ \ldots \circ T_1(x)(s)), \quad s \in J, x \in C(J)$$

and $A_p : C(J) \to C(J)$ by

$$A_p(x)(s) := f(s, T_p \circ \ldots \circ T_1(x)(s)), \ s \in J, x \in C(J).$$

According to inequality (9), in view of (5) of Lemma 1, it suffices to show that

$$\sum_{p=1}^{m-1} \Theta^{m-p}\left(\|(A \cdot B) \circ T_{p-1} \circ \ldots \circ T_1(x_0) - T_p \circ \ldots \circ T_1(x_0)\|\right) +$$

$$\|(A \cdot B) \circ T_{m-1} \circ \ldots \circ T_1(x_0) - T_m \circ \ldots \circ T_1(x_0)\| \leq \varepsilon/2.$$

In view of (11), we have

$$|(A \cdot B) \circ T_{p-1} \circ \ldots \circ T_1(x_0)(t) - T_p \circ T_{p-1} \circ \ldots \circ T_1(x_0)(t)| =$$

$$|(A \cdot B) \circ T_{p-1} \circ \ldots \circ T_1(x_0)(t) - (A \cdot S_p) \circ T_{p-1} \circ \ldots \circ T_1(x_0)(t)| =$$

$$|A_{p-1}(x_0)(t)(B \circ T_{p-1} \circ \ldots \circ T_1(x_0)(t) - S_p \circ T_{p-1} \circ \ldots \circ T_1(x_0)(t))|.$$

Taking into account Remark 2, we infer that $\|A_{p-1}(x)\|$ is bounded, and consequently we get

$$|(A \cdot B) \circ T_{p-1} \circ \ldots \circ T_1(x_0)(t) - T_p \circ T_{p-1} \circ \ldots \circ T_1(x_0)(t)| =$$

$$\left|A_{p-1}(x_0)(t)\left(\int_0^t g(s, T_{p-1} \circ \ldots \circ T_1(x_0)(s))\,ds - \int_0^t P_{n_p}(U_{p-1}(x_0))(s)\,ds\right)\right| \leq$$

$$|A_{p-1}(x_0)(t)| \int_0^t \left|\left(P_{n_p}(U_{p-1}(x_0)) - U_{p-1}(x_0)\right)(s)\right| ds \leq$$

$$\rho \|A_{p-1}(x_0)\| \left\|P_{n_p}(U_{p-1})(x_0) - U_{p-1}(x_0)\right\|.$$

Taking the supremum over t, we get

$$\|(A \cdot B) \circ T_{p-1} \circ \ldots \circ T_1(x_0) - T_p \circ T_{p-1} \circ \ldots \circ T_1(x_0)\| \leq$$

$$\rho M_A \left\|P_{n_p}(U_{p-1})(x_0) - U_{p-1}(x_0)\right\|.$$

Since Θ is a nondecreasing continuous mapping, and taking into account the convergence of the projection operators associated to the Schauder basis, for all $1 \leq p \leq m$ we obtain

$$\Theta^{m-p}\left(\rho M_A \left\|P_{n_p}(U_{p-1}(x_0)) - U_{p-1}(x_0)\right\|\right) \leq \varepsilon/2m,$$

for n_p sufficiently large. Consequently, we consider those $n_1, \ldots, n_m \in \mathbb{N}$ for defining T_1, $T_2, \ldots, T_m$ respectively, and we obtain

$$\sum_{p=1}^{m-1} \Theta^{m-p}\left(\|(A \cdot B) \circ T_{p-1} \circ \ldots \circ T_1(x_0) - T_p \circ \ldots \circ T_1(x_0)\|\right) +$$

$$\|(A \cdot B) \circ T_{m-1} \circ \ldots \circ T_1(x_0) - T_m \circ \ldots \circ T_1(x_0)\| \leq$$

$$\sum_{p=1}^{m-1} \Theta^{m-p}\left(\rho M_A \left\|P_{n_p}(U_{p-1}(x_0)) - U_{p-1}(x_0)\right\|\right) + \rho M_A \left\|P_{n_m}(U_{m-1}(x_0)) - U_{m-1}(x_0)\right\| \leq \varepsilon/2.$$

Now apply Lemma 1, in order to get $\|\tilde{x} - T_m \circ \ldots \circ T_1(x_0)\| < \varepsilon$. □

4.3. Numerical Experiments

This subsection is devoted to providing some examples and their numerical results to illustrate the theorems of the above sections. We will consider $J = [0, 1]$ and the classical Faber-Schauder system in $C(J)$ where the nodes are the naturally ordered dyadic numbers (see Table 1 in [18] and [28,29] for details). In following examples, we will denote $x^* = T_m \circ \ldots \circ T_1(x_0)$ with $m = 4$ and $n_1 = \cdots = n_m = l$ with $l = 9$ or $l = 33$.

Example 1. *Consider the nonlinear differential equation with a nonlocal initial condition*

$$\begin{cases} \dfrac{d}{dt}\left(\dfrac{x(t)}{f(t,x(t))}\right) = ae^{-x(t)}, \ t \in J, \\ x(0) = b\left(\sup_{t \in J}|x(t)| + \dfrac{3}{4}\right), \end{cases} \quad (12)$$

where $0 < a < 1/\log(2)$ and $f(t,x) = \dfrac{b}{1 + ae^{-b}t}$.
Let us define the mappings $g : J \times \mathbb{R} \to \mathbb{R}$ and $\mu : C(J) \to \mathbb{R}$ by

$$g(t,x) = ae^{-x}, \ t \in J, x \in \mathbb{R}$$

and

$$\mu(u) = b\left(\sup_{t \in J}|u(t)| + 3/4\right), \ u \in C(J).$$

Let R be small enough such that $a(\log(2) + R) < 1$. Let $x,y \in [-R,R]$, by an elementary calculus we can show that the functions f and g satisfy the condition (ii), with $\alpha(t) = \varphi(t) = 0$, $\gamma(t) = ae^R(1 - e^{-t})$, and $\psi(t) = t$.
On the other hand, we have that μ is Lipschizian with a Lipschiz constant $L_\mu = b$, and

$$\sup_{x, |x| \leq R} [f(0,x)]^{-1} \leq \delta = \dfrac{1}{b}.$$

Applying Theorem 3, we obtain that (12) has a unique solution in $B_R = \{x \in C(J); \|x\| \leq R\}$ with $R = 3/4$, when a is small enough. In fact the solution is $\tilde{x}(t) = b$. We apply the numerical method for $a = 0.1$, $b = \frac{1}{4}$ and the initial $x_0(t) = \frac{1}{4}\left(\sqrt{bt} + 1\right)$. Table 1 collects the obtained results.

Table 1. Numerical results for (12) with initial $x_0(t) = \frac{1}{4}\left(\sqrt{bt} + 1\right)$.

t	$\tilde{x}(t)$	$x^*(t)$ with $l = 9$	$x^*(t)$ with $l = 33$
0.1	0.25	0.2526360625738145	0.2506238401703868
0.2	0.25	0.2512245431325148	0.2506151528771704
0.3	0.25	0.2510208953229317	0.2506066551064274
0.4	0.25	0.2510087458298449	0.2505983412941664
0.5	0.25	0.2509968386936278	0.2505902060799007
0.6	0.25	0.2509851672563384	0.2505822442972077
0.7	0.25	0.2509737250885047	0.2505744509661791
0.8	0.25	0.2509625059364119	0.2505668212861210
0.9	0.25	0.2509515037642987	0.2505593506272617
1	0.25	0.2509407127451644	0.2505520345235613
$\|x^* - \tilde{x}\|_\infty$		2.86369×10^{-3}	1.0862×10^{-3}

Example 2. *Consider the nonlinear differential equation with a nonlocal initial condition*

$$\begin{cases} \dfrac{d}{dt}\left(\dfrac{x(t)}{f(t,x(t))}\right) = a(x(t))^2, \ t \in J, \\ x(0) = 1/(4b)\sup\limits_{t \in J}|x(t)|^2, \end{cases} \quad (13)$$

where a, b are positive constants such that $ab^2 < 3$ and $f(t,x) = \dfrac{b(t+1)}{1 + \frac{ab^2}{3}(x^3/b^3 - 1)}$.

Let us define the mappings $g: J \times \mathbb{R} \to \mathbb{R}$ and $\mu: C(J) \to \mathbb{R}$ by

$$g(t,x) = ax^2, \ t \in J, x \in \mathbb{R} \text{ and } \mu(u) = 1/(4b)\sup_{t \in J}|u(t)|^2, \ u \in C(J).$$

Let $R > 0$ such that $2b \leq R$ and $\frac{a}{3b}(b^3 + R^3) < 1$. Let $x, y \in [-R, R]$. By an elementary calculus we can show that f and g satisfy the condition (ii) with $\alpha(t) = \dfrac{a(t+1)R^2}{\left(1 - \frac{a}{3b}(R^3 + b^3)\right)^2}$, $\gamma(t) = 2aR$, and $\varphi(t) = \psi(t) = t$.

On the other hand, we have that

$$|\mu(u) - \mu(v)| \leq \frac{R}{2b}\|u - v\|.$$

Consequently, μ is Lipschizian with a Lipschiz constant $L_\mu = \frac{R}{2b}$. It is easy to prove that

$$\sup_{x \in \mathbb{R}, |x| \leq R}[f(0,x)]^{-1} \leq \delta = aR^3/(3b^2) + 1/b.$$

Now, applying Theorem 3, in order to obtain that (13), with a is small enough, has a unique solution in B_R with $R = 1/2$. We can check that the solution is $\tilde{x}(t) = b(t+1)$. Table 2 shows the numerical results of the proposed method for $a = 0.05$, $b = 1/4$ and $x_0(t) = \frac{1}{2}t$.

Table 2. Numerical results for (13) with initial $x_0(t) = \frac{1}{2}t$.

t	$\tilde{x}(t)$	$x^*(t)$ with $l = 9$	$x^*(t)$ with $l = 33$
0.1	0.275	0.2715154513364088	0.2714532970472882
0.2	0.3	0.2961167353030552	0.2961332465465061
0.3	0.325	0.3207837845940706	0.3208140511167786
0.4	0.35	0.3454635279153586	0.3454958547548318
0.5	0.375	0.3701445199310059	0.3701788114857308
0.6	0.40	0.3948268789541488	0.3948630864085328
0.7	0.425	0.4195107187398104	0.4195488540144761
0.8	0.45	0.4441962543294659	0.4442362958308083
0.9	0.475	0.4688837174935067	0.4689256009587782
1	0.5	0.4935733558651244	0.4936169655580174
$\|x^* - \tilde{x}\|_\infty$		6.42664×10^{-3}	6.38303×10^{-3}

5. Nonlinear Integral Equations

This section deals with the nonlinear integral Equation (2). More precisely, we prove the existence and the uniqueness of a solution to Equation (2) under the hypothesis that the mappings $f: J \times \mathbb{R} \to \mathbb{R}$ and $K: J \times J \times \mathbb{R} \to \mathbb{R}$ are such that:

(i) The partial mappings $t \mapsto f(t,x)$ and $(t,s) \mapsto K(t,s,x)$ are continuous.

(ii) There exist $r > 0$, $\gamma : J \times J \to \mathbb{R}$, $\alpha : J \to \mathbb{R}$ two continuous functions and $\varphi, \psi : \mathbb{R}_+ \longrightarrow \mathbb{R}_+$ two nondecreasing continuous functions such that

$$|f(t,x) - f(t,y)| \leq \alpha(t)\varphi(|x-y|), t \in J, \text{ and } x, y \in \mathbb{R} \text{ with } |x|, |y| \leq r,$$

and

$$|K(t,s,x) - K(t,s,y)| \leq \gamma(t,s)\psi(|x-y|), t, s \in J \text{ and } x, y \in \mathbb{R} \text{ with } |x|, |y| \leq r.$$

Throughout this section, Ω will denote the closed ball B_r of $C(J)$, where r is defined in the above assumption (ii).

5.1. Existence and Uniqueness of Solutions

To allow the abstract formulation of Equation (2), we define the following operators on $C(J)$ by

$$
\begin{aligned}
(Ax)(t) &= f(t, x(\sigma(t))), \\
(Bx)(t) &= \left[q(t) + \int_0^{\eta(t)} K(t, s, x(\tau(s))) ds \right], t \in J.
\end{aligned}
\tag{14}
$$

First, we will establish the following result which shows the existence and uniqueness of a solution.

Theorem 5. *Assume that the assumptions (i) and (ii) hold. If*

$$M_A M_B \leq r \text{ and } M_A \rho \|\gamma\|_\infty \psi(t) + M_B \|\alpha\|_\infty \varphi(t) < t, \ \forall t > 0,$$

where

$$M_A = \|\alpha\|_\infty \varphi(r) + \|f(\cdot, \theta)\|_\infty \text{ and } M_B = \|q(\cdot)\|_\infty + \rho(\|K(\cdot, \cdot, 0)\|_\infty + \|\gamma\|_\infty \psi(r)),$$

then the nonlinear integral Equation (2) has a unique solution in Ω.

Proof. By using similar arguments to those in the above section, we can show that A and B define $\mathcal{D}$-lipschitzian mappings from Ω into $C(J)$, with $\mathcal{D}$-functions $\|\alpha\|_\infty \varphi$ and $\rho\|\gamma\|_\infty \psi$, respectively. Also it is easy to see that $A(\Omega)$ and $B(\Omega)$ are bounded with bounds, respectively, M_A and M_B. Taking into account our assumptions, we deduce that $A \cdot B$ maps Ω into Ω.

Notice that $A \cdot B$ defines a nonlinear contraction with $\mathcal{D}$-function

$$\Theta(t) := \rho \|\gamma\|_\infty M_A \psi(t) + \|\alpha\|_\infty M_B \varphi(t), t \geq 0, \text{ i.e.,}$$

$$\|(A \cdot B)(x) - (A \cdot B)(y)\| \leq \Theta(\|x - y\|), \ x, y \in \Omega. \tag{15}$$

Now, an application of Theorem 2 yields that (2) has one and only one solution $\tilde{x}$ in Ω, and for each $x_0 \in \Omega$ we have

$$\lim_{n \to \infty} (A \cdot B)^n (x_0) = \tilde{x}. \tag{16}$$

□

5.2. A Numerical Method to Approximate the Solution

Now we consider a Schauder basis $\{e_n\}_{n\geq 1}$ in $C(J \times J)$ and the sequence of associated projections $\{P_n\}_{n\geq 1}$. Let $p \in \mathbb{N}$, $n_p \in \mathbb{N}$ and consider

$$\begin{cases} S_p : C(J) \longrightarrow C(J) \\ x \longrightarrow S_p(x)(t) = q(t) + \int_0^{\eta(t)} P_{n_p}(U_0(x))(t,s)ds, \end{cases}$$

where $U_0 : C(J) \longrightarrow C(J \times J)$ is defined as $U_0(x)(t,s) = K(t,s,x(\tau(s)))$. Also, we consider the operator $T_p : C(J) \longrightarrow C(J)$, which assigns for all $x \in C(J)$ the valued $T_p(x) \in C(J)$ such that

$$T_p(x)(t) = A(x)(t) S_{n_p}(x)(t), t \in J,$$

where $A : C(J) \longrightarrow C(J)$ is defined as $A(x)(t) = f(t, x(\sigma(t)))$.

Remark 3. *Since for $p \geq 1$,*

$$|T_p(x)(t)| = \left| A(x)(t) \left(q(t) + \int_0^{\eta(t)} P_{n_p}(U_0(x))(t,s)ds \right) \right| \leq$$

$$|f(t, x(\sigma(t)))| \left(|q(t)| + \int_0^{\eta(t)} |P_{n_p}(U_0(x))(t,s)| ds \right),$$

proceeding essentially as in the above section and using the fact that P_{n_p} is a bounded linear operator on $C(J \times J)$, we get

$$|T_p(x)(t)| \leq M_A \left(|q(t)| + \rho \|P_{n_p}(U_0(x))\| \right) \leq$$

$$M_A \left(\|q\|_\infty + \rho \sup_{t,s \in J} |K(t,s,x(\tau(s)))| \right) \leq M_A M_B.$$

Accordingly, under the hypotheses of the Theorem 5, the mapping T_p maps Ω into Ω. In particular, for $m \geq 1$, the operator $T_m \circ \ldots \circ T_1$ maps Ω into Ω.

Analogously as we did in the previous section, the following result allow us to justify it is possible to choose $n_1, n_2, \ldots$ in order that $T_1, T_2, \ldots$ can be used to approximate the unique solution to Equation (2).

Theorem 6. *Let $\tilde{x}$ be the unique solution to the nonlinear Equation (2). Let $x_0 \in \Omega$ and $\varepsilon > 0$, then there exists $m \in \mathbb{N}$ and $n_i \in \mathbb{N}$ to construct T_i for $i = 1, \ldots, m$, such that*

$$\|\tilde{x} - T_m \circ \ldots \circ T_1(x_0)\| \leq \varepsilon.$$

Proof. Let $\varepsilon > 0$, by using (16), there is $m \in \mathbb{N}$ such that

$$\|(A \cdot B)^m(x_0) - \tilde{x}\| \leq \varepsilon/2.$$

For that m, and for $p \in \{1, \ldots, m\}$, we define $U_p : C(J) \to C(J \times J)$ by

$$U_p(x)(t,s) := K(t, s, T_p \circ \ldots \circ T_1(x)(s)), \ t, s \in J, x \in C(J)$$

and $A_p : C(J) \to C(J)$ by

$$A_p(x)(s) := f(s, T_p \circ \ldots \circ T_1(x)(s)), \ s \in J, x \in C(J).$$

Proceeding essentially, as in the Theorem 4, and taking into account (15) together with Remark 3 the desired thesis can be proved. □

5.3. Numerical Experiments

This section is devoted to give some numerical examples to illustrate the previous results using the usual Schauder basis in $C([0,1]^2)$ with the well know square ordering (see Table 1 in [18] and [28,29]). In each example, we will denote $x^* = T_m \circ \ldots \circ T_1(x_0)$ for $m = 4$ and $n_1 = \cdots = n_m = l^2$ with $l = 9$ or $l = 33$.

Example 3. Consider the nonlinear integral equation

$$x(t) = a(t+1)\left[\frac{b}{a} - \frac{b^2}{3}\left((t+1)^3 - 1\right) + \int_0^t (x(s))^2 ds\right], \quad t \in J. \qquad (17)$$

Now we consider the mappings $q : J \to J$, $f : J \times \mathbb{R} \to \mathbb{R}$ and $K : J \times J \times \mathbb{R} \to \mathbb{R}$ such that $q(t) = b/a - \frac{b^2}{3}((t+1)^3 - 1)$, $f(t,x) = a(t+1)$ and $K(t,s,x) = x^2$. Let $R > 0$ and let $x, y \in [-R, R]$. We have that

$$|K(t,s,x) - K(t,s,y)| \le \gamma(t,s)\psi(|x-y|),$$

where $\gamma(t,s) = 2R$, and $\psi(t) = t$. An application of Theorem 5, yields that (17) has a unique solution in B_R, with $R = 3$. In fact the solution is $\tilde{x}(t) = b(t+1)$.

Using the proposed method with $a = 0.1$, $b = 0.1$ and $x_0(t) = t^2$, we obtain Table 3.

Table 3. Numerical results for the (17).

t	$\tilde{x}(t)$	$x^*(t)$ with $l = 9$	$x^*(t)$ with $l = 33$
0.1	0.11	0.1099446333333333	0.1099595576568532
0.2	0.12	0.1198179180577049	0.1199472782251611
0.3	0.13	0.1297511699020331	0.1299327014013851
0.4	0.14	0.1396866403161547	0.1399156114644378
0.5	0.15	0.1496116012197044	0.1498957849652041
0.6	0.16	0.1595251486759711	0.1598729913214837
0.7	0.17	0.1694262809122463	0.1698469898893412
0.8	0.18	0.1793140741901599	0.1798175262525480
0.9	0.19	0.1891875688779072	0.1897843325246908
1	0.2	0.1990457618518603	0.1997471266515799
$\|x^* - \tilde{x}\|_\infty$		9.544238×10^{-4}	2.52873×10^{-4}

Example 4. Consider the nonlinear differential equation

$$x(t) = \left(ae^{-x(t)} + b\right)\left[\frac{t}{ae^{-t}+b} + \frac{1}{1-c}\log(\cos(1-c)t) + \int_0^t \tan((1-c)x(s))ds\right]. \qquad (18)$$

Similarly to that above, (18) can be written as a fixed point problem with the same notations in (14). Let $R > 0$ and let $x, y \in [-R, R]$. By an elementary calculus we can show that the functions f and g satisfy the condition (ii), with $\alpha(t) = ae^R$, $\gamma(t) = (1 + \tan^2(1-c)R)$, and $\varphi(t) = (1 - e^{-t})$ and $\psi(t) = \tan(1-c)t$.

Apply Theorem 5, (18), with a small enough and $c = 1 - a$, has a unique solution in B_R with $R = 3$, in fact the solution is $\tilde{x}(t) = t$. We obtain the results given in Table 4 for $a = 0.01$, $b = 1$, $R = 3$, and $x_0(t) = \sin(t)$.

Table 4. Numerical results for (18) with initial $x_0(t) = \sin(t)$.

t	$\tilde{x}(t)$	$x^*(t)$ with $l = 9$	$x^*(t)$ with $l = 33$
0.1	0.1	0.0999495927525812	0.0999734131829520
0.2	0.2	0.1998269806205324	0.1999419676240642
0.3	0.3	0.2997014781005956	0.2999105694862292
0.4	0.4	0.3995761128223367	0.3998792008487213
0.5	0.5	0.4994508163308592	0.4998478468962116
0.6	0.6	0.5993255387084228	0.5998164954408373
0.7	0.7	0.6992002390137386	0.6997851365136741
0.8	0.8	0.7990748839377436	0.7997537620153589
0.9	0.9	0.8989494465775325	0.8997223654190059
1	1	0.9988239054111422	0.9996909415162489
$\|x^* - \tilde{x}\|_\infty$		1.17609×10^{-3}	3.09058×10^{-4}

Example 5. Consider the problem (2) with

$$f(t,x) = at\left[(b+t)^2 + \frac{t}{(t+1)}\int_0^t \left(1 - e^{-(t+1)(as+1)}\right)ds\right]^{-1},$$

$$K(t,s,x) = \int_0^{x+1} e^{-(t+1)u}du, \qquad (19)$$

$$q(t) = (b+t)^2.$$

Let $0 < R < 1$ and let $x, y \in [-R, R]$. By an elementary calculus, we can show that f and g satisfy the condition (ii), with $\alpha(t) = \varphi(t) = 0$, $\psi(t) = \int_0^{2t} e^{-s}ds$, and $\gamma(t,s) = \frac{1}{t+1}e^{(t+1)(R-1)}$.
Taking $a = 0.1, b = 1$, and applying Theorem 5, the problem has a unique solution in $B_R = \{x \in C([0,1]); \|x\| \leq R\}$, in fact the solution is $\tilde{x}(t) = at$. We obtain the results given in Table 5.

Table 5. Numerical results for (19) with initial $x_0(t) = 1/2\cos(10\pi t)$.

t	$\tilde{x}(t)$	$x^*(t)$ with $l = 9$	$x^*(t)$ with $l = 33$
0.1	0.01	0.0098078897681979	0.0098501736202539
0.2	0.02	0.0191334693414161	0.0197640067592651
0.3	0.03	0.0288588703908235	0.0297138485291223
0.4	0.04	0.0387456185368957	0.0396854768250511
0.5	0.05	0.0486866179763731	0.0496708731179798
0.6	0.06	0.0586657967463166	0.0596654694199951
0.7	0.06	0.0686685394448633	0.0696660302996126
0.8	0.08	0.0786865051341015	0.0796705375310556
0.9	0.09	0.0887140587924687	0.0896776281114000
1	0.09	0.0987473453913395	0.0996863636633998
$\|x^* - \tilde{x}\|_\infty$		1.33705×10^{-3}	3.34982×10^{-4}

6. Conclusions

In this paper we have presented a numerical method, based on the use of Schauder's bases, to solve hybrid nonlinear equations in Banach algebras. To do this, we have used

Boyd-Wong's theorem to establish the existence and uniqueness of a fixed point for the product of two nonlinear operators in Banach algebra (Theorem 2). The method is applied to a wide class of nonlinear hybrid equations such as the ones we have illustrated by means of several numerical examples.

The possibility of applying this process or a similar idea to other types of hybrid equations or systems of such equations is open and we hope to discuss this in the near future.

Author Contributions: Conceptualization, K.B.A. and M.I.B.; methodology, K.B.A., M.I.B. and A.J.; software, K.B.A. and M.I.B.; validation, K.B.A. and M.I.B.; formal analysis, K.B.A., M.I.B. and A.J.; investigation, K.B.A. and M.I.B.; writing—original draft preparation, K.B.A. and M.I.B.; writing—review and editing, K.B.A. and M.I.B.; supervision, K.B.A., M.I.B. and A.J. All authors have read and agreed to the published version of the manuscript.

Funding: The research of Aref Jeribi and Khaled Ben Amara has been partially supported by the University of Sfax (Tunisia). The research of María Isabel Berenguer has been partially supported by Junta de Andalucía (Spain), Project *Convex and numerical analysis*, reference FQM359, and by the *María de Maeztu* Excellence Unit IMAG, reference CEX2020-001105-M, funded by MCIN/AEI/10.13039/501100011033/.

Data Availability Statement: Not applicable.

Acknowledgments: This work was partially carried out during the first author's visit to the Department of Applied Mathematics, University of Granada. The authors wish to thank the anonymous referees for their useful comments. They also acknowledge the financial support of the University of Sfax (Tunisia), the Consejería de Conocimiento, Investigación y Universidad, Junta de Andalucía (Spain) and the *María de Maeztu* Excellence Unit IMAG (Spain).

Conflicts of Interest: The authors declare no conflict of interest.

References

1. Deimling, K. *Nonlinear Functional Analysis*; Springer: Berlin/Heidelberg, Germany, 1985; ISBN 3-540-13928-1.
2. Djebali, S.; Sahnoun, Z. Nonlinear alternatives of Schauder and Krasnosel'skii types with applications to Hammerstein integral equations in L^1-spaces. *J. Differ. Equ.* **2010**, *249*, 2061–2075. [CrossRef]
3. Byszewski, L. Theorems about the existence and uniqueness of solutions of a semilinear evolution nonlocal Cauchy problem. *J. Math. Anal. Appl.* **1991**, *162*, 494–505. [CrossRef]
4. Byszewski, L. *Existence and Uniqueness of Mild and Classical Solutions of Semilinear Functional-Differential Evolution Nonlocal Cauchy Problem*; Selected Problems of Mathematics; Cracow University of Technology: Krakow, Poland, 1995
5. Deng, K. Exponential decay of solutions of semilinear parabolic equations with nonlocal initial conditions. *J. Math. Anal. Appl.* **1993**, *179*, 630–637. [CrossRef]
6. Dhage, B.C. Multi-valued mappings and fixed points I. *Nonlinear Funct. Anal. Appl.* **2005**, *10*, 359–378. [CrossRef]
7. O'Regan, D. New fixed point results for 1-set contractive set-valued maps. *Comput. Math. Appl.* **1998**, *35*, 27–34. [CrossRef]
8. Ben Amar, A.; Chouayekh, S.; Jeribi, A. Fixed point theory in a new class of Banach algebras and application. *Afr. Mat.* **2013**, *24*, 705–724. [CrossRef]
9. Dhage, B.C. On some nonlinear alternatives of Leray-Schauder type and functional integral equations. *Arch. Math. (Brno)* **2006**, *42*, 11–23.
10. Jeribi, A.; Kaddachi, N.; Krichen, B. Existence results for a system of nonlinear integral equations in Banach algebras under weak topology. *Fixed Point Theory* **2017**, *18*, 247–267. [CrossRef]
11. Jeribi, A.; Krichen, B. Nonlinear functional analysis in Banach spaces and Banach algebras: Fixed point theory under weak topology for nonlinear operators and block operator matrices with applications. In *Monographs and Research Notes in Mathematics*; CRC Press/Taylor and Francis: Boca Raton, FL, USA, 2015.
12. Dhage, B.C. On some variants of Schauder's fixed point principle and applications to nonlinear integral equations. *J. Math. Phy. Sci.* **1988**, *25*, 603–611.
13. Cichon, M.; Metwali, M.M.A. On a fixed point theorem for the product of operators. *J. Fixed Point Theory Appl.* **2016**, *18*, 753–770. [CrossRef]
14. Dhage, B.C. On a fixed point theorem in Banach algebras with aplications. *Appl. Math. Lett.* **2005**, *18*, 273–280. [CrossRef]
15. Dhage, B.C. A hybrid fixed point theorem in Banach algebras with applications. *Commun. Appl. Nonlinear Anal.* **2006**, *13*, 71–84.
16. Akyüz-Daşcıoğlu, A.; Sezer, M. Chebyshev polynomial solutions of systems of higher-order linear Fredholm-Volterra integro-differential equations. *J. Frankl. Inst.* **2005**, *342*, 688–701. [CrossRef]
17. Argyros, I.K.; Ezquerro, J.A.; Hernández, M.A.; Hilout, S.; Romero, N.; Velasco, A.I. Expanding the applicability of secant like methods for solving nonlinear equations. *Carphatian J. Math.* **2015**, *31*, 11–30. [CrossRef]

18. Berenguer, M.I.; Gámez, D.; López Linares, A.J. Fixed point techniques and Schauder bases to approximate the solution of the first order nonlinear mixed Fredholm-Volterra integro-differential equation. *J. Comput. Appl. Math.* **2013**, *252*, 52–61. [CrossRef]
19. Berenguer, M.I.; Gámez, D. A computational method for solving a class of two dimensional Volterra integral equations. *J. Comput. Appl. Math.* **2017**, *318*, 403–410. [CrossRef]
20. Dzhumabaev, D.S. On one approach to solve the linear boundary value problems for Fredholm integro differential equations. *J. Comput. Appl. Math.* **2016**, *294*, 342–357. [CrossRef]
21. Heydari, M.H.; Hooshmandasl, M.R.; Mohammadi, F.; Cattani, C. Wavelets method for solving systems of nonlinear singular fractional Volterra integro-differential equations. *Commun. Nonlinear Sci.* **2014**, *19*, 37–48. [CrossRef]
22. Maleknejad, K.; Basirat, B.; Hashemizadeh, E. A Berstein operational matrix approach for solving a system of high order linear Volterra-Fredholm integro-differential equations. *Math. Comput. Model.* **2012**, *55*, 1363–1372. [CrossRef]
23. Micula, S. On some iterative numerical methods for a Volterra functional integral equation of the second kind. *J. Fixed Point Theory Appl.* **2017**, *19*, 1815–1824. [CrossRef]
24. Saberi-Nadjafi, J.; Tamamgar, M. The variational iteration method: A highly promising method for solving the system of integro-differential equations. *Comput. Math. Appl.* **2008**, *56*, 346–351. [CrossRef]
25. Boyd, D.W.; Wong, J.S.W. On nonlinear contractions. *Proc. Am. Math. Soc.* **1969**, *20*, 458–464. [CrossRef]
26. Pata, V. A fixed point theorem in metric spaces. *J. Fixed Point Theory Appl.* **2011**, *10*, 299–305. [CrossRef]
27. Brezis, H. *Functional Analysis, Sobolev Spaces and Partial Differential Equations*; Universitext; Springer: New York, NY, USA, 2011; ISBN 978-0-387-70913-0.
28. Gelbaum, B.R.; Gil de Lamadrid, J. Bases of tensor products of Banach spaces. *Pac. J. Math.* **1961**, *11*, 1281–1286. [CrossRef]
29. Semadeni, Z. Product Schauder bases and approximation with nodes in spaces of continuous functions. *Bull. Acad. Polon. Sci.* **1963**, *11*, 387–391.

Article

Finding an Efficient Computational Solution for the Bates Partial Integro-Differential Equation Utilizing the RBF-FD Scheme

Gholamreza Farahmand [1], Taher Lotfi [1,*], Malik Zaka Ullah [2] and Stanford Shateyi [3,*]

1 Department of Mathematics, Hamedan Branch, Islamic Azad University, Hamedan, Iran; g.r_farahmand@yahoo.com
2 Mathematical Modeling and Applied Computation (MMAC) Research Group, Department of Mathematics, King Abdulaziz University, Jeddah 21589, Saudi Arabia; zmalek@kau.edu.sa
3 Department of Mathematics and Applied Mathematics, School of Mathematical and Natural Sciences, University of Venda, P. Bag X5050, Thohoyandou 0950, South Africa
* Correspondence: lotfi@iauh.ac.ir (T.L.); stanford.shateyi@univen.ac.za (S.S.)

Abstract: This paper proposes a computational solver via the localized radial basis function finite difference (RBF-FD) scheme and the use of graded meshes for solving the time-dependent Bates partial integro-differential equation (PIDE) arising in computational finance. In order to avoid facing a large system of discretization systems, we employ graded meshes along both of the spatial variables, which results in constructing a set of ordinary differential equations (ODEs) of lower sizes. Moreover, an explicit time integrator is used because it can bypass the need to solve the large discretized linear systems in each time level. The stability of the numerical method is discussed in detail based on the eigenvalues of the system matrix. Finally, numerical tests revealed the accuracy and reliability of the presented solver.

Keywords: PIDE; stochastic volatility; semi-discretiztion; RBF-FD; Bates model

MSC: 65M22; 91G60; 91B25

1. Introductory Notes

The Bates model for option pricing considers that the underlying asset S_t, the volatility V_t, the riskless constant r and N_t as the Poisson process satisfy the following system of stochastic differential equations (SDEs) [1]:

$$dS_t = \sqrt{V_t} S_t dW_t^1 + (-\lambda \xi - q + r) S_t dt + (\varrho - 1) S_t dN_t,$$
$$dV_t = \sigma \sqrt{V_t} dW_t^2 + \kappa(-V_t + \theta) dt,$$
(1)

wherein W_t^2 and W_t^1 are standard Brownian motions having $dW_t^1 dW_t^2 = \rho dt$. Here κ is the reversion's rate of the variance V_t, λ is the Poisson process intensity, ξ is the mean jump, q is the dividend, ϱ is the jump size, while θ is the mean level and σ stands for the volatility fixed value.

Financial derivatives such as European call or put options play pioneer roles in the risk management of some portfolios and their pricing as efficiently as possible is of importance. On the other hand for the financial derivative price, since analytical relations are available only in limited settings, one is in need for the construction and the application of fast and stable numerical solvers. More concretely, starting from the initial time zero, we must numerically solve a second-order high-dimensional time-dependent partial integro-differential equation (PIDE) or a partial differential equation (PDE) and then compute the present value of the financial derivative [2–4].

The Heston model, which could be considered as a generalization of the Black–Scholes model [5], can be extended further if one follows the consideration of Bates [1,6] by imposing the jump component into the modeling. In fact, in the stochastic volatility jump (SVJ) model, the price of an option is computed by solving a time-dependent 2D PIDE [7,8]. It is requisite to recall some related models [9,10] discussing stochastic volatility for PDEs in control theory and AI.

The Bates PIDE based on the price function $u(x,y,\tau)$ for European options is expressed by the following [11]:

$$\frac{\partial u(x,y,\tau)}{\partial \tau} = \frac{1}{2}yx^2\frac{\partial^2 u(x,y,\tau)}{\partial x^2} + \frac{1}{2}\sigma^2 y\frac{\partial^2 u(x,y,\tau)}{\partial y^2}$$
$$+ \rho\sigma yx\frac{\partial^2 u(x,y,\tau)}{\partial x \partial y}$$
$$+ (-\lambda\xi - q + r)x\frac{\partial u(x,y,\tau)}{\partial x} + \kappa(\theta - y)\frac{\partial u(x,y,\tau)}{\partial y} \qquad (2)$$
$$- (\lambda + r)u(x,y,\tau) + \lambda \int_0^\infty u(x\varrho,y,\tau)b(\varrho)d\varrho = \mathcal{A}u(x,y,\tau),$$

wherein T is the time to maturity and $\tau = T - t$ is a time transformation to have forward in time PIDE formulation, unlike the original Bates PIDE, which is backward in time. Besides, both the differential and integral parts of the PIDE problem have been encapsulated in the operator $\mathcal{A}$, that is to say, we also can write

$$\mathcal{A}u(x,y,\tau) = \mathcal{A}_D u(x,y,\tau) + \lambda \mathcal{A}_I u(x,y,\tau), \qquad (3)$$

in which $\mathcal{A}_D$ and $\mathcal{A}_I$ stand for the differential and integral portions of the PIDE problem. The probability density function is $b(\varrho) = \frac{1}{\sqrt{2\pi}\hat{\sigma}\varrho}\exp\left[-\frac{(\ln(\varrho)-\gamma)^2}{2\hat{\sigma}^2}\right]$, where it reads $\int_0^\infty b(\varrho)d\varrho = 1$. Here, $\hat{\sigma}$ and γ are the standard deviation and the mean, respectively, which are positive constants. Additionally, we have $\xi = \exp\left(\gamma + \frac{1}{2}\hat{\sigma}^2\right) - 1$.

The so-called payoff which is the the initial condition for the PIDE problem in call-type option pricing can be expressed as [12]:

$$u(x,y,0) = (0, x - K)^+, \qquad (4)$$

wherein K is the strike price. The payoff for a put option could be written similarly. The point is that the initial condition is written only on x and does not rely on the second independent variable of the PIDE, i.e., y.

The side conditions for x and y could be given as follows [12]:

$$u(x,y,\tau) \simeq 0, \qquad x \to 0, \qquad (5)$$
$$u(x,y,\tau) \simeq x_{\max}\exp(-q\tau) - K\exp(-r\tau), \qquad x \to x_{\max}, \qquad (6)$$
$$\frac{\partial u(x,y,\tau)}{\partial y} \simeq 0, \qquad y \to +y_{\max}. \qquad (7)$$

Note that for the case when $y = 0$, the PIDE (2) is degenerate and no boundaries should be incorporated while $x_{\max}$ and $y_{\max}$ are large constants. Similarly for the put option, the boundary conditions are described by the following:

$$u(x,y,\tau) \simeq K\exp(-r\tau) - x_{\max}\exp(-q\tau), \qquad x \to 0, \qquad (8)$$
$$u(x,y,\tau) \simeq 0, \qquad x \to x_{\max}, \qquad (9)$$
$$\frac{\partial u(x,y,\tau)}{\partial y} \simeq 0, \qquad y \to y_{\max}. \qquad (10)$$

The Bates PIDE (2) is given on $(x, y, \tau) \in [0, +\infty) \times [0, +\infty) \times (0, T]$. To solve our high-dimensional linear PDE, we must truncate the unbounded domain while quite delicately ignoring the error caused by imposing the boundary conditions. This can be pursued as follows:

$$\Omega = [0, x_{\max}] \times [0, y_{\max}], \tag{11}$$

wherein $x_{\max}, y_{\max}$ are fixed values. The values for $x_{\max}$, and $y_{\max}$ should be considered large enough to be able to neglect the effect of imposing artificial boundary conditions or imposing the boundary conditions for truncated domains. Some choices are $\Omega = [0, 4K] \times [0, 1]$ or $\Omega = [0, 3K] \times [0, 1]$.

Assume that $\{x_i\}_{i=1}^{m}$ is a mesh of nodes for x. The hyperbolic stretching of nodes [13] can be expressed as follows ($1 \leq i \leq m$):

$$x_i = c \sinh(\beta_i) + K, \tag{12}$$

wherein $c > 0$ stands for a fixed value that controls the density around $x = K$ and $m \gg 3$. In implementations, one can employ c as in [14], i.e., $c = K/5$. This puts a focus around the strike price, in which the initial condition of the PIDE has nonsmoothness. Moreover, $\{\beta_i\}_{i=0}^{m}$ stands for the uniform points given by the following:

$$\beta_i = (i-1)\Delta\beta + \sinh^{-1}\left(-\frac{K}{c}\right), \quad 1 \leq i \leq m, \tag{13}$$

wherein $\Delta\beta = (m-1)^{-1}\left(\sinh^{-1}\left(\frac{S-K}{c}\right) - \sinh^{-1}\left(\frac{-K}{c}\right)\right)$.

Also, if $\{y_j\}_{j=1}^{n}$ is a partition for y, then this stretching strategy can be expressed by the following:

$$y_j = \sinh(\varsigma_j)\nu, \quad 1 \leq j \leq n, \tag{14}$$

wherein $\nu > 0$ is a fixed value that controls the density around $y = 0$ and $n \gg 3$. Basically, we use $\nu = K/500$ [14]. Additionally, the ς_j are equidistant nodes provided by $\varsigma_j = (\Delta\varsigma)(j-1)$, and for any $1 \leq j \leq n$ we have $\Delta\varsigma = \frac{1}{n-1}\sinh^{-1}\left(\frac{K}{\nu}\right)$.

Numerical solution methods generally utilize the discretization means to realize the approximate calculation. When the computational domain/interval is partitioned more finely, the calculated result is closer to the theoretical solution. Indeed, the time required for the calculation increases. For high-dimensional PIDE problems with kink behavior at the initial conditions, sometimes special solvers such as high-order sparse numerical methods are necessary, see, e.g., [15]. Noting finite difference (FD) methods are discussed in [16,17].

In this paper, the main aim is to propose a novel computational method for resolving (2) via the radial basis function generated finite difference (RBF-FD) methodology [18]. This is mostly because (2) is a (1+2)D problem with variable coefficients, in which there is one cross derivatives. Hence, the computational solvers should be constructed for this aim with much attention. In fact, the motivation of this work lies in the fact that literature lacks the application of efficient RBF-FD methodology which result in fast and sparse procedures for solving the Bates PIDE model. Hence, such an application and investigation on the theoretical stability issues will help price option under stochastic volatility in equity markets.

The RBF-FD formulations in this paper, see, e.g., [19], are written so they can be applied to graded meshes in which there is a clear concentration on the hot zone. The procedure taken here is to employ tensor grids and then time discretize the semi-discretized constructed problem. We note that the present work is related to the pioneering works in [20–22]. Meanwhile, these works motivate us to propose a new variant of the RBF-FD scheme for the Bates PIDE problem that competes with these efficient works.

In this paper, after reviewing the well-resulted maps for generating graded meshes along spatial variables with a clear focus around the hot area, the rest of this article is unfolded as follows. The RBF-FD formulas associated with the GMQ RBF are given in

Section 2. Then, the semi-discretization of the two-dimensional PDE (2) is described in Section 3. Then in Section 4, an explicitly quadratically convergent method is taken into account. In fact, an explicit time integrator is used because it can avoid to the need to solve the large discretized linear systems in each time level. It is shown that the proposed solver is fast and conditionally stable. The numerical pieces of evidence are given in Section 5, which overwhelmingly uphold the theoretical discussions of the paper. Concluding notes are provided in Section 6.

2. RBF-FD: The Weights

Generally speaking, for computing the weights α_i in the methodology of the RBF-FD, one must consider L as a linear operator and at $\underline{x} = \underline{x}_p$, for the node locations $\underline{x}_i$, the following is written down [20]:

$$\begin{bmatrix} \Lambda_1(\underline{x}_1) & \Lambda_1(\underline{x}_2) & \cdots & \Lambda_1(\underline{x}_m) \\ \Lambda_2(\underline{x}_1) & \Lambda_2(\underline{x}_2) & \cdots & \Lambda_2(\underline{x}_m) \\ \vdots & \vdots & & \vdots \\ \Lambda_m(\underline{x}_1) & \Lambda_m(\underline{x}_2) & \cdots & \Lambda_m(\underline{x}_m) \end{bmatrix} \begin{bmatrix} \alpha_1 \\ \alpha_2 \\ \vdots \\ \alpha_m \end{bmatrix} = \begin{bmatrix} L\Lambda_1(\underline{x})|_{\underline{x}=\underline{x}_p} \\ L\Lambda_2(\underline{x})|_{\underline{x}=\underline{x}_p} \\ \vdots \\ L\Lambda_m(\underline{x})|_{\underline{x}=\underline{x}_p} \end{bmatrix}, \quad (15)$$

where the underlined $\underline{x}$ shows a vector quantity in the dimension d and $1 \leq k \leq m$ for some set of test functions $\Lambda(\underline{x})$. It is noted that the extension of RBF-FD methodology for solving computational finance models was revived by the works of Soleymani and co-authors, see for instance [23,24].

Now, we consider the famous generalized multiquadric RBF (GMQ RBF) as follows ([25] Chapter 4):

$$\Lambda(r_i) = (p^2 + r_i^2)^l, \quad i = 1, 2, \ldots, \mathrm{m}, \quad (16)$$

where l is a suitable parameter, the parameter of shape is p and $r_i = \|\mathbf{y} - \mathbf{y}_i\|$ shows the Euclidean distance.

It is now focused on computing the weights for the GMQ RBF (in the 1D case without loss of generality). So, we consider a graded mesh including three points along the first spatial variable. For finding the weights of the RBF-FD methodology, by taking into account L as an operator, we could write down [26]:

$$L[\Lambda(y_j)] \simeq \sum_{i=1}^{\psi} \alpha_i \Lambda(y_i), \quad j = 1, 2, \ldots, \psi. \quad (17)$$

This gives us ψ unknowns for ψ equations while the solutions will be α_i. For computing the 1st derivative, three graded nodes are considered ($\psi = 3$) as comes next: $\{y_i - h, y_i, y_i + wh\}$, $w > 0$, $h > 0$, and find (17) as follows:

$$g'(y_i) \simeq \alpha_{i-1} g(y_{i-1}) + \alpha_i g(y_i) + \alpha_{i+1} g(y_{i+1}). \quad (18)$$

Noting that we assume that the function g is smooth sufficiently. In estimating the 1st derivative of a function, the analytical weighting coefficients associated to this RBF can be given as follows [22]:

$$\alpha_{i-1} = \frac{\omega(p^2(9 - 6l) - h^2(l-1)(4(l-5)\omega - 10l + 29))}{3p^2 h(2l-3)(\omega+1)}, \quad (19)$$

$$\alpha_i = \frac{(\omega-1)(p^2(6l-9) + 4h^2(l-5)(l-1)\omega)}{3p^2 h(2l-3)\omega}, \quad (20)$$

$$\alpha_{i+1} = \frac{p^2(6l-9) - h^2(l-1)\omega(2l(5\omega-2) - 29\omega + 20)}{3p^2 h(2l-3)\omega(\omega+1)}. \quad (21)$$

Similarly, in estimating the function's second derivative, we can obtain

$$g''(y_i) \simeq \sum_{j=i-1}^{i+1} \Theta_j g(y_j), \tag{22}$$

along with the following weighting coefficients:

$$\Theta_{i-1} = \frac{2(p^2(6l-9) - h^2(l-1)(4(l-5)\omega^2 + (34-8l)\omega + 10l - 29))}{3p^2h^2(2l-3)(\omega+1)}, \tag{23}$$

$$\Theta_i = \frac{2(p^2(9-6l) + h^2(l-1)(4(l-5)\omega^2 + (25-2l)\omega + 4(l-5)))}{3p^2h^2(2l-3)\omega}, \tag{24}$$

$$\Theta_{i+1} = \frac{2(p^2(6l-9) - h^2(l-1)(2l(\omega(5\omega-4)+2) + \omega(34-29\omega) - 20))}{3p^2h^2(2l-3)\omega(\omega+1)}. \tag{25}$$

Also noting that the given RBF-FD formulations are valid for the interior nodes and at boundary points, similar formulations must be constructed. We give the derivation for the independent variable y and it would be similar for the other cases. The formulations (19)–(21) and (23)–(24) are useful for the rows two to the row before the last one, while for the 1st and the last rows of the derivative matrices (30) and (31), the weighting coefficients could not be valid on boundaries and sided estimations should be incorporated. Hence, by the work [21] on the stencil $\{y_1, y_2, y_3\}$, we have:

$$g'(y_1) = g[y_2, y_1] - g[y_3, y_2] + g[y_3, y_1] + \mathcal{O}\left((y_2 - y_1)^2\right), \tag{26}$$

and

$$g'(y_m) = -g[y_{m-1}, y_{m-2}] + g[y_{m-2}, y_m] + g[y_m, y_{m-1}] + \mathcal{O}\left((y_{m-1} - y_m)^2\right), \tag{27}$$

wherein $g[l, p] = (g(l) - g(p))/(l - p)$. In a similar manner, for the four nodes $\{\{y_1, g(y_1)\}, \{y_2, g(y_2)\}, \{y_3, g(y_3)\}, \{y_4, g(y_4)\}\}$, we can obtain

$$g''(y_1) = \frac{2(\delta y_{1,2} + \delta y_{1,3} + \delta y_{1,4})}{\delta y_{1,2} \delta y_{1,3} \delta y_{1,4}} g(y_1) + \frac{2(\delta y_{3,1} + \delta y_{4,1})}{\delta y_{1,2} \delta y_{2,3} \delta y_{2,4}} g(y_2) \\ + \frac{2(\delta y_{2,1} + \delta y_{4,1})}{\delta y_{1,3} \delta y_{3,2} \delta y_{3,4}} g(y_3) + \frac{2(\delta y_{2,1} + \delta y_{3,1})}{\delta y_{1,4} \delta y_{4,2} \delta y_{4,3}} g(y_4) + \mathcal{O}\left(h^2\right), \tag{28}$$

where $\delta y_{l,q} = y_l - y_q$, h is the maximum space width for the considered stencil nodes. Similarly, we have:

$$g''(y_m) = \frac{2(\delta y_{m-3,m} + \delta y_{m-2,m} + \delta y_{m-1,m})}{\delta y_{m-3,m} \delta y_{m,m-2} \delta y_{m,m-1}} g(y_m) + \frac{2(\delta y_{m-3,m} + \delta y_{m-2,m})}{\delta y_{m-3,m-1} \delta y_{m-1,m-2} \delta y_{m-1,m}} g(y_{m-1}) \\ + \frac{2(\delta y_{m-3,m} + \delta y_{m-1,m})}{\delta y_{m-3,m-2} \delta y_{m-2,m-1} \delta y_{m-2,m}} g(y_{m-2}) + \frac{2(\delta y_{m-2,m} + \delta y_{m-1,m})}{\delta y_{m-2,m-3} \delta y_{m-1,m-3} \delta y_{m,m-3}} g(y_{m-3}) \\ + \mathcal{O}\left(h^2\right). \tag{29}$$

3. A New Solution Method

Let us use the well-known procedure of method of lines (MOL) for semi discretization of the time-dependent problem [27,28] and convert the PIDE problem into a set of linear ordinary differential equations (ODEs). Hence, the following derivative matrices for the

1st and 2nd derivatives of the function in approximating the PDE problem (2) via semi-discretization are considered on non-uniform stencils given in Section 2 as comes next:

$$M_x = \begin{cases} \alpha_{i,j} \text{ using } (19) & i-j=1, \\ \alpha_{i,j} \text{ using } (20) & i-j=0, \\ \alpha_{i,j} \text{ using } (21) & j-i=1, \\ 0 & \text{otherwise,} \end{cases} \qquad (30)$$

and

$$M_{xx} = \begin{cases} \Theta_{i,j} \text{ using } (23) & i-j=1, \\ \Theta_{i,j} \text{ using } (24) & i-j=0, \\ \Theta_{i,j} \text{ using } (25) & j-i=1, \\ 0 & \text{otherwise.} \end{cases} \qquad (31)$$

Consider the $N \times N$ unit matrix $I = I_x \otimes I_y$, while $N = m \times n$, I_x and I_y are unit matrices of appropriate sizes. The MOL can be resulted in the following coefficient matrix for the 1 + 2 dimensional PIDE:

$$\begin{aligned} B = &\frac{1}{2}\mathcal{Y}\mathcal{X}^2(M_{xx} \otimes I_n) + \frac{1}{2}\sigma^2 \mathcal{Y}(I_m \otimes M_{yy}) + \rho\sigma\mathcal{Y}\mathcal{X}M_{x,y} \\ &+ (-\lambda\xi - q + r)\mathcal{X}(M_x \otimes I_n) + \kappa(\theta I_N - \mathcal{Y})(I_m \otimes M_y) - (-\lambda + r)I_N, \end{aligned} \qquad (32)$$

where $\otimes$ stands for the Kronecker product. The square matrices M_x, M_y, M_z, M_{xx}, and M_{yy}, are constructed by the associated weights similarly. Additionally, the sparse diagonal matrices $\mathcal{Y}$ and $\mathcal{X}$ are written as:

$$\mathcal{Y} = I_x \otimes \text{diag}(y_1, y_2, \cdots, y_n), \qquad (33)$$

$$\mathcal{X} = \text{diag}(x_1, x_2, \cdots, x_m) \otimes I_y. \qquad (34)$$

Here the weights corresponding the cross derivative term in the structure of the PIDE (2) can be obtained by employing the Kronecker product as follows:

$$M_{x,y} = M_x \otimes M_y. \qquad (35)$$

Now it is possible to find the following system of ODEs for pricing (2):

$$u'(\tau) = Bu(\tau). \qquad (36)$$

Now, note that we can use the work of [22,29] to discretize the integral part as follows. By a linear interpolation for $u(x\varrho, y, \tau)$ among the adaptive numerical grid nodes, the nonlocal integral given in (2) can be solved using

$$\mathcal{A}_I(u) = \int_0^\infty u(x\varrho, y, \tau)b(\varrho)d\varrho. \qquad (37)$$

Employing $z = x\varrho$, one can transform (37) into the integral below:

$$\mathcal{A}_I(u) = \int_0^\infty u(z, y, \tau) b\left(\frac{z}{x}\right)\left(\frac{1}{x}\right) dz. \qquad (38)$$

Using a linear interpolation for (38), we can find the following:

$$\mathcal{A}_i(u) \simeq \sum_{l=1}^{m-1} Q_{i,l}, \qquad (39)$$

for every node x_i, $i = 2, \ldots, m - 1$, wherein

$$Q_{i,l} = \int_{x_l}^{x_{l+1}} \left(\frac{x_{l+1} - z}{\Delta x_l} u(x_l, y, \tau) + \frac{z - x_l}{\Delta x_l} u(x_{l+1}, y, \tau) \right) b\left(\frac{z}{x_i}\right)\left(\frac{1}{x_i}\right) dz, \quad (40)$$

wherein $\Delta x_l = x_{l+1} - x_l$ is the graded step size. Hence, we have

$$
\begin{aligned}
Q_{i,l} = \frac{1}{2\Delta x_l} &\left(\exp\left(\gamma + \frac{\hat{\sigma}^2}{2}\right) \left(-\operatorname{erf}\left(\frac{-\ln\left(\frac{x_l}{x_i}\right) + \gamma + \hat{\sigma}^2}{\sqrt{2}\hat{\sigma}} \right) \right.\right. \\
+ \operatorname{erf} &\left(\frac{-\ln\left(\frac{x_{l+1}}{x_i}\right) + \gamma + \hat{\sigma}^2}{\sqrt{2}\hat{\sigma}} \right) \Bigg) x_i(u(x_l, y, \tau) - u(x_{l+1}, y, \tau)) + \left(\operatorname{erf}\left(\frac{\gamma - \ln\left(\frac{x_l}{x_i}\right)}{\sqrt{2}\hat{\sigma}} \right) \right. \\
-\operatorname{erf} &\left(\frac{\gamma - \ln\left(\frac{x_{l+1}}{x_i}\right)}{\sqrt{2}\hat{\sigma}} \right) \Bigg) (x_{l+1} u(x_l, y, \tau) - x_l u(x_{l+1}, y, \tau)) \Bigg),
\end{aligned}
\quad (41)
$$

wherein erf($\cdot$) stands for the Gaussian distribution.

So, (36) turns into

$$u'(\tau) = \tilde{B} u(\tau), \quad (42)$$

where $\tilde{B}$ is the system matrix after imposing the integral part. Finally, after considering the boundary conditions, a set of ODEs can be attained as follows:

$$u'(\tau) = F(\tau, u(\tau)) = \tilde{B} u(\tau) + b, \quad (43)$$

wherein b consists of the boundary conditions.

4. The Time-Stepping Solver

Time stepping schemes must be used to solve (43). Although very recently some optimal time stepping solvers have been proposed in literature [30–32] for solving system of ODEs, here we focus on a basic but efficient one. Now it is considered that $\mathbf{u}^\iota$ as an approximation to $u(\tau_\iota)$, then we could derive our final (explicit) time-integrator method. Select $k+1$ uniform temporal nodes and $0 \leq \iota \leq k$, $\tau_{\iota+1} = \tau_\iota + \zeta$, $\zeta = \frac{T}{k} > 0$ with $\mathbf{u}^0 = (4)$, then the second-order RK solver (RK2) also known as the mid-point explicit method is given by [33] (p. 95):

$$\mathbf{u}^{\iota+1} = \mathbf{u}^\iota + \psi_2 + \mathcal{O}(\zeta^3), \quad (44)$$

where

$$\psi_2 = \zeta F\left(\tau_\iota + \frac{1}{2}\zeta, \mathbf{u}^\iota + \frac{1}{2}\psi_1\right), \quad \psi_1 = \zeta F(\tau_\iota, \mathbf{u}^\iota). \quad (45)$$

The approach (44) is useful because its explicit procedure helps programming in lower computational time than many of its competitors from the RK methods. This is a motivation of choosing (44) and not other higher order members of the RK family since their computational cost per time level increases. Anyhow, the investigation for finding the best time-stepping solver from the RK family of an optimal order for our specific PIDE problem remains an open question which could be focused on forthcoming works. Now the most important thing is to investigate that under what conditions this stability can be kept.

Theorem 1. *Let us assume that* (43) *satisfies the Lipschitz condition, then we have a conditional time-stable iteration process using* (44) *for solving* (43).

Proof. Considering the time-stepping method (44) on the set of ODEs (43) gives:

$$\mathbf{u}^{t+1} = \left(\frac{(\zeta \bar{B})^0}{1} + \frac{(\zeta \bar{B})^1}{1} + \frac{(\zeta \bar{B})^2}{2} \right) \mathbf{u}^t. \tag{46}$$

The explicit method (46) is clearly time-stable if the matrix eigenvalues of

$$\left(I + \zeta \bar{B} + \frac{(\zeta \bar{B})^2}{2} \right) \tag{47}$$

have modulus less than or equal to one. Viewing (46) as an iterative map, it would be clear that the eigenvalues of this matrix are $1 + \zeta \bar{B}_i + \frac{(\zeta \bar{B}_i)^2}{2}$, where $\bar{B}_i$ are the eigenvalues of matrix $\bar{B}$. Thus, for $i = 1, 2, \ldots, m$, the A-stability is simplified to

$$\left| 1 + \zeta \bar{B}_i + \frac{(\zeta \bar{B}_i)^2}{2} \right| \leq 1. \tag{48}$$

Therefore, our proposed method is time-stable if the time step size ζ reads as (48). The stability function in (48) shows a conditional stable behavior for (44). Using (48) along with $\zeta > 0$ we have the following:

$$0 < \zeta \leq \frac{2}{\mathrm{Re}(\lambda_{\max}(\bar{B}))}, \tag{49}$$

where $\mathrm{Re}(\cdot)$ is the real part and $\lambda_{\max}(\cdot)$ is the largest eigenvalue (in the absolute value sense). Note that we also obtain

$$-\xi_i \leq \mathrm{Im}(\bar{B}_i) \leq \xi_i, \tag{50}$$

while

$$\xi_i = \left(2 \left(-\frac{\mathrm{Re}(\bar{B}_i)(\zeta \mathrm{Re}(\bar{B}_i) + 2)}{\zeta^3} \right)^{1/2} - \frac{\mathrm{Re}(\bar{B}_i)(\zeta \mathrm{Re}(\bar{B}_i) + 2)}{\zeta} \right)^{1/2}. \tag{51}$$

These inequalities on the real and the imaginary parts of the eigenvalues will determine the conditional time stability bounds of the proposed solver when pricing (2). This ends the proof. □

To discuss about the advantages of the proposed approach, we briefly express that our solver has now been expressed all in matrix notations as in (43) which is a system of linear ODEs. When it couples by the ODE solver (44) with the stability condition (50), it solves (2) and the stability relied only on the largest eigenvalue of the system matrix.

5. Numerical Aspects

The goal here is to resolve (2) for at-the-money options, i.e., the value of u at $x_0 = K$ and also $y_0 = 0.04$ and $K = 100\$$. The comparing methods are given below:

- The 2nd-order FD scheme with equidistant stencils for space and the explicit 1st order Euler's scheme denoted by FDM,
- The method of scalable algebraic multigrid discussed in [34] and shown by AFFT.
- The scheme recently proposed by Soleymani et al. in [21] based on efficient non-uniform procedure denoted by SM.
- The presented solver in Sections 2–4 shown via RBF-FD-PM in this section.

Noting that all the programs have been written carefully under similar conditions in Mathematica 13 [35,36]. Here, the whole CPU time (for constructing the meshes, the derivative matrices, the set of ODEs and employing the time-stepping method) is in second.

We use more number of nodes along x than y, since its computational domain is larger. The criterion given below is used for computing the errors

$$\varepsilon_{i,j,t} = |u_{\text{approx}}(x_i, y_j, \tau_t) - u_{\text{ref}}(x, y, \tau)|, \tag{52}$$

where u_{approx} and u_{ref} are the approximate and exact solutions. u_{ref} is selected from the already well-known literature [14,34].

It is remarked that one efficient way to compute the shape parameter is to calculate it adaptively via the number of discretization points, the numerical domain as well as the structure of the PIDE problem. Hence, here we use ($1 \leq i \leq m-1$):

$$p = 4 \max\{\Delta x_i\}, \tag{53}$$

where Δx_i are the increments along the variable mesh. We can write and use (53) similarly for the other variable. Throughout the tables of this paper, a E-b stands for the scientific notation $a \times 10^{-b}$.

Example 1 ([14]). *Let us investigate the computational results for the call option of* (2) *using the following settings:*

$$\rho = -0.9, \; r = 0.025, \; \lambda = 0, \; \sigma = 0.3, \; \kappa = 1.5, \; \theta = 0.04, \; q = 0, \; T = 1. \tag{54}$$

The reference price, which is obtained by the FFT approach [14], is 8.894869 at the point $(x_0, y_0) = (100, 0.04)$. The numerical truncated domain is $\Omega = [0, 3K] \times [0, 1]$ and $\psi = 1.5$. Economically speaking, the values for the variance (for domain truncating) that are larger than one are not significant. The results in this case are provided in Table 1, which shows the superiority of the proposed solver RBF-FD-PM.

Example 2 ([34]). *Let us investigate the computational results of a European put option for* (2) *using the following settings:*

$$\gamma = -0.5, \; \hat{\sigma} = 0.4, \; \rho = -0.5, \; \lambda = 0.2, \; \sigma = 0.25,$$

$$r = 0.03, \; T = 0.5, \; \kappa = 2.0, \; \theta = 0.04, \; q = 0. \tag{55}$$

Table 1. Numerical results for Example 1.

Solver	m	n	N	$k+1$	u	ε	Time
FDM							
	20	20	400	401	8.700	1.94E-1	0.87
	40	25	1000	2001	8.597	2.97E-1	2.33
	40	40	1600	2001	8.673	2.20E-1	4.92
	65	45	2925	4001	8.860	3.39E-2	14.07
	80	50	4000	10,001	8.874	2.03E-2	31.09
AFFT							
	10	10	100	251	8.346	5.48E-1	0.41
	15	15	225	251	8.698	1.96E-1	0.54
	25	20	500	401	8.860	3.47E-2	0.56
	30	30	900	601	8.870	2.43E-2	1.49
	50	30	1500	2001	8.885	9.62E-3	4.46
	80	30	2400	5001	8.890	4.32E-3	11.49

Table 1. *Cont.*

Solver	m	n	N	k + 1	u	ε	Time
SM							
	10	10	100	251	8.388	5.06E-1	0.55
	15	15	225	251	8.746	1.47E-1	0.81
	25	20	500	401	8.877	1.71E-2	1.83
	30	30	900	601	8.888	6.09E-3	3.64
	80	30	2400	2501	8.894	8.19E-4	27.19
RBF-FD-PM							
	10	10	100	251	8.389	5.05E-1	0.52
	15	15	225	251	5.753	1.41E-1	0.80
	25	20	500	401	8.876	1.88E-2	1.69
	30	30	900	601	8.889	5.56E-3	3.29
	80	30	2400	2501	8.894	6.69E-4	25.74

The reference prices for specific locations of the domain are 11.302917 at (90, 0.04, 0.5), 6.589881 at (100, 0.04, 0.5) and 4.191455 at (110, 0.04, 0.5) using [34]. The convergence results are provided in Tables 2 and 3 and confirm the superiority of the proposed solver with $\psi = 2$ in this paper.

The FDM solver is back-of-the-envelope accounting because it is clear that the uniform grids for the PIDE problem are not a fast calculation to obtain highly accurate prices. To check the stability and positivity of the numerical solution for RBF-FD-PM, the numerical solution for Example 2 is plotted in Figure 1, which shows the stable behavior of RBF-FD-PM using $m = 16, n = 8$ and $k = 1001$.

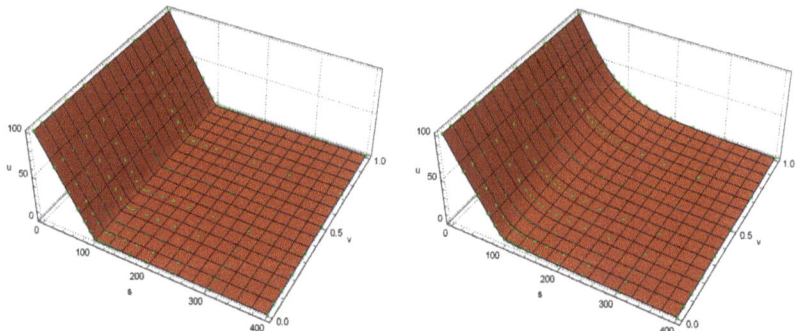

Figure 1. Numerical solution of Example 2 using the RBF-FD-PM solver when $\tau = 0$ on the left and $\tau = 0.5$ on the right. Green points show the location of the graded discretization points on the red curve, which is the numerical solution.

The reason for providing Figure 1 is twofold. We must first reveal that the numerical solution obtained by RBF-FD-PM using some m and n is stable and does not have oscillations. This is important since the PIDE model has a mixed derivative term, which can lead to oscillations in the numerical solution as long as a careless numerical method is employed. Second, we must reveal how the graded meshes (the green points in Figure 1) located on the numerical solution are obtained by employing an automatic interpolation on the obtained solutions.

An inquiry might arise by analyzing the results in Tables 1 and 2. tt is not easy to find out the advantages of the proposed approach since the numerical values are given for different values of the parameters m, n, N and $k + 1$. In fact, larger time step sizes (lower k) are taken for SM and RBF-FD-PM since their ODE solver, i.e., (44), has a larger stability region, and the overall solvers must be compared by fixing an accuracy for the errors and then checking the computational times.

Table 2. Numerical results of the different solvers in Example 2.

Solver	m	n	N	k+1	ε at x = 90	ε at x = 100	ε at x = 110	Time
FDM								
	8	5	40	26	4.54E0	3.10E0	3.56E-1	0.37
	16	8	128	51	1.23E0	1.31E-1	1.02E0	0.52
	32	16	512	101	1.34E-1	2.77E-1	2.26E-1	1.49
	32	32	1024	201	1.25E-1	2.02E-1	2.23E-1	2.93
	64	32	2048	501	5.35E-3	5.85E-2	1.87E-2	9.47
SM								
	8	5	32	51	2.57E-1	7.48E-1	7.13E-1	0.55
	16	8	128	101	7.31E-2	2.51E-1	3.89E-2	0.81
	32	16	512	501	2.18E-3	6.02E-3	5.64E-3	2.40
	64	32	2048	1001	1.79E-3	6.24E-4	1.39E-3	16.71
RBF-FD-PM								
	8	5	32	51	2.49E-1	6.89E-1	7.11E-1	0.50
	16	8	128	101	6.25E-2	2.39E-1	3.84E-2	0.76
	32	16	512	501	2.07E-3	5.44E-3	5.04E-3	2.11
	64	32	2048	1001	1.08E-3	5.81E-4	1.04E-3	15.34

To also show how the instability may ruin the numerical pricing using the stability bound (49), we provide the numerical results of solving (2) by the RBF-FD-PM using $m = 16$ and $n = 8$, but with $k = 25$ uniform discretization nodes along time in Figure 2. This shows that all the involved solvers have some limitations, but the proposed solver sounds more efficient than others.

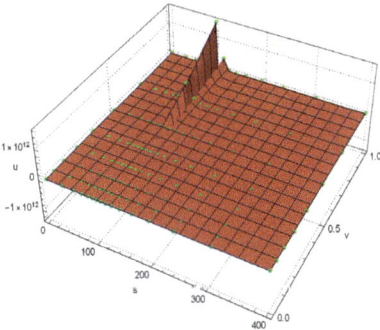

Figure 2. The instable numerical solution of Example 2 at $\tau = 0.5$ using $k = 25$ nodes.

However, due to nonsmoothness at the strike price in the initial condition, it might be useful to employ a time-stepping solver that works on graded meshes over time with more focus at the beginning of the starting time, i.e., zero (the solution near the initial time point has a weak singularity). One such method is the Rannacher time-marching method [37]. Although such an application will help our solver a lot, we will try to focus on this in forthcoming related works.

Table 3. Numerical results of the AFFT solver in Example 2.

Solver	m	n	ε at $x=90$	ε at $x=100$	ε at $x=110$
AFFT	17	9	1.08E0	1.57E0	1.96E-1
	33	17	2.80E-2	5.20E-1	1.38E-1
	65	33	4.78E-3	1.25E-1	2.84E-2
	129	65	7.38E-3	3.09E-2	5.25E-3

6. Concluding Remarks

PIDEs arise in the mathematical modeling of many processes in different fields of engineering and finance. This paper has presented an approximate solution of the linear Bates PIDE with clear application in financial option pricing using a local integral term. The solution method was considered on graded meshes at which there is a clear concentration of the discretization nodes on the financially important are of the problem. Then, an RBF-FD solver using semi-discretization via sparse arrays have been constructed for solving the Bates PIDE. The numerical results were furnished and supported the theoretical discussions. These results have been provided in Tables 1 and 2 which implicitly state that the proposed approach can compete the most efficient solver (SM) for the same purpose. Additionally, the prospects for future research can be focused on how to obtain RBF-FD weights on stencils having five/six adjacent nodes on graded meshes or employing the Rannacher time-marching method in order to obtain higher accuracies for solving the PIDE problem (2).

Author Contributions: Conceptualization, T.L. and G.F.; formal analysis, G.F.; T.L. and S.S.; funding acquisition, M.Z.U. and T.L.; investigation, T.L., M.Z.U. and S.S.; methodology, G.F. and S.S.; supervision, T.L.; validation, M.Z.U. and S.S.; writing—original draft, G.F., M.Z.U. and S.S.; writing—review and editing, T.L., M.Z.U. and S.S. All authors have read and agreed to the published version of the manuscript.

Institutional Review Board Statement: Not applicable.

Informed Consent Statement: Not applicable.

Data Availability Statement: For the data-availability statement, we state that data sharing is not applicable to this article as no new data were created in this study.

Acknowledgments: The third author states that: The Deanship of Scientific Research (DSR) at King Abdulaziz University (KAU), Jeddah, Saudi Arabia, has funded this project, under grant no. (KEP-MSc: 65-130-1443). The authors are very much thankful to three anonymous referees for their suggestions, which helped to improve this paper.

Conflicts of Interest: The authors declare that they have no known competing financial interests or personal relationships that could have appeared to influence the work reported in this paper.

References

1. Bates, D. Jumps and stochastic volatility: The exchange rate processes implicit in Deutsche mark options. *Rev. Fin. Stud.* **1996**, *9*, 69–107. [CrossRef]
2. Itkin, A. *Pricing Derivatives Under Lévy Models: Modern Finite-Difference and Pseudo–Differential Operators Approach, Birkhäuser Basel*; Springer: Berlin/Heidelberg, Germany, 2017.
3. Kim, K.-H.; Sin, M.-G. Efficient hedging in general Black-Scholes model. *Finan. Math. Appl.* **2014**, *3*, 1–9.
4. Ghanadian, A.; Lotfi, T. Approximate solution of nonlinear Black-Scholes equation via a fully discretized fourth-order method. *Aims Math.* **2020**, *5*, 879–893. [CrossRef]
5. Heston, S. A closed-form solution for options with stochastic volatility with applications to bond and currency options. *Rev. Finan. Stud.* **1993**, *6*, 327–343. [CrossRef]
6. Chang, Y.; Wang, Y.; Zhang, S. Option pricing under double Heston jump-diffusion model with approximative fractional stochastic volatility. *Mathematics* **2021**, *9*, 126. [CrossRef]
7. Gómez-Valle, L.; Martínez-Rodríguez, J. Including jumps in the stochastic valuation of freight derivatives. *Mathematics* **2021**, *9*, 154. [CrossRef]
8. Liu, J.; Yan, J. Convergence rate of the high-order finite difference method for option pricing in a Markov regime-switching jump-diffusion model. *Fractal Fract.* **2022**, *6*, 409. [CrossRef]

9. Chen, K.-S.; Huang, Y.-C. Detecting jump risk and jump-diffusion model for Bitcoin options pricing and hedging. *Mathematics* **2021**, *9*, 2567. [CrossRef]
10. Hellmuth, K.; Klingenberg, C. Computing Black Scholes with uncertain volatility-a machine learning approach. *Mathematics* **2022**, *10*, 489. [CrossRef]
11. Ballestra, L.; Sgarra, C. The evaluation of American options in a stochastic volatility model with jumps: An efficient finite element approach. *Comput. Math. Appl.* **2010**, *60*, 1571–1590. [CrossRef]
12. Ballestra, L.; Cecere, L. A fast numerical method to price American options under the Bates model. *Comput. Math. Appl.* **2016**, *72*, 1305–1319. [CrossRef]
13. Kluge, T. Pricing Derivatives in Stochastic Volatility Models Using the Finite Difference Method. Ph.D. Thesis, TU Chemnitz, Chemnitz, Germany, 2002.
14. in 't Hout, K.J.; Foulon, S. ADI finite difference schemes for option pricing in the Heston model with correlation. *Int. J. Numer. Anal. Model.* **2010**, *7*, 303–320.
15. Balajewicz, M.; Toivanen, J. Reduced order models for pricing European and American optionsunder stochastic volatility and jump-diffusion models. *J. Comput. Sci.* **2017**, *20*, 198–204. [CrossRef]
16. Duffy, D. *Finite Difference Methods in Financial Engineering: A Partial Differential Equation Approach*; Wiley: England, UK, 2006.
17. Düring, B.; Fournié, M. High-order compact finite difference scheme for option pricing in stochastic volatility models. *J. Comput. Appl. Math.* **2012**, *236*, 4462–4473. [CrossRef]
18. Soleymani, F.; Ullah, M. A multiquadric RBF-FD scheme for simulating the financial HHW equation utilizing exponential integrator. *Calcolo* **2018**, *55*, 51. [CrossRef]
19. Milovanović, S.; von Sydow, L. A high order method for pricing of financial derivatives using radial basis function generated finite differences. *Math. Comput. Simul.* **2020**, *174*, 205–217. [CrossRef]
20. Milovanović, S.; von Sydow, L. Radial basis function generated finite differences for option pricing problems. *Comput. Math. Appl.* **2018**, *75*, 1462–1481. [CrossRef]
21. Soleymani, F.; Barfeie, M. Pricing options under stochastic volatility jump model: Astable adaptive scheme. *Appl. Numer. Math.* **2019**, *145*, 69–89. [CrossRef]
22. Soleymani, F.; Zhu, S. RBF-FD solution for a financial partial-integro differential equation utilizing the generalized multiquadric function. *Comput. Math. Appl.* **2021**, *82*, 161–178. [CrossRef]
23. Soleymani, F.; Itkin, A. Pricing foreign exchange options under stochastic volatility and interest rates using an RBF-FD method. *J. Comput. Sci.* **2019**, *37*, 101028. [CrossRef]
24. Itkin, A.; Soleymani, F. Four-factor model of quanto CDS with jumps-at-default and stochastic recovery. *J. Comput. Sci.* **2021**, *54*, 101434. [CrossRef]
25. Fasshauer, G. *Meshfree Approximation Methods with MATLAB*; World Scientific Publishing Co.: Singapore, 2007.
26. Bayona, V.; Moscoso, M.; Carretero, M.; Kindelan, M. RBF-FD formulas and convergence properties. *J. Comput. Phys.* **2010**, *229*, 8281–8295. [CrossRef]
27. Meyer, G. *The Time-Discrete Method of Lines for Options and Bonds, A PDE Approach*; World Scientific Publishing: Hackensack, NJ, USA, 2015.
28. Knapp, R. A method of lines framework in Mathematica. *J. Numer. Anal. Indust. Appl. Math.* **2008**, *3*, 43–59.
29. Salmi, S.; Toivanen, J. An iterative method for pricing American options under jump-diffusion models. *Appl. Numer. Math.* **2011**, *61*, 821–831. [CrossRef]
30. Michel, V.; Thomann, D. TVD-MOOD schemes based on implicit-explicit time integration. *Appl. Math. Comput.* **2022**, *433*, 127397.
31. Shymanskyi, V.; Protsyk, Y. Simulation of the heat conduction process in the Claydite-Block construction with taking into account the fractal structure of the material. In Proceedings of the 2018 IEEE 13th International Scientific and Technical Conference on Computer Sciences and Information Technologies (CSIT), Lviv, Ukraine, 11–14 September 2018.
32. Sayfidinov, O.; Bognár, G.; Kovács, E. Solution of the 1D KPZ equation by explicit methods. *Symmetry* **2022**, *11*, 699. [CrossRef]
33. Butcher, J. *Numerical Methods for Ordinary Differential Equations*, 2nd ed.; Wiley: England, UK, 2008.
34. Salmi, S.; Toivanen, J.; von Sydow, L. An IMEX-scheme for pricing options under stochastic volatility models with jumps. *SIAM J. Sci. Comput.* **2014**, *36*, 817–834. [CrossRef]
35. Mangano, S. *Mathematica Cookbook*; O'Reilly Media: Newton, MA, USA, 2010.
36. Wellin, P.; Gaylord, R.; Kamin, S. *An Introduction to Programming with Mathematica*; Cambridge University Press: Cambridge, UK, 2005.
37. Giles, M.; Carter, R. Convergence analysis of Crank-Nicolson and Rannacher time-marching. *J. Comput. Financ.* **2006**, *9*, 89–112. [CrossRef]

Disclaimer/Publisher's Note: The statements, opinions and data contained in all publications are solely those of the individual author(s) and contributor(s) and not of MDPI and/or the editor(s). MDPI and/or the editor(s) disclaim responsibility for any injury to people or property resulting from any ideas, methods, instructions or products referred to in the content.

Article

Hybrid Newton–Sperm Swarm Optimization Algorithm for Nonlinear Systems

Obadah Said Solaiman [1], Rami Sihwail [2,*], Hisham Shehadeh [3], Ishak Hashim [1,4] and Kamal Alieyan [2]

Citation: Said Solaiman, O.; Sihwail, R.; Shehadeh, H.; Hashim, I.; Alieyan, K. Hybrid Newton–Sperm Swarm Optimization Algorithm for Nonlinear Systems. *Mathematics* 2023, 11, 1473. https://doi.org/10.3390/math11061473

Academic Editors: Maria Isabel Berenguer and Manuel Ruiz Galán

Received: 6 February 2023
Revised: 11 March 2023
Accepted: 14 March 2023
Published: 17 March 2023

Copyright: © 2023 by the authors. Licensee MDPI, Basel, Switzerland. This article is an open access article distributed under the terms and conditions of the Creative Commons Attribution (CC BY) license (https:// creativecommons.org/licenses/by/ 4.0/).

[1] Department of Mathematical Sciences, Faculty of Science & Technology, Universiti Kebangsaan Malaysia, Bangi 43600, Selangor, Malaysia; obadah_sy@yahoo.com (O.S.S.); ishak_h@ukm.edu.my (I.H.)
[2] Department of Cyber Security, Faculty of Computer Science & Informatics, Amman Arab University, Amman 11953, Jordan; k.alieyan@aau.edu.jo
[3] Department of Computer Information System, Faculty of Computer Science & Informatics, Amman Arab University, Amman 11953, Jordan; h.shehadeh@aau.edu.jo
[4] Nonlinear Dynamics Research Center (NDRC), Ajman University, Ajman P.O. Box 346, United Arab Emirates
* Correspondence: r.sihwail@aau.edu.jo; Tel.: +962-7-8814-2270

Abstract: Several problems have been solved by nonlinear equation systems (NESs), including real-life issues in chemistry and neurophysiology. However, the accuracy of solutions is highly dependent on the efficiency of the algorithm used. In this paper, a Modified Sperm Swarm Optimization Algorithm called MSSO is introduced to solve NESs. MSSO combines Newton's second-order iterative method with the Sperm Swarm Optimization Algorithm (SSO). Through this combination, MSSO's search mechanism is improved, its convergence rate is accelerated, local optima are avoided, and more accurate solutions are provided. The method overcomes several drawbacks of Newton's method, such as the initial points' selection, falling into the trap of local optima, and divergence. In this study, MSSO was evaluated using eight NES benchmarks that are commonly used in the literature, three of which are from real-life applications. Furthermore, MSSO was compared with several well-known optimization algorithms, including the original SSO, Harris Hawk Optimization (HHO), Butterfly Optimization Algorithm (BOA), Ant Lion Optimizer (ALO), Particle Swarm Optimization (PSO), and Equilibrium Optimization (EO). According to the results, MSSO outperformed the compared algorithms across all selected benchmark systems in four aspects: stability, fitness values, best solutions, and convergence speed.

Keywords: nonlinear systems; Newton's method; iterative methods; sperm swarm optimization algorithm; optimization algorithm

MSC: 65D99; 65H10; 65K10

1. Introduction

Many issues in the natural and applied sciences are represented by systems of nonlinear equations $F(X) = 0$ that require solving, where $F(X) = (f_1, f_2, \ldots, f_n)$ such that f_i is nonlinear for all $i = 1, 2, \ldots, n$. It is well known that determining the precise solution $\alpha = (\alpha_1, \alpha_2, \ldots, \alpha_n)^t$ to the nonlinear system $F(X) = 0$ is a difficult undertaking, especially when the equation comprises terms made up of logarithmic, exponential, trigonometric, or a mix of any transcendental terms. Thus, finding approximate solutions to this type of problem has emerged as a need. The iterative methods, including Newton's method, are some of the most famous methods for finding approximate solutions to nonlinear equation systems (NESs) [1]. Alternatively, optimization algorithms have been applied in attempts to extract the root solution of nonlinear systems.

In the last ten years, various optimization algorithms have been developed. Those methods can be divided into four primary categories: human-based methods, swarm-based methods, physical-based methods, and evolutionary-based methods [2]. Human perception, attitude, or lifestyle influence human-based methods. Examples of these methods are the "Harmony Search Algorithm (HSA)" [3] and the "Fireworks Algorithm (FA)" [4]. Swarm-based methods mimic the behavior of swarms or animals to reproduce or survive. Examples of this algorithm are "Sperm Swarm Optimization (SSO)" [5–8], "Harris Hawks Optimization (HHO)" [9], "The Ant Lion Optimizer (ALO)" [10], and "Butterfly Optimization Algorithm (BOA)" [11]. Some representative swarm intelligence optimization methods and applications have also been proposed; see for example, [12]. Physical-based methods are inspired by both physical theories and the universe's rules. An example of these algorithms is the "Gravitational Search Algorithm (GSA)" [2], and "Equilibrium Optimizer (EO)" [13]. Evolutionary-based methods are inspired by the Darwinian theory of evolution. An example of this method is the "Genetics Algorithm (GA)" [14]. Finally, some advanced optimization methods with applications from the real-life have been proposed, for example [15,16].

The primary objectives of these methods are to yield the optimal solution and a higher convergence rate. Meta-heuristic optimization should be based on exploration and exploitation concepts to achieve global optimum solutions. The exploitation concept indicates the ability of a method to converge to the optimal potential solution. In contrast, exploration refers to the power of algorithms to search the entire space of a problem domain. Therefore, the main goal of meta-heuristic methods is to balance the two concepts.

However, different meta-heuristic methods have been developed to find solutions to various real-life tasks. The use of optimization algorithms for solving NESs is significant and critical. Various optimization algorithms are used in the solution of nonlinear systems. The following may be summarized:

By improving the performance of optimization algorithms, researchers have been able to target more accurate solutions. For example, Zhou and Li [17] provided a unified solution to nonlinear equations using a modified CSA version. FA was modified by Ariyaratne et al. [18], who made it possible to make the root approximation simultaneously with continuity, differentiation, and initial assumptions. Ren et al. [19] proposed another variation by combining GA with harmonic and symmetric individuals. Chang [20] also revised the GA to estimate better parameters for NESs.

Furthermore, complex systems were handled by Grosan and Abraham [21] by putting them in the form of multi-objective optimization problems. Jaberipour et al. [22] addressed NESs using a modified PSO method; the modification aims to overcome the core PSO's drawbacks, such as delayed convergence and trapping at local minimums. Further, NESs have been addressed by Mo and Liu [23], who added the "Conjugate Direction Method (CDM)" into the PSO algorithm. The algorithm's efficiency for solving high-dimensional problems and overcoming local minima was increased by using CDM [24].

Several research methods involved combining two population-based algorithms (PBAs) to achieve more precise results in nonlinear modeling systems. These combinations produce hybrid algorithms that inherit the benefits of both techniques while reducing their downsides [25]. Hybrid ABC [26], hybrid ABC and PSO [27], hybrid FA [28], hybrid GA [29], hybrid KHA [30], hybrid PSO [31], and many others [32–36] are some examples of hybridizing PBAs.

NESs have often been solved using optimization techniques, either using a "Single Optimization Algorithm (SOA)" or a hybrid algorithm that combines two optimization procedures. Only a few researchers have attempted to combine the iterative method and an optimization approach. Karr et al. [37] presented a hybrid method combining Newton's method and GA for obtaining solutions for nonlinear testbed problems. After using GA to identify the most efficient starting solution, Newton's approach was utilized. To solve systems of nonlinear models, a hybrid algorithm described by Luo et al. [38] can be utilized; the combination includes GA, Powell algorithm, and Newton's method. Luo et al. [39] have provided a method for solving NESs by integrating chaos and quasi-Newton techniques. Most of the previous research has concentrated on a specific topic or issue rather than attempting to examine NESs. In a relatively recent study, Sihwail et al. [40] developed a hybrid algorithm known as NHHO to solve arbitrary NESs of equations that combine Harris Hawks' optimization method and Newton's method. Very recently, Sihwail et al. [41] proposed a new algorithm for solving NESs of equations in which Jarratt's iterative approach and the Butterfly optimization algorithm were combined to create the new scheme known as JBOA.

A hybrid algorithm can leverage the benefits of one method while overcoming the drawbacks of the other. However, most hybrid methods face problems with premature convergence due to the technique used in the original algorithms [42]. As a result, choosing a dependable combination of algorithms to produce an efficient hybrid algorithm is a crucial step.

One of the more recent swarm-based methods is Sperm Swarm Optimization (SSO), which is based on the mobility of flocks of sperm to fertilize an ovum. There are various benefits of SSO, which can be listed as follows [2,5,6]:

- The capability of exploitation of SSO is very robust.
- Several kinds of research have validated its simplicity, efficiency, and ability to converge to the optimal solution.
- Its theory can be applied to a wide range of problems in the areas of engineering and science.
- Its mathematical formulation is easy to implement, understand, and utilize.

However, most NESs simulate different data science and engineering problems that have more than one solution. Hence, it is difficult to give accurate solutions to these problems. Like other optimization algorithms, SSO may fall into a local minimum (solution) instead of the optimal solution. As a result, we developed a hybrid approach that incorporates Newton's iterative scheme with the SSO algorithm to mitigate the drawback. It is worth mentioning that Newton's method is the first known iterative scheme for solving nonlinear equations using the successive approximation technique. According to Newton's method, the correct digits nearly double each time a step is performed, referred to as the second order of convergence.

Newton's method is highly dependent on choosing the correct initial point. To achieve good convergence toward the root, the starting point, like other iterative approaches, must be close enough to the root. The scheme may converge slowly or diverge if the initial point is incorrect. Consequently, Newton's method can only perform limited local searches in some cases.

For the reasons outlined above, a hybrid SSO algorithm (MSSO) has been proposed to solve NESs, where Newton's method is applied to improve the search technique and SSO is used to enhance the selection of initial solutions and make global search more efficient.

It is not the concern of this study to demonstrate that hybridizing the SSO and Newton's methods performs better than other optimization algorithms such as PSO or genetic algorithms. However, this work aims to highlight the benefits of hybridizing an optimization algorithm with an iterative method. This is to enhance the iterative method's accuracy in solving nonlinear systems and reduce its complexity. Further, it is also able to overcome several drawbacks of Newton's method, such as initial point selection, trapping in local optima, and divergence problems. Moreover, hybridization in MSSO is beneficial in finding better roots for the selected NSEs. Optimization algorithms alone are unlikely to provide precise solutions compared to iterative methods such as Newton's method and Jarratt's method.

The proposed modification improves the initial solution distribution in the search space domain. Moreover, compared to the random distribution used by the original technique, Newton's approach improves the computational accuracy of SSO and accelerates its convergence rate. Hence, this research paper aims to improve the accuracy of NES solutions. The following are the main contributions of this paper:

1. We present a Modified Newton–Sperm Swarm Optimization Algorithm (MSSO) that combines Newton's method and SSO to enhance its search mechanism and speed up its convergence rate.
2. The proposed MSSO method is intended to solve nonlinear systems of different orders.
3. Different optimization techniques were compared with MSSO, including the original SSO, PSO, ALO, BOA, HHO, and EO. The comparison was made based on multiple metrics, such as accuracy, fitness value, stability, and convergence speed.

The rest of the paper is organized as follows: Section 2 discusses SSO algorithms and Newton's iterative method. Section 3 describes the proposed MSSO. Section 4 describes the experiments on the benchmark systems and their results. Further discussion of the findings is provided in Section 5. Finally, Section 6 presents the study's conclusion.

2. Background
2.1. Standard Sperm Swarm Optimization (SSO) Algorithm

SSO is a newly created swarm-based technique proposed by Shehadeh et al. [2,5,6] that draws inspiration from the actions of a group of sperm as they fertilize an ovum. In the process of fertilization, a single sperm navigates a path against overwhelming odds to merge with an egg (ova). In general, there are 130 million sperm involved in the insemination process. Eventually, one of these sperm will fertilize the ovum. Based on Shehadeh et al. [6], the procedure of fertilization can be summarized as follows:

A male's reproductive system releases the sperm into the cervix, where the fertilization process starts. Each sperm is given a random location inside the cervix to begin the fertilization process as part of this task. Further, every sperm has two velocities on the Cartesian plane. The initial velocity value of sperm denotes this velocity. The procedure of fertilization is demonstrated in Figure 1.

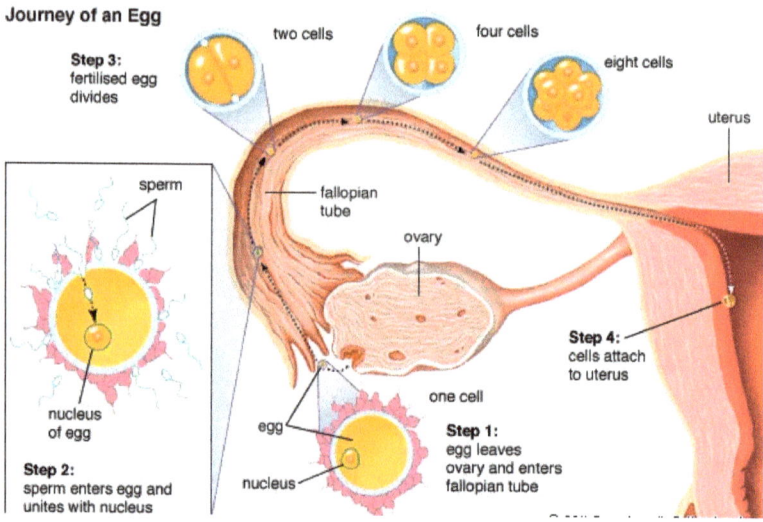

Figure 1. The procedure of fertilization [6].

From this point, every sperm in the swarm is ready to swim until it reaches the outer surface of the ovum. Scientists found that the sperm float on the surface as a flock or swarm, moving from the zone of low temperature to the area of high temperature. Moreover, they observed that the ovum triggers a chemical to pull the swarm; this is known as a chemotactic process. According to researchers, these cells also beat at the same frequency as the tail movements through the grouping. The ovum and its location in the fallopian tubes are illustrated in Figure 1. Based on Shehadeh et al. [6], this velocity is denoted by the personal best velocity of the sperm.

Usually, in a typical scenario, one sperm can fertilize an ovum. Based on that, Shehadeh et al. [2,5–8] calls this sperm the winner. The winner and the flock of sperm are illustrated in Figure 2.

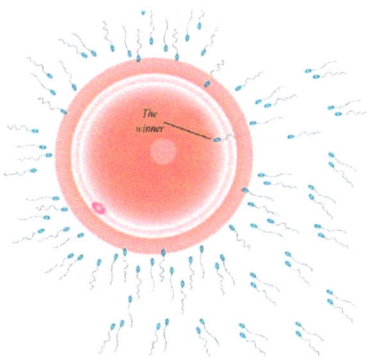

Figure 2. A flock of sperm and the winner [2].

The best answer is found and obtained using this strategy, which makes use of a group of sperm (potential solutions) floating over the whole search area. Concurrently, the possible solutions will consider the most suitable sperm in their path, who will be the victor (the sperm that is closest to the egg). Alternatively, the flock will consider on the winner's position and the position of its prior best solution. Thus, every sperm enhances its initial zone across the optimum area by taking into consideration its current velocity, current location, and the location of both the global's best solution (the winner) and the sperm's best solution. Mathematically speaking, in SSO, the flock updated their sites according to the following formula:

$$x_{i+1}(t) = x_i(t) + v_i(t) \qquad (1)$$

where

- v_i is the velocity of potential solution i at iteration t;
- x_i is the current position of possible solution i at iteration t;

Three velocities can be used to calculate the sperm's velocity: the initial velocity of a potential solution, the personal best solution, and the global best solution.

First is the initial velocity of sperm, which takes a random value based on the velocity dumping parameter and the pH value of the initial location. The model can be calculated by applying the following formula:

$$Initial\_Velocity = D \cdot V_i(t) \cdot Log_{10}(pH\_Rand_1) \qquad (2)$$

Second is a personal best location for the potential solution, adjusted in memory based on the prior location until it is closest to the optimal value. However, this velocity can be changed based on the pH and temperature values. The following formula may be used to calculate this model:

$$Current\_Best\_Solution = Log_{10}(pH\_Rand_2) \cdot Log_{10}(Temp\_Rand_1) \cdot (x_{sbest_i}[] - x_i[]) \qquad (3)$$

Third, the global best solution is simulated by the winner, which is denoted by the closest sperm to the ovum. The mathematical model of the winning velocity of the potential solution $Vi(t)$ can be represented in Equation (4). The flock of sperm and the value of the winner are depicted in Figure 2.

$$Global\_Best\_Solution(the\_winner) = Log_{10}(pH\_Rand_3) \cdot Log_{10}(Temp\_Rand_2) \cdot (x_{sgbest_i}[\,] - x_i[\,]) \quad (4)$$

The symbols of the prior equations are as follows:
- v_i is the velocity of potential solution i at iteration t;
- D is the velocity damping factor and is a random parameter with a range of 0 to 1;
- pH_Rand_1, pH_Rand_2, and pH_Rand_3 are the reached site pH values, which are random parameters that take values between 7 to 14;
- $Temp\_Rand_1$ and $Temp\_Rand_2$ are values of the site temperature, which are random parameters that take values between 35.1 to 38.5;
- x_i is the current position of potential solution i at iteration t;
- x_{sbest} is the personal best location of potential solution i at iteration t;
- x_{sgbest} is the global best location of the flock.

Based on the equations mentioned above, the total velocity rule $V_i(t)$ can be formalized based on velocity initial value, personal best solution, and global best solution as follows [2,5–8]:

$$V_i(t) = Log_{10}(pH\_Rand_1).V_i + Log_{10}(pH\_Rand_2).Log_{10}(Temp\_Rand_1).) \cdot (x_{sbest_i} - x_i(t)) + \\ Log_{10}(pH\_Rand_3).Log_{10}(Temp\_Rand_2).(x_{sbest_i} - x_i(t)) \quad (5)$$

Based on the theory of SSO, both pH and temperature affect the velocity rule. The pH changes depending on the woman's attitude, whether depressed or happy, and on the food consumed. The value of the pH parameter falls in a range between seven and fourteen. Alternatively, the temperature ranges from 35.1 to 38.5 °C according to blood pressure circulation in the reproductive system [7].

Further, SSO is a swarm-based method that simulates the metaphor of natural fertilization. SSO, however, has a few disadvantages in terms of efficiency. Applied to a broad search domain, SSO is prone to getting trapped in local optima [2], which is one of its main drawbacks. Therefore, improvements are needed to enhance the method's exploration process.

2.2. Newton's Method

An iterative technique is a technique (method) for finding an approximate solution by making successive approximations. Iterative approaches usually cannot deliver accurate answers. Accordingly, researchers generally select a tolerance level to distinguish between approximate and exact answers for the solutions obtained through iterative approaches. Newton's method, also known as the Newton–Raphson method, was proposed by Isaac Newton and is the most widely used iterative method. The procedure of Newton's scheme is described by

$$X_{n+1} = X_n - F'^{-1}(X_n).F(X_n), \quad (6)$$

where $F(X)$ is the nonlinear system of equations, and $F'(X_n)$ represents the "Jacobian of $F(X)$". Newton's second-order convergence method may be easily applied to various nonlinear algebraic problems [1]. As a result, mathematical tools such as Mathematica and MATLAB provide built-in routines for finding nonlinear equations' roots based on Newton's scheme.

In Newton's method, many studies and refinements have been performed to improve approximation solutions to nonlinear problems as well as the order of convergence, which impact the speed at which the desired solution can be reached; see, for example, [43–47] and their references.

3. Modified Sperm Swarm Optimization (MSSO)

SSO is a powerful optimization technique that can address various issues. No algorithm, however, is suitable for tackling all problems, according to the "No Free Lunch

(NFL)" theorem [48]. By using Newton's method, the proposed MSSO outperforms the original SSO in terms of solving nonlinear equation systems. In MSSO, Newton's methods are used as a local search to enhance the search process, as shown in Figure 3.

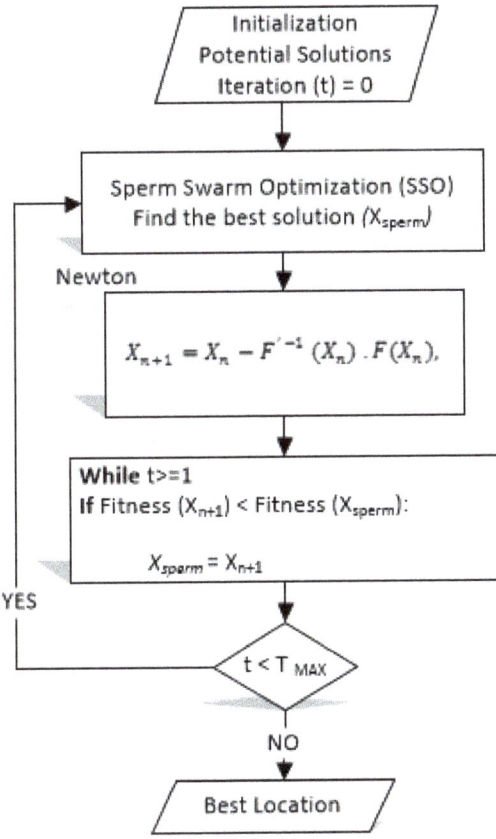

Figure 3. The framework of the proposed MSSO.

When Newton's method is applied to the sperm position, at each iteration, the fitness value of the potential solution is compared to the fitness of the location calculated by Newton's scheme. The newly computed location by Newton's method is shown in Figure 3 as (X_{n+1}).

In each iteration, MSSO employs both the SSO algorithm and Newton's method. The SSO first determines the most optimal sperm location among the twenty initial locations as an optimal candidate location. The optimal candidate location is then fed into Newton's method. In other words, the output from SSO is considered a potential solution or a temporary solution. The obtained solution is then treated as an input for Newton's method. Newton's method as an iterative method calculates the next candidate solution based on Equation (6). Newton's method's ability to find a better candidate is very high since it is a second-order convergence method. However, in order to avoid a local optimal solution, the candidate solution obtained from Newton's method (X_{n+1}) is compared to the solution calculated by SSO (X_{sperm}). Thus, the location with the lowest fitness value determines the potential solution to the problem. The next iteration is then performed based on the current most promising solution. Algorithm 1 shows the pseudocode for the suggested

MSSO algorithm.

Algorithm 1. Modified Sperm Swarm Optimization (MSSO).	
Begin	
Step 1:	Initialize potential solutions.
Step 2:	**for** i = 1: size of flock **do**
Step 3:	apply the fitness for potential solution.
	if obtained fitness > best solution of the potential solution **then**
	give the current value as the best solution of the potential solution.
	end if
	end for
Step 4:	depends on the winner, give the value of winner.
Step 5:	**for** i =1: size of flock **do**
	Perform Equation (5)
	Perform Equation (1).
	end for
Step 6:	Calculate Newton's location X_{n+1} using Equation (6)
	Calculate the fitness of X_{n+1} and X_{sperm} using Equation (7)
	if fitness (X_{n+1}) < fitness (X_{sperm})
	$X_{sperm} = X_{n+1}$
	end if
Step 7:	**while** final iterations is not reached go to **Step 2**.
End.	

The initialization, exploitation, and exploration phases of the SSO method are shown in the algorithm. The alterations specified in the red box are implemented at the end of each iteration. We compare Newton's location with the sperm's optimal location based on their fitness values and select the one that has the best fitness value.

Computational Complexity

The complexity of the new MSSO's can be obtained by adding up the SSO's complexity and Newton's method's complexity. At first glance, Newton's technique is overly complicated compared to optimization methods. At each iteration, one has to solve a $N \times N$ system of linear models, which is time-consuming because every Jacobian calculation requires n^2 scalar function evaluations. As a result, combining Newton's approach with any optimization process is likely to make it more complicated.

On the other hand, combining SSO with Newton's technique did not significantly increase processing time. However, the MSSO can overcome Newton's method limitations, including selecting the starting points and divergence difficulties. As a result, the MSSO is superior at solving nonlinear equation systems.

The MSSO's time complexity is influenced by the initial phase, the process of updating the position of the sperm, and the use of Newton's scheme. The complexity of the initialization process is O(S), where S is the total number of sperm. The updating process, which includes determining the optimal solution and updating sperm positions, has a complexity equal to O(I $\times$ S) + O(I $\times$ S $\times$ M), where I and M represent the maximum number of iterations and the complexity of the tested benchmark equation respectively. Furthermore, Newton's scheme complexity is calculated as O(I $\times$ T), where T is the computation time. Consequently, the proposed MSSO has an overall computational complexity of O(S $\times$ (I + IM + 1) + IT).

Every improvement certainly has a cost. The principal objective of the proposed hybrid algorithm is to enhance the fitness value and the convergence speed of the existing algorithms. However, as a result of adding one algorithm to another, the complexity and the time cost of the hybrid algorithm are increased compared to the original algorithm. Eventually, a tradeoff between the merits and disadvantages should be considered while using any algorithm.

4. Numerical Tests

Eight nonlinear systems of several orders were selected as indicators to clarify the efficiency and capability of the new hybrid MSSO scheme. Comparisons between MSSO and the other six well-known optimization algorithms have been performed. Those optimization algorithms are the original SSO [2], HHO [9], PSO [49], ALO [10], BOA [11], and EO [13]. For consistency, all selected systems used in the comparisons are arbitrary problems that are common in the literature, for instance, [19,21,40,44,50–53].

The comparison between the optimization algorithms is based on the fitness value of each algorithm in each benchmark. A solution with less fitness value is more accurate than a solution with a higher fitness value. Hence, the most effective optimization algorithm is the one that solves with the least fitness value. The fitness function used in the comparison is the Euclidean norm, also called the square norm or norm-2. Using the Euclidean norm, we can determine the distance from the origin, which is expressed as follows:

$$Fitness = \|F(x)\|_2 = \sqrt{f_1^2 + f_2^2 + \ldots + f_n^2}, \tag{7}$$

Similar settings have been used in all benchmarks to guarantee a fair comparison of all selected algorithms. The parameter values of all optimization algorithms have been fine-tuned to improve the performance of the algorithms. The best solution was chosen by every optimization method 30 times. Search agents (population size) have been set to 20 and the maximum iteration to 50. Furthermore, the best solution with the least fitness value is chosen if there is more than one solution for a particular benchmark. In the end, for lack of space, answers are shortened to 11 decimal places.

Calculations were conducted using MATLAB software version R2020a with the default variable precision of 16 digits. This was on an Intel Core i5 processor running at 2.2 GHz and 8 GB of RAM under the Microsoft Windows 8 operating system.

Problem 1: Let us consider the first problem to be the following nonlinear system of two equations:

$$F_1(X) = \begin{cases} x_1 + 1 - e^{x_2} = 0, \\ x_1 + \cos(x_2) - 2 = 0, \end{cases}$$

For this system, the precise solution is given by $\alpha = \{1.3401918575555883401\ldots, 0.8502329164169513268\ldots\}^t$. After running the algorithms 30 times, MSSO significantly surpassed all other optimization algorithms in the comparison. Table 1 shows that the proposed hybrid MSSO algorithm has attained the best solution with the least fitness value equaling zero. This means that the solution obtained by MSSO is an exact solution for the given system.

Table 1. Comparison of different optimization algorithms for Problem 1.

	MSSO	HHO [9]	PSO [49]	ALO [10]	BOA [11]	EO [13]	SSO [2]
x_1	1.34019185756	1.34020535556	1.34019185727	1.34019196042	1.34359319240	1.34019194567	1.34502836805
x_2	0.85023291642	0.85023195766	0.85023291632	0.85023300025	0.85138606082	0.85023289034	0.85355356706
Fitness	0	2.1212×10^{-5}	2.2401×10^{-10}	1.0147×10^{-7}	2.6296×10^{-3}	1.8396×10^{-7}	3.7618×10^{-3}

Problem 2: The second benchmark is the system of two nonlinear equations given by:

$$F_2(X) = \begin{cases} 2 - e^{x_1} + \tan^{-1} x_2 = 0, \\ \tan^{-1}(x_1^2 + x_2^2 - 5) = 0, \end{cases}$$

Here, the exact zero for the system in this problem is given by $\alpha = (1.1290650391602\ldots, 1.9300808629035\ldots)^t$. As shown in Table 2, it is evident that MSSO achieved the exact solution of this system with a fitness value of zero. It also outperformed all other algorithms with a substantial difference, especially in comparison with SSO, BOA, and HHO.

Table 2. Comparison of different optimization algorithms for Problem 2.

	MSSO	HHO [9]	PSO [49]	ALO [10]	BOA [11]	EO [13]	SSO [2]
x_1	1.12906503916	1.12903302177	1.12906503916	1.12906515112	1.12588512395	1.12906504185	1.14402014766
x_2	1.93008086290	1.93011297982	1.93008086290	1.93008085965	1.93375637741	1.93008086329	1.92067058635
Fitness	0	0.000117763	8.01×10^{-15}	4.22×10^{-7}	0.012716315	1.1201×10^{-8}	0.048651092

Problem 3: The third system of nonlinear equations is given by:

$$F_3(X) = \begin{cases} \cos(x_2) - \sin(x_1) = 0, \\ x_3^{x_1} - \frac{1}{x_2} = 0, \\ e^{x_1} - x_3^2 = 0. \end{cases}$$

This NES of three equations has the exact solution $\alpha = \{0.9095694945200448838\ldots,$ $0.6612268322748517354\ldots, 1.575834143906999036\ldots\}^t$. According to Table 3, the proposed MSSO achieved a zero fitness value. The superiority of MSSO is evident in this example, with a significant difference between MSSO and all other compared optimization algorithms.

Table 3. Comparison of different optimization algorithms for Problem 3.

	MSSO	HHO [9]	PSO [49]	ALO [10]	BOA [11]	EO [13]	SSO [2]
x_1	0.90956949452	0.90449212115	0.89176809239	0.85453639710	0.83212389642	0.90775456824	1.03817572093
x_2	0.66122683227	0.66642798414	0.67275154835	0.69673611158	0.69808559231	0.66254037960	0.56914672488
x_3	1.57583414391	1.57229467736	1.56169705842	1.53258611089	1.52262989677	1.57448413869	1.69602879530
Fitness	0	0.005442108	0.004315295	0.013715754	0.036158224	0.000699083	0.061770954

Problem 4: Consider the following system of three nonlinear equations:

$$F_4(X) = \begin{cases} x_2 + x_3 - e^{-x_1} = 0, \\ x_1 + x_3 - e^{-x_2} = 0, \\ x_1 + x_2 - e^{-x_3} = 0. \end{cases}$$

The precise solution of the nonlinear system in this problem is equal to $\alpha = (0.351733711249\ldots,$ $0.351733711249\ldots, 0.351733711249\ldots)^t$. The best solution achieved by the compared schemes for the given system is illustrated in Table 4. The proposed MSSO found a precise answer, with zero as a fitness value. ALO recorded the second-best solution with a fitness value of 2.27×10^{-6}, while the rest of the compared algorithms were far from the exact answer. Again, the proposed MSSO has proved it has an efficient local search mechanism. Hence, it can achieve more accurate solutions for nonlinear systems.

Table 4. Comparison of different optimization algorithms for Problem 4.

	MSSO	HHO [9]	PSO [49]	ALO [10]	BOA [11]	EO [13]	SSO [2]
x_1	0.35173371125	0.36165321762	0.35083292352	0.35172698088	0.38459199838	0.35086562122	0.37260511330
x_2	0.35173371125	0.35137717774	0.35226253114	0.35173655019	0.33171697596	0.35200965295	0.34576550099
x_3	0.35173371125	0.34410796587	0.35213140099	0.35173726704	0.34030291514	0.35226146573	0.33588500543
Fitness	0	0.005300022	0.000379475	2.2674×10^{-6}	0.016625262	0.000294859	0.010254721

Problem 5: The next benchmark is the following system of two nonlinear equations:

$$F_5(X) = \begin{cases} x_1 + e^{x_2} - \cos(x_2) = 0, \\ 3x_1 - \sin(x_1) - x_2 = 0, \end{cases}$$

This nonlinear system has the trivial solution $\alpha = (0,0)^t$. Table 5 illustrates the comparison between the different optimization algorithms for the given system. Compared with the other algorithms, the original SSO and HHO achieved excellent results, with fitness values of 5.36×10^{-15} and 6.92×10^{-14}, respectively. However, MSSO outperformed both of them and delivered the exact solution for the given system.

Table 5. Comparison of different optimization algorithms for Problem 5.

	MSSO	HHO [9]	PSO [49]	ALO [10]	BOA [11]	EO [13]	SSO [2]
x	$3.6298689 \times 10^{-22}$	$1.0162783 \times 10^{-14}$	$-2.0631743 \times 10^{-8}$	$-2.0631743 \times 10^{-8}$	0.00019546601	$-1.0265357 \times 10^{-14}$	$-5.8109345 \times 10^{-16}$
y	$7.2597377 \times 10^{-22}$	$-4.1451213 \times 10^{-14}$	2.4507340×10^{-7}	2.4507340×10^{-7}	1.1132830×10^{-5}	$1.0797593 \times 10^{-13}$	$-3.9989603 \times 10^{-15}$
Fitness	0	6.92×10^{-14}	3.64×10^{-7}	3.64×10^{-7}	4.32×10^{-4}	1.61×10^{-13}	5.36×10^{-15}

Problem 6: The sixth system considered for the comparison is an interval arithmetic benchmark [53] given by the following system of ten equations:

$$F_6(X) = \begin{cases} x_1 - 0.25428722 - 0.18324757 x_4 x_3 x_9 = 0, \\ x_2 - 0.37842197 - 0.16275449 x_1 x_{10} x_6 = 0, \\ x_3 - 0.27162577 - 0.16955071 x_1 x_2 x_{10} = 0, \\ x_4 - 0.19807914 - 0.15585316 x_7 x_1 x_6 = 0, \\ x_5 - 0.44166728 - 0.19950920 x_7 x_6 x_3 = 0, \\ x_6 - 0.14654113 - 0.18922793 x_8 x_5 x_{10} = 0, \\ x_7 - 0.42937161 - 0.21180486 x_2 x_5 x_8 = 0, \\ x_8 - 0.07056438 - 0.17081208 x_1 x_7 x_6 = 0, \\ x_9 - 0.34504906 - 0.19612740 x_{10} x_6 x_8 = 0, \\ x_{10} - 0.42651102 - 0.21466544 x_4 x_8 x_1 = 0, \\ -10 \leq x_1, x_2, \ldots, x_{10} \leq 10. \end{cases}$$

In this benchmark, MSSO has proven its efficiency. Table 6 clearly shows the significant differences between MSSO and the other compared algorithms. MSSO achieved the best solution with a fitness value of 5.21×10^{-17}, while all different algorithms achieved solutions far from the exact answer. When we compare the fitness values of the hybrid MSSO and the original SSO, we can see how substantial modifications were made to the local search mechanism of the original SSO to produce the hybrid MSSO.

Table 6. Comparison of different optimization algorithms for Problem 6.

	MSSO	HHO [9]	PSO [49]	ALO [10]	BOA [11]	EO [13]	SSO [2]
x_1	0.25783339370	0.34365751785	0.25784839865	0.26464526597	0.33136834430	0.25516109743	0.20435054402
x_2	0.38109715460	0.33753782972	0.38110810543	0.40023813660	0.38789340931	0.37760106529	0.28412716608
x_3	0.27874501735	0.29465973836	0.27883198050	0.30288150337	0.21629745964	0.27543881117	0
x_4	0.20066896423	0.25159175619	0.20067772983	0.19561671789	0.11897384735	0.20247039332	$4.6624555 \times 10^{-14}$
x_5	0.44525142484	0.29083336278	0.44529373708	0.42832138835	0.43899648474	0.44562023380	0.21484320995
x_6	0.14918391997	0.17861978035	0.14916957364	0.13017287705	0.11989963467	0.14456849647	0.04811561607
x_7	0.43200969898	0.45287147997	0.43201094116	0.42448051059	0.41892967958	0.43104930617	0.46906778944
x_8	0.07340277778	0.12886919949	0.07336337021	0.08657096366	0.00911718057	0.07245346262	0.04141333025
x_9	0.34596682688	0.41390929124	0.34597891260	0.35142553752	0.31940825594	0.34552658400	0.44010425014
x_{10}	0.42732627599	0.31843020513	0.42732508540	0.40501764912	0.31956474381	0.42687560151	0.45420039449
Fitness	5.21×10^{-17}	0.238337	0.000107027	0.049509462	0.182742367	0.007434684	0.448061654

Problem 7: Consider the model A combustion chemistry problem for a temperature of 3000 °C [21], which can be described by the following nonlinear system of equations:

$$F_7(X) = \begin{cases} x_2 + 2x_6 + x_9 + 2x_{10} - 10^{-5} = 0, \\ x_3 + x_8 - 3 \times 10^{-5} = 0, \\ x_1 + x_3 + 2x_5 + 2x_8 + x_9 + x_{10} - 5 \times 10^{-5} = 0, \\ x_4 + 2x_7 - 10^{-5} = 0, \\ 0.5140437 \times 10^{-7} x_5 - x_1^2 = 0, \\ 0.1006932 \times 10^{-6} x_6 - 2x_2^2 = 0, \\ 0.7816278 \times 10^{-15} x_7 - x_4^2 = 0, \\ 0.1496236 \times 10^{-6} x_8 - x_1 x_3 = 0, \\ 0.6194411 \times 10^{-7} x_9 - x_1 x_2 = 0, \\ 0.2089296 \times 10^{-14} x_{10} - x_1 x_2^2 = 0, \\ -10 \leq x_1, x_2, \ldots, x_{10} \leq 10. \end{cases}$$

In Table 7, the comparison for this system shows that MSSO has the least fitness value of 7.09×10^{-21}, while PSO and EO have fitness values of 2.85×10^{-9} and 3.45×10^{-8}, respectively.

Table 7. Comparison of different optimization algorithms for Problem 7.

	MSSO	HHO [9]	PSO [49]	ALO [10]	BOA [11]	EO [13]	SSO [2]
x_1	1.8492683×10^{-7}	4.8416050×10^{-6}	1.9790922×10^{-5}	1.0594162×10^{-5}	1×10^{-22}	1.0078652×10^{-5}	1×10^{-22}
x_2	1.5794030×10^{-7}	1×10^{-22}	$1.3635593 \times 10^{-15}$	3.3602174×10^{-7}	1×10^{-22}	3.5661155×10^{-8}	1×10^{-22}
x_3	1.3864372×10^{-5}	1.6731599×10^{-5}	3.1002047×10^{-5}	3.0337169×10^{-5}	4.1974292×10^{-6}	3.0993197×10^{-5}	3.8503515×10^{-6}
x_4	$7.1476236 \times 10^{-11}$	9.8490309×10^{-6}	$5.7239289 \times 10^{-10}$	1.4332843×10^{-8}	6.9533835×10^{-6}	9.9663562×10^{-6}	8.9634004×10^{-7}
x_5	$6.6527288 \times 10^{-21}$	1×10^{-22}	$1.3480554 \times 10^{-18}$	1×10^{-22}	1×10^{-22}	$1.0400080 \times 10^{-22}$	1×10^{-22}
x_6	2.4773409×10^{-6}	1×10^{-22}	4.8969622×10^{-6}	2.6156272×10^{-7}	2.6521256×10^{-6}	1.0305788×10^{-9}	2.7036389×10^{-7}
x_7	4.9999643×10^{-6}	1×10^{-22}	4.9991846×10^{-6}	5.0388691×10^{-6}	1×10^{-22}	$9.0975075 \times 10^{-10}$	4.1982561×10^{-6}
x_8	1.7135628×10^{-5}	1.1426668×10^{-5}	$1.1003359 \times 10^{-10}$	7.7891263×10^{-7}	2.1564327×10^{-5}	$2.1008819 \times 10^{-22}$	2.2239423×10^{-5}
x_9	4.7151213×10^{-7}	5.6143966×10^{-6}	2.0556945×10^{-7}	7.7518075×10^{-6}	3.3294486×10^{-6}	9.9131258×10^{-6}	6.2906500×10^{-6}
x_{10}	2.2079329×10^{-6}	2.4214874×10^{-6}	$2.7225791 \times 10^{-15}$	6.7696638×10^{-7}	1×10^{-22}	1.9269643×10^{-8}	1×10^{-22}
Fitness	7.09×10^{-21}	3.23×10^{-6}	2.85×10^{-9}	1.73×10^{-7}	6.22×10^{-6}	3.45×10^{-8}	6.91×10^{-6}

Problem 8: The last benchmark is an application from neurophysiology [52], described by the nonlinear system of six equations:

$$F_8(X) = \begin{cases} x_1^2 + x_3^2 - 1 = 0 \\ x_2^2 + x_4^2 - 1 = 0 \\ x_5 x_3^3 + x_6 x_4^3 = 0 \\ x_5 x_1^3 + x_6 x_2^3 = 0 \\ x_5 x_1 x_3^2 + x_6 x_2 x_4^2 = 0, \\ x_5 x_3 x_1^2 + x_6 x_4 x_2^2 = 0 \end{cases} \quad -10 \leq x_1, x_2, \ldots, x_6 \leq 10.$$

There is more than one exact solution to this system. Table 8 shows that the proposed MSSO algorithm achieved the most accurate solution with a fitness value of 1.18×10^{-24}, and the PSO algorithm achieved second place with a fitness value of 5.26×10^{-7}. In contrast, the rest of the algorithms recorded answers that differ significantly from the exact solution. Further, NESs in problems 6–8 prove the flexibility of the proposed hybrid MSSO as it remains efficient even in a wide interval $[-10, 10]$.

Table 8. Comparison of different optimization algorithms for Problem 8.

	MSSO	HHO [9]	PSO [49]	ALO [10]	BOA [11]	EO [13]	SSO [2]
x_1	0.68279148724	0.52702319411	0.76960300904	0.28887548289	0.95829879077	0.26693676403	1.00511003439
x_2	0.50647432076	0.29250343550	0.66834059064	0.24588295652	0.10377244360	0.73023242916	−0.14156714998
x_3	−0.7306132937	0.84391409892	0.63852284443	−0.95725516399	0.20563151204	−0.96364982722	0.12921880541
x_4	−0.8622550449	0.96128971140	−0.74385526431	0.96902915055	−0.98879741269	0.68370357562	0.99423873612
x_5	$3.8805276 \times 10^{-19}$	−0.01763142313	$-5.5341563 \times 10^{-7}$	0.00262835607	−0.02586929684	−0.00260602535	0.01451788346
x_6	$-3.013005 \times 10^{-19}$	−0.00227648751	$-2.3175063 \times 10^{-7}$	0.00282255517	0.01218071672	−0.00190637065	−0.00244565414
Fitness	1.18×10^{-24}	0.020764231	5.26×10^{-7}	0.001489	0.048684	0.002456	0.032031

The comparison results in all benchmarks confirm the hypothesis that we have mentioned in the first section; that is, that the hybridization of two algorithms inherits the efficient merits of both algorithms (SSO and Newton's methods). This can be seen by looking at the comparison results between the MSSO and the original SSO, where the MSSO has outperformed the original SSO in all selected benchmarks. The reason for this remarkable performance is the use of Newton's method as a local search, which strengthens the hybrid's capability to avoid the local optimum in Problems 1–5 (where MSSO has obtained the exact solution), and significantly improves the obtained fitness values in Problems 6-8. The comparisons indicate that the proposed hybrid algorithm MSSO has avoided being trapped in the local optima in all problems, compared with the majority of the other algorithms.

5. Results and Analysis

5.1. Stability and Consistency of MSSO

Table 9 shows the average fitness value of the MSSO and the other algorithms compared in the previous benchmarks. This is when each problem is run 30 times to illustrate the continuous efficiency and power of the proposed MSSO algorithm.

Table 9. The comparison results of the average 30-run solution for all problems.

	MSSO	HHO [9]	PSO [49]	ALO [10]	BOA [11]	EO [13]	SSO [2]
Problem 1	2.2709×10^{-16}	0.0022869	2.2927×10^{-6}	6.2912×10^{-7}	0.039573	9.3817×10^{-5}	0.050354
Problem 2	4.7855×10^{-16}	0.13913	0.037009	0.11703	0.12076	0.060332	0.27432
Problem 3	1.1842×10^{-16}	0.038848	2.1189×10^{-12}	7.5657×10^{-6}	0.20288	3.3604×10^{-5}	0.14209
Problem 4	1.1102×10^{-17}	0.052119	0.0055764	0.042144	0.063878	0.015678	0.12467
Problem 5	0	2.706×10^{-9}	0.011783	0.058917	0.0035033	0.011783	2.1635E-09
Problem 6	5.2147×10^{-17}	0.37777	0.00092349	0.16493	0.36299	0.037007	0.56687
Problem 7	4.7872×10^{-9}	4.4292×10^{-5}	2.5874×10^{-6}	3.4687×10^{-6}	2.0904×10^{-5}	2.3701×10^{-6}	1.1393×10^{-5}
Problem 8	0.010581	0.18797	0.01278	2.9582	0.13696	0.014989	0.11305
Mean (F-test)	1	5.375	2.625	4.375	5.5	3.375	5.625
Rank	1	5	2	4	6	3	7

According to Table 9, MSSO has surpassed all other compared algorithms. The average fitness values of MSSO and the original SSO show a significant difference in all benchmarks. Consequently, this improvement confirms the flexibility of the hybrid MSSO in seeking the best solution without being entrapped by local optima. Furthermore, as shown in Table 9, MSSO outperforms all of the other compared algorithms, particularly for problems 2, 4, 6, and 8.

Additionally, the algorithm is considered consistent and stable if it maintains consistency over 30 runs. The average of the solutions must, therefore, be the same as or very close to the best solution in order to achieve consistency. It has been demonstrated in this study that MSSO consistency has been maintained for all selected problems. Moreover, the average standard deviation achieved by each algorithm is shown in Table 10, in which smaller values of standard deviation indicate more stability. The hybrid MSSO demonstrated stable results in most of the selected problems.

Table 10. The average standard deviation for all problems.

	MSSO	HHO [9]	PSO [49]	ALO [10]	BOA [11]	EO [13]	SSO [2]
Problem 1	7.7097×10^{-16}	0.0035697	4.4735×10^{-6}	8.3914×10^{-7}	0.046935	0.00012725	0.030655
Problem 2	1.1592×10^{-16}	0.062883	0.021589	0.069769	0.058383	0.058383	0.085942
Problem 3	3.4857×10^{-16}	0.039902	3.889×10^{-12}	8.6567×10^{-6}	0.18297	5.8122×10^{-5}	0.069194
Problem 4	6.0809×10^{-17}	0.031155	0.0043532	0.039841	0.022589	0.045526	0.082401
Problem 5	0	9.7731×10^{-9}	0.064539	0.13399	0.0026465	0.064539	4.3991×10^{-9}
Problem 6	0	0.076223	0.00068543	0.061743	0.064055	0.038589	0.07177
Problem 7	6.8883×10^{-9}	2.0068×10^{-5}	4.9339×10^{-6}	2.582×10^{-6}	1.0476×10^{-5}	2.8284×10^{-6}	2.3389×10^{-6}
Problem 8	0.057522	0.11493	0.0348	12.8391	0.051742	0.016544	0.050028
Mean (F-test)	1.5	5.25	2.875	4.625	4.875	3.75	4.875
Rank	1	7	2	4	5.5	3	5.5

Furthermore, the significance of MSSO improvements was examined using the statistical t-test in Table 11. Improvements were considered significant if the *p*-value was less than 0.05; otherwise, they were not. Results show that all algorithms have *p*-values lower than 0.05 in all tested problems, except for HHO, which has a single value above 0.05 in Problem 5. It is evident from this that MSSO has a higher level of reliability than competing algorithms. Further, MSSO's solutions are significantly more accurate than those of other algorithms since the majority of its *p*-values are close to 0. The results demonstrate that the MSSO is a robust search method capable of finding precise solutions. Moreover, it is able to avoid local optimal traps and immature convergence.

Table 11. *p*-values for the fitness based on the *t*-test.

	HHO [9]	PSO [49]	ALO [10]	SSO [2]	EO [13]	BOA [11]
Problem 1	7.425×10^{-5}	0.0032362	7.305×10^{-5}	6.322×10^{-11}	0.00053712	0.032655
Problem 2	1.396×10^{-8}	0.0078581	0.00018975	7.512×10^{-17}	0.0053228	0.002542
Problem 3	2.1404×10^{-8}	0.00038876	1.7706×10^{-6}	2.171×10^{-13}	5.5596×10^{-5}	0.000194
Problem 4	6.4406×10^{-10}	5.0472×10^{-5}	1.2494×10^{-7}	6.948×10^{-11}	0.013013	6.918×10^{-11}
Problem 5	0.32558	9.7628×10^{-8}	0.0012288	0.32563	0.001503	4.3991×10^{-6}
Problem 6	1.8665×10^{-26}	3.7433×10^{-5}	1.1361×10^{-16}	2.345×10^{-26}	2.9061×10^{-10}	2.855×10^{-22}
Problem 7	3.7355×10^{-12}	0.0044676	3.9777×10^{-9}	7.247×10^{-21}	0.00029067	2.3389×10^{-6}
Problem 8	2.3479×10^{-12}	0.049502	0.00014768	1.574×10^{-9}	2.3043×10^{-6}	0.000028

Moreover, one of the criteria that is considered when comparing algorithms is their speed of convergence. Figure 4 indicates that MSSO enhanced the convergence speed of the original SSO in all problems. It also shows that MSSO achieves the best solution with much fewer iterations than the other algorithms. Consequently, the superiority of the proposed MSSO is confirmed.

It is known that any optimization method has some constraints that slow down the algorithm from finding the optimum solution or, in some cases, prevent it from finding the solution. HHO, for instance, probably attains local optima instead of the optimal answer. SSO quickly falls into a local minimum of systems of nonlinear equations, which consists of a set of models [2]. PSO has some drawbacks, such as a lack of population variety and the inability to balance local optima and global optima [54]. The EO method, on the other hand, does not function well for large-scale situations [55].

The novel hybrid algorithm MSSO's convergence speed is attributed to combining Newton's iterative method as a local search and the SSO algorithm. On the one hand, MSSO benefits from the originality of Newton's method, which was developed to find solutions to nonlinear equation systems. On the other hand, SSO ensures appropriate initial solutions for Newton's method by employing search agents. Furthermore, Newton's method features a second-order of convergence, which implies that the scheme converges to approximately two significant digits in each iteration [1]. Thus, the hybridization between Newton's method and the SSO algorithm inherits the merits from both sides to produce an efficient algorithm that can overcome the main disadvantages [56,57].

It is worth noting that the default precision value of the variable in MATLAB was used for all calculations in this study, which is 16 digits of precision. This precision is timesaving compared with more significant digits. However, in some situations, this may impact the outcome. In MATLAB, the function "vpa" may be used to enhance variable precision. Thus, increasing the number of digits can improve the accuracy of the findings, but this is a time-consuming operation. More details and examples of this case can be seen in [40]. In this research, the use of "vpa" has increased the accuracy of the results in Problem 5, Problem 7, and Problem 8.

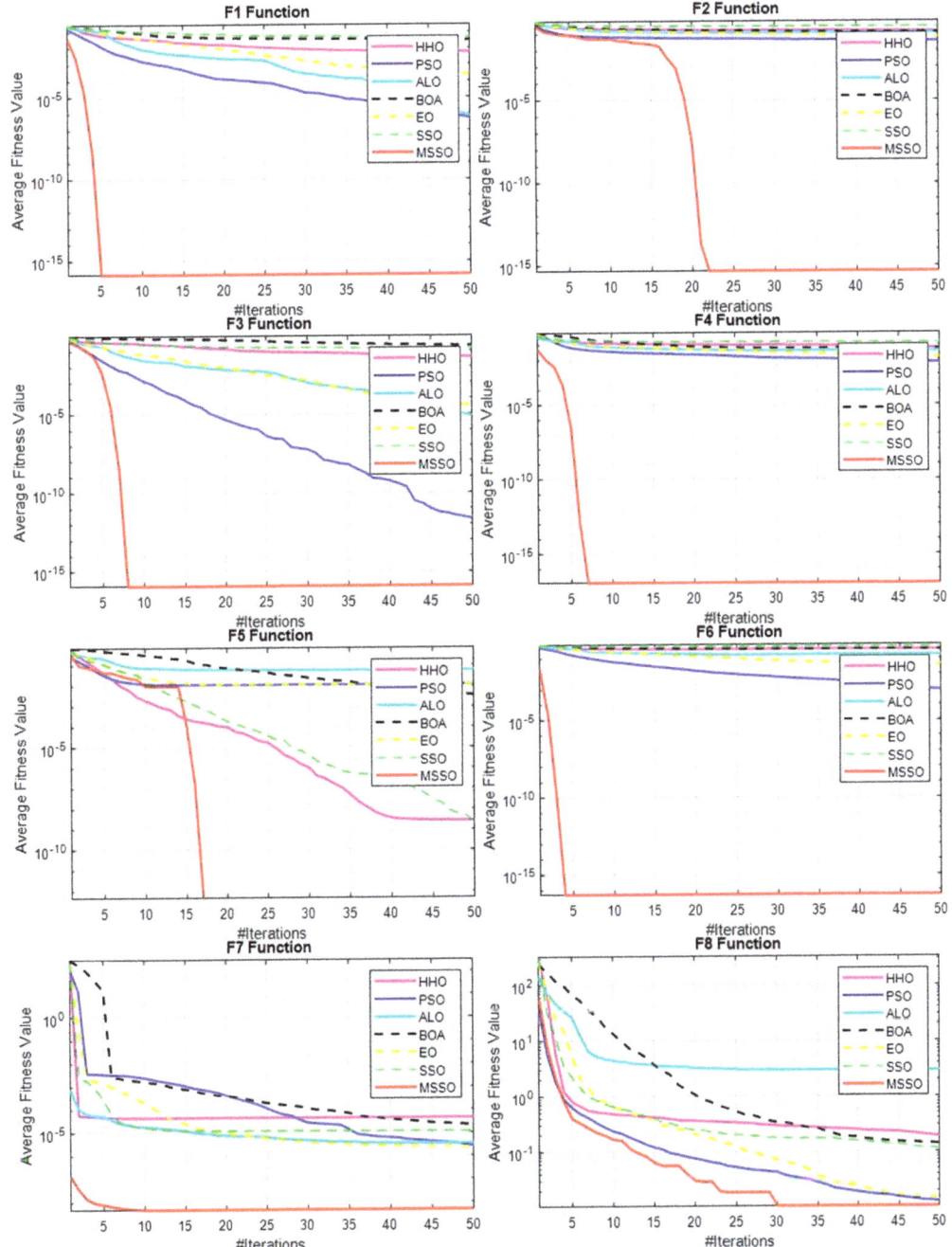

Figure 4. The convergence speed for the eight problems based on an average of 30 runs.

5.2. Comparison between MSSO and Newton's Method

The effectiveness of MSSO is demonstrated by the correctness of the generated solutions and its ability to avoid local optima compared to Newton's method. Accordingly, both strategies were examined for problems 1–4. Tables 12–15 compare the fitness values achieved by MSSO and Newton's method using three randomly chosen starting points. We examined both strategies for comparison purposes at iteration 5, iteration 7, and iteration 10. In addition, variables of 1200-digit precision in all selected problems were used to clarify the solutions' accuracy. If, as noted earlier, the number of digits is increased, the findings may also improve.

Table 12. A comparison of Newton's method and MSSO for Problem 1.

Iteration	Newton $x_0=(0,0)$	Newton $x_0=(1.5,0.5)$	Newton $x_0=(1,1)$	MSSO
5	1.14×10^{-17}	1.17×10^{-24}	3.01×10^{-35}	0
7	2.08×10^{-70}	2.26×10^{-98}	9.97×10^{-141}	0
10	1.20×10^{-562}	2.34×10^{-786}	3.33×10^{-1125}	0

Table 13. A comparison of Newton's method and MSSO for Problem 2.

Iteration	Newton $x_0=(1.5,2)$	Newton $x_0=(1,1.5)$	Newton $x_0=(2,2)$	MSSO
5	6.38×10^{-9}	Diverge	Diverge	0
7	2.61×10^{-37}	Diverge	Diverge	0
10	1.92×10^{-302}	Diverge	Diverge	0

Table 14. A comparison of Newton's method and MSSO for Problem 3.

Iteration	Newton $x_0=(0,0,0)$	Newton $x_0=(1,0,0.5)$	Newton $x_0=(1,1,1)$	MSSO
5	4.68×10^{-4}	Not Applicable	6.15×10^{-8}	2.82×10^{-16}
7	6.10×10^{-13}	Not Applicable	1.67×10^{-28}	8.09×10^{-57}
10	7.68×10^{-96}	Not Applicable	2.35×10^{-220}	0

Table 15. A comparison of Newton's method and MSSO for Problem 4.

Iteration	Newton $x_0=(0,0,0)$	Newton $x_0=(1,0,0.5)$	Newton $x_0=(1,1,1)$	MSSO
5	Not Applicable	1.72×10^{-17}	1.45×10^{-35}	1.12×10^{-45}
7	Not Applicable	4.77×10^{-68}	1.73×10^{-144}	3.76×10^{-183}
10	Not Applicable	1.85×10^{-538}	4.22×10^{-1161}	0

MSSO surpassed Newton's approach in all of the chosen problems, as shown in Tables 12–15. Newton's method, like all other iterative methods, is extremely sensitive to the starting answer x_0. Choosing an incorrect starting point can slow down the convergence of Newton's method (see Tables 12 and 14) or cause Newton's method to diverge (see Table 13). Further, a singularity in the Jacobian in Newton's method's denominator can be caused by the improper selection of the initial point. The Jacobian's inverse does not thus exist. Therefore, it is impossible to utilize Newton's approach (refer to Tables 14 and 15).

Tables 12–15 show a considerable improvement in MSSO outcomes compared with Newton's technique. The primary issue with Newton's starting point has been addressed by relying on 20 search agents at the early stages of the hybrid MSSO. This is rather than picking one point as Newton does. The MSSO selects several random starting points, called search agents, unlike Newton's method. MSSO examines each search agent's fitness value, then chooses the search agent with the lowest fitness value as an initial guess. Selecting the starting point in this manner is crucial for improving the accuracy of the answer.

The previous experiments show that the proposed MSSO outperforms Newton's method in selected problems. As opposed to Newton's method, which normally starts with one initial point, MSSO starts with 20 search agents. The superiority of the MSSO is demonstrated by the accuracy of its solutions. In addition, the time required to reach the convergence criteria is less in MSSO. Having 20 random initial solutions clearly requires more time for Newton's method. Therefore, this is another reason why hybridizing both SSO and Newton's method is better than depending on one of them.

Moreover, the speed of convergence towards the best solution is astonishing. MSSO can choose the best initial point in a few iterations and move quickly toward the global optima. Figure 5 shows the convergence speed of problems 1–4 for the first five iterations on an average of 30 runs.

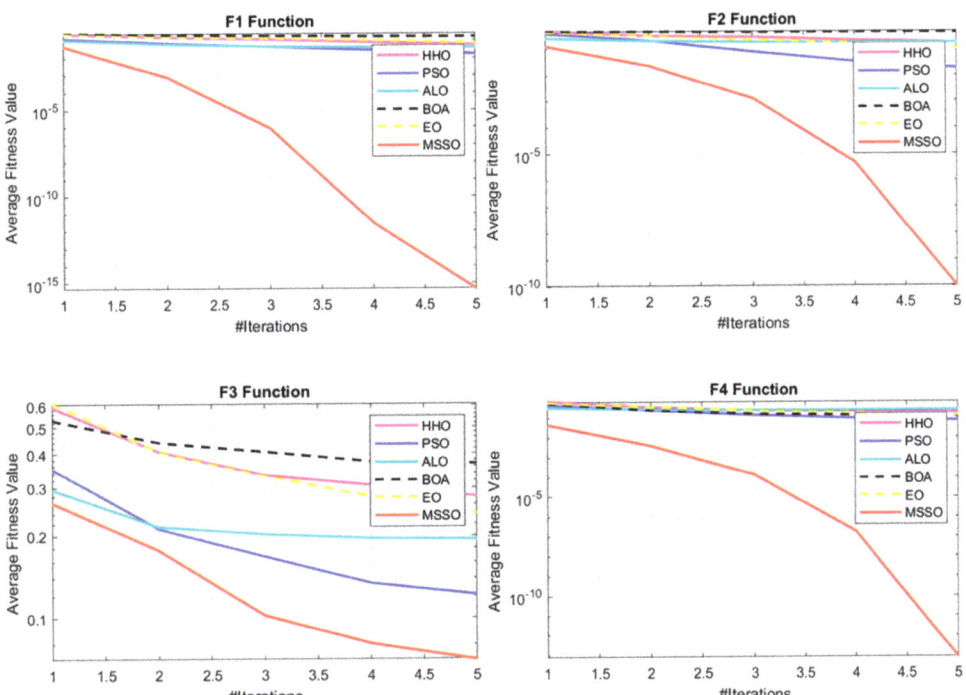

Figure 5. The convergence speed of problems 1–4 for five iterations based on an average of 30 runs.

To clarify the significant improvements of MSSO over Newton's iterative method, a comparison between Newton's technique and MSSO for Problems 1, 2, 3, and 4 were performed. Table 16 shows the CPU-time needed for Newton's technique and MSSO to attain the stopping criterion ($\varepsilon \leq 1 \times 10^{-15}$).

Table 16. Comparing Newton's method and MSSO in terms of average time (in seconds).

Problem	Newton			MSSO
	Initial Guess	Iteration	$\varepsilon \leq 1 \times 10^{-15}$	$\varepsilon \leq 1 \times 10^{-15}$
Problem 1	{0,0}	5	1.389	0.283
Problem 2	{1.5,1.5}	5	1.871	0.179
Problem 3	{1,1,1}	8	2.497	0.234
Problem 4	{0.5,0.5}	4	2.137	0.244

Based on the results, an apparent enhancement has been added to Newton's method by using the hybridized MSSO. The CPU-time needed to satisfy the selected stopping limit is much better for MSSO than Newton's method. Even though Newton's method is a part of the proposed MSSO, MSSO showed better results because of the mechanism of SSO in selecting the best initial guess for Newton's technique as a local search inside the hybrid algorithm.

It is well known that choosing a starting point that is far from the root of the system could negatively affect the convergence of Newton's method. Therefore, since Newton's method is included in the MSSO, this could negatively affect MSSO's convergence as well. However, based on the mechanism of the MSSO, the algorithm randomly selects 20 agents that are considered as initial points within a specific interval. In general, optimization algorithms have more choices to start with compared to Newton's method. Iterative methods can benefit from hybridization in selecting initial points because optimization algorithms can have many initial points. On the other hand, optimization algorithms can benefit from the fast and accurate convergence of iterative methods.

6. Conclusions

In this work, a hybrid method known as MSSO was introduced for solving systems of nonlinear equations using Newton's iterative method as a local search for the Sperm Swarm Optimization algorithm SSO. The main goal of the MSSO is to solve the problem of Newton's method's initial guess, the achievement of which results in a better selection of initial points, enabling it to be applied to a wider variety of real-world applications. Moreover, Newton's scheme was used in MSSO as a local search, which improved the accuracy of the tested solutions. In addition, the MSSO's convergence speed is substantially improved.

Eight nonlinear systems of varying orders were utilized to illustrate the effectiveness of the proposed MSSO. The novel MSSO was also compared to six well-known optimization methods, including the original SSO, BOA, ALO, EO, HHO, and PSO. The Euclidean norm has been utilized as a fitness function in all benchmarks. According to the results, MSSO outperforms all other compared algorithms in four metrics: fitness value, solution accuracy, stability, and speed of convergence. In addition, the consistency of the MSSO is confirmed by running the methods thirty times. Additionally, the standard deviation showed that MSSO was the most stable optimization algorithm.

Additionally, we compared the performance of MSSO and Newton's method on four problems from the benchmarks. Across all four datasets, the MSSO outperformed Newton's method. The MSSO method also overcomes some of Newton's scheme's limitations, such as divergence and selection of initial guesses.

Future work can address some related issues, such as how the suggested method performs against common optimization benchmarks. Future research will also focus on solving nonlinear equations arising from real-world applications, such as Burgers' Equation. In addition, future work needs to address the efficiency of the proposed algorithm when solving big systems. Finally, the use of a derivative-free iterative method instead of Newton's method reduces the computational complexity resulting from the need to evaluate Newton's method in each iteration and is an interesting topic that needs to be focused on in the future.

Author Contributions: Conceptualization, O.S.S. and R.S.; methodology, O.S.S., R.S. and H.S.; validation, K.A. and I.H.; formal analysis, O.S.S. and R.S.; investigation, O.S.S. and R.S.; resources, O.S.S., R.S. and H.S.; data curation, O.S.S. and R.S.; writing—original draft preparation, O.S.S., R.S. and H.S.; writing—review and editing, K.A. and I.H.; visualization, R.S.; supervision, O.S.S., R.S. and I.H.; project administration, O.S.S., R.S. and I.H.; funding acquisition, I.H. All authors have read and agreed to the published version of the manuscript.

Funding: This research and the APC were funded by Universiti Kebangsaan Malaysia, grant number DIP-2021-018.

Data Availability Statement: The data that support the findings of this study are available on request from the corresponding author, Sihwail, R.

Conflicts of Interest: The authors declare that there is no conflict of interest regarding the publication of this paper.

References

1. Traub, J.F. *Iterative Methods for the Solution of Equations*; Prentice-Hall: Englewood Cliffs, NJ, USA, 1964.
2. Shehadeh, H.A. A Hybrid Sperm Swarm Optimization and Gravitational Search Algorithm (HSSOGSA) for Global Optimization. *Neural Comput. Appl.* **2021**, *33*, 11739–11752. [CrossRef]
3. Gupta, S. Enhanced Harmony Search Algorithm with Non-Linear Control Parameters for Global Optimization and Engineering Design Problems. *Eng. Comput.* **2022**, *38*, 3539–3562. [CrossRef]
4. Zhu, F.; Chen, D.; Zou, F. A Novel Hybrid Dynamic Fireworks Algorithm with Particle Swarm Optimization. *Soft Comput.* **2021**, *25*, 2371–2398. [CrossRef]
5. Shehadeh, H.A.; Ahmedy, I.; Idris, M.Y.I. Empirical Study of Sperm Swarm Optimization Algorithm. *Adv. Intell. Syst. Comput.* **2018**, *869*, 1082–1104. [CrossRef]
6. Shehadeh, H.A.; Ahmedy, I.; Idris, M.Y.I. Sperm Swarm Optimization Algorithm for Optimizing Wireless Sensor Network Challenges. In Proceedings of the 6th International Conference on Communications and Broadband Networking, Singapore, 24–26 February 2018; pp. 53–59. [CrossRef]
7. Shehadeh, H.A.; Idris, M.Y.I.; Ahmedy, I.; Ramli, R.; Noor, N.M. The Multi-Objective Optimization Algorithm Based on Sperm Fertilization Procedure (MOSFP) Method for Solving Wireless Sensor Networks Optimization Problems in Smart Grid Applications. *Energies* **2018**, *11*, 97. [CrossRef]
8. Id, H.A.S.; Yamani, M.; Idris, I.; Ahmedy, I. Multi-Objective Optimization Algorithm Based on Sperm Fertilization Procedure (MOSFP). *Symmetry* **2017**, *9*, 241. [CrossRef]
9. Heidari, A.A.; Mirjalili, S.; Faris, H.; Aljarah, I.; Mafarja, M.; Chen, H. Harris Hawks Optimization: Algorithm and Applications. *Future Gener. Comput. Syst.* **2019**, *97*, 849–872. [CrossRef]
10. Mirjalili, S. The Ant Lion Optimizer. *Adv. Eng. Softw.* **2015**, *83*, 80–98. [CrossRef]
11. Arora, S.; Singh, S. Butterfly Optimization Algorithm: A Novel Approach for Global Optimization. *Soft Comput.* **2018**, *23*, 715–734. [CrossRef]
12. Zhang, Y.; Wang, Y.H.; Gong, D.W.; Sun, X.Y. Clustering-Guided Particle Swarm Feature Selection Algorithm for High-Dimensional Imbalanced Data With Missing Values. *IEEE Trans. Evol. Comput.* **2022**, *26*, 616–630. [CrossRef]
13. Faramarzi, A.; Heidarinejad, M.; Stephens, B.; Mirjalili, S. Equilibrium Optimizer: A Novel Optimization Algorithm. *Knowl.-Based Syst.* **2020**, *191*, 105190. [CrossRef]
14. Holland, J.H. Genetic Algorithms. *Sci. Am.* **1992**, *267*, 66–72. [CrossRef]
15. Liu, K.; Hu, X.; Yang, Z.; Xie, Y.; Feng, S. Lithium-Ion Battery Charging Management Considering Economic Costs of Electrical Energy Loss and Battery Degradation. *Energy Convers. Manag.* **2019**, *195*, 167–179. [CrossRef]
16. Liu, K.; Zou, C.; Li, K.; Wik, T. Charging Pattern Optimization for Lithium-Ion Batteries with an Electrothermal-Aging Model. *IEEE Trans. Ind. Inform.* **2018**, *14*, 5463–5474. [CrossRef]
17. Zhou, R.H.; Li, Y.G. An Improve Cuckoo Search Algorithm for Solving Nonlinear Equation Group. *Appl. Mech. Mater.* **2014**, *651–653*, 2121–2124. [CrossRef]
18. Ariyaratne, M.K.A.; Fernando, T.G.I.; Weerakoon, S. Solving Systems of Nonlinear Equations Using a Modified Firefly Algorithm (MODFA). *Swarm Evol. Comput.* **2019**, *48*, 72–92. [CrossRef]
19. Ren, H.; Wu, L.; Bi, W.; Argyros, I.K. Solving Nonlinear Equations System via an Efficient Genetic Algorithm with Symmetric and Harmonious Individuals. *Appl. Math. Comput.* **2013**, *219*, 10967–10973. [CrossRef]
20. Chang, W. der An Improved Real-Coded Genetic Algorithm for Parameters Estimation of Nonlinear Systems. *Mech. Syst. Signal Process.* **2006**, *20*, 236–246. [CrossRef]
21. Grosan, C.; Abraham, A. A New Approach for Solving Nonlinear Equations Systems. *IEEE Trans. Syst. Man Cybern. Part A Syst. Hum.* **2008**, *38*, 698–714. [CrossRef]
22. Jaberipour, M.; Khorram, E.; Karimi, B. Particle Swarm Algorithm for Solving Systems of Nonlinear Equations. *Comput. Math. Appl.* **2011**, *62*, 566–576. [CrossRef]
23. Mo, Y.; Liu, H.; Wang, Q. Conjugate Direction Particle Swarm Optimization Solving Systems of Nonlinear Equations. *Comput. Math. Appl.* **2009**, *57*, 1877–1882. [CrossRef]
24. Sihwail, R.; Omar, K.; Ariffin, K.A.Z. An Effective Memory Analysis for Malware Detection and Classification. *Comput. Mater. Contin.* **2021**, *67*, 2301–2320. [CrossRef]
25. Sihwail, R.; Omar, K.; Zainol Ariffin, K.; al Afghani, S. Malware Detection Approach Based on Artifacts in Memory Image and Dynamic Analysis. *Appl. Sci.* **2019**, *9*, 3680. [CrossRef]
26. Jadon, S.S.; Tiwari, R.; Sharma, H.; Bansal, J.C. Hybrid Artificial Bee Colony Algorithm with Differential Evolution. *Appl. Soft Comput. J.* **2017**, *58*, 11–24. [CrossRef]
27. Jia, R.; He, D. Hybrid Artificial Bee Colony Algorithm for Solving Nonlinear System of Equations. In Proceedings of the 2012 8th International Conference on Computational Intelligence and Security, CIS 2012, Guangzhou, China, 17–18 November 2012; pp. 56–60.

28. Aydilek, İ.B. A Hybrid Firefly and Particle Swarm Optimization Algorithm for Computationally Expensive Numerical Problems. *Appl. Soft Comput. J.* **2018**, *66*, 232–249. [CrossRef]
29. Nasr, S.; El-Shorbagy, M.; El-Desoky, I.; Hendawy, Z.; Mousa, A. Hybrid Genetic Algorithm for Constrained Nonlinear Optimization Problems. *Br. J. Math. Comput. Sci.* **2015**, *7*, 466–480. [CrossRef]
30. Abualigah, L.M.; Khader, A.T.; Hanandeh, E.S.; Gandomi, A.H. A Novel Hybridization Strategy for Krill Herd Algorithm Applied to Clustering Techniques. *Appl. Soft Comput. J.* **2017**, *60*, 423–435. [CrossRef]
31. El-Shorbagy, M.A.; Mousa, A.A.A.; Fathi, W. *Hybrid Particle Swarm Algorithm for Multiobjective Optimization: Integrating Particle Swarm Optimization with Genetic Algorithms for Multiobjective Optimization*; Lambert Academic: Saarbrücken, Germany, 2011.
32. Goel, R.; Maini, R. A Hybrid of Ant Colony and Firefly Algorithms (HAFA) for Solving Vehicle Routing Problems. *J. Comput. Sci.* **2018**, *25*, 28–37. [CrossRef]
33. Turanoğlu, B.; Akkaya, G. A New Hybrid Heuristic Algorithm Based on Bacterial Foraging Optimization for the Dynamic Facility Layout Problem. *Expert Syst. Appl.* **2018**, *98*, 93–104. [CrossRef]
34. Skoullis, V.I.; Tassopoulos, I.X.; Beligiannis, G.N. Solving the High School Timetabling Problem Using a Hybrid Cat Swarm Optimization Based Algorithm. *Appl. Soft Comput. J.* **2017**, *52*, 277–289. [CrossRef]
35. Chen, X.; Zhou, Y.; Tang, Z.; Luo, Q. A Hybrid Algorithm Combining Glowworm Swarm Optimization and Complete 2-Opt Algorithm for Spherical Travelling Salesman Problems. *Appl. Soft Comput. J.* **2017**, *58*, 104–114. [CrossRef]
36. Marichelvam, M.K.; Tosun, Ö.; Geetha, M. Hybrid Monkey Search Algorithm for Flow Shop Scheduling Problem under Makespan and Total Flow Time. *Appl. Soft Comput. J.* **2017**, *55*, 82–92. [CrossRef]
37. Karr, C.L.; Weck, B.; Freeman, L.M. Solutions to Systems of Nonlinear Equations via a Genetic Algorithm. *Eng. Appl. Artif. Intell.* **1998**, *11*, 369–375. [CrossRef]
38. Luo, Y.Z.; Yuan, D.C.; Tang, G.J. Hybrid Genetic Algorithm for Solving Systems of Nonlinear Equations. *Chin. J. Comput. Mech.* **2005**, *22*, 109–114.
39. Luo, Y.Z.; Tang, G.J.; Zhou, L.N. Hybrid Approach for Solving Systems of Nonlinear Equations Using Chaos Optimization and Quasi-Newton Method. *Appl. Soft Comput. J.* **2008**, *8*, 1068–1073. [CrossRef]
40. Sihwail, R.; Said Solaiman, O.; Omar, K.; Ariffin, K.A.Z.; Alswaitti, M.; Hashim, I. A Hybrid Approach for Solving Systems of Nonlinear Equations Using Harris Hawks Optimization and Newton's Method. *IEEE Access* **2021**, *9*, 95791–95807. [CrossRef]
41. Sihwail, R.; Said Solaiman, O.; Zainol Ariffin, K.A. New Robust Hybrid Jarratt-Butterfly Optimization Algorithm for Nonlinear Models. *J. King Saud Univ.—Comput. Inf. Sci.* **2022**, *34 Pt A*, 8207–8220. [CrossRef]
42. Sihwail, R.; Omar, K.; Ariffin, K.A.Z.; Tubishat, M. Improved Harris Hawks Optimization Using Elite Opposition-Based Learning and Novel Search Mechanism for Feature Selection. *IEEE Access* **2020**, *8*, 121127–121145. [CrossRef]
43. Said Solaiman, O.; Hashim, I. Efficacy of Optimal Methods for Nonlinear Equations with Chemical Engineering Applications. *Math. Probl. Eng.* **2019**, *2019*, 1728965. [CrossRef]
44. Said Solaiman, O.; Hashim, I. An Iterative Scheme of Arbitrary Odd Order and Its Basins of Attraction for Nonlinear Systems. *Comput. Mater. Contin.* **2020**, *66*, 1427–1444. [CrossRef]
45. Said Solaiman, O.; Hashim, I. Optimal Eighth-Order Solver for Nonlinear Equations with Applications in Chemical Engineering. *Intell. Autom. Soft Comput.* **2021**, *27*, 379–390. [CrossRef]
46. Said Solaiman, O.; Hashim, I. Two New Efficient Sixth Order Iterative Methods for Solving Nonlinear Equations. *J. King Saud Univ. Sci.* **2019**, *31*, 701–705. [CrossRef]
47. Said Solaiman, O.; Ariffin Abdul Karim, S.; Hashim, I. Dynamical Comparison of Several Third-Order Iterative Methods for Nonlinear Equations. *Comput. Mater. Contin.* **2021**, *67*, 1951–1962. [CrossRef]
48. Adam, S.P.; Alexandropoulos, S.A.N.; Pardalos, P.M.; Vrahatis, M.N. No Free Lunch Theorem: A Review. *Springer Optim. Its Appl.* **2019**, *145*, 57–82. [CrossRef]
49. Kennedy, J.; Eberhart, R. Particle Swarm Optimization. In Proceedings of the ICNN'95—International Conference on Neural Networks, Perth, WA, Australia, 27–1 December 1995; pp. 1942–1948. [CrossRef]
50. El-Shorbagy, M.A.; El-Refaey, A.M. Hybridization of Grasshopper Optimization Algorithm with Genetic Algorithm for Solving System of Non-Linear Equations. *IEEE Access* **2020**, *8*, 220944–220961. [CrossRef]
51. Wang, X.; Li, Y. An Efficient Sixth-Order Newton-Type Method for Solving Nonlinear Systems. *Algorithms* **2017**, *10*, 45. [CrossRef]
52. Verschelde, J.; Verlinden, P.; Cools, R. Homotopies Exploiting Newton Polytopes for Solving Sparse Polynomial Systems. *SIAM J. Numer. Anal.* **1994**, *31*, 915–930. [CrossRef]
53. van Hentenryck, P.; Mcallester, D.; Kapur, D. Solving Polynomial Systems Using a Branch and Prune Approach. *SIAM J. Numer. Anal.* **1997**, *34*, 797–827. [CrossRef]
54. Ridha, H.M.; Heidari, A.A.; Wang, M.; Chen, H. Boosted Mutation-Based Harris Hawks Optimizer for Parameters Identification of Single-Diode Solar Cell Models. *Energy Convers. Manag.* **2020**, *209*, 112660. [CrossRef]
55. Elgamal, Z.M.; Yasin, N.M.; Sabri, A.Q.M.; Sihwail, R.; Tubishat, M.; Jarrah, H. Improved Equilibrium Optimization Algorithm Using Elite Opposition-Based Learning and New Local Search Strategy for Feature Selection in Medical Datasets. *Computation* **2021**, *9*, 68. [CrossRef]

56. Shehadeh, H.A.; Mustafa, H.M.J.; Tubishat, M. A Hybrid Genetic Algorithm and Sperm Swarm Optimization (HGASSO) for Multimodal Functions. *Int. J. Appl. Metaheuristic Comput.* **2021**, *13*, 1–33. [CrossRef]
57. Shehadeh, H.A.; Shagari, N.M. Chapter 24: A Hybrid Grey Wolf Optimizer and Sperm Swarm Optimization for Global Optimization. In *Handbook of Intelligent Computing and Optimization for Sustainable Development*; John Wiley & Sons, Inc.: Hoboken, NJ, USA, 2022; pp. 487–507. [CrossRef]

Disclaimer/Publisher's Note: The statements, opinions and data contained in all publications are solely those of the individual author(s) and contributor(s) and not of MDPI and/or the editor(s). MDPI and/or the editor(s) disclaim responsibility for any injury to people or property resulting from any ideas, methods, instructions or products referred to in the content.

MDPI
St. Alban-Anlage 66
4052 Basel
Switzerland
www.mdpi.com

Mathematics Editorial Office
E-mail: mathematics@mdpi.com
www.mdpi.com/journal/mathematics

Disclaimer/Publisher's Note: The statements, opinions and data contained in all publications are solely those of the individual author(s) and contributor(s) and not of MDPI and/or the editor(s). MDPI and/or the editor(s) disclaim responsibility for any injury to people or property resulting from any ideas, methods, instructions or products referred to in the content.

www.ingramcontent.com/pod-product-compliance
Lightning Source LLC
LaVergne TN
LVHW070655100526
838202LV00013B/971